W9-BBS-561

The One Year Book of POETRY

Philip Comfor

Compiled and written by

and Daniel Partner

Tyndale House Publishers, Inc.
WHEATON, ILLINOIS

Visit Tyndale's exciting Web site at www.tyndale.com

Edited by Steve Benson

Designed by Timothy R. Botts

Library of Congress Cataloging-in-Publication Data

Printed in the United States of America

06 05 04 03 02 01 00 99
8 7 6 5 4 3 2 1

for Georgia

P.C.

for Margaret

D.P.

INTRODUCTION

Reading poetry. Some people do this with pleasure; others, with difficulty. Either way, if you spend one year with this book, you will love poetry more or begin to like it for the first time.

For your enjoyment and enrichment we have selected many of the greatest poetical works ever composed. John Milton's *Paradise Lost* and John Bunyan's *Pilgrim's Progress* top the list, followed closely by William Blake's "The Tyger" and "The Lamb," John Donne's Holy Sonnets, and George Herbert's "Easter Wings" and "The Altar." Because these poems develop biblical themes, it is quite likely that reading this book will challenge your faith and cause you to grow in your knowledge of and devotion to the God of our Lord Jesus Christ.

But like anything that is rewarding, you must make the effort to understand. The meaning of some of the poems will be easy to pick up. Others are hard nuts to crack, but once opened, they are sweetly nourishing. Our comments and devotional insights on these poems do not always explain them stanza by stanza, line by line. Rather, they are tools—nutcrackers to help you pry open the shell of the poems.

By way of another metaphor, within each of these poems is buried a treasure. Our comments serve as a map to point out where to dig. But you must do the digging. If you do, you will find the treasure and exclaim, "Aha! I understand."

As you read this book you will notice that we have selected poems from a broad chronology (from the third to the twentieth century). In addition, the poets come from a variety of Christian backgrounds (Catholic mystics to Protestant preachers). You may come across a poet and say, "I didn't know he [or she] was a Christian." We feel that it is difficult to judge the condition of a person's soul before God. Remember what the Lord said to Samuel: "Don't judge by his appearance or height. . . . People judge by outward appearance, but the Lord looks at a person's thoughts and intentions" (1 Samuel 16:7). So we have selected each poem for the virtue of its content. These are Christian poems or, at the very least, compatible with biblical Christianity. Our desire is that you enjoy them and so enrich your spiritual and intellectual life.

PHILIP COMFORT
DANIEL PARTNER

The Lamb

Little Lamb, who made thee?
Dost thou know who made thee?
Gave thee life, and bid thee feed
By the stream and o'er the mead;
Gave thee clothing of delight,
Softest clothing, wooly, bright;
Gave thee such a tender voice,
Making all the vales rejoice?
Little Lamb, who made thee?
Dost thou know who made thee?

Little Lamb, I'll tell thee
Little Lamb, I'll tell thee:
He is callèd by thy name,
For he calls himself a Lamb.
He is meek, and he is mild;
He became a little child.
I a child, and thou a lamb,
We are callèd by his name.
Little Lamb, God bless thee!
Little Lamb, God bless thee!

WILLIAM BLAKE (1757–1827)

WILLIAM BLAKE was an English poet who lived and wrote during the romantic period (1798–1832). Although we are not sure whether Blake was a Christian, a few of his poems are based on biblical themes.

In this poem Blake plays on the biblical image of the lamb. He first presents the children of God as lambs (see John 21:15-17), and then he presents Jesus Christ as the Lamb of God (see John 1:29, 36). Thus, all the little children of God, as lambs, share the same name as the Lamb of God. But the connotation in Scripture is quite different for each of these. The term *lambs* or *sheep*—when applied to God's people—refers to their dependence on God for provision and protection (see John 10). The term *Lamb of God* designates Christ as God's provision for sin. Nearly all of the biblical passages on lambs speak of sacrifice. Characteristically, the lamb takes away one's sin by sacrificing its life.

Blake's poem, however, has more to do with God's care as a shepherd than with Christ's death for our sins. In fact, when we read this poem, our mind fastens quickly on the image of Jesus Christ as the Good Shepherd who cares for his sheep. His care is nowhere better pictured than in Psalm 23, to which Blake alludes in the lines "Gave thee life, and bid thee feed by the stream and o'er the mead."

As a New Year's prayer of gratitude, thank Christ that he gave you his life and sustains yours.

Messenger of good news, shout to Zion from the mountaintops! Shout louder to Jerusalem—do not be afraid. Tell the towns of Judah, "Your God is coming!" Yes, the Sovereign Lord is coming in all his glorious power. He will rule with awesome strength. See, he brings his reward with him as he comes. He will feed his flock like a shepherd. He will carry the lambs in his arms, holding them close to his heart. He will gently lead the mother sheep with their young. Isaiah 40:9-11

The Three Kings PART ONE

Three Kings came riding from far away,
Melchior and Gaspar and Baltasar;
Three Wise Men out of the East were they.
And they travelled by night and they slept by day
For their guide was a beautiful, wonderful star.

The star was so beautiful, large, and clear,
That all the other stars of the sky
Became a white mist in the atmosphere.
And by this they knew that the coming was near
Of the Prince foretold in prophecy.

Three caskets they bore on their saddlebows,
Three caskets of gold with golden keys;
Their robes were of crimson silk with rows
Of bells and pomegranates and furbelows,
Their turbans like blossoming almond-trees.

And so the Three Kings rode into the West,
Through the dusk of night, over hill and dell,
And sometimes they nodded with beard on breast,
And sometimes talked, as they paused to rest,
With the people they met at some wayside well.

"Of the child that is born," said Baltasar,
"Good people, I pray you, tell us the news;
For we in the East have seen his star,
And have ridden fast, and have ridden far,
To find and worship the King of the Jews."

And the people answered, "You ask in vain;
We know of no king but Herod the Great!"
They thought the Wise Men were men insane,
As they spurred their horses across the plain,
Like riders in haste, and who cannot wait.

And when they came to Jerusalem,
Herod the Great, who had heard this thing,
Sent for the Wise Men and questioned them;
And said, "Go down unto Bethlehem,
And bring me tidings of this new king."

(continued in next day's reading)

HENRY WADSWORTH LONGFELLOW (1807–1882)

HENRY WADSWORTH LONGFELLOW was an American poet and linguist. He is best known as the author of *Paul Revere's Ride* and *The Song of Hiawatha.* However, several of his lesser-known works were written on Christian subjects, as was this one.

Longfellow romanticizes the story of the wise men from Matthew 2:1-12. This poem expresses many modern-day misconceptions about these men. For instance, the title says that there were three wise men. The first three stanzas describe the wise men as richly dressed and traveling at night by starlight. The Bible does not give us this much detail about these men. No one knows who they were, where exactly they came from, or how many of them made the journey.

The star they followed is an equal mystery. It seems to have led them as far as Jerusalem. Apparently they had lost sight of the star while there (Matthew 2:9), for they asked King Herod, "Where is the newborn king of the Jews?" (Matthew 2:2).

Herod had no idea what to tell them, so he called in the priests and religious teachers of Jerusalem. They knew where Christ was to be born, quoting Micah 5:2. They also knew that these strangers had come to find the long awaited Messiah. If there was a possibility that the Christ could be found at that moment in Bethlehem, why didn't they go with the travelers? Instead, they did nothing.

Although this story has many unknowns, we do know this: Those who should have welcomed the Messiah missed out on their opportunity, while foreigners—perhaps even kings—traveled far to honor the king of the Jews, the King of kings.

Jesus was born in the town of Bethlehem in Judea, during the reign of King Herod. About that time some wise men from eastern lands arrived in Jerusalem, asking, "Where is the newborn king of the Jews? We have seen his star as it arose, and we have come to worship him."
Matthew 2:1-2

The Three Kings PART TWO

So they rode away; and the star stood still,
The only one in the gray of morn;
Yes, it stopped,—it stood still of its own free will,
Right over Bethlehem on the hill,
The city of David, where Christ was born.

And the Three Kings rode through the gate and the guard,
Through the silent street, till their horses turned
And neighed as they entered the great inn yard;
But the windows were closed and the doors were barred,
And only a light in the stable burned.

And cradled there in the scented hay,
In the air made sweet by the breath of kine,
The little child in the manger lay,
The child that would be king one day
Of a kingdom not human but divine.

His mother Mary of Nazareth
Sat watching beside his place of rest,
Watching the even flow of his breath,
For the joy of life and the terror of death
Were mingled together in her breast.

They laid their offerings at his feet:
The gold was their tribute to a King,
The frankincense, with its odor sweet,
Was for the Priest, the Paraclete,
The myrrh for the body's burying.

And the mother wondered and bowed her head,
And sat as still as a statue of stone;
Her heart was troubled yet comforted,
Remembering what the Angel had said
Of an endless reign and of David's throne.

Then the Kings rode out of the city gate,
With a clatter of hoofs in proud array;
But they went not back to Herod the Great,
For they knew his malice and feared his hate,
And returned to their homes by another way.

HENRY WADSWORTH LONGFELLOW (1807–1882)

FROM TIME to time Christians have intense interest in the second coming of Christ. They study the Bible, gather evidence, and read and reread the signs of the times.

The wise men arrived at the time of the Lord's first appearing. Yet their story provides some hints about the Second Coming. We can learn two lessons from the religious leaders in Jerusalem: First, working in collusion with political powers may prevent us from seeing the Lord. Second, Bible knowledge alone will not secure our preparedness to meet the Lord when he returns.

How can we be wise about Christ's return? These men from the East show us. First, look for his star as it arises (Matthew 2:2). As the apostle Paul says, long for his appearing (2 Timothy 4:8). Second, expect nothing for yourself. The wise men came to worship the king (Matthew 2:2), bringing gifts for him. We—and all we have—should be his now, and later, when he returns.

After this interview the wise men went their way. Once again the star appeared to them, guiding them to Bethlehem. It went ahead of them and stopped over the place where the child was. When they saw the star, they were filled with joy! Matthew 2:9-10

Lulla, My Sweet Little Baby PART ONE

Lulla, la lulla, lulla lullaby.
My sweet little baby, what meanest thou to cry?
Be still, my blessed babe, though cause thou hast to mourn,
Whose blood most innocent to shed the cruel king hath sworn.
And lo, alas, behold what slaughter he doth make,
Shedding the blood of infants all, sweet Savior, for thy sake
A King is born, they say, which King this king would kill.
Oh woe, and woeful heavy day, when wretches have their will!

Lulla, la lulla, lulla lullaby.
My sweet little baby, what meanest thou to cry?
Three kings this King of kings to see are come from far,
To each unknown, with offerings great, by guiding of a star.
And shepherds heard the song which angels bright did sing,
Giving all glory unto God for coming of this King,
Which must be made away, King Herod would him kill.
Oh woe, and woeful heavy day, when wretches have their will!

(continued in next day's reading)

WILLIAM BYRD (1543–1623)

WILLIAM BYRD was the most famous and versatile English composer of his day. He wrote many musical works for the Anglican and Roman Catholic churches in England. It is no wonder that he wrote a song for Jesus.

Each stanza of this poem begins with a question reminiscent of many a lullaby—"My sweet little baby, what meanest thou to cry?" Its beautiful meter seeks a partnership with a lovely tune, but its theme revolves around royal intrigue and murder.

At the time of Jesus' birth, who knew that the promised Christ had been born? Probably no one but Mary, Joseph, Elizabeth, and some shepherds at first (Matthew 1:18-25; Luke 1:49-56; 2:8-20). Certainly not Herod the Great. The news that a king had been born in his realm came to him through strangers from the East. It was hardly more than hearsay. But Herod took the news seriously. He feared any political rival, even a newborn baby. Out of this fear came the infamous slaughter of the innocents. William Byrd's use of a lovely poetic form—the lullaby—helps us to see clearly the horrendous uselessness of Herod's action.

Despite its form, this poem is more of a lament over the "woeful heavy day, when wretches have their will" than it is a lullaby. But the final stanza contains hope. God's Son will triumph over wretches: "Oh joy, and joyful happy day, when wretches want their will!" Just as Herod's bloody rage could not prevent Christ's incarnation, nothing can hinder his return. Until then, we can pray, "How long, Sovereign Lord, holy and true?" (Revelation 6:10, NIV).

Herod was furious when he learned that the wise men had outwitted him. He sent soldiers to kill all the boys in and around Bethlehem who were two years old and under, because the wise men had told him the star first appeared to them about two years earlier. Matthew 2:16

Lulla, My Sweet Little Baby PART TWO

Lulla, la lulla, lulla lullaby.
My sweet little baby, what meanest thou to cry?
Lo, my little babe, be still, lament no more;
From fury thou shalt step aside, help have we still in store.
We heavenly warning have some other soil to seek,
From death must fly the Lord of life, as lamb both mild and meek.
Thus must my babe obey the king that would him kill.
Oh woe, and woeful heavy day, when wretches have their will!
Lulla, la lulla, lulla lullaby.
My sweet little baby, what meanest thou to cry?
But thou shalt live and reign as Sibyls have foresaid,
As all the prophets prophesy, whose mother, yet a maid
And perfect virgin pure, with her breasts shall upbreed
Both God and man, that all hath made, the Son of heavenly seed,
Whom caitiffs none can 'tray, whom tyrants none can kill.
Oh joy, and joyful happy day, when wretches want their will!

WILLIAM BYRD (1543–1623)

CONSIDER the scene of this poem: An angel appears to Joseph and says, "Get up and flee to Egypt with the child and his mother, . . . because Herod is going to try to kill the child" (Matthew 2:13). Joseph arises in the dark of night, lights a lamp, rouses his wife, and whispers to her the angel's urgent, dreamlike message. They quickly move about the room, dressing and planning. What do they take for the trip to Egypt? What must they abandon in Bethlehem? Then the baby awakens.

Joseph kneels by the crib. "Lulla, la lulla, lulla lullaby," he sings in a whisper, lips close to the child's warm forehead. "Lulla, la lulla, lulla lullaby. My sweet little baby, what meanest thou to cry?"

Joseph's song to Jesus remembers the extraordinary events of the boy's short life. The father sings of the slaughter that is soon to come upon Bethlehem—a lullaby of murder and martyrdom. He weaves into the melody the strange story of the visitors from the East, whose gifts would soon be sold to finance the family's flight. He also relates the account of the shepherds' hurried visit—these rough men who were the first of the human race to worship the Savior.

"Lulla, la lulla, lulla lullaby. My sweet little baby, what meanest thou to cry?" The baby had plenty to cry about. While his father sang of the lovely mother who was to nurture "the Son of heavenly seed," armed soldiers were assembling nearby, preparing to kill him. And Joseph lilted of the prophecies foretelling the baby's kingly life and reign while he hustled the bundled mother and son out of Bethlehem toward Egypt. "Lulla, la lulla, lulla lullaby."

"Get up and flee to Egypt with the child and his mother," the angel said. "Stay there until I tell you to return, because Herod is going to try to kill the child." That night Joseph left for Egypt with the child and Mary, his mother, and they stayed there until Herod's death. Matthew 2:13-15

Epiphany

"Lord Babe, if Thou art He
We sought for patiently,
Where is Thy court?
Hither may prophecy and star resort;
Men heed not their report."—
"Bow down and worship, righteous man:
This Infant of a span
Is He man sought for since the world began!"—
"Then, Lord, accept my gold, too base a thing
For Thee, of all kings King."—

"Lord Babe, despite Thy youth
I hold Thee of a truth
Both Good and Great:
But wherefore dost Thou keep so mean a state,
Low-lying desolate?"—
"Bow down and worship, righteous seer:
The Lord our God is here
Approachable, Who bids us all draw near."—
"Wherefore to Thee I offer frankincense,
Thou Sole Omnipotence."—

"But I have only brought
Myrrh; no wise afterthought
Instructed me
To gather pearls or gems, or choice to see
Coral or ivory."—
"Not least thine offering proves thee wise:
For myrrh means sacrifice,
And He that lives, this Same is He that dies."—
"Then here is myrrh: alas! yea, woe is me
That myrrh befitteth Thee."—

Myrrh, frankincense, and gold:
And lo! from wintry fold
Good-will doth bring
A Lamb, the innocent likeness of this King
Whom stars and seraphs sing:
And lo! the bird of love, a Dove
Flutters and coos above:

And Dove and Lamb and Babe agree in love:—
Come all mankind, come all creation hither,
Come, worship Christ together.

CHRISTINA ROSSETTI (1830-1894)

CHRISTINA ROSSETTI was a devout follower of Christ. She spent most of her life writing sacred poetry and preparing devotional manuals for her church. Her first volume of poems, *Goblin Market, and Other Poems* (1862), was much praised for its style and originality. Following her death, her brother William collected her unpublished poems and published them as *New Poems* (1896).

In this poem Rossetti commemorates epiphany, which means "appearing"—specifically the appearing of God in the person of Jesus Christ. Paul spoke of this "epiphany" in his Pastoral Epistles. He said, "It is God who saved us and chose us to live a holy life. He did this not because we deserved it, but because that was his plan long before the world began—to show his love and kindness to us through Christ Jesus. And now he has made all of this plain to us by the coming [epiphany] of Christ Jesus, our Savior, who broke the power of death and showed us the way to everlasting life through the Good News" (2 Timothy 1:9-10; see also 1 Timothy 3:16; Titus 2:13-14).

What a marvelous thought: We were blessed in Christ before the world began because God saw us in his Son, as his children (see Ephesians 1:3-6). We did not deserve God's appearance or God's gift of immortality. Our thanks to him is the best gift we can give in return.

And they said, "We give thanks to you, Lord God Almighty, the one who is and who always was, for now you have assumed your great power and have begun to reign." Revelation 11:17

Epiphanytide

Trembling before Thee we fall down to adore Thee,
Shamefaced and trembling we lift our eyes to Thee:
O First and with the last! annul our ruined past,
Rebuild us to Thy glory, set us free
From sin and from sorrow to fall down and worship Thee.

Full of pity view us, stretch Thy sceptre to us,
Bid us live that we may give ourselves to Thee:
O faithful Lord and True! stand up for us and do,
Make us lovely, make us new, set us free—
Heart and soul and spirit—to bring all and worship Thee.

CHRISTINA ROSSETTI (1830–1894)

IN THIS POEM Rossetti celebrates the appearing of God in the person of Jesus. She glorifies the eternal one, Jesus Christ, calling him the "First and with the last." She also honors his steadfast testimony by calling him "faithful Lord and True." These titles come from the book of Revelation, where Jesus said, "I am the First and the Last" (1:17). This means that he lives from eternity and endures through eternity (see Isaiah 41:4; 44:6; 48:12).

This eternal one is the King of kings, the very Lord of glory. It is no wonder the poet wrote, "Trembling before Thee we fall down to adore Thee, shamefaced and trembling we lift our eyes to Thee."

John the apostle (who wrote the book of Revelation) was overcome with the same kind of fear and awe when he saw Jesus as the First and the Last, the Alpha and Omega, and the King of kings (see Revelation 19:16; 22:13).

But this King does not come to conquer or subdue us. Rather, he comes to rebuild us, to restore us, to set us free. Knowing this about her King, the poet seeks permission to approach him. This is implicit in the lines "Full of pity view us, stretch Thy scepter to us, bid us live that we may give ourselves to Thee."

In ancient times no one could approach a king if the king did not extend his scepter to that person. If a person approached and the king refused to extend his scepter, that person would be killed.

Fortunately for us, we have an approachable King, who extended his scepter to us on the cross! Let us come to him and worship. As we do so, he will renew us and stand up for us.

➻ *We look forward to that wonderful event when the glory of our great God and Savior, Jesus Christ, will be revealed. He gave his life to free us from every kind of sin, to cleanse us, and to make us his very own people, totally committed to doing what is right.* Titus 2:13-14

Earth Has Many a Noble City

Earth has many a noble city;
Bethlehem, thou dost all excel;
Out of thee the Lord from heaven
Came to rule His Israel.

Fairer than the sun at morning
Was the star that told His birth,
To the world its God announcing
Seen in fleshly form on earth.

Eastern sages at His cradle
Make oblations rich and rare;
See them give, in deep devotion,
Gold and frankincense and myrrh.

Sacred gifts of mystic meaning:
Incense doth their God disclose;
Gold the King of kings proclaimeth;
Myrrh His sepulcher foreshows.

Jesus, whom the Gentiles worshiped
At Thy glad epiphany,
Unto Thee, with God the Father
And the Spirit, glory be.

AURELIUS CLEMENS PRUDENTIUS (348–c. 410)
Translated by Edward Caswall (1814–1878)

PRUDENTIUS was a lawyer and a governor of Spain around the end of the Roman Empire. At the age of fifty-seven, he ended his successful career in politics to devote his life to Christ. It was then that he published several major works that had great influence on future Christian poets.

A few of his poems have been translated into English and set to music, including this one, "Earth Has Many a Noble City." The poem extols Bethlehem as being the most excellent city because that is where the Savior Jesus was born. In this poem Prudentius calls us to join the sages from the East to come to this city, bring our gifts to the newborn King, and kneel before him in worship.

Each of the gifts the wise men brought Jesus typifies a spiritual truth. The gold symbolizes divinity and loyalty—"the King of kings proclaimeth." All the kings of Israel wore gold or procured gold to display their royalty. Solomon, who had more gold than any king of Israel, had the most glorious display of them all (see 1 Kings 10:14-22). It was only fitting that the Eastern sages offer gold to Jesus, the King of kings.

Incense symbolizes the prayer that brings people into God's presence (see Revelation 8:3-4). And myrrh symbolizes suffering, because this spice was used for Jesus' burial (see John 19:39-40). As the poet wrote, "Myrrh His sepulcher foreshows."

These gifts helped sustain Joseph and Mary when they had to flee to Egypt (for two years) to avoid King Herod. So the gifts had practical, as well as spiritual, value. Perhaps they also serve as a model for the kinds of gifts we should give to our Lord and his people—spiritual and material offerings.

When [the wise men] saw the star, they were filled with joy! . . . Then they opened their treasure chests and gave him gifts of gold, frankincense, and myrrh. Matthew 2:10-11

Jerusalem the Golden

Jerusalem the golden,
With milk and honey blest!
Beneath thy contemplation
Sink heart and voice oppressed;
I know not, oh, I know not
What joys await me there;
What radiancy of glory,
What bliss beyond compare.

They stand, those halls of Zion,
All jubilant with song,
And bright with many an angel,
And all the martyr throng;
The Prince is ever in them,
The daylight is serene;
The pastures of the blessed
Are decked in glorious sheen.

There is the throne of David;
And there, from care released,
The song of them that triumph,
The shout of them that feast;
And they, who with their Leader
Have conquered in the fight,
Forever and forever
Are clad in robes of white.

O sweet and blessed country,
The home of God's elect!
O sweet and blessed country
That eager hearts expect!
Jesus, in mercy bring us
To that dear land of rest;
Who art, with God the Father,
And Spirit, ever blest.

BERNARD OF CLUNY (fl. mid–12th c.)
Translated by John Neale (1818–1866)

BERNARD was a Benedictine monk who lived at the monastery of Cluny, near Lyons, France. He is remembered most for his poetry, in particular "De Contemptu Mundi" ("In Contempt of the World"). Full of apocalyptic scenes and vivid descriptions of the afterworld, this satire is credited for influencing Dante, an Italian poet who wrote *The Divine Comedy,* an epic poem about hell, purgatory, and heaven.

In "Jerusalem the Golden" Bernard expresses his longing to reside in the new Jerusalem, the eternal city of God. This is the city that exists (in some fashion) even now in heaven, for Paul calls it the Jerusalem that is above (Galatians 4:26). This Jerusalem will eventually come down from heaven—perhaps concurrent with the descent of God's people to earth. Thus, the new Jerusalem will be the eternal dwelling of God and man.

Bernard contemplated this glorious city in times of depression: "Beneath thy contemplation sink heart and voice oppressed." He also asked God for the privilege to participate in the golden city: "Jesus, in mercy bring us to that dear land of rest." Although the joy that awaited him there was beyond his understanding, his poem wonderfully depicts all the joys one might experience there: jubilation, triumph, feasting, and rest. But the greatest joy is the presence of God: Father, Son, and Spirit.

May we, like Bernard, put our minds on the things of heaven and pray that we, too, may have a part in the New Jerusalem. For there we will see our Lord face-to-face and experience "bliss beyond compare."

And I saw the holy city, the new Jerusalem, coming down from God out of heaven like a beautiful bride prepared for her husband. I heard a loud shout from the throne, saying, "Look, the home of God is now among his people! He will live with them, and they will be his people. God himself will be with them." Revelation 21:2-3

Love Constraining to Obedience

No strength of Nature can suffice
To serve the Lord aright:
And what she has, she misapplies,
For want of clearer light.

How long beneath the law I lay
In bondage and distress!
I toil'd the precept to obey,
But toil'd without success.

Then to abstain from outward sin
Was more than I could do;
Now, if I feel its pow'r within,
I feel I hate it too.

Then all my servile works were done
A righteousness to raise;
Now, freely chosen in the Son,
I freely choose his ways.

What shall I do, was then the word,
That I may worthier grow?
What shall I render to the Lord?
Is my enquiry now.

To see the Law by Christ fulfill'd,
And hear his pard'ning voice;
Changes a slave into a child,
And duty into choice.

WILLIAM COWPER (1731–1800)

WILLIAM COWPER was the son of John Cowper, an Anglican rector, and Anne Donne, who belonged to the same family as John Donne, the seventeenth-century poet and preacher. Cowper was nominated to two administrative posts in the House of Lords but was so frightened by having to take an oral examination that he attempted suicide and emerged from the ordeal mentally unbalanced.

Cowper spent years searching for recovery from intermittent sieges of depression and insanity. *The Task,* book 3, refers to his mental problems: "I was a stricken deer that left the herd." In a private hospital he took up Bible reading and was converted to Christianity.

His Christian life, as expressed in his poetry, was filled with the ups and downs that most Christians experience. This poem reminds us of what Paul explained in Romans 7–8 about his inability to keep the law by his own power—until he laid hold of the powerful Spirit of Jesus Christ. Cowper expresses what all Christians feel—that they cannot do the things they know they should do and therefore feel guilty for not doing them. But Christ fulfilled the law and set us free from its demands on us. Furthermore, Christ's Spirit gives us the power to overcome the law of sin and death. His new life, residing in us, enables us to live like children of God, no longer enslaved to sin.

So now there is no condemnation for those who belong to Christ Jesus. For the power of the life-giving Spirit has freed you through Christ Jesus from the power of sin that leads to death. Romans 8:1-2

To the Infant Martyrs

Go smiling souls, your new built cages break,
In Heaven you'll learn to sing ere here to speak,
Nor let the milky fonts that bathe your thirst,
Be your delay;
The place that calls you hence, is at the worst
Milk all the way.

RICHARD CRASHAW (C. 1613–1649)

RICHARD CRASHAW was an English poet with an interesting religious background. His father was a Puritan minister who despised Roman Catholics. Crashaw was attracted to Catholicism. He eventually left the Puritan church for the Anglican. Five years before his death, he converted to Roman Catholicism.

As a poet, Crashaw dedicated himself to writing sacred verse. He employed the genre of "emblem," which brings together pictures (engraving) and poetry. The short poem or motto interpreted the picture. Emblem gained popularity throughout Europe in the sixteenth and seventeenth centuries. Religious poets often used this genre to illustrate stages of the soul.

This poem came from Crashaw's first collection of sacred poetry, *Steps to the Temple* (1646). In this emblem poem, Crashaw memorialized the infants who were murdered by Herod's soldiers in an attempt to kill the newborn king of the Jews (Matthew 2:13-16). Herod was the Jews' king at the time of Christ's birth. When he learned about Jesus, he wanted to rid himself of any contenders to the throne. In this ferocious act, Herod was as crafty as he was cruel. He took sweeping measures to ensure that he would not miss his mark. He thought this mass murder would take care of his single victim. And it would have if Jesus had been there. But his parents had fled with him to Egypt.

The infants died for Jesus' sake and, therefore, Crashaw considered them martyrs. Released from their young bodies and transported to heaven, they experienced singing before speaking, and an abundance of pure spiritual milk (see 1 Peter 2:2).

Herod was furious when he learned that the wise men had outwitted him. He sent soldiers to kill all the boys in and around Bethlehem who were two years old and under, because the wise men had told him the star first appeared to them about two years earlier. Matthew 2:16

Eternal Light

Eternal Light! Eternal Light!
How pure the soul must be
When, placed within Thy searching sight,
It shrinks not, but with calm delight
Can live, and look on Thee!

The Spirits that surround Thy throne
May bear the burning bliss;
But that is surely theirs alone,
Since they have never, never known
A fallen world like this.

Oh how shall I, whose native sphere
Is dark, whose mind is dim,
Before the Ineffable appear,
And on my naked spirit bear
That uncreated beam?

There is a way for man to rise
To that sublime abode,—
An Offering and a Sacrifice
A Holy Spirit's energies,
An advocate with God:

These, these prepare us for the sight
Of holiness above;
The sons of ignorance and night
May dwell in the Eternal Light,
Through the Eternal Love.

THOMAS BINNEY (1798–1874)

THOMAS BINNEY was a minister of Weigh House Chapel, a congregational church in London. He is well known for introducing the Nonconformist or non-Anglican churches to liturgical worship. He is also known for composing this poem, which was used as a hymn.

Here, Binney laments his inability to enter into the brightness of God's pure light. To understand the radiance of God, consider this: People cannot stare at the sun, which is a small part of God's creation, without going blind. How much less can they look upon the inexpressible glory of God and "bear the burning bliss"? To come into his very presence would mean instant death.

This is not Binney's only concern, though. He also expresses his reluctance to expose his soul to that light, to "bear that uncreated beam." But there is good news: The Son of God brought this light to people in such a way that they could receive it without perishing. This is why John says, "In him was life, and the life was the light of all people" (John 1:4, NRSV).

Binney rejoices in the provision that now "there is a way for man to rise to that sublime abode" where God dwells in blazing light. Both the Son and the Spirit are our Advocates, to bring us into the presence of God. And one day we will look upon the Lord as he really is and rejoice in his radiant presence (Matthew 5:8; 1 Corinthians 13:12; 1 John 3:2; Revelation 22:4).

For at the right time Christ will be revealed from heaven by the blessed and only almighty God, the King of kings and Lord of lords. He alone can never die, and he lives in light so brilliant that no human can approach him. No one has ever seen him, nor ever will. To him be honor and power forever. Amen. 1 Timothy 6:15-16

Live to Love

Since Life in sorrow must be spent,
So be it—I am well content,
And meekly wait my last Remove,
Seeking only growth in Love.

No bliss I seek but to fulfill
In life, in death, thy lovely will,
No succour in my woes I want,
Save what thou art pleas'd to grant.

Our days are number'd, let us spare
Our anxious hearts a needless care,—
'Tis thine to number out our days,
Ours to give them to thy praise.

Love is our only bus'ness here,
Love, simple, constant and sincere,
Oh blessed days thy servants see,
Spent O Lord, in pleasing Thee!

MADAME GUYON (1648–1717)

JEANNE-MARIE BOUVIER GUYON is quite well known, even to this day, because she revealed so much about herself and her spiritual experiences in a lengthy autobiography.

At age fifteen she was forced to learn inward prayer because her mother-in-law made her marriage miserable. Guyon was widowed at the age of twenty-eight. Four years later, she had an intense spiritual experience that she interpreted as a special, mystical union with God. Thereafter she spent her life communing with God, absorbed in his love. During this time, she wrote numerous poems, many of which were translated into English by William Cowper. These poems reveal a soul who was so completely attached to Christ that nothing mattered to her but Jesus' love. She knew by experience that life is sad and painful. The only way to carry on in this life is to love the Lord in the midst of the sadness:

Since Life in sorrow must be spent,
So be it—I am well content,
And meekly wait my last Remove,
Seeking only growth in Love.

Though we may not be as mystical or intense as Guyon, we can still deepen our love for Jesus by desiring him and devoting our heart to him. A story in the Gospel of Luke illustrates this kind of love. A sinful woman, forgiven by Jesus, poured out her love and gratitude on him while he was dining with Simon—to whom Jesus said:

Look at this woman kneeling here. When I entered your home, you didn't offer me water to wash the dust from my feet, but she has washed them with her tears and wiped them with her hair. You didn't give me a kiss of greeting, but she has kissed my feet again and again from the time I first came in. You neglected the courtesy of olive oil to anoint my head, but she has anointed my feet with rare perfume. I tell you, her sins—and they are many—have been forgiven, so she has shown me much love. Luke 7:44-47

Tell Me the Old, Old Story

Tell me the old, old story of unseen things above,
Of Jesus and His glory, of Jesus and His love.
Tell me the story simply, as to a little child,
For I am weak and weary, and helpless and defiled.

Tell me the story slowly, that I may take it in—
That wonderful redemption, God's remedy for sin.
Tell me the story often, for I forget so soon;
The "early dew" of morning has passed away at noon.

Tell me the story softly, with earnest tones and grave;
Remember, I'm the sinner whom Jesus came to save.
Tell me the story always, if you would really be,
In any time of trouble, a comforter to me.

Tell me the same old story when you have cause to fear
That this world's empty glory is costing me too dear.
Yes, and when that world's glory is dawning on my soul,
Tell me the old, old story: "Christ Jesus makes thee whole."

ARABELLA CATHERINE HANKEY (1834–1911)

ARABELLA CATHERINE HANKEY grew up in a well-to-do London suburb. Eager to spread God's Good News, she began a Bible class for girls in the neighborhood. At the age of eighteen, Hankey went to London to teach the Bible to the girls who worked in the factories. This continued for several years until in her early thirties, she became seriously ill and was confined to a year of bed rest. During this long convalesence, she wrote two lengthy poems. The first poem, printed in part here, was "Tell Me the Old, Old Story." The second poem is titled "I Love to Tell the Story." Both poems were later turned into hymns.

After ten months she felt strong enough to visit her brother in the jungles of South America, where she preached the Good News. She soon returned to her Bible classes in London and continued to tell the story of Jesus.

In this poem Hankey calls upon other believers to tell and retell her the story of God's salvation so that her appreciation for Jesus' love for her will be continually refreshed.

We who are Christians should never tire of hearing the Good News. It doesn't have to be "new" to be "good." The same old story should always be music to our ears.

So I am eager to come to you in Rome, too, to preach God's Good News. For I am not ashamed of this Good News about Christ. It is the power of God at work, saving everyone who believes—Jews first and also Gentiles. Romans 1:15-16

The H. Scriptures I

Oh Book! infinite sweetness! let my heart
Suck every letter, and a honey gain,
Precious for any grief in any part;
To clear the breast, to mollify all pain.

Thou art all health, health thriving till it make
A full eternity: thou art a mass
Of strange delights, where we may wish and take.
Ladies, look here; this is the thankful glass,
That mends the lookers' eyes: this is the well
That washes what it shows. Who can endear
Thy praise too much? thou art heaven's ledger
here,
Working against the states of death and hell.

Thou art joy's handsell: heaven lies flat in thee,
Subject to every mounter's bended knee.

GEORGE HERBERT (1593–1633)

GEORGE HERBERT was a brilliant man from a well-to-do Welsh family. He went to Cambridge at age fifteen and specialized in oratory. Herbert became a country priest and devoted his life to the church and to writing poetry of faith. *The Temple* (1633), published two months after Herbert's death, contains almost all of his poetry.

This poem is an uplifting presentation of Herbert's joyous relationship with God's Word. His expression of joy is similar to that of the psalmist who wrote Psalm 119. The psalmist found joy in the discovery of God's Word as one who had found a pearl of great price (see Matthew 13:45-46). He told the Lord, "I have chosen your precepts." This was his preference over all other objects of delight. The psalmist also expressed his longings for God's words and his dependence on God for the fleshing out of those words in appropriate, righteous actions. Not only did the psalmist carefully reflect on God's precepts, but God's Word became a mirror that reflected the actions and motives of his heart. Herbert speaks of this in his poem, as did James, who said, "Be doers of the word, and not hearers only" (1:22, RSV).

Simply reading (or hearing) the Bible will not profit us if we do not do what it says. Those who read the Word and don't follow it are like people who look at themselves in a mirror and then forget what they look like. God's Word accurately exposes the reality of man's inner nature in the same way that a mirror reminds us of the imperfections of our physical features. Once we see who we are, the very same Word can cleanse us (see John 15:3; Ephesians 5:26).

And remember, it is a message to obey, not just to listen to. . . . For if you just listen and don't obey, it is like looking at your face in a mirror but doing nothing to improve your appearance. . . . But if you keep looking steadily into God's perfect law—the law that sets you free—and if you do what it says and don't forget what you heard, then God will bless you for doing it. James 1:22-25

The Windhover TO CHRIST OUR LORD

I caught this morning morning's minion, king-
dom of daylight's dauphin, dapple-dawn-drawn
Falcon, in his riding
Of the rolling level underneath him steady air,
and striding
High there, how he rung upon the rein of a
wimpling wing
In his ecstasy! then off, off forth on swing,
As a skate's heel sweeps smooth on a bow-bend:
the hurl and gliding
Rebuffed the big wind. My heart in hiding
Stirred for a bird,—the achieve of, the mastery of the
thing!

Brute beauty and valour and act, oh, air, pride, plume,
here
Buckle! AND *the fire that breaks from thee then, a*
billion
Times told lovelier, more dangerous, O my
chevalier!

No wonder of it: shéer plód makes plough down
sillion
Shine, and blue-bleak embers, ah my dear,
Fall, gall themselves, and gash gold-vermilion.

GERARD MANLEY HOPKINS (1844–1889)

GERARD MANLEY HOPKINS was a Jesuit priest who struggled with whether or not he should write poetry. When he entered the Jesuit order, he burned all his poems and resolved not to write any more unless his superiors gave him permission. However, nothing could keep back this gifted poet. In 1875 he wrote his first well-known poem, "The Wreck of the Deutschland," a lament for the death of four nuns. In the following years he wrote several other great poems, including "The Windhover."

In his poetry Hopkins intently examined the characteristics that constitute the outward reflection of the inner nature of a living being. He always sought the principle that gave to any object its delicate and surprising uniqueness. To explain his poetic mission, he coined the words *inscape* and *instress.* Simply put, inscape is the individual essence of a living being. Instress is an outward expression of that essence. Through his unique study of life, Hopkins was able to appreciate the Lord and his character in nature. When speaking of a bluebell, Hopkins said: "I know the beauty of our Lord by it."

In this poem Hopkins sees qualities of Christ his Lord exhibited in the falcon. As he watches the "brute beauty and valour and act" of a falcon in flight, his senses catch fire, as it were, with a revelation of how much "lovelier" and "more dangerous" Christ, his "chevalier" (that is, his chivalrous one), is.

May God grant us mercy to catch glimpses of Christ through the world he created.

From the time the world was created, people have seen the earth and sky and all that God made. They can clearly see his invisible qualities—his eternal power and divine nature. So they have no excuse whatsoever for not knowing God. Romans 1:20

To Heaven

Good, and great God, can I not think of thee,
But it must, straight, my melancholy be?
Is it interpreted in me disease,
That, laden with sins, I seek for ease?
O, be thou witness, that the reins dost know,
And hearts of all, if I be sad for show,
And judge me after: if I dare pretend
To ought but grace, or aim at other end.
As thou art all, so be thou all to me,
First, midst, and last, converted one, and three;
My faith, my hope, my love: and in this state,
My judge, my witness, and my advocate.
Where have I been this while exiled from thee?
And whither raped, now thou but stoopst to me?
Dwell, dwell here still O, being every-where,
How can I doubt to find thee ever, here?
I know my state, both full of shame, and scorn,
Conceived in sin, and unto labor born,
Standing with fear, and must with horror fall,
And destined unto judgement, after all.
I feel my griefs too, and there scarce is ground,
Upon my flesh t'inflict another wound.
Yet dare I not complain, or wish for death
With holy Paul, lest it be thought the breath
Of discontent; or that these prayers be
For weariness of life, not love of thee.

BEN JONSON (1572–1637)

ONE OF THE MOST brilliant writers of English drama, Ben Jonson was a descendant of the Scottish Johnstones. He was educated at Westminster, worked as a bricklayer, served as a soldier, and eventually became an actor. In 1598 he was put on trial for murdering another actor in a duel, but he was acquitted with the help of some clergy.

In this poem Jonson makes honest confession to the Lord about his spiritual condition, aspirations, and fears. The overall tone of the poem is weariness. He's weary of his sin, weary of suffering, and weary of life. Because of this weariness and discontent, he wants to end his life and be with his Lord. Yet this isn't his only motive for departure. He does love the Lord, and because of that love he wants to leave this earth and go to heaven. Paul expresses the same desire: "For to me, living is for Christ, and dying is even better. . . . I'm torn between two desires: Sometimes I want to live, and sometimes I long to go and be with Christ" (Philippians 1:21-23).

This is one of the paradoxes of the Christian life. We desire heaven for both selfish and pure reasons. It is our hope that by the time we meet the Lord, our motives will be pure. Nonetheless, the hope is still sure. Our destiny is to see Jesus and live with him in eternity.

Yes, dear friends, we are already God's children, and we can't even imagine what we will be like when Christ returns. But we do know that when he comes we will be like him, for we will see him as he really is. And all who believe this will keep themselves pure, just as Christ is pure. 1 John 3:2-3

Morning Hymn

New every morning is the love
Our wakening and uprising prove;
Through sleep and darkness safely brought,
Restored to life, and power, and thought.

New mercies, each returning day,
Hover around us while we pray;
New perils past, new sins forgiven,
New thoughts of God, new hopes of heaven.

If, on our daily course, our mind
Be set to hallow all we find,
New treasures still, of countless price,
God will provide for sacrifice.

The trivial round, the common task,
Will furnish all we ought to ask;
Room to deny ourselves, a road
To bring us daily nearer God.

Only, O Lord, in thy dear love
Fit us for perfect rest above;
And help us this and every day
To live more nearly as we pray.

JOHN KEBLE (1792–1866)

JOHN KEBLE had played a key role in the Oxford movement of 1833, which aimed its furor at the apathy of the church in England. Of course, the church retaliated and opposed the Oxford movement. As a result, Keble was not permitted to become a professor, which is what he desired to be. So he spent the rest of his life in rural ministries. His devotional life, faithful visitation, teaching the church members, and attentiveness to the church services provided a model of the Oxford movement's principles. During this time, he produced *The Christian Year* (1827). This book, which became a devotional classic, includes poems for believers to use in worship throughout the church year. An extremely modest man, Keble published this book anonymously.

In this poem, taken from *The Christian Year,* Keble focuses on how each new morning provides an opportunity for renewed spiritual awakenings. Every believer can come to Christ anew and find his presence refreshing, like the morning dawn over a bubbling brook. This renewal can stay with us the whole day through if we set our mind on the things of the Spirit (Romans 8:6). This is clearly stated in the lines "If, on our daily course, our mind be set to hallow all we find." Instead of dreading the mundane chores and tasks of everyday life, we can take delight in communing with God while carrying out our daily activities: *"The trivial round, the common task, will furnish all we ought to ask; . . . to bring us daily nearer God."*

As we awake each day, we can decide from the start to live for Christ, refusing to waste the day complaining or living for self-fulfillment. By turning our heart and mind to Christ, we will not only gain a fresh knowledge of God but also mature in our faith and relationship with him.

Great is his faithfulness; his mercies begin afresh each day.
Lamentations 3:23

Recessional

God of our fathers, known of old—
Lord of our far-flung battle-line—
Beneath whose awful Hand we hold
Dominion over palm and pine—
Lord God of Hosts, be with us yet
Lest we forget—lest we forget!

The tumult and the shouting dies—
The Captains and the Kings depart—
Still stands Thine ancient Sacrifice,
An humble and a contrite heart.
Lord God of Hosts, be with us yet,
Lest we forget—lest we forget!

Far-called, our navies melt away—
On dune and headland sinks the fire—
Lo, all our pomp of yesterday
Is one with Nineveh and Tyre!
Judge of the Nations, spare us yet,
Lest we forget—lest we forget!

If, drunk with sight of power, we loose
Wild tongues that have not Thee in awe—
Such boasting as the Gentiles use
Or lesser breeds without the Law—
Lord God of Hosts, be with us yet,
Lest we forget—lest we forget!

For heathen heart that puts her trust
In reeking tube and iron shard—
All valiant dust that builds on dust,
And guarding calls not Thee to guard—
For frantic boast and foolish word,
Thy mercy on Thy People, Lord!

RUDYARD KIPLING (1865–1936)

RUDYARD KIPLING is famous for his books *Barrack-Room Ballads* and *The Jungle Book.* He was also a noteworthy poet. In 1897, when England was celebrating the diamond jubilee of Queen Victoria's reign, the editors of the London *Times* asked Kipling to compose a special poem for the occasion. The celebration was characterized by great processions and pompous displays of Britain's power.

Kipling struggled with this poem. He said, "It gave me more trouble than anything I had ever written." After Kipling had thrown away draft after draft, his wife picked one from the wastepaper basket and sent it to the *Times.* The paper published it. The poem was quite controversial because Kipling belittled Britian's power, as in the lines, "Lo, all our pomp of yesterday is one with Nineveh and Tyre!" Instead of praising his country's military prowess, Kipling called upon God for mercy and justice. This was a bold but needed prayer in the midst of the heyday of British imperialism. The proud heart—and proud nation—can easily forget its need for the sovereign Lord, the King of all nations.

And they were singing the song of Moses, the servant of God, and the song of the Lamb: "Great and marvelous are your actions, Lord God Almighty. Just and true are your ways, O King of the nations. Who will not fear, O Lord, and glorify your name? For you alone are holy. All nations will come and worship before you, for your righteous deeds have been revealed." Revelation 15:3-4

Shepherd of Eager Youth

Shepherd of eager youth,
Guiding in love and truth
Through devious ways—
Christ, our triumphant King,
We come Thy name to sing;
Hither Thy children bring
Tributes of praise.

Thou art our Holy Lord,
The all-subduing Word,
Healer of strife;
Thou didst Thyself abase
That from sin's deep disgrace
Thou mightest save our race
And give us life.

Ever be near our side,
Our shepherd and our guide,
Our staff and song;
Jesus, Thou Christ of God,
By Thy enduring Word
Lead us where Thou hast trod,
Make our faith strong.

CLEMENT OF ALEXANDRIA (c. 170–c. 220)
Translated by Henry Martyn Dexter (1821–1890)

TITUS FLAVIUS CLEMENT, born in Athens, Greece, of pagan parents, became a Christian after studying philosophy. He traveled to the centers of learning in the Greek-speaking East and then joined Pantaenus's school in Alexandria. Impressed by Pantaenus's ability to interpret Scripture, Clement remained in Alexandria and took over the leadership of this school when Pantaenus left Alexandria, never to return. Clement worked hard to establish this small school as the center of Christian study and mission. By A.D. 200 he had built up a flourishing community of well-educated Alexandrian Christians. But Clement fled Alexandria in 202 because of savage persecution. Origen took over after Clement and established a well-known school of Christian scholars.

This history is significant because it tells us that Clement was among the leading Christian scholars of the second century. During his years as a teacher in Alexandria (190–202), Clement wrote most of his works. In them he tried to show that God's revelation to humanity became clearer and clearer through the ages. God's revelation of himself came first through the Greek poets, then through the philosophers, and then through the Hebrew prophets. But the highest revelation of them all is the "Divine Word," the Christ of God. This is the one that Clement extols in this poem as "Shepherd," "Christ," "triumphant King," "Holy Lord," "all-subduing Word," and "Healer of strife." Here, Clement also personally thanks Jesus, his Great Shepherd, for having found him when he was an "eager youth" (that is, one eager to know the truth) and for guiding him "through devious ways" (that is, through many philosophies) to the truth.

Let us join Clement in asking Christ, our Shepherd, for his guidance into all truth.

Once you were wandering like lost sheep. But now you have turned to your Shepherd, the Guardian of your souls. 1 Peter 2:25

Take Time to Be Holy

Take time to be holy,
Speak oft with thy Lord;
Abide in Him always,
And feed on His Word.
Make friends of God's children;
Help those who are weak;
Forgetting in nothing
His blessing to seek.

Take time to be holy,
The world rushes on;
Much time spend in secret
With Jesus alone;
By looking at Jesus,
Like Him thou shalt be;
Thy friends in thy conduct
His likeness shall see.

Take time to be holy,
Let Him be thy guide,
And run not before Him
Whatever betide;
In joy or in sorrow
Still follow the Lord,
And, looking to Jesus,
Still trust in His Word.

Take time to be holy,
Be calm in thy soul;
Each thought and each motive
Beneath His control;
Thus led by His Spirit
To fountains of love,
Thou soon shalt be fitted
For service above.

WILLIAM DUNN LONGSTAFF (1822–1894)

THOUGH William Longstaff was the son of a wealthy English shipowner, he was a humble and devout Christian. He was also a close friend and dedicated supporter of the evangelistic team headed by D. L. Moody and Ira Sankey, whose evangelistic campaigns stirred England in the late 1800s. In one of these meetings, Longstaff heard a message about 1 Peter 1:16: "Be holy because I am holy." He was so moved by what he heard that he wrote down, in poetic form, what holiness meant to him. The poem was printed in a Christian newspaper in 1882. Many years later, the composer George Stebbins remembered the poem when he was asked if there was a good hymn on living a holy life. Finding the poem in the newspaper he had kept, he turned it into a hymn.

Holiness means to be completely separate from all that is common. Only God is completely "holy" because he alone is uniquely divine. But we are called upon to emulate him by partaking of his divine nature and expressing his holiness (2 Peter 1:3-4). The first stanza tells some of the things we can do to attain this holiness. We can spend time with the Lord in prayer, abide in his presence, feed on his Word, fellowship with other Christians, and do good to others. The second stanza tells us what will happen if we do these things: We will become like Jesus. What a wonderful outcome—to be like Christ! May God grant us all that we need to be transformed into the likeness of his blessed Son.

Obey God because you are his children. Don't slip back into your old ways of doing evil; you didn't know any better then. But now you must be holy in everything you do, just as God—who chose you to be his children—is holy. For he himself has said, "You must be holy because I am holy." 1 Peter 1:14-16

Samson Agonistes

Oh, how comely it is, and how reviving
To the spirits of just men long oppressed,
When God into the hands of their deliverer
Puts invincible might
To quell the mighty of the earth, th' oppressor,
The brute and boisterous force of violent men,
Hardy and industrious to support
Tyrannic power, but raging to pursue
The righteous, and all such as honor truth!
He all their ammunition
And feats of war defeats,
With plain heroic magnitude of mind
And celestial vigor armed;
Their armories and magazines contemns,
Renders them useless, while
With wingèd expedition
Swift as the lightning glance he executes
His errand on the wicked, who, surprised,
Lose their defense, distracted and amazed.
But patience is more oft the exercise
Of saints, the trial of their fortitude,
Making them each his own deliverer,
And victor over all
That tyranny or fortune can inflict.
Either of these is in thy lot,
Samson, with might endued
Above the sons of men; but sight bereaved
May chance to number thee with those
Whom patience finally must crown.

JOHN MILTON (1608–1674)

JOHN MILTON was an extraordinary man who experienced great success as well as terrible tragedy. But he is remembered most for his poetry, in particular his epic poem *Paradise Lost.* In 1671 he published *Samson Agonistes,* a poem about Samson's tribulation and triumph, in the form of Greek tragedy.

In *Samson Agonistes* John Milton focuses on Samson's last heroic act. Samson had performed many heroic acts on behalf of Israel in their constant struggle against the Philistines. The Spirit of the Lord was with this man from the beginning to the end. This was first manifest in Samson's bare-handed killing of the lion (Judges 14:6). Other mighty feats of strength showed the working of the Lord's Spirit in Samson (see, for example, Judges 14:19; 15:14; 16:3). But the greatest act occurred in the last moment of Samson's life (see Judges 16:23-30). Having been deceived by Delilah, captured by the Philistines, blinded, and then put on public display, it seemed as if his life was going to end in tragic defeat. But not so. As Samson stood in a temple full of Philistines, God enabled him to push over the pillars that held up the roof, destroying the temple, thousands of Philistines, and Samson. In Samson's final feat, more Philistines died than during all his earlier exploits.

Despite its appearance, Samson's premeditated act was not motivated by thoughts of a vindictive suicide. Rather, he wanted one last chance to show that God was with him in his fight against the Philistines. In fact, he must be regarded as one who died for his country's cause. Samson is ranked among the ancient heroes of the faith (Hebrews 11:32).

Then Samson put his hands on the center pillars of the temple and pushed against them with all his might. "Let me die with the Philistines," he prayed. And the temple crashed down on the Philistine leaders and all the people. So he killed more people when he died than he had during his entire lifetime. Judges 16:29-30

Death, Be Not Proud

Death, be not proud, though some have callèd thee
Mighty and dreadful, for thou are not so;
For those whom thou think'st thou dost overthrow
Die not, poor Death, nor yet canst thou kill me.
From rest and sleep, which but thy pictures be,
Much pleasure; then from thee much more must flow,
And soonest our best men with thee do go,
Rest of their bones, and soul's delivery.
Thou art slave to fate, chance, kings, and desperate men,
And dost with poison, war, and sickness dwell,
And poppy or charms can make us sleep as well
And better than thy stroke; why swell'st thou then?
One short sleep past, we wake eternally
And death shall be no more; Death, thou shalt die.

JOHN DONNE (1572–1631)

JOHN DONNE was not only one of the greatest metaphysical poets of his time, he was also one of the greatest preachers. His sermons were so powerful and popular that they were reproduced throughout England and preached by other ministers. Today, a complete collection of Donne's sermons fills ten volumes. His most famous passage is found in *Devotions upon Emergent Occasions* (1624). It begins with the line "No man is an island," and ends with "Ask not for whom the bell tolls; it tolls for thee." This was a reminder to all that the death of one person is not an isolated event. All share the same fate.

This poem, "Death, Be Not Proud," takes an opposite view. Instead of admitting that we all are mortal and must succumb to death, Donne proclaims the defeat of death and the end of mortality. Speaking to death as if it were a person, Donne confronts death with its ultimate demise. With poignant irony, the last line jabs: "Death, thou shalt die." Death cannot be proud because it will suffer what it has done to all others.

This language and tone echo those used by the apostle Paul, who taunted death, asking: "O death, where is your victory? O death, where is your sting?" The answer is potent: "Death is swallowed up in victory."

And who swallowed up death? Jesus, by experiencing death himself and overcoming it through his resurrection (see 1 Corinthians 15:54-57).

As believers in Christ's power over death, we can rest assured that our death will not be the end of us. We will have "one short sleep" and then "wake eternally." Therefore, we can live in peace, for our last enemy—death—has been conquered (1 Corinthians 15:26).

But all who receive God's wonderful, gracious gift of righteousness will live in triumph over sin and death through this one man, Jesus Christ. Romans 5:17

My Faith Looks Up to Thee

My faith looks up to thee,
Thou Lamb of Calvary,
Saviour divine!
Now hear me while I pray,
Take all my guilt away,
Oh, let me, from this day,
Be wholly thine!

May thy rich grace impart
Strength to my fainting heart,
My zeal inspire;
As thou hast died for me,
Oh! may my love to thee
Pure, warm, and changeless be,
A living fire!

While life's dark maze I tread
And griefs around me spread,
Be thou my Guide;
Bid darkness turn to day,
Wipe sorrow's tears away,
Nor let me ever stray
From thee aside.

When ends life's transient dream,
When death's cold, sullen stream
Shall o'er me roll;
Blest Saviour, then, in love,
Fear and distrust remove;
Oh, bear me safe above,
A ransomed soul.

RAY PALMER (1808–1887)

THIS POEM was written by Ray Palmer when he was a young man, long before he became a well-known American evangelist. Before he entered the ministry, he struggled with his inadequacies. During that time of frustration, he read a German poem about a sinner kneeling before Jesus' cross. He translated the poem into English and added some of his own verses. This is what he said about that composition:

> It is well-remembered when writing the last line, "O bear me safe above, a ransomed soul!" the thought that the whole work of redemption and salvation was involved in those words, and suggested the theme of eternal praises, and this brought me to a degree of emotion that brought abundant tears.

Palmer kept this poem in a notebook he carried with him and read it from time to time during devotions. A few years later, Lowell Mason, the well-known hymn writer, asked Palmer if he'd like to contribute a new hymn to a hymnal Mason was working on. Palmer gave him a copy of this poem. In his memoirs, Palmer recalled the incident:

> The little book containing the poem was shown him, and he asked for a copy. . . . Two or three days afterward, we met again in the street, when scarcely waiting to salute me, he earnestly exclaimed, "Mr. Palmer, you may live many years and do many good things, but I think you will be best known to posterity as the author of 'My Faith Looks Up to Thee.'"

We can be thankful that Palmer shared his poem, so that we, too, can be inspired to lift our heart and soul to him who was lifted up on the cross for our sins.

To you, O Lord, I lift up my soul. Psalm 25:1

On Dinah

When Dinah's careless eye was grown too lavish
To entertain, Shechem found time to ravish:
It is no less than silent invitation,
Although we scorn the sin, to give th' occasion:
Sure, Dinah's resolution was too strong,
Or to admit, or not resist a wrong,
And scorns to stoop to the adulterer's arms;
We often burn, intending but to warm's:
She went but out to see; perchance, to hear
What lust could say: What harm to lend an ear?
Another's sin, sometimes, procures our shames:
It stains our bodies; or, at least, our names.

FRANCIS QUARLES (1592–1644)

FRANCIS QUARLES, a metaphysical poet of the seventeenth century, wrote many poems that recounted biblical narratives. In this poem he retells a story that most Bible readers would rather forget: the rape of Dinah, the daughter of Jacob (Genesis 34:2-4).

Quarles believed that this was not a sudden happening but the result of lust getting the best of her. It's likely that she had been freely mixing in Shechem's society often and in so doing had been flattered by his attentions. Therefore, Quarles's poem implies that it should have come as no surprise when Shechem sexually forced himself upon Dinah.

Jacob, as a father and a good man, must have been deeply distressed when he found out about this. But he could do little, for his clan was small in number compared with the surrounding nations. Also, he was more concerned about the status of his family and their safety than about their honor. In addition, according to the custom of his day, it wasn't Jacob's responsibility to avenge his daughter. It was the full brothers who were supposed to protect their sister. They were the guardians of a sister's welfare and the avengers of her attackers. It was for this reason that Simeon and Levi, the two brothers of Dinah by Leah, avenged her by killing all the men of Shechem's nation. But this extermination could not erase the stain on Dinah's reputation—as the last two lines so poignantly charge: "Another's sin, sometimes, procures our shames: It stains our bodies; or, at least, our names."

Obviously, no woman deserves to experience the horrible and violent act of rape. But men and women alike do flirt with many other sinful situations. May God keep us from situations that give sin a free reign in our life. May we never sully the name of Christ.

➻ *And don't let us yield to temptation, but deliver us from the evil one.* Matthew 6:13

Like to the Arctic Needle

Like to the arctic needle, that doth guide
The wand'ring shade by his magnetic pow'r,
And leaves his silken gnomon to decide
The question of the controverted hour,
First frantics up and down from side to side,
And restless beats his crystal'd iv'ry case,
With vain impatience jets from place to place,
And seeks the bosom of his frozen bride;
At length he slacks his motion, and doth rest
His trembling point at his bright pole's beloved breast.

E'en so my soul, being hurried here and there,
By ev'ry object that presents delight,
Fain would be settled, but she knows not where;
She likes at morning what she loathes at night:
She bows to honour; then she lends an ear
To that sweet swan-like voice of dying pleasure,
Then tumbles in the scatter'd heaps of treasure;
Now flatter'd with false hope, now foil'd with fear.
Thus finding all the world's delight to be
But empty toys, good God, she points alone to thee. . . .

Eternal God! O thou that only art
The sacred fountain of eternal light,
And blessed loadstone of my better part,
O thou, my heart's desire, my soul's delight!
Reflect upon my soul, and touch my heart,
And then my heart shall prize no good above thee;
And then my soul shall know thee; knowing, love thee;
And then my trembling thoughts shall never start
From thy commands, or swerve the least degree,
Or once presume to move, but as they move in thee.

FRANCIS QUARLES (1592–1644)

AS WITH ALL the metaphysical poets, Quarles selected one physical image—that of a needle in a compass pointing to the north pole—to express a higher spiritual truth. In this poem (for which stanzas one, two, and five are printed opposite), Quarles uses this image to represent his desire to stay focused on God. The poet compares himself to the arctic needle (the needle on a compass that points to the north), which is subject to all kinds of forces. The "gnomon," basically a synonym for this needle, is a shaft in the compass that is perpendicular to the east/west horizon, and thus it guides the traveler by pointing north.

Like the needle, the poet finds himself moving all around, following this whim and that. What his soul finds attractive in the morning, it "loathes at night." Every desire pulls him in one direction or another. Finally, he is pulled by the greatest attraction of all—God himself! Until then, he is anything but "pointed" toward true north.

Doesn't this sound a lot like you and me? When we aren't focused on God, we are drawn to anything and everything that can possibly pique our interest. The needle on our compass points anywhere but true north. How we need God to attract us, to keep us on the right course!

[Jesus said,] "And when I am lifted up on the cross, I will draw everyone to myself." John 12:32

Eve PART ONE

'While I sit at the door,
Sick to gaze within,
Mine eye weepeth sore
For sorrow and sin:
As a tree my sin stands
To darken all lands;
Death is the fruit it bore.

'How have Eden bowers grown
Without Adam to tend them!
How have Eden flowers blown,
Squandering their sweet breath,
Without me to tend them!
The Tree of Life was ours,
Tree twelvefold-fruited,
Most lofty tree that flowers,
Most deeply rooted:
I chose the Tree of Death.

'Hadst thou but said me nay,
Adam, my brother,
I might have pined away;
I, but none other:
God might have let thee stay
Safe in our garden
By putting me away
Beyond all pardon.

'I, Eve, sad mother
Of all who must live,
I, not another,
Plucked bitterest fruit to give
My friend, husband, lover.
O wanton eyes run over;'

(continued in next day's reading)

CHRISTINA ROSSETTI (1830–1894)

CHRISTINA ROSSETTI began to write poetry at an early age. She wrote on many biblical themes and retold general Bible stories in poetic verse.

In this poem Rossetti presents us with the fallen Eve lamenting her sin and its consequences. She had been tempted by the serpent and had fallen for his lies. When he told her that her eyes would be opened if she ate the fruit of the tree of the knowledge of good and evil, he was promising her that she would see things not visible to human eyes (see 2 Kings 6:17). He aroused her natural desire for knowledge and prompted the thought that she might have supernatural wisdom, like that of the angels. When Eve saw that the tree was good for food, her imagination and feelings were completely won. The fall of Eve was soon followed by that of Adam.

The process of every temptation, and of every sin, is essentially the same. It begins with an attraction to a forbidden object. A person then becomes confused about right and wrong. Passionate desire increases and triumphs over moral reason. Finally, the person commits the sinful act, which ends in the degradation, slavery, and ruin of the soul (James 1:15; 1 John 2:16). May God protect us from the deceitfulness of sin.

"You won't die!" the serpent hissed. "God knows that your eyes will be opened when you eat it. You will become just like God, knowing everything, both good and evil." Genesis 3:4-5

Eve PART TWO

'Who but I should grieve?—
Cain hath slain his brother:
Of all who must die mother,
Miserable Eve!'

Thus she sat weeping,
Thus Eve our mother,
Where one lay sleeping
Slain by his brother.
Greatest and least
Each piteous beast
To hear her voice
Forgot his joys
And set aside his feast.
The mouse paused in his walk
And dropped his wheaten stalk;
Grave cattle wagged their heads
In rumination;
The eagle gave a cry
From his cloud station:
Larks on thyme beds
Forbore to mount or sing;
Bees drooped upon the wing;
The raven perched on high
Forgot his ration;
The conies in their rock,
A feeble nation,
Quaked sympathetical;
The mocking-bird left off to mock;
Huge camels knelt as if
In deprecation;
The kind hart's tears were falling;
Chattered the wistful stork;
Dove-voices with a dying fall
Cooed desolation
Answering grief by grief.
Only the serpent in the dust,
Wriggling and crawling,
Grinned an evil grin, and thrust
His tongue out with its fork.

CHRISTINA ROSSETTI (1830–1894)

IN THESE TWO STANZAS, the ultimate consequence of Adam and Eve's sin becomes readily apparent. Perhaps Adam and Eve thought the serpent didn't lie when he said they wouldn't die if they ate the fruit from the tree of the knowledge of good and evil. After all, both of them were still alive. But death—even murder—now raised its ugly head, as their first son, Cain, murdered their second son, Abel.

Rossetti depicts Eve as weeping over her dead son. And all creation—except the serpent—joins in her lament, because the fall of man affected the whole creation. This is graphically portrayed in Rossetti's images:

Bees drooped upon the wing; . . .
Huge camels knelt as if
In deprecation;
The kind hart's tears were falling; . . .

The earth—and all living things in it—was cursed when Adam and Eve sinned (see Genesis 3). But the earth—and all living things in it—will participate in man's redemption. It is no accident that Paul (in Romans 8) speaks of the redemption of nature as coinciding with the redemption of man's body—that physical part of his being that links him with the material creation. The world as we know it will not be annihilated; rather, the present universe will be completely transformed so that the world will then be able to fulfill the purpose for which God had created it.

All creation anticipates the day when it will join God's children in glorious freedom from death and decay. For we know that all creation has been groaning as in the pains of childbirth right up to the present time. And even we Christians, although we have the Holy Spirit within us as a foretaste of future glory, also groan to be released from pain and suffering. We, too, wait anxiously for that day when God will give us our full rights as his children, including the new bodies he has promised us. Romans 8:21-23

Teach Me, My God and King

Teach me, my God and King,
In all things Thee to see,
And what I do in anything,
To do it as for Thee.

A man that looks on glass,
On it may stay his eye,
Or, if he pleaseth, through it pass,
And then the heav'n espy.

All may of Thee partake:
Nothing can be so mean
Which with this motive, "For Thy sake,"
Will not grow bright and clean.

This is the famous stone
That turneth all to gold;
For that which God doth touch and own
Cannot for less be told.

GEORGE HERBERT (1593–1633)

GEORGE HERBERT devoted his life to the church and to writing poetry of faith. *The Temple* (1633), published two months after Herbert's death, contains almost all of his poetry.

In this poem he urges Christians to not stand apart from God but to partake of him and live for him. If a person keeps looking at himself or herself all the time (as in a mirror), the image will not change. But if people look beyond the "glass," to seek the Lord of heaven, they will be transformed into his very image—no matter how vile and "mean" they are. This concept is drawn from the apostle Paul, who said that we will be transformed into the image of the Lord as we gaze upon him.

The last stanza contains an allusion to the "philosopher's stone." Some believed that when this stone touched a baser metal, the stone turned it to gold. Thus, Herbert is saying that when we are touched by God, we are transformed by him, "the famous stone."

As the Spirit of the Lord works within us, we become more and more like him and reflect his glory even more. 2 Corinthians 3:18

Ode

The spacious firmament on high
With all the blue ethereal sky,
And spangled heavens, a shining frame,
Their great original proclaim:
The unwearied sun, from day to day,
Does his creator's power display,
And publishes to every land
The work of an almighty hand.

Soon as the evening shades prevail,
The moon takes up the wondrous tale,
And nightly to the listening earth
Repeats the story of her birth:
Whilst all the stars that round her burn,
And all the planets in their turn,
Confirm the tidings as they roll,
And spread the truth from pole to pole.

What though, in solemn silence, all
Move round the dark, terrestrial ball?
What though nor real voice nor sound
Amid their radiant orbs be found?
In reason's ear they all rejoice,
And utter forth a glorious voice,
For ever singing, as they shine,
'The hand that made us is divine'.

JOSEPH ADDISON (1672–1719)

JOSEPH ADDISON was an English statesman, known mostly for his essays that appeared in his periodical, *The Spectator*. He was also a successful playwright, poet, and politican. At one point he was secretary of state under King George I.

The title of this poem is "Ode." An ode is a lyric on a single theme, set in stanzas, and often of considerable length. Addison's poem is too short to be a true ode. The ode he refers to in his title is probably not the poem itself but its subject—the voice of creation, which chants, "The hand that made us is divine."

How long have the heavens declared the glory of God and the skies proclaimed the work of his hands (Psalm 19:1)? Since the fourth day of creation, when God said, "Let bright lights appear in the sky" (Genesis 1:14). Every day is a strictly patterned stanza. As the psalmist said, "Day after day they continue to speak; night after night they make him known" (Psalm 19:2). This chant is "their voice [which] goes out into all the earth" (Psalm 19:4, NIV). Invisible though they are, God's power and nature "have been understood and seen through the things he has made" (Romans 1:20, NRSV), for "there is no speech or language where their voice is not heard" (Psalm 19:3, NIV).

Many of us pray that family and friends will be open to God and believe in Jesus Christ. We hope that their ears will be opened to hear the gospel. But here's an idea: Let's pray that they first hear the greatest preacher of all—God's own creation. Everyday, without fail, "in reason's ear they all rejoice, and utter forth a glorious voice, for ever singing, as they shine, 'the hand that made us is divine.' "

From the time the world was created, people have seen the earth and sky and all that God made. They can clearly see his invisible qualities—his eternal power and divine nature. So they have no excuse whatsoever for not knowing God. Romans 1:20

Huswifery

Make me, O Lord, Thy spining wheel complete.
Thy Holy Word my distaff make for me.
Make mine affections Thy swift flyers neat
And make my soul Thy holy spool to be.
My conversation make to be Thy reel
And reel the yarn thereon spun of Thy wheel.

Make me Thy loom then, knit therein this twine:
And make Thy Holy Spirit, Lord, wind quills:
Then weave the web Thyself. The yarn is fine.
Thine ordinances make my fulling mills.
Then dye the same in heavenly colors choice,
All pinked with varnished flowers of paradise.

Then clothe therewith mine understanding, will,
Affections, judgment, conscience, memory,
My words, and actions, that their shine may fill
My ways with glory and Thee glorify.
Then mine apparel shall display before Ye
That I am clothed in holy robes for glory.

EDWARD TAYLOR (1642–1729)

EDWARD TAYLOR came to America seeking religious freedom. In 1668 he embarked on a ship headed for the Bay Colony (Massachusetts). After arriving in Massachusetts, Taylor attended Harvard College and graduated in 1671. He intended to stay at Harvard as a resident scholar, but instead he answered a call to become a minister for the church in Westfield, a small town one hundred miles west of Boston. He remained there until his death fifty-eight years later.

Taylor was also a metaphysical poet who wrote in the tradition of George Herbert. He contributed to our American heritage of Christian poetry and is credited with being the first American poet. This recognition did not come until the twentieth century, when his poetry was discovered in the Yale University library.

In this poem, Taylor uses metaphysical language to symbolize his desire for God to transform him. He asks the Lord to make him "Thy spining wheel complete." He requests that the Word would be his "distaff" (a staff used to hold the material for spinning), and he asks the Holy Spirit to "wind quills" (to wind yarn or thread around a spindle). With the Word and the Holy Spirit working in his life, the poet becomes the machine used by God to weave a garment displaying God's glory. Thus, the poet is both the spinning wheel and the woven cloth. These images, common in Taylor's day, take on an elevated meaning when likened to spiritual realities.

Jesus was also fond of using common items to depict spiritual truths. He used parables about men sowing seed and women baking bread to illustrate aspects of his kingdom. This method helps people to understand abstract concepts in concrete ways. May God enable us to see common things in a way that helps us understand spiritual realities.

"The Kingdom of Heaven is like yeast used by a woman making bread. Even though she used a large amount of flour, the yeast permeated every part of the dough. Matthew 13:33

Faith

The Father of the Faithful said,
At God's first calling, 'Here am I';
Let us by his example swayed,
Like him submit, like him reply,

'Go take thy son, thine only son,
And offer him to God thy King.'
The word was given: the work begun,
'The altar pile, the victim bring.'

But lo! th' angelic voice above
Bade the great Patriarch stop his hands;
'Know God is everlasting love,
And must revoke such harsh commands.'

Then let us imitate the Seer,
And tender with compliant grace
Ourselves, our souls, and children here,
Hereafter in a better place.

CHRISTOPHER SMART (1722–1771)

CHRISTOPHER SMART had an incredible prayer life. He thought nothing of kneeling in public to pray. Eventually this habit got him committed to a madhouse. While there, he began writing a new style of poetry that wasn't appreciated until the nineteenth century.

In this poem, Smart retells the story of Abraham's journey to Mount Moriah to sacrifice his son Isaac. In the biblical story, God asked Abraham to offer up his son as a sacrifice, and then at the last minute God sent his angel to prevent Abraham from doing so. What is amazing about this story is that Abraham was obedient from the moment he heard God's command. He made preparations for the sacrifice before setting out—gathering the materials and the knife and choosing the servants who would convey them.

During the three-day journey, Abraham kept the painful secret pent up in his chest. On the third day, the father and son ascended the hill, one bearing the knife, and the other, the wood for the sacrifice. But there was no victim, and to Isaac's insightful question, Abraham replied, "My son, God will provide himself a lamb for a burnt offering" (Genesis 22:8, KJV). Abraham spoke evasively to his son, who was unaware of the situation. Yet he also spoke in confidence. Abraham believed that if he sacrificed Isaac, God would miraculously restore him (Hebrews 11:19).

When God saw that Abraham would go through with the sacrifice, he stopped Abraham from carrying it out. God declared his acceptance of Abraham's sacrifice in the highest terms of approval, so much so that the New Testament speaks of it as though Abraham completed it (Hebrews 11:17; James 2:21).

It was by faith that Abraham offered Isaac as a sacrifice when God was testing him. . . . Abraham assumed that if Isaac died, God was able to bring him back to life again. Hebrews 11:17-19

The Tyger

Tyger! Tyger! burning bright
In the forests of the night,
What immortal hand or eye
Could frame thy fearful symmetry?

In what distant deeps or skies
Burnt the fire of thine eyes?
On what wings dare he aspire?
What the hand dare seize the fire?

And what shoulder, & what art,
Could twist the sinews of thy heart?
And when thy heart began to beat,
What dread hand? & what dread feet?

What the hammer? what the chain?
In what furnace was thy brain?
What the anvil? what dread grasp
Dare its deadly terrors clasp?

When the stars threw down their spears
And water'd heaven with their tears,
Did he smile his work to see?
Did he who made the Lamb make thee?

Tyger! Tyger! burning bright
In the forests of the night,
What immortal hand or eye
Dare frame thy fearful symmetry?

WILLIAM BLAKE (1757–1827)

IN THIS POEM Blake asks a compelling question: Could the same God who made a meek and mild lamb also make a ferocious and dreaded "tyger"? Another way to put the question is: Did God create both good and evil? Wisely, Blake doesn't explicitly answer the question. Rather, he implies that it was a daring act for God to make a counterpart to the Lamb. Why was this daring? Because the tiger (representing the devil and/or evil) could easily conquer the lamb. But in the end it is the Lamb of God who is the conquerer. According to the book of Revelation, the Lamb of God conquers all evil—even the devil himself (see 17:3-14; 19:11-21).

Still another way to understand what Blake did here is to look at his poem as a presentation of an incomprehensible God—one who makes both mild lambs and devouring tigers. Even Christ himself has both dispositions. He is as gentle as a lamb but as ferocious as a tiger. This dual picture of Christ is presented nowhere more dramatically than in Revelation 5. The Lamb of God, slaughtered for the sins of the world, is called "the Lion of the tribe of Judah," because he who died is now alive to become the conquering one!

Then I wept because no one could be found who was worthy to open the scroll and read it. But one of the twenty-four elders said to me, "Stop weeping! Look, the Lion of the tribe of Judah, the heir to David's throne, has conquered. He is worthy to open the scroll and break its seven seals." I looked and I saw a Lamb that had been killed but was now standing between the throne and the four living beings and among the twenty-four elders. Revelation 5:4-5

Walking with God

OH! for a closer walk with GOD,
A calm and heav'nly frame;
A light to shine upon the road
That leads me to the Lamb!

Where is the blessedness I knew
When first I saw the LORD?
Where is the soul-refreshing view
Of JESUS, and his word?

What peaceful hours I once enjoy'd!
How sweet their mem'ry still!
But they have left an aching void,
The world can never fill.

Return, O holy Dove, return,
Sweet messenger of rest;
I hate the sins that made thee mourn,
And drove thee from my breast.

The dearest idol I have known,
Whate'er that idol be;
Help me to tear it from thy throne,
And worship only thee.

So shall my walk be close with GOD,
Calm and serene my frame;
So purer light shall mark the road
That leads me to the Lamb.

WILLIAM COWPER (1731–1800)

AFTER YEARS of fighting depresssion and insanity, William Cowper started reading the Bible and eventually found peace in Christ. But this solace and peace never lasted for Cowper. He moved in and out of depression and struggled constantly with insanity. The precious simplicity of Jesus' presence that he first experienced eluded him time and again. The yearning for a closer, more constant walk with God is what prompted this poem.

Cowper thought that God's presence had left him because of his sin: "I hate the sins that . . . drove thee from my breast." Many believers share the same feelings. They long for the presence of the Lord when they think they have done something to offend him. David, the psalmist, knew this painfully well. Having committed adultery and murder, he asked the Lord for forgiveness and for the Lord's presence to return to him.

➻ *Oh, give me back my joy again; you have broken me—now let me rejoice. Don't keep looking at my sins. Remove the stain of my guilt. Create in me a clean heart, O God. Renew a right spirit within me. Do not banish me from your presence, and don't take your Holy Spirit from me. Restore to me again the joy of your salvation, and make me willing to obey you.* Psalm 51:8-12

To Learn the Transport by the Pain

To learn the Transport by the Pain—
As Blind Men learn the sun!
To die of thirst—suspecting
That Brooks in Meadows run!

To stay the homesick—homesick feet
Upon a foreign shore—
Haunted by native lands, the while—
And blue—beloved air!

This is the Sovereign Anguish!
This—the signal woe!
These are the patient "Laureates"
Whose voices—trained—below—

Ascend in ceaseless Carol—
Inaudible, indeed,
To us—the duller scholars
Of the Mysterious Bard!

EMILY DICKINSON (1830–1886)

EMILY DICKINSON lived a life of self-confinement. She never married and rarely left her family home in Amherst, Massachusetts. Though physically limited, her imagination soared, and her poems are among the most sublime, earning her a reputation as the greatest American female poet.

In this phenomenal poem, Dickinson tells us, line after line, that experiential pain and suffering are our earthly teachers. Indeed, they are the "patient 'Laureates' " (poets) that sing to us of a higher life. They tell us of "the Mysterious Bard," who allows us to experience trials so that we might long for something else.

If all were well now on this earth, we would never desire a different life. We would want to keep the one we have. But pain and suffering instill in our souls a "homesick" longing to be transported to a world where there is no pain. In truth, pain and suffering are part of God's sovereign plan to make us yearn for paradise.

The life that pain and suffering cause us to anticipate is found in eternity, in the New Jerusalem. There God will live with his people, and they with him. In this new world, God will wipe away all tears from our eyes and take away all remembrance of our past pain. In the meantime, pain and suffering prompt us to look heavenward.

Look, the home of God is now among his people! He will live with them, and they will be his people. God himself will be with them. He will remove all of their sorrows, and there will be no more death or sorrow or crying or pain. For the old world and its evils are gone forever. Revelation 21:3-4

I Shall Know Why

I shall know why—when Time is over—
And I have ceased to wonder why—
Christ will explain each separate anguish
In the fair schoolroom of the sky—

He will tell me what "Peter" promised—
And I—for wonder at his woe—
I shall forget the drop of Anguish
That scalds me now—that scalds me now!

EMILY DICKINSON (1830–1886)

NOT MUCH is known about Dickinson's personal life, but apparently it was lonely and painful. Whatever her particular pains were, she believed that one day she would know why she had suffered. This poem is an expression of her belief. In the first stanza she wrote, "Christ will explain each separate anguish in the fair schoolroom of the sky." Dickinson knew that while she was alive she would probably never know why she suffered. She would have to wait until she met Christ in heaven to get an answer to that question.

But, more important, Dickinson realized that her sufferings were nothing compared to Christ's. Thus, in awe of Jesus' woe, she would "forget the drop of Anguish that scalds me now."

Most of us want a full explanation *now* for our present sufferings. But this is not always possible. As Paul wrote in 1 Corinthians, "Now we see things imperfectly as in a poor mirror" (13:12). Mirrors in Paul's time were made of polished brass or other metals. They gave a hazy or blurred reflection, which is expressed by the Greek word *enigma,* an appropriate description of so much of this life. Although we cannot see things clearly now, we will one day. Paul assured the Corinthians—and us—that in the future "we will see everything with perfect clarity" (13:12). When that day comes, we will not only know why all things happened but also soon forget the anguish we have experienced in this life. And, like Dickinson, we will see Christ's sufferings as greater than our own.

Now we see things imperfectly as in a poor mirror, but then we will see everything with perfect clarity. All that I know now is partial and incomplete, but then I will know everything completely, just as God knows me now. 1 Corinthians 13:12

I Love to Tell the Story

I love to tell the story of unseen things above,
Of Jesus and His glory, of Jesus and His love.
I love to tell the story, because I know 'tis true;
It satisfies my longings as nothing else can do.

I love to tell the story, more wonderful it seems
Than all the golden fancies of all our golden dreams.
I love to tell the story, it did so much for me;
And that is just the reason I tell it now to thee.

I love to tell the story, 'tis pleasant to repeat
What seems, each time I tell it, more wonderfully sweet.
I love to tell the story, for some have never heard
The message of salvation from God's own Holy Word.

I love to tell the story, for those who know it best
Seem hungering and thirsting to hear it like the rest.
And when, in scenes of glory, I sing the new, new song,
'Twill be the old, old story that I have loved so long.

ARABELLA CATHERINE HANKEY (1834–1911)

WHEN ARABELLA CATHERINE HANKEY became extremely sick, she was confined to a year of bed rest. During this long, lonely period, she wrote two substantial poems. The first poem was "Tell Me the Old, Old Story." The second poem, printed in part here, was "I Love to Tell the Story." Both poems were later turned into hymns.

In this poem, Hankey overflows with exuberant joy and delight in one special privilege: She can proclaim the story of God's salvation! This is good news for all who will hear and accept it. It is also good news for those who have never heard it and for those who need to hear it again and again. It is food for those who hunger and thirst for God.

The gospel is spiritual food for those who preach it as well. Recall the story of Jesus and the Samaritan woman in John 4. The disciples had gone into town looking for food. Jesus stayed by the well, where he encountered the woman. There he preached the gospel to her, and she drank in this living water. Although Jesus was physically hungry, as he preached he was nourished. The disciples wondered who had fed Jesus when he refused to eat the food they brought him. But Jesus explained to them that he was "fed" by doing the will of his Father. As Christ's example shows us, nothing is more satisfying than proclaiming the Good News.

➻ *How can they call on [the Lord] to save them unless they believe in him? And how can they believe in him if they have never heard about him? And how can they hear about him unless someone tells them? And how will anyone go and tell them without being sent? That is what the Scriptures mean when they say, "How beautiful are the feet of those who bring good news!"* Romans 10:14-15

God's Grandeur

The world is charged with the grandeur of God.
It will flame out, like shining from shook foil;
It gathers to a greatness, like the ooze of oil
Crushed. Why do men then now not reck his rod?
Generations have trod, have trod, have trod;
And all is seared with trade; bleared, smeared with toil;
And wears man's smudge and shares man's smell: the soil
Is bare now, nor can foot feel, being shod.

And for all this, nature is never spent;
There lives the dearest freshness deep down things;
And though the last lights off the black West went
Oh, morning, at the brown brink eastward, springs—
Because the Holy Ghost over the bent
World broods with warm breast and with ah! bright wings.

GERARD MANLEY HOPKINS (1844–1889)

HOPKINS was always intent on examining the characteristics that constitute the outward reflection of the inner nature of a living being. He was always looking for the principle that gave to any object its delicate and surprising uniqueness. Writing in his journal, Hopkins said, "I thought how sadly beauty of inscape was unknown and buried away from simple people and yet how near at hand it was if they had eyes to see it and it could be called out everywhere again" (for an explanation of *inscape,* see January 16).

Of all his poems, this is the best example of Hopkins's desire to show that the vitality of all living things emanates from a supernatural inner essence. As he put it: "There lives the dearest freshness deep down things."

This poem also celebrates the resilience of nature to overcome human exploitation. This theme speaks to our age, when we are painfully aware of how much damage industrialization has done to our environment. Yet life will prevail! The Holy Spirit, who gave birth to this creation (Genesis 1:2), still broods over it—to generate life anew. This is exquisitely expressed in the last stanza:

And though the last lights off the black West went
Oh, morning, at the brown brink eastward, springs—
Because the Holy Ghost over the bent
World broods with warm breast and with ah! bright wings.

➼ *In the beginning God created the heavens and the earth. The earth was empty, a formless mass cloaked in darkness. And the Spirit of God was hovering over its surface.* Genesis 1:1-2

Sun of My Soul, Thou Savior Dear

Sun of my soul, Thou Savior dear,
It is not night if Thou be near;
O may no earthborn cloud arise
To hide Thee from Thy servant's eyes.

When the soft dews of kindly sleep
My wearied eyelids gently steep,
Be my last thought, how sweet to rest
Forever on my Savior's breast.

Abide with me from morn till eve,
For without Thee I cannot live;
Abide with me when night is nigh,
For without Thee I dare not die.

If some poor wandering child of Thine
Has spurned, today, the voice divine,
Now, Lord, the gracious work begin;
Let him no more lie down in sin.

Watch by the sick; enrich the poor
With blessings from Thy boundless store;
Be every mourner's sleep tonight,
Like infants' slumbers, pure and light.

Come near and bless us when we wake,
Ere through the world our way we take,
Till in the ocean of Thy love
We lose ourselves in heaven above.

JOHN KEBLE (1792–1866)

KEBLE was the author of a nineteenth-century devotional classic titled *The Christian Year* (1827). This book contained poems, such as "Sun of My Soul," for believers to use in worship throughout the church year.

This poem highlights a common biblical theme—namely, that Christ came into the world to give light. Believers are children of light, who live in the light and depend on the light. They have been transferred from the kingdom of darkness into the kingdom of light. Keble said it well when he told the Lord, "It is not night if Thou be near."

One of the most precious and profound stanzas of the poem is the third:

Abide with me from morn till eve,
For without Thee I cannot live;
Abide with me when night is nigh,
For without Thee I dare not die.

Here, Keble asks for the Lord's presence every waking moment because he cannot live without him. He also asks for the Lord's presence in his sleep, which is a foreshadowing of death.

Every night we take our leave from this life. One day we will take our leave forever. In both day and night, we need Christ with us. In both life and death, we want to live with Christ. This is not far from what Paul said when he proclaimed, "For to me, to live is Christ" (Philippians 1:21, NIV). May this also be our aspiration and daily reality.

Life itself was in him, and this life gives light to everyone. The light shines through the darkness, and the darkness can never extinguish it. John 1:4-5

Psalm 103: 'Praise the Lord, O My Soul'

Praise, my soul, the King of heaven;
To his feet thy tribute bring;
Ransomed, healed, restored, forgiven,
Who like thee his praise should sing?
Praise him, praise him,
Praise the everlasting King.

Praise him for his grace and favour
To our fathers in distress;
Praise him still the same for ever,
Slow to chide, and swift to bless:
Praise him, praise him,
Glorious in his faithfulness.

Father-like he tends and spares us;
Well our feeble frame he knows;
In his hands he gently bears us,
Rescues us from all our foes:
Praise him, praise him,
Widely as his mercy flows.

Angels, help us to adore him,
Ye behold him face to face;
Sun and moon, bow down before him;
Dwellers all in time and space,
Praise him, praise him.
Praise with us the God of grace.

HENRY LYTE (1793–1847)

HENRY LYTE was a minister in Ireland and England. Throughout his life he struggled with ill health. He often traveled to other countries, seeking moderate climates and possible cures for his illnesses. He died in Nice, a French town located on the Mediterranean coast, and was buried there in the British cemetery.

Lyte's poems and hymns often expressed dependence on God that grew out of his experiences of suffering. Some of his hymns were published in *Poems Chiefly Religious* (1833). He published his metrical psalms in *Spirit of the Psalter* (1834).

This work, "Psalm 103: 'Praise the Lord, O My Soul,' " is one of the best poems from his book *Spirit of the Psalter.* It is based on a psalm in which David praises God for all the good things God had given him.

David knew that God is the true King, worthy of praise and adoration. God, our King, is not cruel. He is kind and just. He is "slow to chide, and swift to bless." That is because he knows our weaknesses, our shortcomings, and our frailties. David, though a mighty warrior, was also a weak sinner who relied on God's grace, favor, and faithfulness. We, too, rely on God, our kind King, for many things, such as forgiveness of sins, healing of diseases, justice for the oppressed, and even life itself. Let us gladly join David and Henry in praising our everlasting King.

Praise the Lord, I tell myself; with my whole heart, I will praise his holy name. Praise the Lord, I tell myself, and never forget the good things he does for me. He forgives all my sins and heals all my diseases. He ransoms me from death and surrounds me with love and tender mercies. He fills my life with good things. My youth is renewed like the eagle's! Psalm 103:1-5

The Caged Skylark

As a dare-gale skylark scanted in a dull cage
Man's mounting spirit in his bone-house, mean house, dwells—
That bird beyond the remembering his free fells;
This in drudgery, day-labouring-out life's age.

Though aloft on turf or perch or poor low stage,
Both sing sometímes the sweetest, sweetest spells,
Yet both droop deadly sómetimes in their cells
Or wring their barriers in bursts of fear or rage.

Not that the sweet-fowl, song-fowl, needs no rest—
Why, hear him, hear him babble and drop down to his nest,
But his own nest, wild nest, no prison.

Man's spirit will be flesh-bound when found at best,
But uncumberèd: meadow-down is not distressed
For a rainbow footing it nor he for his bónes rísen.

GERARD MANLEY HOPKINS (1844–1889)

IN THIS POEM Hopkins compares the skylark in a cage to the human spirit in a mortal body. Neither is at home. Both are bound. As the skylark needs to live in the wild to set its spirit singing, so people will need a new, resurrected body to suit their new life after death and resurrection.

We see this vividly in the resurrection of Jesus. His resurrected body was altogether different from the one that was buried. In death he had been sown like a seed in corruption, dishonor, and weakness. But in resurrection he came forth in perfection, glory, and power. The natural body that Jesus possessed as a man became a spiritual body when he rose from the dead.

When God made the first man, Adam, he created him to be a living soul with a physical body. The last Adam, Jesus, became life-giving spirit with a spiritual body (1 Corinthians 15:40-45). One day all Christians will have a resurrected, spiritual body for their new spiritual life in glory. This is wonderful news! We will become uncaged, new-bodied skylarks!

It is the same way for the resurrection of the dead. Our earthly bodies, which die and decay, will be different when they are resurrected, for they will never die. Our bodies now disappoint us, but when they are raised, they will be full of glory. They are weak now, but when they are raised, they will be full of power. They are natural human bodies now, but when they are raised, they will be spiritual bodies. For just as there are natural bodies, so also there are spiritual bodies.
1 Corinthians 15:42-44

In Memoriam CXXVI (126)

Love is and was my lord and king,
And in his presence I attend
To hear the tidings of my friend,
Which every hour his couriers bring.

Love is and was my king and lord,
And will be, though as yet I keep
Within the court on earth, and sleep
Encompassed by his faithful guard,

And hear at times a sentinel
Who moves about from place to place,
And whispers to the worlds of space,
In the deep night, that all is well.

ALFRED, LORD TENNYSON (1809–1892)

ALFRED, LORD TENNYSON, is considered one of the greatest and most popular poets of his time. He devoted himself to the craft of poetry while living in Cambridge in the late 1820s. There he also became a close friend of Arthur Henry Hallam. In 1833 Hallam died suddenly at the age of twenty-two. His death inspired Tennyson to write a long sequence of elegies that became the poem *In Memoriam.*

In this section of *In Memoriam,* Tennyson draws heavily upon palace imagery. His king, which is Love, is in the heavenly palace. Tennyson's friend (presumably Hallam) has already gone to heaven to be in the presence of the King. Tennyson waits outside in the earthly court to hear about how his friend is doing. The King sends him couriers with news, gives him a guard to protect him, and even a sentinel to keep him during the night. The poet is still separated from his beloved friend, as well as from the King himself. But Love keeps him hoping and trusting. Nothing would separate him from Love.

Paul expounded on the same theme in his letter to the Romans, where he declared that "nothing in all creation will ever be able to separate us from the love of God that is revealed in Christ Jesus our Lord" (8:39). In context, he was speaking of all the trials life brings—including the ultimate trial, death. No trial, no matter how grievous, can separate us from Christ's love. Rather, we are victorious over these trials "through Christ, who loved us." Paul was convinced of this reality, as we should be. But words can't convince us; only life experience can.

And I am convinced that nothing can ever separate us from his love. Death can't, and life can't. The angels can't, and the demons can't. Our fears for today, our worries about tomorrow, and even the powers of hell can't keep God's love away. Romans 8:38

The Thief

Thou rob'st my Daies of bus'nesse and delights.
Of sleep thou rob'st my Nights;
Ah, Lovely Thiefe, what wilt thou doe?
What? Rob me of Heaven too?
Thou, even my prayers thou hauntest me;
And I, with wild Idolatry,
Begin, to God, and end them all, to Thee.

Is it a Sinne to Love, that it should thus,
Like an ill Conscience, torture us?
What ere I do, where ere I go,
(None Guiltless ere was haunted so)
Still, still, methinks thy face I view,
And still thy shape does me pursue,
As if, not you Mee, but I had murthered You.

From books I strive some remedy to take,
But thy Name all the Letters make;
What ere 'tis writ, I find that there,
Like Points and Comma's every where,
Me blesst for this let no man hold;
For I, as Midas did of old,
Perish by turning every thing to Gold.

What do I seek, alas, or why do I
Attempt in vain from thee to fly;
From making thee my Deitie,
I gave thee then Ubiquitie.
My pains resemble Hell in this;
The divine presence there too is,
But to torment Men, not to give them blisse.

ABRAHAM COWLEY (1618–1667)

ABRAHAM COWLEY was a Royalist who was imprisoned during Cromwell's regime but managed to survive by pretending to conform to Cromwell. An extremely erudite man, he wrote sophisticated metaphysical poetry and even introduced the Pindaric ode to English verse.

This poem is fascinating, for it depicts the poet's struggle with loving someone (or perhaps something) more than he loves God. The "Lovely Thief" seems to be both the person loved and the presence of God—or God's Spirit activating the poet's conscience. The poet can escape from neither. Both are everywhere. The more he loves this person or thing, the more guilty he feels—even haunted by God. In his struggle to be free from guilt, the poet questions, "Is it a [sin] to love?" Apparently so, because God seems to be pursuing him as if he were a criminal, even a murderer. But how had he "murdered" God? Apparently he had done so by giving his love to someone or something other than God. At least this is the way the poet felt. In any event, the result was psychological "hell" and torment for the poet. He felt as if he was guilty of idolatry.

Many Christians who sincerely love the Lord have struggled with these feelings. They wonder if they have slighted God by loving their spouse or children with a fervor that seems to be greater than their love for God. This is well worth examining. But the truth is, those who are concerned about this are those who love God to the utmost. If they didn't, they would not struggle with this issue. May God direct our heart to love him the most and keep us from loving anyone or anything else more than him.

You must love the Lord your God with all your heart, all your soul, all your mind, and all your strength. Mark 12:30

The Soul That Loves God Finds Him Everywhere

Oh thou, by long experience tried,
Near whom no grief can long abide
My Love! how full of sweet content
I pass my years of banishment.

All scenes alike engaging prove
To souls impress'd with sacred love,
Where'er they dwell, they dwell in thee,
In heav'n, in earth or on the sea.

To me remains nor place nor time,
My country is in ev'ry clime,
I can be calm and free from care
On any shore, since God is there.

While place we seek, or place we shun,
The soul finds happiness in none,
But with a God to guide our way,
'Tis equal joy to go or stay.

Could I be cast where thou art not,
That were indeed a dreadful, lot,
But regions none remote I call,
Secure of finding God in all.

My country, Lord, art thou alone,
Nor other can I claim or own,
The point where all my wishes meet,
My law, my love, life's only sweet.

MADAME GUYON (1648–1717)

MADAME GUYON is known for her mystical experiences with God. As a result of this relationship, she believed she had authority and insight beyond that of official church leaders. Guyon traveled extensively throughout France, making both disciples and enemies.

In 1686 Guyon went to Paris and became influential at court. During that time the church began to suppress all those it considered to be unorthodox mystic spiritualists. For example, Miguel de Molinos, a deviant Spanish priest, was condemned by the church and imprisoned for his writings on the meditative life. In 1687 Father Lacombe—Guyon's closest disciple and confessor—was arrested. Eventually Guyon herself was confined to a convent; she calls this her "years of banishment." In exile from her own country, Guyon experienced God as her "country": "My country, Lord, art thou alone, nor other can I claim or own." As is evident in this poem (only the first six stanzas are printed opposite), she enjoyed God's presence as her domain. It did not matter where she went, for she was at home in God wherever she was.

As Guyon's experience illustrates, those who truly seek God are often misunderstood and mistreated. They can become exiles in their own country. But as God's Word tells us, those people are "no more than foreigners and nomads here on earth" (Hebrews 11:13). Their real home is heaven. Their comfort on earth is God's presence, which is everywhere for those who seek him. This was David's realization when he penned these beautiful words:

If I go up to heaven, you are there; if I go down to the place of the dead, you are there. If I ride the wings of the morning, if I dwell by the farthest oceans, even there your hand will guide me, and your strength will support me. Psalm 139:8-10

Love II

Immortal Heat, O let thy greater flame
Attract the lesser to it: let those fires,
Which shall consume the world, first make it tame,
And kindle in our hearts such true desires,

As may consume our lusts, and make thee way.[a]
Then shall our hearts pant thee;[b] *then shall our brain*
All her invention on thine Altar lay,
And there in hymns send back thy fire again.

Our eyes shall see thee, which before saw dust;
Dust blown by wit, till that they both were blind:
Thou shalt recover all thy goods in kind,
Who wert disseized[c] *by usurping lust:*

All knees shall bow to thee, all wits shall rise,
And praise him who did make and mend our eyes.

GEORGE HERBERT (1593–1633)

[a] make way for you [b] pant for [c] dispossessed by force

GEORGE HERBERT is generally considered one of the greatest metaphysical poets. He wrote his poetry during the years he was a priest at Bemerton. Almost all of Herbert's poetry is contained in *The Temple* (1633), which was published two months after his death. The book concludes with a group of poems on the Last Things, culminating with "Love III." This, the penultimate poem in the book, extols the virtues of God's love.

In typical metaphysical fashion, the poet compares God to fire. Of course, Herbert wasn't the first one to make this comparison. The writer of Hebrews said, "For our God is a consuming fire" (Hebrews 12:29). But whereas the writer of Hebrews was speaking of God's ability to consume the disobedient, Herbert was recognizing God's ability to consume our lusts, our vain wittiness, and our mental inventions. Herbert calls upon God to consume all the small fires in our soul—our lusts and vain imaginations—with God's great fire. Having been purged thereby, we can have pure hearts to see God and pure spirits to worship him.

This poem echoes what Peter said about God's fire. One day it will sweep through the world in complete, consuming judgment. For now, it moves through the household of God, purging us and purifying our souls (see 1 Peter 4:12-17; 2 Peter 3:11-12). This is the love of God for us. This is his passion: to make us pure.

May we pray, with Herbert, that all our "lesser" flames would be taken over by God, the "Immortal Heat," the "greater flame." He will then consume whatever consumes us and make us free to love him.

God blesses those whose hearts are pure, for they will see God.
Matthew 5:8

Holy Sonnet XIV

Batter my heart, three-personed God; for you
As yet but knock, breathe, shine, and seek to mend;
That I may rise and stand, o'erthrow me, and bend
Your force to break, blow, burn, and make me new.
I, like an usurped town, to another due,
Labor to admit you, but O, to no end;
Reason, your viceroy in me, me should defend,
But is captived, and proves weak or untrue.
Yet dearly I love you, and would be loved fain,
But am betrothed unto your enemy.
Divorce me, untie or break that knot again;
Take me to you, imprison me, for I,
Except you enthrall me, never shall be free,
Nor ever chaste, except you ravish me.

JOHN DONNE (1572–1631)

JOHN DONNE was one of the greatest English poets and preachers of the 1600s. His deep intellect and fiery emotions are evident in both his poetry and sermons.

A descendant of Saint Thomas More, Donne was raised a Roman Catholic, but in the 1590s he became a member of the Church of England. In 1597 he became secretary to Sir Thomas Egerton. He fell in love with Egerton's niece, Ann More, and they eloped in 1601. Ann's father disapproved of the marriage and caused Egerton to dismiss Donne from his job. Thereafter, Donne struggled with poverty, which ended only in 1615 when Donne accepted the king's invitation to become an Anglican priest.

These experiences of poverty and failure caused Donne to rely on God and cherish his love. This poem expresses the poet's desire for God—the entire Triune God—to take over his being. Donne compares himself to a captive town that can never be free unless God captures the capturer (the enemy) and sets Donne free. And with pungent, dramatic irony, Donne declares that he can never be "chaste"—a spiritual virgin—unless God ravishes him. Wooing had not worked. Donne needed God to take violent action, to batter down his heart and take it over completely.

Sometimes we need to ask God to take over our heart and mind in a radical way. In doing so, he will not enslave us or usurp us. Rather, he will free us. Until God completely occupies us, we will be occupied with everything but God.

I will make you my wife forever, showing you righteousness and justice, unfailing love and compassion. I will be faithful to you and make you mine, and you will finally know me as Lord.
Hosea 2:19-20

Paradise Lost BOOK I, LINES 1–16

Of man's first disobedience, and the fruit
Of that forbidden tree whose mortal taste
Brought death into the world, and all our woe,
With loss of Eden, till one greater Man
Restore us, and regain the blissful seat,
Sing, Heavenly Muse, that on the secret top
Of Oreb, or of Sinai, didst inspire
That shepherd who first taught the chosen seed
In the beginning how the heavens and earth
Rose out of Chaos: or, if Sion hill
Delight thee more, and Siloa's brook that flowed
Fast by the oracle of God, I thence
Invoke thy aid to my adventurous song,
That with no middle flight intends to soar
Above th' Aonian mount, while it pursues
Things unattempted yet in prose or rhyme.

JOHN MILTON (1608–1674)

THE SUBJECT of Milton's grand poem is made clear in the opening five lines. His intent was to explain how Adam and Eve lost Paradise, which was then regained through Jesus, the "greater Man."

Milton asks for extraordinary inspiration for his literary design of pursuing "things unattempted yet in prose or rhyme." Alluding to classical Greek and biblical images, he calls upon the "Heavenly Muse" to give him inspiration that superseded that which came from the "Aonian mount" (a mountain sacred to the muses). In poetic fashion he asks that the inspiration come from one of two different mountains—both with biblical significance: Mt. Horeb (which is the same as Mt. Sinai), the place where the Law was given; or Mt. Zion, the hill on which Jerusalem, the city of God, was built. God had inspired Moses ("that shepherd") to write of the beginnings of the world in Genesis 1–3. Milton asked that same divine Inspirer to be with him in his composition of *Paradise Lost.*

When composing this epic poem, Milton did not follow the biblical sequence of events in his account. Instead he used flashbacks and flash-forwards to rearrange the chronology of the creation story, which is presented as: (1) the war in heaven; (2) the creation of the universe; (3) Adam and Eve in Paradise; (4) the temptation and fall of humankind; and (5) the aftermath of the Fall, which is human history.

The Bible doesn't go into as much detail as Milton does in covering these events. In fact, much of *Paradise Lost* is just story. But it is based on the truth of God's Word and, ultimately, glorifies God. Take time to read Milton's classic and the God-inspired classic it is based on—the Bible.

All Scripture is inspired by God and is useful to teach us what is true. 2 Timothy 3:16

Paradise Lost BOOK III, LINES 1–6

Hail, holy Light, offspring of Heaven first-born!
Or of th' Eternal coeternal beam,
May I express thee unblamed? since God is light,
And never but in unapproachèd light
Dwelt from eternity, dwelt then in thee,
Bright effluence of bright essence increate!

John Milton (1608–1674)

IN THESE LINES that begin the third book of *Paradise Lost,* Milton wonders if he is qualified to explain the mystery of God's being light: "May I express thee unblamed? since God is light." Nonetheless, Milton captures three aspects of light that are revealed in Scripture. The first is that God has been light forever. He has never lived in anything but unapproachable light. The second is that the Son of God (the "coeternal beam") has also been light forever. He has always been the "bright effluence" of God's glory. The third aspect is stated in the first line: the light that God created on the first day of creation ("offspring of Heaven first-born").

The light of creation is enjoyed by all living beings, especially human beings. This light is but a picture of the real light, who is God himself. We cannot comprehend or withstand the brilliance of this light. That is why Paul wrote that God dwells in unapproachable light (1 Timothy 6:16); the psalmist sang that the eternal God is clothed in light (Psalm 104:2); and John stated that "God is light" (1 John 1:5).

To experience God is to experience being illumined, enlightened, and even exposed, by Christ. His goodness and righteousness expose our faults and sins. This is the normal experience of those who live in the light through close fellowship with God. Such people will not deny that they are sinners (1 John 1:8-10) and will gladly say that they have seen who their Savior is: Jesus Christ the righteous (2:1).

Life itself was in him, and this life gives light to everyone. The light hines through the darkness, and the darkness can never extinguish it.
John 1:4-5

"Father, thy word is passed, man shall find grace;
And shall Grace not find means, that finds her way,
The speediest of thy wingèd messengers,
To visit all thy creatures, and to all
Comes unprevented, unimplored, unsought?
Happy for man, so coming! He her aid
Can never seek, once dead in sins and lost;
Atonement for himself, or offering meet,
Indebted and undone, hath none to bring.
Behold me, then: me for him, life for life,
I offer; on me let thine anger fall;
Account me man: I for his sake will leave
Thy bosom, and this glory next to thee
Freely put off, and for him lastly die
Well pleased; on me let Death wreak all his rage;
Under his gloomy power I shall not long
Lie vanquished. Thou hast given me to possess
Life in myself forever; by thee I live."

JOHN MILTON (1608–1674)

THESE LINES give us a glimpse into the eternal councils of God. In this council, the Son of God tells his Father that he is willing to die for the sins of the world. When the Godhead first decided to create humans, the Son must have known that this would be his destiny—for it must have been foreknown that people would need redemption.

Redemption could not have been accomplished if Jesus had not become flesh and blood—that is, mortal. Because God is immortal, he cannot die. Therefore, he had to become human to be mortal. To become human would also require the Son to leave his Father: "I for his sake will leave thy bosom, and this glory next to thee freely put off, and for him lastly die." The Son willingly relinquished his divine prerogatives and equality with the Father to accomplish redemption (see Philippians 2:5-11). Why would he give up so much for humankind? The Son did it because he loved the Father (John 14:31).

While on earth, Jesus must have longed to return home and recapture that special fellowship he had enjoyed with the Father. It must have been difficult for Jesus to leave that divine, eternal communion to join the human race. We believers must thank him for that sacrifice of love. He paved the way for us to have restored fellowship with God. We who had been alienated from God due to the Fall can now return to God our Father. Christ's death was not an afterthought or a mere remedy but the fulfillment of the determined counsel and foreknowledge of God (Acts 2:23). God foreknew the Fall, and he foresaw the need for redemption and salvation. Even more, he foreknew and predestined all those who would come to believe in his Son. Not only was the Lamb's destiny foreordained, so was our salvation.

God paid for you with the precious lifeblood of Christ, the sinless, spotless Lamb of God. God chose him for this purpose long before the world began. 1 Peter 1:19-20

Paradise Lost BOOK III, LINES 138–142, 167–170

Beyond compare the Son of God was seen
Most glorious; in him all his Father shone
Substantially expressed; and in his face
Divine compassion visibly appeared,
Love without end, and without measure grace;

To whom the great Creator thus replied:
"O Son, in whom my soul hath chief delight,
Son of my bosom, Son who art alone
My word, my wisdom, and effectual might."

JOHN MILTON (1608–1674)

HERE, MILTON depicts the Father and Son in eternity. Long before creation, the Father and Son enjoyed perfect fellowship with each other. We know this because the Bible tells us so—but not in great detail. For the most part, the Scriptures are silent about this scene. Yet there are a few verses that give us a glimpse into that sublime relationship that always existed between the Father and the Son.

Of all the books in the Bible, the Gospel of John has the most to say about their relationship. We read from the outset, "In the beginning was the Word, and the Word was with God, and the Word was God" (John 1:1, NIV). The Greek conveys something more picturesque: "In the beginning was the Word and the Word was face-to-face with God, and the Word was himself God." In Koine Greek, the expression *face-to-face* signifies intimate fellowship, which is what the Father and Son had enjoyed from eternity.

After the Son became man and began his ministry, he spoke of his eternal relationship with the Father, what he had seen and heard (see John 3:11; 8:38). Jesus longed to return to that glorious sphere. In his prayer before going to the cross, he asked the Father to glorify him with the glory he had with the Father before the world began (John 17:5). Jesus wanted to recapture his equality with the Father—something he had willingly relinquished for the sake of his Father's plan (see Philippians 2:6-7). As he prayed, a wonderful utterance escaped from his lips: "Father . . . you loved me even before the world began" (John 17:24). God's unique Son was the single object of the Father's love. One day Jesus will allow all of God's sons and daughters to share in this glorious relationship.

[Jesus prayed,] "Father, I want these whom you've given me to be with me, so they can see my glory. You gave me the glory because you loved me even before the world began!" John 17:24

Paradise Lost BOOK XI, LINES 500–514

"O miserable mankind, to what fall
Degraded, to what wretched state reserved!
Better end here unborn. Why is life giv'n
To be thus wrested from us? Rather why
Obtruded on us thus? Who if we knew
What we receive, would either not accept
Life offered, or soon beg to lay it down,
Glad to be so dismissed in peace. Can thus
Th' image of God in man, created once
So goodly and erect, though faulty since,
To such unsightly sufferings be debased
Under inhuman pains? Why should not man,
Retaining still divine similitude
In part, from such deformities be free,
And for his Maker's image sake exempt?"

JOHN MILTON (1608–1674)

WHEN PEOPLE hear the name John Milton, they think of a brilliant poet who wrote the masterpiece *Paradise Lost.* But this brilliant poet was also a man of God who endured many trials. Milton's family life was not tranquil. His first wife, Mary Powell, left him a few months after they were married. She returned to him three years later and died several years after that, giving birth to their third child, John. He then died one month after his mother.

Unfortunately these were not the only family members Milton lost. His second wife, Katherine Woodcock, died a few months after giving birth to a daughter. The baby girl died as well. Between these losses, Milton had another—his sight.

If all of these personal losses were not enough, Milton also faced political persecution. He had served as secretary for foreign languages under Oliver Cromwell, who had briefly deposed England's monarchy. When Cromwell died, the heir to England's throne, Charles II, returned from exile. Milton went into hiding. He was eventually arrested and stood trial. But influential friends intervened on his behalf and spared his life.

Milton knew what it meant to suffer. When he penned these lines spoken by Adam, he was drawing from his own experience. Milton, with Adam—as with any thinking person—asks the age-old, perplexing question: "Why would God allow human beings, created in his image, to suffer the corrupting and deforming experiences of mortality?" The answer is twofold: (1) because humankind sinned and reaped the grim consequences—mortality and all its ill effects and (2) because death must precede eternal life. Paul speaks of this in the fifteenth chapter of 1 Corinthians.

➻ *Our bodies now disappoint us, but when they are raised, they will be full of glory. . . . Just as we are now like Adam, the man of the earth, so we will someday be like Christ, the man from heaven.* 1 Corinthians 15:43, 49

"O goodness infinite, goodness immense!
That all this good of evil shall produce,
And evil turn to good; more wonderful
Than that which by creation first brought forth
Light out of darkness! Full of doubt I stand,
Whether I should repent me now of sin
By me done and occasioned, or rejoice
Much more, that much more good thereof shall spring,
To God more glory, more good will to men
From God, and over wrath grace shall abound."

JOHN MILTON (1608–1674)

MILTON wrote this epic poem "to justify the ways of God to men." Near the end of this poem, the archangel Michael tells Adam what good will come from Adam's sin: A Savior will come to remedy sin and bring grace to all humankind. Adam, in response, praises God that "evil [will] turn to good." Had Adam not sinned, he would not have needed a Savior, and a Savior would not have had to come. Thus, some theologians have called Adam's sin *felix culpa*—the fortunate fall.

Paul dealt with the fortunate fall in the book of Romans. This verse is the crux of the argument: "And what a difference between our sin and God's generous gift of forgiveness. For this one man, Adam, brought death to many through his sin. But this other man, Jesus Christ, brought forgiveness to many through God's bountiful gift" (Romans 5:15). By "many" Paul meant the mass of humankind represented respectively by Adam and Christ. A single act on the part of each influenced the whole human race. Death was the end result of Adam's sin, life the end result of Christ's righteousness.

This life we receive through Christ's righteousness is an act of God's grace toward humanity. It is an absolution not only from the guilt of that first offense (mysteriously attached to every individual of the human race) but from the countless offenses committed by each person. God's grace is not only rich in its character but also in its detail. His grace is so expansive that it can redeem any person from sin even though he or she is loaded with a myriad of offenses.

➻ *The sin of this one man, Adam, caused death to rule over us, but all who receive God's wonderful, gracious gift of righteousness will live in triumph over sin and death through this one man, Jesus Christ.*

Yes, Adam's one sin brought condemnation upon everyone, but Christ's one act of righteousness makes all people right in God's sight and gives them life. Romans 5:17-18

Paradise Lost BOOK XII, LINES 607–624, 641–649

Descended, Adam to the bow'r where Eve
Lay sleeping ran before, but found her waked;
And thus with words not sad she him received:

"Whence thou return'st, and whither went'st, I know;
For God is also in sleep, and dreams advise,
Which he hath sent propitious, some great good
Presaging, since with sorrow and heart's distress
Wearied I fell asleep. But now lead on;
In me is no delay; with thee to go,
Is to stay here; without thee here to stay,
Is to go hence unwilling; thou to me
Art all things under heav'n, all places thou,
Who for my wilful crime art banished hence.
This further consolation yet secure
I carry hence; though all by me is lost,
Such favor I unworthy am vouchsafed,
By me the Promised Seed shall all restore."

So spake our mother Eve, and Adam heard. . . .

They, looking back, all th' eastern side beheld
Of Paradise, so late their happy seat,
Waved over by that flaming brand, the gate
With dreadful faces thronged and fiery arms.
Some natural tears they dropped, but wiped them soon;
The world was all before them, where to choose
Their place of rest, and Providence their guide:
They hand in hand, with wand'ring steps and slow,
Through Eden took their solitary way.

JOHN MILTON (1608–1674)

PARADISE LOST is considered by many to be the most moving poetry in the English language. A poem by Samuel Barrow, included in the 1674 edition of Milton's epic work, aptly asks, "He who reads *Paradise Lost,* what does he read but everything? All things and the origin of all things."

In these last lines of the epic poem Adam has just returned to Eve after hearing how the plan of salvation would unfold. Eve has been told the same thing in a dream.

God created Adam and Eve to have fellowship with him. He also wanted them to have sons and daughters with whom he could fellowship. No other creatures in the universe were suited for this purpose. Created in the image of God (Genesis 1:26), they alone enjoyed daily fellowship with him (implicit in Genesis 3:8). According to Genesis 2 and 3, Adam and Eve could have partaken of the tree of life (2:9; 3:22), obtaining immortality and the everlasting bliss of unbroken fellowship with God.

Deceived by the serpent, Adam and Eve disobeyed God. They ate fruit from the tree of the knowledge of good and evil. Through this disobedience, sin and death entered the human race (Romans 5:12). People lost the chance to live forever. Even worse, they became consciously separate from God.

But all was not lost. God had promised that the woman's seed would crush the enemy. That seed would be the Savior, Jesus Christ (see Galatians 3:16). A long time had to pass, however, before the Son of God would come to accomplish redemption. The believers in the Old Testament anticipated that day (see John 8:56; Hebrews 11), a day when the Savior would defeat Satan, the enemy of God and humankind.

After banishing them from the garden, the Lord God stationed mighty angelic beings to the east of Eden. And a flaming sword flashed back and forth, guarding the way to the tree of life. Genesis 3:24

Echo of Songs in the Night

To live of Thee—blest source of deepest joy!
To hear e'en now by faith Thy voice of love—
Thou living spring of bliss without alloy,
Bright inlet to the light of heaven above!

Come, fill my soul! Thy light is ever pure,
And brings from heaven what Thou alone canst give,
Yea, brings Thyself, the revelation sure
Of heaven's eternal bliss; in Thee we live.

I hail Thee, Lord! Of Thee my song shall speak—
Poor and unworthy strains, yet still of Thee;
Yes, fill my soul! 'tis this my heart doth seek—
To dwell in love, and God my dwelling be.

Thou'st made the Father known; Him have we seen
In Thy blest Person—infinite delight!
Yes, it suffices: though we here but glean
Some foretaste of His love, till all be light.

O, dwell with me; let no distracting thought
Intrude to hide from me that heavenly light.
Be Thou my strength! Let not what Thou hast brought
Be chased by idle nature's poor delight.

Father, Thou lov'st me. Favour, all divine,
Rests on my soul, a cloudless favour! There
Thy face shines on me, as it still doth shine
On Thy blest Son! His image I shall bear!

But now, e'en now, Thy love can fill my soul—
That love that soars beyond all creature thought—
In spirit bring where endless praises roll,
And fill my longing heart till there I'm brought.

Thee will I hail, O Lord, in whose blest face
God's glory shines unveiled! Thee will I praise,
Whose love has brought me nigh in righteous grace,
And soon wilt come, eternal songs to raise!

JOHN NELSON DARBY (1800–1882)

JOHN NELSON DARBY was the gifted leader of the Brethren movement, a prolific writer, and a Bible translator. In this poem Darby overflows with delight concerning his expectation of seeing Jesus and being like him on that glorious day: "Thy face shines on me, as it still doth shine on Thy blest Son! His image I shall bear!"

Although we have been given the promise that we will be like Jesus, this transformation takes years and involves an inward renewal of our mind. Paul told the Roman believers: "Be transformed by the renewing of your mind" (Romans 12:2, NIV). As our Christian life progresses, we should gradually notice our thought life changing from Christ*less*ness to Christ*like*ness.

We are transformed into Christ's image gradually as we spend time beholding him in intimate fellowship. Eventually we will begin to mirror the one we behold. Transformation does not happen overnight—regeneration is instantaneous but transformation is not. Paul wrote: "All of us . . . are being transformed into the same image from one degree of glory to another; for this comes from the Lord, the Spirit" (2 Corinthians 3:18, NRSV). As we behold the Lord, who is the indwelling Spirit, we begin to reflect his image. This does not come from conscious imitation but from enjoyable communion with our Lord. One day we shall see him as he really is, for we will be like him (1 John 3:2).

Concurrent with the inward process of transformation, each maturing believer must undergo conformation. There is no escape, for this was predetermined for every child of God. God's desire and plan is to have many children, each one conforming to the prototype, Jesus.

For God knew his people in advance, and he chose them to become like his Son, so that his Son would be the firstborn, with many brothers and sisters. Romans 8:29

Am I Thy Gold? . . . CANTICLES II

Am I thy gold? Or purse, Lord, for thy wealth;
Whether in mine or mint refined for thee?
I'm counted so, but count me o'er thyself,
Lest gold-washed face, and brass in heart I be.
I fear my touchstone touches when I try
Me, and my counted gold too overly.

Am I new-minted by thy stamp indeed?
Mine eyes are dim; I cannot clearly see.
Be thou my spectacles that I may read
Thine image and inscription stamped on me.
If thy bright image do upon me stand,
I am a golden angel in thy hand.

Lord, make my soul thy plate: thine image bright
Within the circle of the same enfoil.
And on its brims in golden letters write
Thy superscription in an holy style.
Then I shall be thy money, thou my hoard:
Let me thy angel be, be thou my Lord.

EDWARD TAYLOR (1642–1729)

EDWARD TAYLOR was a metaphysical poet who wrote in the tradition of George Herbert, but he was not as polished and refined as Herbert or other great metaphysical poets such as Donne and Crashaw. Nonetheless, he made a significant contribution to our American heritage of Christian poetry and is credited with being the first American poet.

In this poem Taylor expresses his desire to be transformed into the image of Christ. Using metaphysical language— giving physical objects spiritual value—to communicate his desire, he asks the Lord to make him a gold coin stamped with Jesus' image. In this way his life could become an expression—a representative—for the Lord.

Perhaps Taylor was thinking of the opening lines in the book of Hebrews, where the Son of God is called the express image of God's substance. The Greek expression *express image* denotes the image engraved or stamped on a coin. In this context it means that Christ is the "exact representation" of God the Father's being (NIV), the very "stamp of his nature" (RSV). Since God's essence, nature, and being are invisible, the Son's function is to be the express image, the exact visible likeness of God to humankind.

As a son of God, Taylor also wanted to be stamped with God's image. So should each one of us who are called to be the sons and daughters of God. We should share Taylor's prayer:

> *Lord, make my soul thy plate: thine image bright*
> *Within the circle of the same enfoil.*
> *And on its brims in golden letters write*
> *Thy superscription in an holy style.*

➻ *[The Son] is the reflection of God's glory and the exact imprint of God's very being.* Hebrews 1:3, NRSV

To See a World in a Grain of Sand

To see a world in a grain of sand
And a heaven in a wild flower,
Hold infinity in the palm of your hand
And eternity in an hour.

WILLIAM BLAKE (1757–1827)

WILLIAM BLAKE had a vivid imagination. It was this imagination that enabled him to write such elegant yet pithy poems as this one. Every line of "To See a World in a Grain of Sand" is packed with metaphor. In the first line, Blake compares our world to a grain of sand. Our world, like the grain of sand, is round, stony, and one of a trillion orbs. Heaven is compared to a wildflower in that it is beautiful, enchanting, and not the product of human cultivation.

The beauty of these two metaphors is that the "macro" (world and heaven) can be seen and experienced in the "micro" (sand and flower). Likewise, God's character and eternal power, while difficult to explain, can be seen in his creation. The apostle Paul wrote that all of visible creation exhibits God's "invisible qualities—his eternal power and divine nature" (Romans 1:20). In other words, we experience the grandeur of God and his universe in small created things. Thus, when we pick up a grain of sand, we "hold infinity in the palm of [our] hand." May God open our eyes to see his touch of divinity in every aspect of nature.

From the time the world was created, people have seen the earth and sky and all that God made. They can clearly see his invisible qualities—his eternal power and divine nature. So they have no excuse whatsoever for not knowing God. Romans 1:19-20

My Cocoon Tightens, Colors Tease

My Cocoon tightens—Colors tease—
I'm feeling for the Air—
A dim capacity for Wings
Demeans the Dress I wear—

A power of Butterfly must be—
The Aptitude to fly
Meadows of Majesty implies
And easy Sweeps of Sky—

So I must baffle at the Hint
And cipher at the Sign
And make much blunder, if at last
I take the clue divine—

EMILY DICKINSON (1830–1886)

DICKINSON uses the image of a caterpillar in chrysalis form as a metaphor of Christian transformation. The desire in the caterpillar to become what it should be is seen throughout. Thus, the change in colors "tease." It feels "for the Air." It knows it has a "capacity for Wings" and the "Aptitude to fly." Eventually, that inherent power will burst forth from the chrysalis with full-spread wings. Then the butterfly, with "easy Sweeps" of its wings will be the majestic master of the meadows.

What a wonderful picture God has given us in the butterfly—a worm transfigured into a beautiful flying creature! A similar transformation is taking place in the lives of those of us who are Christians. At present, we are like the caterpillar in the chrysalis. We have a new, divine life within us that is transforming us into the likeness of Christ. When he returns, we will shed our imperfect body and sinful nature like a butterfly breaking out of its chrysalis. Until then, we endure a slow and sometimes painful transformation.

But let me tell you a wonderful secret God has revealed to us. Not all of us will die, but we will all be transformed. It will happen in a moment, in the blinking of an eye, when the last trumpet is blown. For when the trumpet sounds, the Christians who have died will be raised with transformed bodies. And then we who are living will be transformed so that we will never die. For our perishable earthly bodies must be transformed into heavenly bodies that will never die.
1 Corinthians 15:51-53

At the Name of Jesus

At the name of Jesus
Every knee shall bow,
Every tongue confess Him
King of glory now;
'Tis the Father's pleasure
We should call Him Lord,
Who from the beginning
Was the mighty Word.

At His voice creation
Sprang at once to sight,
All the angel faces,
All the hosts of light,
Thrones and dominations,
Stars upon their way,
All the heavenly orders,
In their great array.

Humbled for a season,
To receive a name
From the lips of sinners
Unto whom He came,
Faithfully He bore it
Spotless to the last,
Brought it back victorious
When from death He passed.

In your hearts enthrone Him;
There let Him subdue
All that is not holy,
All that is not true:
Crown Him as your captain
In temptation's hour;
Let His will enfold you
In its light and power.

CAROLINE MARIA NOEL (1817–1877)

CAROLINE MARIA NOEL had tried her hand at poetry as a youth, but then gave it up. But when she became seriously ill at the age of forty, she began to write again. Her poetry was published in a volume called *At the Name of Jesus, and Other Verses for the Sick and Lonely.* "At the Name of Jesus" was eventually transformed into a hymn.

The poem is basically a paraphrase of Philippians 2:6-11. In this portion of Scripture—perhaps an early Christian hymn—we are presented with Jesus' humiliation prior to his glorification. We see him willingly leaving his position of glory in heaven, becoming God's servant as a man, dying on the cross, and returning to his glorious state as the God-man. Because of Jesus' willingness, God the Father enthroned and exalted him above all—giving him the highest name in the universe. What higher praise could we give Jesus than to exalt him as our Savior and enthrone him in our heart as our Lord?

Though he was God, he did not demand and cling to his rights as God. He made himself nothing; he took the humble position of a slave and appeared in human form. And in human form he obediently humbled himself even further by dying a criminal's death on a cross. Because of this, God raised him up to the heights of heaven and gave him a name that is above every other name, so that at the name of Jesus every knee will bow, in heaven and on earth and under the earth, and every tongue will confess that Jesus Christ is Lord, to the glory of God the Father. Philippians 2:6-11

Bermudas

Where the remote Bermudas ride,
In th' ocean's bosom unespied,
From a small boat that rowed along,
The listening winds received this song:

"What should we do but sing his praise
That led us through the wat'ry maze
Unto an isle so long unknown,
And yet far kinder than our own?
Where he the huge sea monsters wracks,
That lift the deep upon their backs;
He lands us on a grassy stage,
Safe from the storms, and prelate's rage.
He gave us this eternal spring
Which here enamels everything,
And sends the fowls to us in care,
On daily visits through the air;
He hangs in shades the orange bright,
Like golden lamps in a green night,
And does in the pomegranates close
Jewels more rich than Ormus[a] *shows;*
He makes the figs our mouths to meet,
And throws the melons at our feet;
But apples[b] *plants of such a price,*
No tree could ever bear them twice;
With cedars, chosen by his hand,
From Lebanon, he stores the land;
And makes the hollow seas that roar
Proclaim the ambergris[c] *on shore;*
He cast (of which we rather boast)
The Gospel's pearl upon our coast,
And in these rocks for us did frame
A temple, where to sound his name.
O let our voice his praise exalt
Till it arrive at heaven's vault,
Which, thence (perhaps) rebounding, may
Echo beyond the Mexique Bay."[d]

Thus sung they in the English boat
An holy and a cheerful note
And all the way, to guide their chime,
With Falling oars they kept the time

ANDREW MARVELL (1621–1678)

[a]Hormuz, on the Persian Gulf, a center for the pearl trade [b]pineapples [c]fragrant substance taken from the sperm whale [d]the Gulf of Mexico

TODAY when we think of the Bermudas, we think of honeymoons and vacations. In Marvell's day, the Bermudas were a refuge for persecuted Puritans and a symbol of remoteness, associated with Paradise. Marvell, like Milton, was a poet for the Puritan cause. His loyalties can be seen in a few poems he wrote in honor of the Puritan leader Oliver Cromwell: "An Horatian Ode: Upon Cromwell's Return from Ireland" (1650), "The First Anniversary of the Government under His Highness the Lord Protector" (1655), and "A Poem upon the Death of His Late Highness the Lord Protector" (1658).

From this poem we gather that the Puritans weren't just looking for safe passage from "the storms" at sea. They were fleeing from the "prelate's rage"—that is, persecution from the Church of England. As they fled, they considered it their duty to spread the gospel. They had been blessed by receiving the "pearl" (see Matthew 13:45-46) cast on their shore around the eighth century (A.D. 700–800). It was now their turn to take the gospel elsewhere—even beyond the Gulf of Mexico, where the Good News could be taken to the Native Americans.

Upon what "shore" can you cast the "pearl"?

And then [Jesus] told them, "Go into all the world and preach the Good News to everyone, everywhere." Mark 16:15

The Tree of Life PART ONE

Soon we taste the endless sweetness
Of the Tree of life above;
Taste its own eternal meetness
For the heavenly land we love.

In eternal counsels founded,
Perfect now in fruit divine;
When the last blest trump has sounded,
Fruit of God for ever mine!

Fresh and ever new are hanging
Fruits of life on that blest Tree;
There is stilled each earnest longing,
Satisfied my soul shall be.

Safety, where no foe approaches;
Rest, where toil shall be no more;
Joy, whereon no grief encroaches;
Peace, where strife shall all be o'er—

Various fruits of richest flavour
Offers still the Tree divine;
One itself, the same for ever,
All its various fruits are mine.

Where deceiver ne'er can enter,
Sin-soiled feet have never trod,
Free, our peaceful feet may venture
In the paradise of God;

Drink of life's perennial river,
Feed on life's perennial food,
Christ, the fruit of life, and Giver—
Safe through His redeeming blood.

Object of eternal pleasure,
Perfect in Thy work divine!
Lord of glory! Without measure,
Worship, joy, and praise are Thine!

(continued in next day's reading)

JOHN NELSON DARBY (1800–1882)

DARBY advocated "thinking in Scripture." This meant to become so absorbed with the Scriptures that one's thought processes align with God's will as revealed in the Bible. This poem is an excellent example of his thinking. Filled with biblical allusions, the poem looks forward to the day when all believers will enjoy the tree of life in the paradise of the New Jerusalem.

The Bible begins and ends with paradise, in the midst of which is a tree of life. The way to the tree of life, which was closed in Genesis 3, opens again—in Revelation—for God's people. Following the picture in Ezekiel 47:7-12, the language in Revelation 22:1-2 depicts several trees on both sides of the river, all collectively called the tree of life. The fruit on these trees varies and is replenished each month, providing an endless variety and supply for God's people to feed on.

The poem also speaks of the river of life, which is also depicted in Revelation 22:1-2. This river probably symbolizes the flow of Christ's Spirit, out from God, to supply his people with life (see John 7:37-39). Whether the river is real, symbolic, or both, it is the final reality of the rivers mentioned in Ezekiel 47:1-2 and Zechariah 14:8. The continuous flow of these waters from the God-man, who is the fountain of life, symbolizes the uninterrupted flow of life to the believers. This flow brings life in fullness of joy as well as in perpetual vitality.

And the angel showed me a pure river with the water of life, clear as crystal, flowing from the throne of God and of the Lamb, coursing down the center of the main street. On each side of the river grew a tree of life, bearing twelve crops of fruit, with a fresh crop each month.
Revelation 22:1-2

The Tree of Life PART TWO

But, my soul, hast thou not tasted
Of that Tree of life on high?
As through desert lands thou'st hasted,
Eschol's grapes been never nigh?

Ah! that Tree of life was planted,
Rooted deep in love divine,
Ere the sons of God had chanted
Worlds where creature glories shine.

Love divine without a measure
Godhead glory must reveal;
In the Object of its pleasure
All its ways of grace must seal.

As a tender sucker, rising
From a dry and stony land,
Object of man's proud despising,
Grew the Plant of God's right hand.

Grace and truth, in love unceasing,
Rivers on the thirsty ground—
Every step to God well pleasing—
Spread their heavenly savour round.

He the Father's Self revealing—
Heavenly words none else could tell,
Words of grace, each sorrow healing,
On the ear of sorrow fell.

Yes! that Tree of life is planted;
Sweetest fruit e'en here has borne;
To its own rich soil transplanted,
Waits alone the eternal morn—

Fruits that our own souls have tasted
By the Spirit from above,
While through desert lands we've hasted,
Fruits of perfect, endless love!

JOHN NELSON DARBY (1800–1882)

THE SECOND PART of this poem focuses on the theme that the tree of life—never partaken of by humanity because of its sin—is now available in Jesus Christ. God placed the tree of life in the midst of Eden (Genesis 2:8-9). He had told Adam that he could eat from every tree in the Garden except the tree of the knowledge of good and evil (Genesis 2:16-17). When Adam and Eve disobeyed God by eating from this tree, God expelled them from the Garden lest they "take also of the tree of life, and eat, and live for ever" (Genesis 3:22, KJV).

The Genesis narrative suggests that God intended the tree of life to provide Adam and Eve with "eternal life" in fellowship with and dependence on him. Human life, as distinguished from that of the animals, was much more than biological. It was also spiritual and found its deepest significance in fellowship with God. Life in the fullness of its physical and spiritual dimensions, however, could remain humankind's possession only as long as Adam and Eve remained obedient to God's command (Genesis 2:17). It seems that Adam and Eve could have eaten of the tree of life and gained eternal life, but by their fall they were banished from Paradise and severed from the tree of life.

Jesus Christ came to earth to offer eternal life to those who believe in him. By doing so, he was offering the world access to the tree of life again. The book of Revelation makes this clear. Those who have sought forgiveness for their sin through Christ's redemptive work have the right to eat from the tree of life—as a foretaste now and as a full taste in eternity (Revelation 22:14). Let us enjoy this privilege!

Blessed are those who wash their robes so they can enter through the gates of the city and eat the fruit from the tree of life. Revelation 22:14

I Wake and Feel the Fell of Dark, Not Day

I wake and feel the fell of dark, not day.
What hours, O what black hoürs we have spent
This night! what sights you, heart, saw; ways you went!
And more must, in yet longer light's delay.

With witness I speak this. But where I say
Hours I mean years, mean life. And my lament
Is cries countless, cries like dead letters sent
To dearest him that lives alas! away.

I am gall, I am heartburn. God's most deep decree
Bitter would have me taste: my taste was me;
Bones built in me, flesh filled, blood brimmed the curse.

Selfyeast of spirit a dull dough sours. I see
The lost are like this, and their scourge to be
As I am mine, their sweating selves; but worse.

GERARD MANLEY HOPKINS (1844–1889)

THIS POEM could be called Hopkins's "dark night of the soul." Exposing himself in all his naked weakness, Hopkins gets a full taste of himself as if it were a taste of death. In so doing, he knows what it must be like for those who are lost. But their situation is worse than his because he still has faith in the living God—even though his God, at the time, seems far away.

What Hopkins went through and expressed in this poem was a struggle with spiritual dryness. This happens in the lives of those who intensely seek to live in God's presence every day. As Ignatius said in his classic book *Spiritual Exercises,* such periods of dryness are bound to happen and must, in order for the believer to mature in faith. During such times, Ignatius said, the soul will experience desolation and even the sense of abandonment. Desolation is the human shuddering recoil from the strain of intense spiritual seeking. It brings a sourness, hopelessness, and sadness—almost a suspension of faith itself—that makes the person feel that he or she has been abandoned by God. Thus, Hopkins confesses that he has made his pleas "like dead letters sent to dearest him that lives alas! away."

In this condition Hopkins was miserable beyond compare. But so are we all. For what are we without God but flesh experiencing "the curse." Without God, we are lost. Jesus temporarily experienced this separation from God when he died on the cross, because he took the sins of the world on himself. Fortunately, we will not remain separated from God, just as Jesus didn't. But we may experience spiritual dryness that can seem like death. When we do, we can keep in mind that these times serve to increase our faith in the God who resurrects the dead.

At about three o'clock, Jesus called out with a loud voice, "Eli, Eli, lema sabachthani?" which means, "My God, my God, why have you forsaken me?" Matthew 27:46

Isaac: A Poise

His sun's arms and grappling
hooks and spears
stripping him
fleabane bare
on its abstract field—

in the fume-like shimmer and blur.

A kiln-pure sky
the cypresses touch.
'His eyes like the dying moon.'
His hope at home in the finally darkness
where what should happen would.

He waited.

Blood on the wood
where his head had been.
Where the body buried what its father had planned.
Spirit.
Thicket.

The strained way home.

'A host'
it says.
A host of them shouting
Praise Him.
goat-meat and ox-ash and noise.

With fire, and whisper, and gall.

A host.
While the gold tackle tore at his will.
Consigned.
Among thistle and rubble,
and caper

and dill.

PETER COLE (b. 1957)

IT IS DIFFICULT to understand why God asked Abraham to kill Isaac. But remember, Abraham was the father of faith. And here is what he believed: "Isaac is the son through whom your descendants will be counted" (Hebrews 11:18). Yet faith's father trudged up Mount Moriah to sacrifice Isaac at God's command. In so doing, Abraham would have destroyed his descendants—who number as the stars in the sky and the sand on the seashore (Genesis 22:17). Did he stop believing God's promise as he ascended the mountain? No. Abraham still "believed that God would keep his promise" (Hebrews 11:11).

Abraham's faith was expressed in his response to Isaac's question, "Where is the lamb for the sacrifice?" Abraham said, "God will provide a lamb, my son" (Genesis 22:7-8). And God did. As Isaac lay bound on the altar and Abraham raised the knife to sacrifice his son, God interrupted. A little way off, a ram was entangled in a thicket (Genesis 22:8-13). A powerful creature had become defenseless, its horns caught in the underbrush.

Is this not a picture of Christ? When Jesus was born, the almighty God became forever entangled in the crooked thicket of humanity. He was exactly like us in human form and vulnerable to death. Although we are all sinners and should have to pay the price for our sin, Christ took the penalty upon himself. He was the sacrifice for our sin.

The words of Abraham foretell Christ's story: "God will provide a lamb." While the ram was the substitute for Isaac, so "Christ also suffered for sins once for all, the righteous for the unrighteous, in order to bring you to God" (1 Peter 3:18, NRSV).

Then Abraham looked up and saw a ram caught by its horns in a bush. So he took the ram and sacrificed it as a burnt offering on the altar in place of his son. Genesis 22:13

Ash Wednesday

My God, my God, have mercy on my sin,
For it is great; and if I should begin
To tell it all, the day would be too small
To tell it in.

My God, Thou wilt have mercy on my sin
For Thy Love's sake: yea, if I should begin
To tell This all, the day would be too small
To tell it in.

Good Lord, today
I scarce find breath to say:
Scourge, but receive me.
For stripes are hard to bear, but worse
Thy intolerable curse;
So do not leave me.

Good Lord, lean down
In pity, tho' Thou frown;
Smite, but retrieve me:
For so Thou hold me up to stand
And kiss Thy smiting hand,
It less will grieve me.

CHRISTINA ROSSETTI (1830–1894)

ACCORDING TO TRADITION, Ash Wednesday comes four days before the beginning of Lent. Hence, it falls on a Wednesday. On this day Christians are sprinkled with ashes, dress in sackcloth, and commence a period of self-denial in preparation for the Easter season. Christians are encouraged to emulate Jesus' forty-day fast in the wilderness in order to identify with him in his sufferings. In this poem Rossetti asks Christ to help her suffer for him. This is why she asks the Lord to scourge her and to smite her: so she may identify experientially with his sufferings.

We must remember that our sufferings add nothing to Christ's with respect to redemption. He himself accomplished redemption by his death on the cross. Nevertheless, we can learn from him how to suffer and accept his grace when we do.

When sufferings come—and they will—we need to understand that they come from God's hand. As Peter said, "Dear friends, don't be surprised at the fiery trials you are going through, as if something strange were happening to you. Instead, be very glad—because these trials will make you partners with Christ in his suffering. . . . Be happy if you are insulted for being a Christian, for then the glorious Spirit of God will come upon you" (1 Peter 4:12-14).

Our suffering should be on Christ's account, not on account of our sins (2:20). If we are reproached for Christ's sake, we can cope with curses and insults because God's glorious Spirit rests on us as it did upon Christ. In addition, we can be happy because the Spirit and the glory that is inseparable from it will be ours before God. Let us attribute praise and honor to God since it is he who counts us worthy of identifying with the name of Christ.

This suffering is all part of what God has called you to. Christ, who suffered for you, is your example. Follow in his steps. 1 Peter 2:21

On Lazarus Raised from Death

Where am I, or how came I here, hath death
Bereaved me of my breath,
Or do I dream?
Nor can that be, for sure I am
These are no ensigns of a living man,
Beside, the stream
Of life did fly
From hence, and my blessed soul did soar on
And well remember I,
My friends on either hand
Did weeping stand
To see me die;
Most certain then it is my soul was fled
Forth of my clay, and I am buried.

These linens plainly show this cave did keep
My flesh in its dead sleep,
And yet a noise
Me-thought I heard, of such strange force
As would have raised to life the dullest corse,[a]
So sweet a voice
As spite of death
Distilled through every vein a living breath,
And sure I heard it charge
Me by my name, even thus
O Lazarus
Come forth at large,
And so nought hinders, I will straightway then
Appear, (though thus dressed) ere it call again. . . .

HENRY COLMAN (fl. 1640)

[a]an archaic form of *corpse*

"OUR FRIEND LAZARUS has fallen asleep," said Jesus, as he prepared to visit Bethany in this well-known story about death and resurrection (John 11:11). But what Jesus Christ called sleep we call death. This is the subject that Henry Colman chose to write about in this marvelous poem.

The perspective Colman used is unique. He wrote in the voice of Lazarus, whose body lay lifeless in the grave. The story of Lazarus had never been told from the grave before. And since John—the author of the Gospel that records this account—did not interview Lazarus, the sleep of death remains a mystery to the living. In fact, the gospel's task is not to explain death. Instead, it reveals the way to eternal life. But Colman chose as the center of his poem one thing about death that we know for certain: "The dead will hear the voice of the Son of God and those who hear will live" (John 5:25, NIV). Lazarus, in Colman's poem, describes this experience: "So sweet a voice as spite of death distilled through every vein a living breath."

This view of death provides a stark contrast to the world's view. Death is, and always has been, a major preoccupation of humanity. In the past, death was greatly feared, and this fear was useful for religious and superstitious manipulation. Today death has been sensationalized, packaged as entertainment, and used as a sales gimmick. But the gospel will have none of this. The truth about death for Christ's followers is presented simply in this story: Lazarus fell asleep, and upon hearing the voice of the Son of God, he woke up! This is our hope as Christians, as well: to be resurrected from the dead when Christ says, "Come forth."

Then Jesus shouted, "Lazarus, come out!" And Lazarus came out, bound in graveclothes, his face wrapped in a headcloth. Jesus told them, "Unwrap him and let him go!" John 11:43-44

The Man of Sorrows PART ONE

O ever homeless Stranger,
Thus, dearest Friend to me;
An outcast in a manger,
That Thou might'st with us be!

How rightly rose the praises
Of heaven that wondrous night,
When shepherds hid their faces
In brightest angel-light!

More just those acclamations,
Than when the glorious band
Chanted earth's deep foundations,
Just laid by God's right hand.

Come now, and view that manger—
The Lord of glory see,
A houseless, homeless Stranger
In this poor world for thee—

To God, in the highest, glory,
And peace on earth to find;
And learn that wondrous story,
Good pleasure in mankind.

How blessed those heavenly spirits,
Who joy increasing find,
That spite of our demerits
God's pleasure's in mankind;

And chant the highest glory
Of Him they praise above,
In telling out the story
Of God come down in love!

(continued in next day's reading)

JOHN NELSON DARBY (1800–1882)

THROUGH ARDENT study of the Bible, John Nelson Darby came to know Christ and felt that he should devote himself to God's work. From then on, he served the Lord tirelessly. He wrote commentaries on every book of the Bible, was founder of the Brethren movement in England and Europe, and traveled around the world, teaching and preaching the Scriptures.

Some of Darby's views were a bit extreme. For example, he considered the church to be in a state of ruin—soon after its inception—as a result of human failure. In addition, he thought that it was presumptuous for anyone to try to recover the early church, which several men in the Brethren movement were trying to do. This position caused a great deal of disagreement between himself and other Bible teachers. In 1866, Darby was severely criticized by close friends because he had taught certain views that appeared to be unorthodox. As a result, he was alienated. This painful experience prompted the writing of "The Man of Sorrows" (in 1867).

The poem traces the life of Jesus, from the manger to the cross, and focuses on each aspect that caused the Lord of glory pain. "No room in the inn" was not just a No Vacancy sign. It signaled the beginning of a life of rejection. It is sad but true: The Creator of this earth was not welcome in it. A birth in a manger (a feeding trough for animals) was a presage for an unusual, homeless life. It is no wonder Jesus said, "Foxes have holes, and birds of the air have nests; but the Son of Man has nowhere to lay his head" (Luke 9:58, NRSV).

As you read the rest of this poem, focus your thoughts on what it meant for Jesus to suffer. May the words of Paul be true for you, too, as you meditate on the sufferings of the Savior.

For I decided to know nothing among you except Jesus Christ, and him crucified. 1 Corinthians 2:2, NRSV

The Man of Sorrows PART TWO

Oh, strange yet fit beginning
Of all that life of woe,
In which Thy grace was winning
Poor man his God to know!

Bless'd Babe! who lowly liest
In manger-cradle there;
Descended from the highest,
Our sorrows all to share.

Oh, suited now in nature
For Love's divinest ways,
To make the fallen creature
The vessel of Thy praise!

O Love, all thought surpassing!
That thou should'st with us be,
Nor yet in triumph passing,
But human infancy!

We cling to Thee in weakness—
The manger and the cross;
We gaze upon Thy meekness,
Through suffering, pain, and loss;

There see the Godhead glory
Shine through that human veil,
And, willing, hear the story
Of Love that's come to heal.

(continued in next day's reading)

JOHN NELSON DARBY (1800–1882)

IN THIS POEM, Darby retraces the path of Jesus' life of suffering—beginning with the Incarnation and concluding with the Crucifixion. One would not think that the manger was a source of suffering to Jesus, only the cross. But both experiences—one at the beginning of his life and the other at the end—involved alienation and humiliation. Christ's birth in a stable, with a manger (a feeding trough for animals) for a bed, shows how unwelcome he was in this world. His dying on a cross demonstrates even more how the world rejected him:

We cling to Thee in weakness—

The manger and the cross;
We gaze upon Thy meekness,
Through suffering, pain, and loss.

Think of the loss the Son of God endured when he became human. He gave up so much to leave heaven and come to earth. What an act of humility! What's more, he didn't just become a normal man who lived out a normal existence. He became a poor man who eventually died the most humiliating death—and a criminal's death at that. The steps of humility the Son of God took to accomplish the Father's will are expressed in Paul's words in Philippians (cited below). Christ sacrificed much to accomplish our salvation. As you read the following passage, think about a sacrifice of praise that you can offer him. Then praise Jesus Christ—the humble Savior of the world.

Though he was God, [Jesus Christ] did not demand and cling to his rights as God. He made himself nothing; he took the humble position of a slave and appeared in human form. And in human form he obediently humbled himself even further by dying a criminal's death on a cross. Because of this, God raised him up to the heights of heaven and gave him a name that is above every other name. Philippians 2:6-9

The Man of Sorrows PART THREE

My soul in secret follows
The footsteps of His love;
I trace the Man of sorrows,
His boundless grace to prove.

A child in growth and stature,
Yet full of wisdom rare;
Sonship, in conscious nature,
His words and ways declare.

Yet still in meek submission
His patient path He trod,
To wait His heavenly mission,
Unknown to all but God.

But who, Thy path of service,
Thy steps removed from ill,
Thy patient love to serve us,
With human tongue can tell?

Midst sin and all corruption,
Where hatred did abound,
Thy path of true perfection
Was light on all around.

In scorn, neglect, reviling,
Thy patient grace stood fast;
Man's malice unavailing
To move Thy heart to haste.

O'er all, Thy perfect goodness
Rose blessedly divine;
Poor hearts oppressed with sadness
Found ever rest in Thine.

(continued in next day's reading)

JOHN NELSON DARBY (1800–1882)

JOHN NELSON DARBY was a loyal servant of the Lord all the days of his adult life. He translated the entire Bible into three languages (English, French, German), wrote commentaries on every book of the Bible (*The Synopsis of the Bible*), and was founder of the Brethren movement in England and Europe. He traveled worldwide until his eightieth year—teaching the Bible, encouraging the priesthood of all believers, and advocating the return of Christian worship and service to scriptural simplicity. Darby died, having never married, in Bournemouth, England, remarking that Christ had been the object of his life.

Throughout his many years, he won and lost many friends because of his extreme views. From the year 1866 until his death, he suffered a great deal of alienation. During this period he wrote his best poems, including "The Man of Sorrows."

In this section of the poem, we come to realize that it wasn't just Jesus' death that brought him suffering. His entire human life was one of suffering, because he who is God gave up his divine rights in order to become a lowly human being. And as a human among humans, he did not live a reclusive, standoffish life. Rather, he took all human sorrows upon himself. That is why the prophet Isaiah called him "a man of sorrows."

He was despised and rejected—a man of sorrows, acquainted with bitterest grief. We turned our backs on him and looked the other way when he went by. He was despised, and we did not care. Yet it was our weaknesses he carried; it was our sorrows that weighed him down. And we thought his troubles were a punishment from God for his own sins! But he was wounded and crushed for our sins. He was beaten that we might have peace. He was whipped, and we were healed! Isaiah 53:3-5

The Man of Sorrows PART FOUR

The strong man in his armour
Thou mettest in Thy grace,
Did'st spoil the mighty charmer
Of our unhappy race.

The chains of man, his victim,
Were loosened by Thy hand;
No evils that afflict him
Before Thy power could stand.

Disease, and death, and demon,
All fled before Thy word,
As darkness the dominion
Of day's returning lord!

The love that bore our burden
On the accursèd tree,
Would give the heart its pardon,
And set the sinner free!

Love, that made Thee a mourner
In this sad world of woe,
Made wretched man a scorner
Of grace—that brought Thee low.

Still in Thee love's sweet savour
Shone forth in every deed,
And showed God's loving favour
To every soul in need.

(continued in next day's reading)

JOHN NELSON DARBY (1800–1882)

IN THIS SECTION of the poem, Darby focuses on what Jesus accomplished in his struggle against the devil ("the strong man" and "the mighty charmer of our unhappy race") and the evils of this world. Jesus took on Satan, our ancient foe, and released those who were in bondage to him: "The chains of man, his victim, were loosened by Thy hand; no evils that afflict him before Thy power could stand."

Jesus exercised his power over "disease, and death, and demon"—"all fled before [his] word" because his kingdom was more powerful than Satan's. Satan's demise came when Jesus, by his death on the cross, destroyed him who had the power of death. In the ultimate irony, Jesus died to kill death. His resurrection proved that death (the devil's most powerful force against humanity) had been defeated.

This was the greatest grace God could have given the human race. It was motivated by love and demonstrated in Christ's ultimate sacrifice. But think of it—while Jesus was dying on the cross to save people from their worst enemy, those standing around the cross were behaving like Jesus' worst enemies. Instead of thanking him, they scorned him: "Love, that made Thee a mourner in this sad world of woe, made wretched man a scorner of grace—that brought Thee low."

Though Jesus' grace was scorned, he accomplished deliverance for all who will believe in him and thank him for his love. Hallelujah! Now, we no longer have to fear the devil, who used to have the power of death.

Because God's children are human beings—made of flesh and blood—Jesus also became flesh and blood by being born in human form. For only as a human being could he die, and only by dying could he break the power of the Devil, who had the power of death. Only in this way could he deliver those who have lived all their lives as slaves to the fear of dying. Hebrews 2:14-15

The Man of Sorrows PART FIVE

I pause:—for in Thy vision
The day is hastening now,
When for our lost condition
Thy holy head shall bow;

When, deep to deep still calling,
The waters reach Thy soul,
And—death and wrath appalling—
Their waves shall o'er Thee roll.

O day of mightiest sorrow,
Day of unfathomed grief!
When Thou should'st taste the horror
Of wrath without relief.

O day of man's dishonour!
When, for Thy love supreme,
He sought to mar Thine honour,
Thy glory turn to shame.

O day of our confusion!
When Satan's darkness lay,
In hatred and delusion,
On ruined nature's way.

(continued in next day's reading)

JOHN NELSON DARBY (1800–1882)

IN THIS SECTION of the poem, Darby comes to a most dreadful vision—that of Jesus dying on the cross. This is not a pretty sight: a man stripped naked, dying a most humiliating, agonizingly slow death. And this was *the Son of God* who was dying there.

The prophet Isaiah had predicted the Messiah's death seven hundred years before it actually occurred. In Isaiah 53 we learn that the Messiah would be "despised and rejected" by humanity. Indeed, the Lord's own people didn't receive him (John 1:12). Even more, they turned away from him as if he were a leper. Isaiah said, "He was despised, and we did not care. Yet it was our weaknesses he carried; it was our sorrows that weighed him down" (53:3-4).

He carried the world's sorrows on his shoulders when he carried the cross to Golgotha. He did it alone because only he could do away with the sin of the world. This is why Isaiah wrote, "He was wounded and crushed for our sins. He was beaten that we might have peace. He was whipped, and we were healed!" (53:5). The Messiah in his perfect humanity was bodily afflicted for us. Our sorrows became his. Since sin and sickness were often connected as cause and effect in Scripture (John 5:14; James 5:15), when Christ accepted our guilt, he also received the divine punishment connected with it (Isaiah 53:5).

To receive this punishment in our stead, he was "wounded"—the Messiah's hands, feet, and side were pierced (Psalm 22:16). He acquiesced to this torture for our sins (Romans 4:25; 2 Corinthians 5:21; 1 Peter 3:18) so that we could have peace with God.

[Jesus] personally carried away our sins in his own body on the cross so we can be dead to sin and live for what is right. You have been healed by his wounds! 1 Peter 2:24

The Man of Sorrows PART SIX

Thou soughtest for compassion—
Some heart Thy grief to know,
To watch Thine hour of passion—
For comforters in woe.

No eye was found to pity,
No heart to bear Thy woe;
But shame, and scorn, and spitting—
None cared Thy name to know.

The pride of careless greatness
Could wash its hands of Thee;
Priests, that should plead for weakness,
Must Thine accusers be!

Man's boasting love disowns Thee;
Thine own Thy danger flee;
A Judas only owns Thee
That Thou may'st captive be.

O man! How hast thou provèd
What in thy heart is found;
By grace divine unmovèd,
By self in fetters bound.

(continued in next day's reading)

JOHN NELSON DARBY (1800–1882)

IN THIS SECTION the poet focuses on Jesus' experience of being abandoned, forsaken, and betrayed during the last hours before his crucifixion. This section does not follow the chronology Darby had set thus far, in that it goes back to the hours prior to Christ's crucifixion, which Darby covered in previous stanzas. But this is allowed in poetry because it is not bound by chronology. Even in this section, the poet does not follow the pre-Crucifixion events as they are presented in the Gospels.

The first stanza alludes to Jesus' time with James, John, and Peter in the Garden of Gethsemane. While Jesus prayed, the disciples slept. The second stanza relates the humiliation Jesus endured at the hands of Roman guards just before he was led away to be crucified. The third stanza focuses on the Jewish leaders' betrayal of their Messiah and Pilate's public declaration of innocence concerning Jesus' crucifixion. The fourth stanza is about Judas Iscariot's betrayal of Jesus for thirty pieces of silver.

In chronological order, Judas betrayed Jesus; Jesus prayed in the Garden of Gethsemane; Jesus was arrested and tried by the Sanhedrin and Pilate; and then Jesus went to the cross. What holds all of these stanzas together isn't the chronology but the theme: Jesus was abandoned to suffer all these disgraces alone. No wonder he is called "the man of sorrows." Let us praise him and adore him for what he suffered for our sake.

He was despised and rejected—a man of sorrows, acquainted with bitterest grief. We turned our backs on him and looked the other way when he went by. He was despised, and we did not care. Isaiah 53:3

The Man of Sorrows PART SEVEN

Yet with all grief acquainted,
The Man of sorrows view,
Unmoved—by ill untainted—
The path of grace pursue.

In death, obedience yielding
To God His Father's will,
Love still its power is wielding
To meet all human ill.

On him who had disowned Thee
Thine eye could look in love—
'Midst threats and taunts around Thee—
To tears of grace to move.

What words of love and mercy
Flow from those lips of grace,
For followers that desert Thee,
For sinners in disgrace!

The robber learned beside Thee,
Upon the cross of shame—
While taunts and jeers deride Thee—
The savour of Thy name.

Then, finished all, in meekness
Thou to Thy Father's hand
(Perfect Thy strength in weakness)
Thy spirit dost commend.

(continued in next day's reading)

JOHN NELSON DARBY (1800–1882)

THE DEATH OF CHRIST on the cross was motivated by God's love for humanity, as well as by the Son's love for his Father. The Son desired to please the Father by becoming the sacrifice that would take away the sins of the world. The Father had an adventurous plan: His Son's death would not only atone for humankind's sin, but it would also demonstrate his love to the world, thereby attracting his people to love him in return.

God was anxious to have his people approach him in worship and for fellowship. But the Israelites, as a whole, had little appreciation for God and did not come to him. As much as God wanted to be their loving Father, his visitations incited fear rather than love (see Exodus 20:18; Hebrews 12:18-21). While God was drawing near, the Israelites were falling away into idolatry.

This one-sided love affair characterizes the Old Testament narrative. God's love for his people was rarely reciprocated and frequently slighted. How often God lamented Israel's idolatrous harlotry! No matter what God did to attract his people to himself, they were not enchanted. He approached them again and again. He wooed them and warned them. He loved them, but they (as a whole) had little or no love for him. Fortunately, God had a better plan in store for his people—a plan that would attract those who truly desired to love him.

When the time was ripe, God sent his beloved Son to die on the cross. In pursuing humankind, God went all the way to show how much he loved us. Let us do our best to return his love by giving ourselves to him completely.

God showed his great love for us by sending Christ to die for us while we were still sinners. Romans 5:8

O Lord! Thy wondrous story
My inmost soul doth move;
I ponder o'er Thy glory—
Thy lonely path of love!

But, O divine Sojourner
'Midst man's unfathomed ill,
Love, that made Thee a mourner,
It is not man's to tell!

We worship, when we see Thee
In all Thy sorrowing path;
We long soon to be with Thee
Who bore for us the wrath.

Come then, expected Saviour;
Thou Man of sorrows, come!
Almighty, blest Deliverer!
And take us to Thee—home.

JOHN NELSON DARBY (1800–1882)

IN THE CONCLUDING portion of this poem, Darby explodes with praise from his inmost soul. He praises the Lord for the "lonely path of love" he took in order to secure our salvation. Most people (like Darby) are not brought to salvation by understanding the legal ramifications of redemption. They are saved, experientially, by the profound and compelling display of God's love as manifested in the crucified Jesus. Millions have been drawn to God by the constraining power manifested in Christ's cross. Paul, as if speaking for all of us who have known that love, exclaimed, "The love of Christ urges us on, because we are convinced that one has died for all . . . so that those who live might live no longer for themselves, but for him who died and was raised for them" (2 Corinthians 5:14-15, NRSV).

Mysteriously, the cross of Christ has become an attracting force, drawing peoples' hearts to God like a great magnet. Christ knew that when he was lifted up on the cross, he would draw all men to him. He declared this prior to his crucifixion (see John 12:32). The Greek word underlying "draw" is the same word used for drawing in a fishnet.

This is illustrated by the way fishermen from Ghana draw in a net. After a net is let out into the ocean, two groups of men on shore pull it in. It takes at least three hours to draw in a net full of fish.

Those who have been captivated by Jesus are like fish caught in a net. The cross draws people to Christ for various reasons, but it is the wide net of his love that captures them. And once we have been captured, there is no alternative except to joyfully surrender our life to him.

[Jesus said,] "And when I am lifted up on the cross, I will draw everyone to myself." John 12:32

His Metrical Prayer

Let them bestow on ev'ry airth a limb;
Open all my veins, that I may swim
To Thee my Savior, in that crimson lake;
Then place my par-boiled head upon a stake;
Scatter my ashes, throw them in the air:
Lord (since Thou knowst where all these atoms are)
I'm hopeful, once Thou'lt recollect my dust,
And confident Thou'lt raise me with the just.

JAMES GRAHAM, MARQUESS OF MONTROSE
(1612–1650)

THIS IS a gruesome poem of hope written by James Graham, Marquis of Montrose, a man of war. This Scotsman had joined the Bishops' Wars (1639–40) against the religious policies of King Charles I. During the English Civil Wars (1642–51), he became a Royalist and led Scottish armies against the Parliament-backed Covenanters. His military career followed the convoluted path of this tragic conflict until he was betrayed to Parliament and hanged in 1650, at the age of thirty-eight.

The night before his execution he wrote these lines. Consider their images: To "bestow on ev'ry airth a limb" meant to disembowel his body and cut it up into four parts. Opening every vein in his body would produce a "crimson lake" in which he would swim to his Savior—that is, bleed to death. He also included an image of decapitation and cremation.

Obviously, Graham did not fear a painful or grotesque execution. Was this because he practiced seventeenth-century politics and warfare? was surprised and defeated by Lord Newark at Philiphaugh (1645) and fled to exile? rallied an army and invaded Scotland, where most of his troops were lost at sea and the clans would not join him? Or was it the sight of his final defeat at Carbisdale that hardened him to the sight of blood?

More likely it was Graham's faith in Christ and the resurrection of the dead that gave him the courage to face a gruesome death at such a young age. It was this faith that gave him hope in the dark hours before his execution. Graham knew that his death was not the end. One day God would recollect his dust and raise him with the just.

And if we have hope in Christ only for this life, we are the most miserable people in the world. But the fact is that Christ has been raised from the dead. He has become the first of a great harvest of those who will be raised to life again. 1 Corinthians 15:19-20

Stupendous Love! All Saints' Astonishment!

JOHN VI:55: "For my flesh is meat indeed,
and my blood is drink indeed."

Stupendous love! All saints' astonishment!
Bright angels are black motes in this sun's light.
Heaven's canopy, the pantile to God's tent,
Can't cover't neither with its breadth nor height.
Its glory doth all glory else outrun,
Beams of bright glory to't are motes i'the sun.

My soul had caught an ague, and like hell
Her thirst did burn: she to each spring did fly,
But this bright blazing love did spring a well
Of aqua vigae in the Deity,
Which on the top of heaven's high hill outburst
And down came running thence t'allay my thirst.

But how it came, amazeth all communion.
God's only Son doth hug humanity
Into his very person. By which union
His human veins its golden gutters lie.
And rather than my soul should die by thirst,
These golden pipes, to give me drink, did burst.

This liquor brewed, thy sparkling art divine,
Lord, in thy crystal vessels did up run,
(Thine ordinances) which all earth o'ershine,
Set in thy rich wine cellars out to run.
Lord, make thy butler draw, and fill with speed
My beaker full: for this is drink indeed.

Whole butts of this blest nectar shining stand
Locked up with sapph'rine taps, whose splendid flame
Too bright do shine for brightest angels' hands
To touch, my Lord. Do thou untap the same.
Oh! make thy crystal butts of red wine bleed
Into my crystal glass this is drink indeed.

How shall I praise thee then? My blottings jar
And wrack my rhymes to pieces in thy praise.
Thou breath'st thy vein still in my porringer,
To lay my thirst, and fainting spirits raise.
Thou makest glory's chiefest grape to bleed
Into my cup: And this is drink indeed.

Nay, though I make no pay for this red wine,
And scarce do say I thank ye for't; strange thing!
Yet were thy silver skies my beer bowl fine,
I find my Lord would fill it to the brim.
Then make my life, Lord, to thy praise proceed
For thy rich blood, which is my drink indeed.

EDWARD TAYLOR (1642–1729)

EDWARD TAYLOR wrote many spiritual meditations in preparation for the Lord's Supper. In this poem Taylor celebrates the outpouring of Jesus' blood as if it were an outpouring of divine liquor, which Taylor drinks to his fill. The language of the poem is filled with drinking imagery. His soul "had caught an ague" (that is, he was ill), causing him to burn with thirst. The "aqua vigae [living water] in the Deity" came running down from heaven to allay his thirst. And how did it come down? It came when God became a man, with blood running through his veins:

God's only Son doth hug humanity

Into his very person. By which union
His human veins its golden gutters lie.
And rather than my soul should die by thirst,
These golden pipes, to give me drink, did burst.

Taylor calls this drink a "liquor brewed, [God's] sparkling art divine . . . this red wine." The blood that flowed from Jesus' veins is divine drink to the thirsty sinner because it satisfies the deepest desire: to be right with God and have communion with him.

➻ *[Jesus said,] "I assure you, unless you eat the flesh of the Son of Man and drink his blood, you cannot have eternal life within you."* John 6:53

The Deer's Cry PART ONE

I arise to-day
Through a mighty strength, the invocation of the Trinity,
Through belief in the threeness,
Through confession of the oneness
Of the Creator of Creation.

I arise to-day
Through the strength of Christ's birth with His baptism,
Through the strength of His crucifixion with His burial,
Through the strength of His resurrection with His ascension,
Through the strength of His descent for the judgement of Doom.

I arise to-day
Through the strength of the love of Cherubim,
In obedience of angels,
In the service of archangels,
In hope of resurrection to meet with reward,
In prayers of patriarchs,
In predictions of prophets,
In preachings of apostles,
In faiths of confessors,
In innocence of holy virgins,
In deeds of righteous men.

(continued in next day's reading)

SAINT PATRICK (c. 390–c. 461)
Translators: Whitley Stokes, John Strachan, Kuno Meyer

As THE SON of a British deacon, life was quite normal for Patrick until, at the age of sixteen, he was captured in a raid by Irish pirates and sold into slavery. After six years he escaped to Gaul, where he became a monk. While Patrick was visiting his family, God gave him a vision to preach the gospel to the Irish.

After becoming a bishop, he took a group of missionaries with him to Ireland in 431. One hostile reception after another drove him up the east coast to Strangford Lough. There he set up his base until he had converted all the Ulstermen to Christianity. Among his converts was his old slave master, Milchu.

It was Patrick's custom to make converts by first converting the chiefs of the Irish clans. He would then use their influence to reach their people. Patrick employed this practice on the many missionary journeys he made throughout Ireland.

These journeys were dangerous for Patrick, whose message was not always well received. As strange as it may seem, the story goes that Patrick composed this poem and then sang it to deceive assassins lying in wait for him into thinking that he and his companions were a herd of deer passing—hence, the title "The Deer's Cry."

In this poem we see Patrick's orthodox Christianity in his proclamation of the Trinity (stanza one), his confession of the basic tenets of the Christian faith (stanza two), and his dependence on others—whether in heaven or on earth—to live a full Christian life (stanza three).

May we also "arise to-day" in the strength of the Trinity, the power of Christ, and the help of those in his body—the church—to live this day for our Savior.

May the Lord make your love grow and overflow to each other and to everyone else, just as our love overflows toward you.
1 Thessalonians 3:12

The Deer's Cry PART TWO

I arise to-day
Through the strength of heaven:
Light of sun,
Radiance of moon,
Splendor of fire,
Speed of lightning,
Swiftness of wind,
Depth of sea,
Stability of earth,
Firmness of rock.

I arise to-day
Through God's strength to pilot me:
God's might to uphold me,
God's wisdom to guide me,
God's eye to look before me,
God's ear to hear me,
God's word to speak for me,
God's hand to guard me,
God's way to lie before me,
God's shield to protect me,
God's host to save me
From snares of devils,
From temptations of vices,
From every one who shall wish me ill,
Afar and anear,
Alone and in multitude.

(continued in next day's reading)

SAINT PATRICK (c. 390–c. 461)
Translators: Whitley Stokes, John Strachan, Kuno Meyer

PATRICK'S primary literary work is the *Confessions.* These confessions were written to silence critics who attacked him concerning a moral lapse when he was fifteen. Later versions of these writings were embellished by others to elevate Patrick to an intellectual status he never had. Other legends were associated with him. The best known is the story of his expelling snakes from Ireland. Popular tradition ascribed to him sainthood, though he was never formally canonized by Rome. What we know for sure about his life is that he did Christianize most of Ireland, whereby it became a center of Christian influence throughout Europe.

Patrick is also said to have written this poem. As mentioned yesterday, he sang it to deceive assassins lying in wait for him. In this second part of the poem, Patrick sings of two divine provisions that strengthen him day by day. The first is the created universe, which was made by the God of heaven for humans' life on earth. The universe God created not only sustains life but is a marvelous work to explore and to behold.

The second provision is not something God made for us, but it is still something that we can enjoy. That is, God's very own presence. God has—in his own person—what we need for a spiritual life day by day. His strength pilots us; his might upholds us; his wisdom guides us; his eye sees for us; his ear hears us; his word speaks for us; his hand guards us; his shield protects us; while his "host" (his spiritual armies) keeps us from evil. Let us joyously thank God for these two wonderful provisions that minister to us daily.

I love you, Lord; you are my strength. The Lord is my rock, my fortress, and my savior; my God is my rock, in whom I find protection. He is my shield, the strength of my salvation, and my stronghold.
Psalm 18:1-2

The Deer's Cry PART THREE

I summon to-day all these powers between me and those evils,
Against every cruel merciless power that may oppose my body and soul,
Against incantations of false prophets,
Against black laws of pagandom,
Against false laws of heretics,
Against craft of idolatry,
Against spells of women and smiths and wizards,
Against every knowledge that corrupts man's body and soul.

Christ to shield me to-day
Against poison, against burning,
Against drowning, against wounding,
So that there may come to me abundance of reward.
Christ with me, Christ before me, Christ behind me,
Christ in me, Christ beneath me, Christ above me,
Christ on my right, Christ on my left,
Christ when I lie down, Christ when I sit down, Christ when I arise.
Christ in the heart of every man who thinks of me,
Christ in the mouth of every one who speaks of me,
Christ in every eye that sees me,
Christ in every ear that hears me.

I arise to-day
Through a mighty strength, the invocation of the Trinity,
Through belief in the threeness,
Through confession of the oneness
Of the Creator of Creation.

SAINT PATRICK (c. 390–c. 461)
Translators: Whitley Stokes, John Strachan, Kuno Meyer

THIS FINAL SECTION of Patrick's poem is a genuine, all-encompassing request for protection from evil. According to the story behind the composition of this poem, Patrick created it to protect himself and his companions from assassins (see reading on March 17). Patrick could have prayed, "Father, deliver me from evil." But here we see a list of potential threats against Patrick's life and missionary efforts: "incantations of false prophets," "black laws of pagandom," "false laws of heretics," "craft of idolatry," and "spells of women and smiths and wizards." What a window into fifth-century Ireland!

Patrick then prays for protection from bodily harm, whether by poisoning, burning, drowning, or wounding. Those who take the gospel to hostile people need Christ to shield them.

This poem is also remarkable in that it reveals a man's complete commitment to Christ. Patrick was a man who lived for Christ and by Christ. He was not a man dedicated to a religion; he was a man devoted to the living God, Jesus Christ. Reread part of his prayer: "Christ with me, Christ before me, Christ behind me, Christ in me, Christ beneath me, Christ above me, Christ on my right, Christ on my left, Christ when I lie down, Christ when I sit down, Christ when I arise."

All Patrick wanted all day long was Christ. But he didn't just want Christ for himself. He also wanted his listeners to have Christ. And so he prayed: "Christ in the heart of every man who thinks of me, Christ in the mouth of every one who speaks of me."

Patrick did not want people to think of St. Patrick when they thought of him or spoke of him, but to think of Christ and to speak of Christ. May God give us the same ambition.

For to me, to live is Christ. Philippians 1:21, NIV

"O, My Heart Is Woe"

"O, my heart is woe!" Mary she said so,
"For to see my dear son die, and sons I have no mo."

"When that my sweet son was thirty winter old,
Then the traitor Judas waxed very bold:
For thirty plates of money his master he had sold.
But when I it wist,[a] *Lord, my heart was cold!*

"Upon Shere Thursday[b] *then truly it was*
On my son's death that Judas did compass.
Many were the false Jews that followed him by trace;
And there before them all he kissed my son's face.

"My son before Pilate brought was he,
And Peter said three times he knew him not, pardee.[c]
Pilate said unto the Jews: 'What say ye?'
Then they cried with one voice: 'Crucify!'

"On Good Friday, at the mount of Calvary,
My son was done on the cross, nailed with nails three.
Of all the friends that he had, never one could he see
But gentle John the Evangelist, that still stood him by.

"Though I were sorrowful, no man have at it wonder;
For huge was the earthquake, horrible was the thunder.
I looked on my sweet son on the cross that I stood under;
Then came Longeus with a spear and cleft his heart in
sunder."

ANONYMOUS

[a]past tense of *wit;* that is, knew, perceived [b]Maundy Thursday, the day before Good Friday when liturgical churches commemorate the institution of the Eucharist (Communion) in the Last Supper [c]indeed

THIS POEM was written in the voice of Jesus' mother, Mary, and is a beautiful reminder of Jesus' humanity. The tone of the poem is conversational. It is as if we have met Mary on the street or in a park. She is an old woman in a housedress, leaning on a cane or sitting on a bench. We listen to her tell the story of her son's death, just as any elderly woman might do.

Contrary to a popular view that Mary was wise, the poem depicts her as uneducated. For example, she says "sons I have no mo." She also refers to the pieces of silver as "plates of money."

In addition, Mary's rendition does not contain a spiritual perspective. To Mary, the result of Jesus' death was not wonderful redemption. Rather, it was heartache from the loss of her "sweet son." She reveals that her heart went cold when she heard that Judas had betrayed Jesus. When she speaks of the Crucifixion, we can sense anger or bitterness in her voice—particularly when she says, "My son was done on the cross." If Jesus' death wasn't bad enough, she notes that only one of his friends was there to watch him die. And she appears to have known the soldier who stabbed Jesus to make sure he was dead. Perhaps Longeus lived in her neighborhood.

Of course there is no record of Mary's reactions to Jesus' betrayal and death. This is only a poem from an artist's imagination. But with skill, this artist has portrayed a mother's love for her son. It is this portrayal that helps us appreciate Jesus as a man and as a son of Mary.

But when they came to Jesus, they saw that he was dead already, so they didn't break his legs. One of the soldiers, however, pierced his side with a spear, and blood and water flowed out. John 19:33-34

And He Answered Them Nothing

O Mighty Nothing! unto thee,
Nothing, we owe all things that be.
God spake once when he all things made,
He saved all when he Nothing said.
The world was made of Nothing then;
'Tis made by Nothing now again.

RICHARD CRASHAW (c. 1613–1649)

AS A POET, Crashaw used sensuous and often violent imagery, exaggeration, and paradox to describe experiences of mysticism and religious passion. He was also a master at saying a lot with only a few words. In this poem, he brings us from creation to redemption in four lines.

Another striking aspect about this poem is the poet's insight. Crashaw points out that in creation God spoke but in redemption God was silent. The poet's insight is especially striking since nothing exists without God's speaking: "By faith we understand that the worlds were prepared by the word of God" (Hebrews 11:3, NRSV). Plus, we know God only because we know the divine Word: "God spoke to our ancestors in many and various ways by the prophets, but in these last days he has spoken to us by a Son" (Hebrews 1:1-2, NRSV). But our redemption—the redemption of the entire creation—did not come so easy. Words could not accomplish this incredible task. It required the physical presence and sacrifice of the incarnate God. His perfect blood was not a verbal utterance but a real, rich, red liquid.

So much can be learned about God and from him in the contrast of these two events: creation and redemption. For instance, we might draw conclusions on when to speak and when to act. How many of us would have been silent if we were falsely accused of a capital crime and were facing brutal execution? At such a time, even the reticent can find eloquence. Yet Christ remained silent because his work on the cross would say it all.

Pilate asked Jesus, "Are you the King of the Jews?" Jesus replied, "Yes, it is as you say." Then the leading priests accused him of many crimes, and Pilate asked him, "Aren't you going to say something? What about all these charges against you?" But Jesus said nothing, much to Pilate's surprise. Mark 15:2-5

Good Friday Morning "BEARING HIS CROSS"

Up Thy Hill of Sorrows
Thou all alone,
Jesus, man's Redeemer,
Climbing to a Throne:
Thro' the world triumphant,
Thro' the Church in pain,
Which think to look upon Thee
No more again.

Upon my hill of sorrows
I, Lord, with Thee,
Cheered, upheld, yea, carried,
If a need should be:
Cheered, upheld, yea, carried,
Never left alone,
Carried in Thy heart of hearts
To a throne.

CHRISTINA ROSSETTI (1830–1894)

IN THIS POEM, Christina Rossetti pictures Jesus climbing up the hill of Golgotha to the cross, which is a throne. Who would ever think of a cross as a throne? Evidently Jesus did. He often spoke of how he would be "lifted up," which meant being "taken up to the cross" but also being "exalted on a throne." Prior to his death and resurrection, no one knew this but him. The irony is that people thought his crucifixion was his tragic downfall, not his glorious uprising. The people at that time could never have thought that Jesus was about to enter into glory via death and resurrection. As he entered Jerusalem for the last time, millions were hailing him. That should have been the moment for Jesus to seize the hour!

But the hour had come for the Son of Man to be "lifted up." The hour had come for him, like a grain of wheat, to be buried in the earth. He would forego the momentary glory for the eternal. The buried grain would eventually bring forth many grains in resurrection—more fruit than could have been produced had he then and there taken the kingship on earth. If Jesus had not gone to Calvary, he would have remained single and alone, like an unplanted grain. But his burial, like a planting, brought germination and multiplication.

How many grains have come from that one seed! How many are there now who lift their hands in praise to him? Jesus, through being lifted up on the cross, is King in the heart of millions!

[Jesus said,] "And just as Moses lifted up the serpent in the wilderness, so must the Son of Man be lifted up, that whoever believes in him may have eternal life. And I, when I am lifted up from the earth, will draw all people to myself." John 3:14-15; 12:32, NRSV

Good Friday

Lord Jesus Christ, grown faint upon the Cross,
A sorrow beyond sorrow in Thy look,
The unutterable craving for my soul;
Thy love of me sufficed
To load upon Thee and make good my loss
In face of darkened heaven and earth that shook:—
In face of earth and heaven, take Thou my whole
Heart, O Lord Jesus Christ.

GOOD FRIDAY EVENING
"Bring Forth the Spear."

No Cherub's heart or hand for us might ache,
No Seraph's heart of fire had half sufficed:
Thine own were pierced and broken for our sake,
O Jesus Christ.

Therefore we love Thee with our faint good-will,
We crave to love Thee not as heretofore,
To love Thee much, to love Thee more, and still
More and yet more.

CHRISTINA ROSSETTI (1830–1894)

IN THESE POEMS, Rossetti remembers two aspects of Christ's death on the cross: (1) when he grew faint prior to death and (2) when he was pierced with a spear after he had died. Near the end of Jesus' crucifixion, he, "knowing that all things were now accomplished" said, "I thirst." This fulfilled the Scriptures (John 19:28, NRSV, from Psalm 69:21) and revealed that Jesus was quite weary.

Because Jesus died quickly, the soldiers didn't need to break his legs. This also fulfilled Scripture: "Not a bone of him shall be broken" (John 19:36, NASB, from Psalm 34:20; see also Exodus 12:46; Numbers 9:12). Instead of breaking Jesus' legs, one of the soldiers pierced his side, from which blood and water then issued. This also fulfilled prophecy: "They shall look on him whom they pierced" (John 19:37, NASB, from Zechariah 12:10).

Jesus' death fulfilled Scripture, but it did so much more. His death was a display of God's great love for us. How can we not give him our whole heart and tell him that we love him?

You love him even though you have never seen him. Though you do not see him, you trust him; and even now you are happy with a glorious, inexpressible joy. 1 Peter 1:8

Palm Sunday

"He treadeth the winepress of the
fierceness and wrath of Almighty God."

I lift mine eyes, and see
Thee, tender Lord, in pain upon the tree,
Athirst for my sake and athirst for me.

"Yea, look upon Me there,
Compassed with thorns and bleeding everywhere,
For thy sake bearing all, and glad to bear."

I lift my heart to pray:
Thou Who didst love me all that darkened day,
Wilt Thou not love me to the end alway?

"Yea, thee My wandering sheep,
Yea, thee My scarlet sinner slow to weep,
Come to Me, I will love thee and will keep."

Yet am I racked with fear:
Behold the unending outer darkness drear,
Behold the gulf unbridgeable and near!

"Nay, fix thy heart, thine eyes,
Thy hope upon My boundless sacrifice:
Will I lose lightly one so dear-bought prize?"

Ah, Lord; it is not Thou,
Thou that wilt fail; yet woe is me, for how
Shall I endure who half am failing now?

"Nay, weld thy resolute will
To Mine: glance not aside for good or ill:
I love thee; trust Me still and love Me still."

Yet Thou Thyself hast said,
When Thou shalt sift the living from the dead
Some must depart shamed and uncomforted.

"Judge not before that day:
Trust Me with all thy heart, even tho' I slay:
Trust Me in love, trust on, love on, and pray."

CHRISTINA ROSSETTI (1830–1894)

THE SCRIPTURE under the title of this poem, "He treadeth the winepress of the fierceness and wrath of Almighty God," seems to be an odd companion to the title "Palm Sunday." How do the two match? The Scripture comes from Isaiah 63:1-3, which is again referred to in Revelation 19:13. In Isaiah the image is of the conquering Lord God, who executes judgment on his enemies like one smashing grapes. In this image, the vinedresser is pictured with red all over his clothes. A similar image in Revelation 19:13-14 shows Christ the Conqueror with his clothes dipped in blood. Thus, the execution of judgment was already carried out when Christ died on the cross to conquer Satan.

But the poet fears that the Lord will still judge her on the last day, as we gather from the conversation she has with Jesus in this poem. He assures her, however, that he has died for her to win her soul and, therefore, will not "lose lightly one so dear-bought prize." Like the poet, we need to trust in Jesus for our eternal salvation.

I give [my sheep] eternal life, and they will never perish.
John 10:28

O Sacred Head, Now Wounded

O sacred Head, now wounded,
With grief and shame weighed down;
Now scornfully surrounded
With thorns, Thine only crown;
O sacred Head, what glory,
What bliss till now was Thine!
Yet, though despised and gory,
I joy to call Thee mine.

What Thou, my Lord, hast suffered
Was all for sinners' gain:
Mine, mine was the transgression,
But Thine the deadly pain.
Lo, here I fall, my Saviour!
'Tis I deserve Thy place;
Look on me with Thy favor,
Vouchsafe to me Thy grace.

What language shall I borrow
To thank Thee, dearest Friend:
For this Thy dying sorrow,
Thy pity without end!
O make me Thine forever;
And should I fainting be,
Lord, let me never, never
Outlive my love to Thee.

BERNARD OF CLAIRVAUX (1090–1153)
Translated from Latin into German by Paul Gerhardt (1607–1676) and translated into English by James Waddell Alexander (1804–1859)

CHRISTIANS of all denominations appreciate Bernard for his poetry, hymns, and mystical piety. His motto, which has been adopted by others throughout the ages, was this: To Know Jesus and Jesus Crucified.

Bernard spent most of his life in a monastery at Clairvaux ("bright valley") that he and a few close relatives established. He experienced continual tension between a life of ascetic retirement and a life of Christian involvement in the world. Bernard challenged popes and princes about the quality of their Christian practice and called all Christians to a life of mystical devotion. Such a life was pictured as a separation of soul and body, an emptying of worldly desire, and a final union of the soul with God.

Racked by ill health in his later years, he was urged to retire to a hut near the monastery. It was here that his writings first evolved. They contain a strange but pleasing mixture of sayings from the church fathers, biblical symbols, analogies, etymologies, and alliterations. Most are marked with poetic genius. Thus, he has been called the "greatest master of language in the Middle Ages." In addition, the writings of Bernard of Clairvaux have continued to influence the church.

One such writing is this poem, "O Sacred Head, Now Wounded." It is the most famous poem Bernard composed. The original contained seven parts, each focusing on a different area of Christ's crucified body (his feet, knees, hands, side, breast, heart, and head). This part obviously compels us to look at Christ's head, which is surrounded by a crown of thorns and weighed down with "grief and shame." As we gaze upon the suffering Savior in this poem, let us be overcome with appreciation for the love that motivated him to suffer and die for us.

But God showed his great love for us by sending Christ to die for us while we were still sinners. Romans 5:8

I Am Not Skilled to Understand

I am not skilled to understand
What God hath willed, what God hath planned;
I only know at His right hand
Stands One who is my Savior.

I take Him at His word and deed:
"Christ died to save me," this I read;
And in my heart I find a need
Of Him to be my Savior.

That He should leave His place on high
And come for sinful man to die,
You count it strange? so once did I
Before I knew my Savior.

And O that He fulfilled may see
The travail of His soul in me,
And with His work contented be,
As I with my dear Savior!

Yes, living, dying, let me bring
My strength, my solace, from this spring,
That He who lives to be my King
Once died to be my Savior!

DORA GREENWELL (1821–1882)

DORA GREENWELL was born into an affluent English family. But her father died when she was young, and the family estate had to be sold. Thereafter, she suffered bad health as she lived alone in London. Greenwell included this poem, "I Am Not Skilled to Understand," in a book she compiled, titled *Songs of Salvation.*

Dora knew what it meant to suffer. And like all human beings, she wanted to know the meaning of suffering but realized she couldn't. Yet what amazed her the most was not her suffering but God's. Thus, in this poem she asks why "He should leave His place on high and come for sinful man to die." She does not give us an answer that will satisfy human reason, but she does declare that the answer is found in knowing Jesus as our Savior.

You can be sure that the more we suffer for Christ, the more God will shower us with his comfort through Christ. So when we are weighed down with troubles, it is for your benefit and salvation! For when God comforts us, it is so that we, in turn, can be an encouragement to you. Then you can patiently endure the same things we suffer.
2 Corinthians 1:5-6

Redemption

Having been tenant long to a rich lord,
Not thriving, I resolvèd to be bold,
And make a suit unto him, to afford
A new small-rented lease, and cancel th' old.

In heaven at his manor I him sought:
They told me there that he was lately gone
About some land which he had dearly bought
Long since on earth, to take possession.

I straight returned, and knowing his great birth,
Sought him accordingly in great resorts—
In cities, theaters, gardens, parks, and courts:
At length I heard a ragged noise and mirth

Of thieves and murderers; there I him espied,
Who straight, "Your suit is granted," said, and died.

GEORGE HERBERT (1593–1633)

HERBERT'S main volume of poetry, *The Temple* (1633), has several poems about Christ's death on the cross. In this poem, Herbert provides an interesting perspective on the meaning of Christ's death as the means of redemption.

In order to understand what Herbert was getting at, we need to understand the meaning of redemption. In legal terms, redemption signifies "the liberation of any possession, object, or person, usually by payment of a ransom." In Old Testament times, redemption occurred quite frequently. When a person lost a piece of property, that person's next-of-kin had both the right and the obligation to redeem the property. This right of redemption protected the family inheritance. An Israelite who was forced to sell himself into slavery to pay his debts could be redeemed by a close relative or even by himself (Leviticus 25:47-49). Land might also be redeemed in the same fashion (Leviticus 25:25-28; Jeremiah 32:6-9). In the New Testament, the term *redemption* means a freeing from the slavery of sin—with the ransom, or price paid for this freedom, being Christ himself on the cross.

With this in mind, Herbert compares himself to a person in need of a redeemer to cancel his old debt and make a new lease for him. He sought the Lord in heaven to make this transaction, but the Lord had gone to earth—to live among the lowly and to die on the cross to pay the price for Herbert's (as well as our own) redemption. The rich Lord had lowered himself—all the way to death—to grant Herbert's request.

➻ *For even I, the Son of Man, came here not to be served but to serve others, and to give my life as a ransom for many.* Mark 10:45

His Savior's Words, Going to the Cross

Have, have ye no regard, all ye
Who pass this way, to pity me,
Who am a man of misery!

A man both bruised, and broke, and one
Who suffers not here for mine own,
But for my friends transgression!

Ah! Sion's Daughters, do not fear
The Cross, the Cords, the Nails, the Spear,
The Myrrh, the Gall, the Vinegar:

For Christ, your loving Savior, hath
Drunk up the wine of God's fierce wrath;
Only, there's left a little froth,

Less for to taste, than for to show,
What bitter cups had been your due,
Had He not drank them up for you.

ROBERT HERRICK (1591–1674)

ROBERT HERRICK, a goldsmith's son, initially pursued his father's trade but then went to Cambridge. He was ordained in 1623 and was appointed by King Charles I to be Dean Prior of Devonshire. He was dismissed from this post in 1647 but was reinstated after the Restoration of 1660. In 1648 he published a book of poems called *Hesperides* and thereby established himself as one of the great English lyrical poets.

In this poem Herrick recreates the scene of Jesus' crucifixion. Many who surrounded Jesus were mocking him and deriding him while he was dying for their sins. The poem (beginning with the third stanza) also recaptures the words of Jesus to the women of Jerusalem as he was going to the cross (see Luke 23:26-31). These women (called "Sion's Daughters"—Sion being Zion, the hill Jerusalem is built on) were weeping for Jesus as he was carrying the cross to Golgotha, where he would be crucified. He told them, "Daughters of Jerusalem, don't weep for me, but weep for yourselves and for your children."

Jesus drank the bitter cup of God's eternal wrath against sin. But he left a little for us to drink. That is, each one of us has to endure our own portion of suffering so that we might never forget what it meant for Jesus to suffer. Our small sufferings should remind us of his great suffering for us.

Jesus walked away, about a stone's throw, and knelt down and prayed, "Father, if you are willing, please take this cup of suffering away from me. Yet I want your will, not mine." Luke 22:41-42

Good Friday

Am I a stone and not a sheep
That I can stand, O Christ, beneath Thy Cross,
To number drop by drop Thy Blood's slow loss,
And yet not weep?

Not so those women loved
Who with exceeding grief lamented Thee;
Not so fallen Peter weeping bitterly;
Not so the thief was moved;

Not so the Sun and Moon
Which hid their faces in a starless sky,
A horror of great darkness at broad noon—
I, only I.

Yet give not o'er,
But seek Thy sheep, true Shepherd of the flock;
Greater than Moses, turn and look once more
And smite a rock.

CHRISTINA ROSSETTI (1830–1894)

IN THIS POEM Christina decries her inability to express emotion for Jesus' death on the cross. Her impassiveness, when compared to the emotion of all those who witnessed Jesus' death, is all the more remarkable. Thus, she asks Christ, who is greater than Moses, to smite her like Moses smote the rock in the wilderness so that the waters (her tears) might burst forth.

This imagery also points us to the biblical image of Jesus' death being compared to the smitten rock. This is brought out in John 7:37-39. On the last day, the great day of the Festival of Tabernacles, Jesus stood and cried, "If you are thirsty, come to me! If you believe in me, come and drink! For the Scriptures declare that rivers of living water will flow out from within." Jesus became the true smitten Rock by being crucified on the cross. There, life-giving water flowed, figuratively speaking, from his sacrifice. His wounds became the founts of blessing.

May Christ smite our hard heart too, so we might weep for the anguish we have caused our Lord and Savior.

[God told Moses], "Strike the rock, and water will come pouring out. Then the people will be able to drink." Moses did just as he was told; and as the leaders looked on, water gushed out. Exodus 17:6

Upon Our Savior's Tomb Wherein Never Man Was Laid

How Life and Death in thee
Agree!
Thou hadst a virgin Womb
And Tomb.
A Joseph did betroth
Them both.

RICHARD CRASHAW (c. 1613–1649)

THE SON of a zealous and well-educated Puritan minister, Crashaw was educated at Cambridge, where he learned Latin, Greek, Hebrew, Spanish, and Italian. During the civil war of 1642–1651, he began to side with the Roman Catholics and thereby lost all favor with the Puritans. In 1644 he moved to France and became a Roman Catholic. During these years, he prepared his books of poems, *Steps to the Temple* and *Sacred Poems,* both of which contained religious and secular poems in Latin and English. Crashaw then published *Carmen Deo Nostro* ("Hymn to Our Lord"), illustrated with twelve drawings.

Although he is often linked with the metaphysical poets of England, his poetry resembles that of the Italian and Spanish mystics. He sought to focus the senses and imaginations on various religious themes that would evoke the spiritual emotions: the wounds and blood of the crucified Lord, the sorrows and sufferings of Mary, the tears of Mary Magdalene, or the sufferings and joys of Teresa of Avila.

In this short poem Crashaw celebrates the interesting fact that Jesus was conceived in a virgin womb and laid to rest in a virgin tomb—that is, a tomb never occupied before. Furthermore, two men, both called Joseph, were involved with Jesus' birth and death. Joseph (of Galilee) married Mary the virgin, the mother of Jesus (see Matthew 1:18-25), and another Joseph (of Arimathea) buried Jesus in a newly hewn tomb, which Joseph had made for himself but then gave for Jesus' body (see Matthew 27:57-60; John 19:38-42).

Now this is how Jesus the Messiah was born. His mother, Mary, was engaged to be married to Joseph. But while she was still a virgin, she became pregnant by the Holy Spirit. . . . As evening approached, Joseph, a rich man from Arimathea who was one of Jesus' followers, went to Pilate and asked for Jesus' body. . . . Joseph took the body and wrapped it in a long linen cloth. He placed it in his own new tomb.
Matthew 1:18; 27:57-60

Easter Wings

Lord, who createdst man in wealth and store,
Though foolishly he lost the same,
Decaying more and more
Till he became
Most poor:
With thee
O let me rise
As larks, harmoniously,
And sing this day thy victories:
Then shall the fall further the flight in me.
My tender age in sorrow did begin:
And still with sicknesses and shame
Thou didst so punish sin,
That I became
Most thin.
With thee
Let me combine,
And feel this day thy victory;
For, if I imp my wing on thine,
Affliction shall advance the flight in me.

GEORGE HERBERT (1593–1633)

IN THIS POEM Herbert explains that God had exceedingly blessed the people he had created but that they had foolishly lost the abundance of his blessings when they sinned. The consequences of that loss are cumulative, bringing about continual corruption of soul and depletion of body. The poem's visual form depicts this depletion—beginning with a broad line in each stanza that narrows in each of the first two sections to the lines "Most poor" and "Most thin."

The recovery from this poor, thin condition begins when one joins him or herself to Christ. This is visually depicted in both stanzas of the poem in the words "With thee." The poet asks for union with Christ: "With thee O let me rise" and "With thee let me combine." The image, of course, is that of flying on Jesus' Easter wings. The verb *imp* is perfect for this image because it means "to graft a falcon's wing with a feather." Herbert needed this imping—grafting—because he could not fly on his own. During the days Herbert wrote this poem, he was struggling with bad health. He needed Christ's resurrected wings to sustain him and take him into eternal life. Herbert knew that if he put his afflicted life on the wings of the Lord, he would rise up.

But for you who fear my name, the Sun of Righteousness will rise with healing in his wings. Malachi 4:2

Long Barren

Thou who didst hang upon a barren tree,
My God, for me;
Tho' I till now be barren, now at length,
Lord, give me strength
To bring forth fruit to Thee.

Thou who didst bear for me the crown of thorn,
Spitting and scorn;
Tho' I till now have put forth thorns, yet now
Strengthen me Thou
That better fruit be borne.

Thou Rose of Sharon, Cedar of broad roots,
Vine of sweet fruits,
Thou Lily of the vale with fadeless leaf,
Of thousands Chief,
Feed Thou my feeble shoots.

CHRISTINA ROSSETTI (1830–1894)

GAZING upon a barren tree in winter may remind us of the stark cross on which Jesus died. In fact, many poets have used this image as a symbol for Christ's cross. Others picture the cross as a vine giving forth sweet wine. Rossetti uses both of these images in her poem to illustrate her spiritual condition and her need for Christ.

In the first two stanzas Rossetti compares her life to two things that brought Christ pain—the cross and the crown of thorns. As the poet is painfully aware, Christ did not suffer and die so that his followers would remain spiritually barren. She knows she should produce more than thorns. But how? The only way her life will produce fruit is by abiding in Christ, the true Vine.

The image of the true Vine is drawn from John 15, where Jesus says, "I am the vine; you are the branches." Each branch that remains in the vine continues to bear fruit (15:5). Some commentators say the fruit is new converts, while others think it is "the fruit of the Spirit" (Galatians 5:22-23). The devotional writer Andrew Murray said, "The essential idea of fruit is that it is the silent natural restful produce of our inner life." Simply put, it is the outward expression of Christ's work in a believer's life.

Rossetti desired to produce this fruit and prayed, "Strengthen me Thou that better fruit be borne. . . . vine of sweet fruits . . . feed Thou my feeble shoots." If we, like Rossetti, long to produce more than thorns, we must depend on Christ to nourish us. May Christ strengthen us to bear better fruit. May he feed our feeble shoots.

I am the vine; you are the branches. Those who remain in me, and I in them, will produce much fruit. For apart from me you can do nothing. . . . My true disciples produce much fruit. This brings great glory to my Father. John 15:5, 8

Crucifying

By miracles exceeding power of man,
He faith in some, envy in some begat,
For, what weak spirits admire, ambitious, hate;
In both affections many to him ran,
But Oh! the worst are most, they will and can,
Alas, and do, unto the immaculate,
Whose creature fate is, now prescribe a fate,
Measuring self-life's infinity to a span,
Nay to an inch. Lo, where condemned he
Bears his own cross, with pain, yet by and by
When it bears him, he must bear more and die.
Now thou art lifted up, draw me to thee,
And at thy death giving such liberal dole,
Moist, with one drop of thy blood, my dry soul.

JOHN DONNE (1572–1631)

IN THE PAST, public executions drew large crowds. Donne, aware of this fact, wrote about the people who came to witness Christ's crucifixion. Two kinds of people, who form a pair, appear within the first three lines of this poem—those Christ inspires to faith and those he incites to envy. The spectators knew that Jesus' power exceeded that of a mere man. Weak spirits admired him for this, while ambitious spirits hated him. People of both persuasions hurried to see Christ die. The former hoped he would miraculously come down from the cross. The latter hoped he never would.

These hostile people—the poet notes—made up the majority of those who witnessed the Crucifixion. In arrogance, they prescribed the Lord's fate: They measured his life and found only a span or less. In other words, to them Jesus was nothing more than a man, albeit a powerful one. Therefore, they came, they gazed, they walked away.

Perhaps if one of them were to measure Jesus' hand, it would actually come to nine inches. After all, he is human. As Donne wrote, Jesus bore his own cross with pain. Then he was lifted up, and the cross bore him. But the poet does not stop there in describing the significance of Christ and his crucifixion. Jesus' death was not meaningless. Rather, his death redeemed humanity. Unlike the first two groups of people, those who acknowledge their need for redemption are drawn to the crucified Son of Man for the right reason. Donne was one such person. He recognized his need for redemption. In the last three lines of the poem Donne places himself at the foot of the cross and asks Christ to moisten his dry soul with one drop of blood. May we, like Donne, come to Christ for this reason.

It was nine o'clock in the morning when the crucifixion took place. Mark 15:25

Christ's Passion PART ONE

Enough, my Muse, of earthly things,
And inspirations but of wind,
Take up thy lute, and to it bind
Loud and everlasting strings;
And on 'em play and to 'em sing,
The happy mournful stories,
The lamentable glories,
Of the great Crucified King.
Mountainous heap of wonders! which dost rise
Till earth thou joinest with the skies!
Too large at bottom, and at top too high,
To be half seen by mortal eye.
How shall I grasp this boundless thing?
What shall I play? what shall I sing?
I'll sing the mighty riddle of mysterious love,
Which neither wretched men below, nor blessed spirits above
With all their comments can explain;
How all the Whole World's Life to die did not disdain.

I'll sing the searchless depths of the compassion divine,
The depths unfathomed yet
By reasons plummet, and the line of wit,
Too light the plummet, and too short the line,
How the Eternal Father did bestow
His own Eternal Son as ransom for his Foe,
I'll sing aloud, that all the world may hear,
The triumph of the buried conquerer.
How hell was by its prisoner captive led,
And the great slayer Death slain by the dead.

(continued in next day's reading)

ABRAHAM COWLEY (1618–1667)

THE ENGLISH metaphysical poet and essayist Abraham Cowley, who published his first volume of poems at the age of fifteen (*Poetical Blossoms,* 1633), led a colorful life. During the English Civil War he was cipher secretary to Henrietta Maria, queen consort of England, in Paris. Later he was a Royalist spy, a botanist, and a founder of the Royal Society. After the Restoration he retired to the English countryside.

Cowley describes the accumulated stories and glories of the great crucified King as a "mountainous heap of wonders." This mountain is so broad at the bottom and so high at the top that it cannot be entirely seen by the human eye. Cowley also looks into the "searchless depths of the compassion divine" and finds that our capacity to fathom these depths is severely limited. If all human wit and reason could compose the plumb line used for this measurement, he wrote, the line of wit is too short and the plummet of reason would be too light to perform the task.

Such images describe a love and a death that are far beyond our understanding. Consider with Cowley these incomprehensible wonders: The Bread of Life did not refuse to die (John 6:51); the eternal Father gave his eternal Son as the ransom for his foe (Hebrews 2:14-15); hell was captured by its own prisoner (Ephesians 4:8); and Death was slain by the dead (Hebrews 2:14). In the light of this mystery, even Paul, who was most articulate, could only write:

Oh, what a wonderful God we have! How great are his riches and wisdom and knowledge! How impossible it is for us to understand his decisions and his methods! For who can know what the Lord is thinking? Who knows enough to be his counselor? And who could ever give him so much that he would have to pay it back? For everything comes from him; everything exists by his power and is intended for his glory. To him be glory evermore. Amen. Romans 11:33-36

Christ's Passion PART TWO

Me thinks I hear of murdered men the voice,
Mixed with the murderers' confused noise,
Sound from the top of Calvary;
My greedy eyes fly up the hill, and see
Who 'tis hangs there midmost of the three;
Oh how unlike the others he!
Look how he bends head with blessings from the Tree!
His gracious hands ne'er stretched but to do good,
Are nailed to the infamous wood:
And sinful Man does fondly bind
The arms, which he extends t'embrace all human kind.

Unhappy, canst thou stand by, and see
All this as patient, as he?
Since he thy sins does bear,
Make thou his sufferings thine own,
And weep, and sigh, and groan,
And beat thy breast, and tear,
Thy garments, and thy hair,
And let thy grief, and let thy love
Through all thy bleeding bowels move.
Dost thou not see thy Prince in purple clad all o'er,
Not purple brought from the Sidonian shore,
But made at home with richer gore?
Dost thou not see the roses, which adorn
The thorny garland, by him worn?
Dost thou not see the livid traces
Of the sharp scourges rude embraces?
If yet thou feelest not the smart
Of thorns and scourges in thy heart,
If that be yet not crucified,
Look on his hands, look on his feet, look on his side.

Open, Oh! open wide the fountains of thine eyes,
And let 'em call
Their stock of moisture forth, where e'er it lies,
For this will ask it all.
'Twould all (alas) too little be,
Though thy salt tears came from a sea:
Canst thou deny him this, when he

Has opened all his vital springs for thee?
Take heed; for by his sides mysterious flood
May well be understood,
That he will still require some waters to his blood.

ABRAHAM COWLEY (1618–1667)

IN PART 1 of this poem Cowley posed the question, "How shall I grasp this boundless thing?" He was referring to Christ's love for fallen humanity, which is a mystery indeed.

The apostle Paul may have understood the ways of God better than anyone since Jesus Christ. It has been said that without Paul's writings there would be no Christian theology. Yet Paul, like Cowley, admitted that he only partially understood the truth. In fact, Paul once made this request: "Pray also for me, so that when I speak, a message may be given to me to make known with boldness the mystery of the gospel" (Ephesians 6:19, NRSV). Elsewhere he wrote: "We know only a little. . . . We see things imperfectly as in a poor mirror. . . . All that I know now is partial and incomplete" (1 Corinthians 13:9, 12). It may surprise us to learn that even Paul needed prayer so God would grant him the words to convey something that, while beautifully simple, is most difficult to express.

In light of this let's pray: *Dear heavenly Father, save me from the arrogance of thinking that I could ever entirely understand you. Please give me a humble heart that pursues the truth of the gospel, knowing that it can never be completely grasped. I love you and look forward to the day when I will see you face-to-face, when I will know in full, even as I have been fully known. Amen.*

➻ *The Lord answered Job from the whirlwind: . . . "Where were you when I laid the foundations of the earth? Tell me, if you know so much.* Job 38:1, 4

A Bruised Reed Shall He Not Break

I will accept thy will to do and be,
Thy hatred and intolerance of sin,
Thy will at least to love, that burns within
And thirsteth after Me:
So I will render fruitful, blessing still
The germs and small beginnings in thy heart,
Because thy will cleaves to the better part. —
Alas, I cannot will.

Dost not thou will, poor soul? Yet I receive
The inner unseen longings of the soul,
I guide them turning towards Me; I control
And charm hearts till they grieve:
If thou desire, it yet shall come to pass,
Tho' thou but wish indeed to choose My love;
For I have power in earth and heaven above. —
I cannot wish, alas!

What, neither choose nor wish to choose? and yet
I still must strive to win thee and constrain:
For thee I hung upon the cross in pain,
How then can I forget?
If thou as yet dost neither love, nor hate,
Nor choose, nor wish,—resign thyself, be still
Till I infuse love, hatred, longing, will. —
I do not deprecate.

CHRISTINA ROSSETTI (1830–1894)

HAVE you ever felt like such a spiritual failure that you thought the Lord might just cut you off and throw you away? This poem speaks about this feeling.

As its title indicates, the Lord will not dispose of or "deprecate" a believer who displeases him. Rather, he will "infuse" that person with fresh spiritual desires. The title "A Bruised Reed Shall He Not Break" comes from a prominent messianic prophecy in Isaiah, which is quoted in Matthew (see below).

The Messiah-Servant would execute judgment in a gentle way, not with ruthlessness or ill regard toward people. Whereas one rough touch breaks a bruised reed or quenches the smoldering wick, the Messiah's touch is tender, loving, and skillful. His touch lifts up the meek, comforts the mourning, and says to the fearful heart, "Be strong, fear not."

This was to fulfill what had been spoken through the prophet Isaiah: "Here is my servant, whom I have chosen, my beloved, with whom my soul is well pleased. I will put my Spirit upon him, and he will proclaim justice to the Gentiles. He will not wrangle or cry aloud, nor will anyone hear his voice in the streets. He will not break a bruised reed or quench a smoldering wick until he brings justice to victory."
Matthew 12:17-20, NRSV

On the Inscription . . . PART ONE

I am that Savior that vouchsafed to die
For sin-sick souls, behold me it is I
Even unto my self that was content to be
Scourged, buffeted, despised, bethorned for yE
Suffered the death o'th'Cross, suffered no less
Than all my Father's wrath that happineS
Unto the world might come, and peace ensue
To those that would repent, to heaven be trU
Suffer I did such wounds, such killing groans
As would have moved to ruth[a] *the senseless stoneS*

O let it pity then move in you so
As may constrain you to repentance gO
Ferret remorse, and that enjoin you doff
Sin's damned garment, and all vice put ofF

No more let sin abound, but may contrition
For me, and for your sins make good remissioN
All else in vain I suffer, and Abba
In vain you cry not having learned your A
Zeal is but cold in you, howe'er the blaze
May make such as your self with wonder gaZ
All your devotion is not worth a flea
Unless it have more than an outward pleA
Repent then quickly that my sepulcher
May bury all your sins, and may you eveR
Ever remember him that did deny
No pains, no torments, that might remediE
The misery of you; for my sake set
Light by all pleasure, and let no man freT
Himself with the world's business, I am nigh
To all that love me, will assist from higH

(continued in next day's reading)

HENRY COLMAN (fl. 1640)

[a]related to *rue* and means "pity" or "compassion"

HENRY COLMAN called his poem an anacrostica—that is, a backward acrostic. An acrostic is a poetic form in which the first letter of each line, when taken in order, spells out a word or motto. Notice that the poet arranged his poem so that both the first and the final letter of each couplet combine to spell I[J]ESUS OF NAZARETH THE KING OF THE I[J]EWES (see tomorrow's reading for the last half).

This eloquent inscription fastened to the cross declares Jesus' rightful title. Jesus was the Jews' true king. Ironically, his claim to be God's Son violated Jewish law (John 5:18; 19:7). It was blasphemous for a man to claim equality with God. Therefore, the Jewish leaders condemned him to die. But because they did not have the authority to carry out the sentence, they brought Jesus to Pilate, the Roman governor of Palestine.

Pilate couldn't find Jesus guilty of any offense and wanted to release him. The Jewish leaders, however, reminded Pilate that to do so would offend Caesar (John 19:12). For a peasant to claim kingship was a political offense. The wonder of it all is that Jesus is man and God, peasant and king.

As Jesus hung from the cross, he said, "Forgive them, for they do not know what they are doing" (Luke 23:34, NIV). So true. The subjects did not know they were killing their ruler. The creatures did not know they were destroying their Creator. To them only a troublesome man was dying there. But in dying, the gracious King made a way for his true subjects to enter a paradise of everlasting joy and peace with him.

➺ *It was now about noon of the day of preparation for the Passover. And Pilate said to the people, "Here is your king!" "Away with him," they yelled. "Away with him—crucify him!"* John 19:14-15

On the Inscription . . . PART TWO

Trust not in worldly wealth for cankered rust
Will soon consume it, but among the jusT
Heap up your treasure, for in heaven nor moth,
Nor thief, nor can consume, nor pilfer dotH
Earth, and its choicest pleasures are but dross
And rob the soul of bliss, then fly such lossE

Knit, and ingrafted into me, the rack
Ye need not fear, though whips furrow your bacK
I will be with you still, pity your cry
Wipe off your tears, make your tormentors dI
Not death it self shall hurt you, I upon
Your heads (in spite of death) will set the CrowN
Glory shall be your reward, every dreg
Of frail mortality, and pollution's raG

Off you shall purged be, and you shall know
Eternal pleasures, 'stead of these belO
Fear not then quickly for my sake to doff
Sin's damned garment, and all vice put ofF

Then shall you welcome be, for I was sent
Only to save such as are penitenT
Heal such as seek for ease, bestow new birth
On the repentant and obedient eartH
Even for such, and none but such I give
Freely my life that they may ever livE

I will revenge my blood on those that fly
Far from my love, for ever let them frI
Even in the flames of hell, and may a curse
Fall on them greater if there may be worsE
Well I am come to heal, and as I bow
For sinners, so I would have them to voW
Eternally themselves to me, and keep
Those vows most constant, then though now I weepE
Sorrow shall be exiled, and I no less
Happy in death, than you in happineS

HENRY COLMAN (fl. 1640)

"IN THE BEGINNING the Word already existed. He was with God, and he was God" (John 1:1). Jesus Christ is called "the Word." "So the Word became human and lived here on earth among us" (1:14). He himself was the speaking, the expression, of God. We are told: "Long ago God spoke many times and in many ways to our ancestors through the prophets. But now in these final days, he has spoken to us through his Son. . . . The Son reflects God's own glory, and everything about him represents God exactly" (Hebrews 1:1-3). It is not Christ's speaking, his words, which qualifies him as the Word. The Word is what Jesus is.

As the Word, Jesus didn't need Pilate's help to make his true identity known. But that is exactly what Pilate did. In posting this inscription, which was a common practice in crucifixion, Pilate unwittingly proclaimed the truth. What he meant as a mockery was true in reality. This man, beaten bloody, whose full weight hung from his arms, saying nearly nothing as he was about to die, represented God exactly. According to the inscription, he was someone named Jesus from Nazareth. He was a foolish boaster who said he was a king or some kind of god. This was all the people saw hanging from that cross near Jerusalem. But now we know that this was God speaking to us through his Son. This tortured man was the Word who became human and dwelt among us.

And Pilate posted a sign over him that read, "Jesus of Nazareth, the King of the Jews." The place where Jesus was crucified was near the city; and the sign was written in Hebrew, Latin, and Greek, so that many people could read it. John 19:19-20

Upon the Ass That Bore Our Savior

Hath only anger an omnipotence
In eloquence?
Within the lips of love and joy doth dwell
No miracle?
Why else had Balaam's ass a tongue to chide
His masters pride?
And thou (Heaven-burdened beast) hast ne'er a word
To praise thy Lord?
That he should find a tongue and vocal thunder,
Was a great wonder.
But o methinks 'tis a far greater one
That thou find'st none.

RICHARD CRASHAW (c. 1613–1649)

THE BIBLE gives us a lot to think about. For example, Richard Crashaw wondered why Balaam's donkey spoke (Numbers 22:28-30), yet the donkey that carried Jesus into Jerusalem did not.

When Jesus rode into Jerusalem, "all of his followers began to shout and sing as they walked along, praising God for all the wonderful miracles they had seen" (Luke 19:37). Then "some of the Pharisees among the crowd said, 'Teacher, rebuke your followers for saying things like that!'" (v. 39). In Jesus' answer we gain a peek into the order of God's creation: "If they kept quiet," he said, "the stones along the road would burst into cheers!" (v. 40).

Scripture illustrates that creation is not severed from humanity. In fact, when humanity fell (Genesis 3), it dragged the entire creation down with it. Romans 8:20 says: "Against its will, everything on earth was subjected to God's curse."

Yet Romans 8:21 continues: "All creation anticipates the day when it will join God's children in glorious freedom from death and decay." When humanity fully enters into God's redemption, it will be joined by the rest of creation.

Getting back to Crashaw's question, there was no need for the donkey to praise the Lord; it would have been out of place if it had begun to cheer. The humans who were present did that job well and so advanced this world toward the day when everything will be fully redeemed. But perhaps the donkey groaned, not under the weight of Jesus but as described in Romans 8:22: "For we know that all creation has been groaning as in the pains of childbirth right up to the present time." The donkey and all creation are waiting to be released from their bondage.

Jesus found a young donkey and sat on it, fulfilling the prophecy that said: "Don't be afraid, people of Israel. Look, your King is coming, sitting on a donkey's colt." John 12:14-15

Wisdom

Ere God had built the mountains,
Or raised the fruitful hills;
Before he filled the fountains
That feed the running rills;
In me, from everlasting,
The wonderful I AM,
Found pleasures never-wasting,
And Wisdom is my name.

When, like a tent to dwell in,
He spread the skies abroad,
And swathed about the swelling
Of Ocean's mighty flood;
He wrought by weight and measure,
And I was with him then:
Myself the Father's pleasure,
And mine, the sons of men.

Thus Wisdom's words discover
Thy glory and thy grace,
Thou everlasting lover
Of our unworthy race!
Thy gracious eye surveyed us
Ere stars were seen above;
In wisdom thou hast made us,
And died for us in love.

And couldst thou be delighted
With creatures such as we,
Who, when we saw thee, slighted
And nailed thee to a tree?
Unfathomable wonder,
And mystery divine!
The voice that speaks in thunder,
Says, "Sinner, I am thine!"

WILLIAM COWPER (1731–1800)

"AND THIS is eternal life, that they may know you, the only true God" (John 17:3, NRSV). Yet the world has not been able to know God through its own wisdom (1 Corinthians 1:21). Why? It is true that wisdom is not the same as knowledge. Wisdom involves a developed intuition and accumulated experience combined with keen knowledge. But this is still *human* wisdom. If someone is to know God through wisdom, it must be *God's* wisdom, and this is impossible for a person to attain. It is entirely beyond human comprehension.

What is God's wisdom? Scripture answers this question: "Christ . . . the wisdom of God" (1 Corinthians 1:24). William Cowper has wonderfully described Christ as wisdom. Reading this poem in its meter and rhyme uplifts the heart. Read it aloud and sense even more the joy of God's wisdom.

Now let's assess our situation thus far: (a) To know God is to have eternal life; (b) through human wisdom it is impossible to know God; (c) what we need is God's wisdom; (d) God's wisdom is Christ. This is good, but something is missing: (e) To have God's wisdom we must have Christ. "[God] is the source of your life in Christ Jesus, *who became for us wisdom from God*" (1 Corinthians 1:30, NRSV, italics added). The apostle proclaimed Christ crucified, who came to us through his death, and he is ours—the wisdom of God. And in God's wisdom we sing, "Thy gracious eye surveyed us ere stars were seen above; in wisdom thou hast made us, and died for us in love."

As the Scriptures say, "I will destroy human wisdom and discard their most brilliant ideas." So where does this leave the philosophers, the scholars, and the world's brilliant debaters? God has made them all look foolish and has shown their wisdom to be useless nonsense. Since God in his wisdom saw to it that the world would never find him through human wisdom, he has used our foolish preaching to save all who believe. 1 Corinthians 1:19-21

A Ballad of Trees and the Master

Into the woods my Master went,
Clean forspent,[a] *forspent.*
Into the woods my Master came,
Forspent with love and shame.
But the olives they were not blind to Him,
The little gray leaves were kind to Him:
The thorn-tree had a mind to Him
When into the woods He came.

Out of the woods my Master went,
And he was well content.
Out of the woods my Master came,
Content with death and shame.
When Death and Shame would woo Him last,
From under the trees they drew Him last:
'Twas on a tree they slew Him—last
When out of the woods He came.

SIDNEY LANIER (1842–1881)

[a]exhausted

THE AMERICAN poet, novelist, and musician Sidney Lanier was the outstanding southern poet of the late nineteenth century. Lanier's best-known poems include "Corn" (1875), "The Symphony" (1875), "The Revenge of Hamish" (1878), and "A Ballad of Trees and the Master" (1880).

The Garden of Gethsemane is the setting for this poem. Gethsemane was a favorite retreat of Jesus'. He took his disciples there often, most likely to rest and pray. It is only fitting that he prayed there the night before his crucifixion. As Lanier recounts this scene, he emphasizes three points. The first is Christ's physical state: Christ was "clean forspent" as he entered the woods. The last week of Christ's life was physically and emotionally exhausting. Yet he still had to face the most terrible events of his life.

Second, creation took notice of Christ's condition. While the Bible makes it clear that Christ received strength from an angel from heaven (Luke 22:43), Lanier romanticizes the role the trees played in comforting the Master. The olives noticed his suffering, and the leaves were kind to him. Perhaps Lanier thought Christ may have taken comfort in the familiar surroundings of the garden. The peace and solitude of this place were probably what Christ needed during this agonizing time.

Lanier's third point is finality. The word *last* appears three times in the second stanza. Why? The purpose for which Christ came to earth was about to be fulfilled. He would die as *the* sacrifice for everyone's sins. But perhaps what Lanier had in mind was that Christ was also the last person who had to die forsaken by God. Everyone who died after him could die in peace with God through faith in Christ. That is why the Good News is called the "gospel of peace" (Ephesians 6:15).

➻ *Then, accompanied by the disciples, Jesus left the upstairs room and went as usual to the Mount of Olives.* Luke 22:39

Woefully Arrayed PART ONE

Woefully arrayed,
My blood, man,
For thee ran,
It may not be nayed:
My body blue and wan,
Woefully arrayed.

Behold me, I pray thee, with all thine whole reason,
And be not hard-hearted for this encheason,[a]
That I for thy soul's sake was slain in good season,
Beguiled and betrayed by Judas' false treason,
Unkindly entreated,
With sharp cords sore fretted,
The Jewës me threated,
They mowed,[b] *they spitted and despised me*
Condemned to death, as thou mayst see.

Thus naked am I nailed, O man, for thy sake.
I love thee, then love me. Why sleepest thou? Awake!
Remember my tender heart-root for thee brake,
With pains my veins constrained to crack.
Thus was I defaced,
Thus was my flesh rased,[c]
And I to death chased,
Like a lamb led unto sacrifice,
Slain I was in most cruel wise.

(continued in next day's reading)

JOHN SKELTON? (c. 1460–1529)

a cause; occasion **b** a *mow* is a wry or derisive grimace **c** razed

JOHN SKELTON could not have chosen a more perfect title for this poem. Why? Crucifixion was one of the cruelest and most humiliating forms of punishment in the ancient world. Jesus' experience was no exception.

First, a Roman soldier tied Jesus to a post and flogged him with a short whip of heavy, leather thongs. The thongs often had two small lead balls attached to the ends. The first few blows cut through the skin only. But as the blows continued, they cut deeper into the underlying muscles, leaving Christ's back a mass of torn, bleeding tissue.

Then mocking Roman soldiers threw a robe across Christ's shoulders and placed a stick in his hand for a scepter. They pressed a crown of thorny branches into his scalp. The soldiers continued their mockery by grabbing the stick from Christ's hand and striking him across the head, driving the thorns deeper into his scalp. Finally, they tore the robe from his back, and the wounds began to bleed again.

Next the soldiers tied the heavy beam of the cross across Jesus' shoulders, and a procession began its slow journey 650 yards to Golgotha. The weight of the heavy wooden beam combined with the shock from blood loss caused Jesus to stumble and fall. The rough beam gouged the lacerated skin and muscles of his shoulders. Christ's human muscles were pushed beyond endurance. The soldiers pressed Simon of Cyrene, an onlooker from North Africa, to carry the beam. Jesus followed, bleeding and sweating in cold, clammy shock.

The scene was indeed woeful. Jesus Christ, a real human being, felt all the pain of his excruciating death. Forget the cinematic images and artful representations of the Crucifixion; they only sentimentalize and sanitize the most cruel and necessary death of all human history.

Many were amazed when they saw him—beaten and bloodied, so disfigured one would scarcely know he was a person. Isaiah 52:14

Woefully Arrayed PART TWO

Of sharp thorn I have worn a crown on my head
So rubbed, so bobbed, so rueful, so red;
Sore pained, sore strained, and for thy love dead,
Unfeigned, not deemed, my blood for thee shed;
My feet and hands sore
With sturdy nails bore.
What might I suffer more
Than I have suffered, man, for thee.
Come when thou wilt and welcome to me!

Dear brother, none other thing I desire
But give me thy heart free, to reward mine hire.
I am he that made the earth, water and fire.
Sathanas,[a] *that sloven, and right loathly sire,*
Him have I overcast
In hell-prison bound fast,
Where aye his woe shall last.
I have purveyed a place full clear
For mankind, whom I have bought dear.

JOHN SKELTON? (c. 1460–1529)

[a]Satan

ON GOLGOTHA Christ's torment continued. There, Simon placed the cross beam on the ground, and a soldier threw Jesus backward against the wood. The soldier then drove a wrought-iron nail through Christ's wrist into the beam. He repeated this on the other side, careful to allow some flexion of the arms. Next he and some other soldiers lifted the beam—with Jesus attached—to the top of a pole.

Finally, the soldier took Christ's left foot, pressed it backward against the right, and drove one last nail through the arch of each foot, leaving the knees moderately flexed. As Jesus slowly sagged down, the nails in his wrists put pressure on his median nerves, causing excruciating pain along his fingers and up his arms. Jesus pushed himself upward to avoid this torment, placing his full weight on the nail in his feet. This nail tore through the nerves between the metatarsal bones, causing searing agony.

As Christ's arms fatigued, his pectoral muscles were paralyzed, and the intercostal muscles were unable to act. Jesus could draw air into his lungs but couldn't exhale. Carbon dioxide built up in his lungs and bloodstream, and the cramps partially subsided. Spasmodically, Jesus pushed himself upward to breathe.

Someone lifted a sponge soaked in sour wine to Jesus' lips, but he refused it. By now Jesus felt the chill of death in his tissues, and he whispered, "It is finished."

A soldier drove his lance between Jesus' ribs, upward through the fluid-filled sac surrounding the heart. Blood and water flowed out, but Jesus Christ was already dead.

As Skelton's poem portrays, the Crucifixion was not a pretty sight. It was depressing, disgusting. But death was not the end—"I have purveyed a place full clear for mankind, whom I have bought dear."

➻ *My life is poured out like water, and all my bones are out of joint. My heart is like wax, melting within me.* Psalm 22:14

The Agony

Philosophers have measured mountains,
Fathomed the depths of seas, of states, and kings,
Walked with a staff to heav'n, and traced fountains:
But there are two vast, spacious things,
The which to measure it doth more behove:
Yet few there are that sound them; Sin and Love.

Who would know Sin, let him repair
Unto Mount Olivet; there shall he see
A man so wrung with pains, that all his hair,
His skin, his garments bloody be.
Sin is that press and vice, which forceth pain
To hunt his cruel food through ev'ry vein.

Who knows not Love, kept him assay
And taste that juice, which on the cross a pike
Did set again abroach; then let him say
If ever he did taste the like.
Love is that liquor sweet and most divine,
Which my God feels as blood; but I, as wine.

GEORGE HERBERT (1593–1633)

ALMOST all of Herbert's poetry is included in *The Temple* (1633), which was published two months after his death. The collection begins with poems that focus on the basis of humanity's relationship with God—Christ's sacrifice. Eucharistic imagery runs throughout the entire collection.

In this poem Herbert compares two unfathomable realities: sin and love. There had been so much sin committed on earth that no one could measure it. Consequently, it took a tremendous amount of love to absorb all this sin. And this is what Jesus did when he died on the cross. As the Scriptures say, "God made Christ, who never sinned, to be the offering for our sin" (2 Corinthians 5:21). What motivated God to do this? His love for us. Scripture says: "God showed his great love for us by sending Christ to die for us while we were still sinners" (Romans 5:8).

Christ's death was a bitter cup for him to drink, but a sweet one for us. He bore the brunt of the pike so that we could enjoy the sweet liquor of his love.

The soldiers came and broke the legs of the two men crucified with Jesus. But when they came to Jesus, they saw that he was dead already, so they didn't break his legs. One of the soldiers, however, pierced his side with a spear, and blood and water flowed out. John 19:32-34

On the Strange Apparitions . . .

What strange unusual prodigy is here,
The height of day and yet no sun appear,
Nothing but darkness to be seen? what fright
Hath caused the day thus to be turned to night?
Sure th'old Chaos, or the Day of Doom,
Heaven, and earth's fabric to dissolve is come,
For so graves open, and in every street
The dead are seen to stand upon their feet,
Nor is the Temple safe, its vale[a] *in sunder*
Is rent,[b] *by a prodigious clap of thunder,*
And all disordered is: God's Son is dead.
No marvel then, the Sun doth hide its head.
Black death hath seized upon the God of light,
'Tis equal then day mourn in sable night.
Nor is it fit the graves should peopled be
With dead, when earth receives eternity.
The Temple's vale must rent in pieces be
Lest there should want a winding-sheet for thee.
Nor is 't a wonder that all things do lie
Disordered, and are sick when God can die.

HENRY COLMAN (fl. 1640)

[a]archaic spelling of *veil* [b]"its vale in sunder is rent" refers to the tearing of the curtain that divided the Holy Place from the holiest of all within the temple (Matthew 27:51).

AFTER READING this poem we may think that perhaps we don't understand Christ's death as well as we thought. We look at the world around us and see its beauty *and* its hideousness. We do our best to live in such a world with our conscience clear toward God and all people (Acts 24:16) and to hate what is evil and hold fast to what is good (Romans 12:9). We hope to do the things we have learned and heard and seen in the apostle Paul's example (Philippians 4:9), so that when the time of our departure comes, like him we can say, "I have fought the good fight, I have finished the race, I have kept the faith" (2 Timothy 4:7, NIV).

Henry Colman's poem points out the disorder and sickness of the world—so disordered and sick that it was possible for God to receive a death sentence, hang from a pole by his arms, and suffocate under the weight of his own body. Let's put aside the victory of resurrection and triumph of ascension for now. Banish for a moment the joy of our own salvation. Look upon the terror of that day, which revealed that "all things do lie disordered, and are sick when God can die."

There may come a time in our life when we fear Christ's return. We may wonder, *How can I possibly be ready to meet the Lord?* It is then that we should pray, *Lord, I don't care what happens to me. Please come back and heal the earth and its inhabitants.* Let us join the apostle Paul in longing for the Lord's appearing (2 Timothy 4:8), praying with John, "Amen! Come, Lord Jesus!" (Revelation 22:20).

For I am not ashamed of this Good News about Christ. It is the power of God at work, saving everyone who believes—Jews first and also Gentiles. Romans 1:16

An Easter Carol

Spring bursts today,
For Christ is risen and all the earth's at play.

Flash forth, thou Sun,
The rain is over and gone, its work is done.

Winter is past,
Sweet Spring is come at last, is come at last.

Bud, Fig and Vine,
Bud, Olive, fat with fruit and oil and wine.

Break forth this morn
In roses, thou but yesterday a Thorn.

Uplift thy head,
O pure white Lily thro' the Winter dead.

Beside your dams
Leap and rejoice, you merry-making Lambs.

All Herds and Flocks
Rejoice, all Beasts of thickets and of rocks.

Sing, Creatures, sing,
Angels and Men and Birds and everything.

All notes of Doves
Fill all our world: this is the time of loves.

CHRISTINA ROSSETTI (1830–1894)

CHRISTINA ROSSETTI was one of the most gifted female poets of the nineteenth century. She was a devout Christian and wrote many religious works. Ironically, she was known more for these works during her lifetime than she was for her poetry.

This poem is so simple that a child could understand it, yet so fresh that an adult can appreciate it. Rossetti celebrates the coincidence of spring and Christ's resurrection. Just as spring sets nature free from winter, Christ's resurrection gives all creation the hope of being set free from the bondage of sin and corruption (Romans 8).

The poem also ties in various images from Song of Songs, especially the passage where the beloved asks his lover to join him in celebrating spring's arrival after a long winter. Again, Christ's resurrection can be seen in a similar way. When Christ arose from the grave, sin's long, cold dominion over humanity ended, and new life burst forth in the hearts of his followers. Rossetti writes: "Spring bursts today, for Christ is risen and all the earth's at play." What a glorious truth! As we enter this season of new life, let us not only be glad winter is past, but let us rejoice that Christ is risen!

My lover said to me, "Rise up, my beloved, my fair one, and come away. For the winter is past, and the rain is over and gone. The flowers are springing up, and the time of singing birds has come, even the cooing of turtledoves. The fig trees are budding, and the grapevines are in blossom. How delicious they smell! Yes, spring is here! Arise, my beloved, my fair one, and come away." Song of Songs 2:10-13

Godhead Here in Hiding PART ONE

Godhead here in hiding, whom I do adore
Masked by these bare shadows, shape and nothing more,
See, Lord, at thy service low lies here a heart
Lost, all lost in wonder at the God thou art.

Seeing, touching, tasting are in thee deceived;
How says trusty hearing? that shall be believed;
What God's Son has told me, take for true I do;
Truth himself speaks truly or there's nothing true.

On the cross thy godhead made no sign to men;
Here thy very manhood steals from human ken:
Both are my confession, both are my belief,
And I pray the prayer of the dying thief.

(continued in next day's reading)

THOMAS AQUINAS (c. 1225–1274)

THOMAS AQUINAS was an Italian theologian and philosopher. He wrote prolifically, leaving us poetry and two major theological works: the *Summa theologiae* and *Summa contra gentiles.*

This poem reveals Aquinas's wonder at how Christ embodied the triune God. It seems all the more amazing that the godhead made no sign to those watching Christ die. To them Jesus was simply another lawbreaker dying a miserable death. But one of the crucified criminals saw deeper. Aquinas interprets the criminal's request as a confession of belief in the deity of Jesus Christ. According to Luke, that criminal entered the kingdom because he recognized the Lord. But this creates a theological dilemma. Jesus said, "Unless your righteousness exceeds that of the scribes and Pharisees, you will never enter the kingdom of heaven" (Matthew 5:20, NRSV). The scribes and Pharisees were extremely careful to live according to Old Testament law. The criminal could never come close to their righteousness—much less exceed it. Yet he was promised paradise.

To solve this dilemma we must answer this question: What was it that Christ stole from human experience while on the cross? The apostle Paul wrote: "For our sake [God] made [Christ] to be sin who knew no sin" (2 Corinthians 5:21a, NRSV). This was Christ's theft. He stole our sin "so that in him we might become the righteousness of God" (2 Corinthians 5:21b, NRSV). This righteousness exceeds that of the scribes and Pharisees. Through faith in Christ, we have been made righteous before God. This righteousness is our entrance—along with the criminal's—into the kingdom.

The other criminal protested, "Don't you fear God even when you are dying? We deserve to die for our evil deeds, but this man hasn't done anything wrong." Then he said, "Jesus, remember me when you come into your Kingdom." Luke 23:40-42

I am not like Thomas, wounds I cannot see,
But can plainly call thee God and Lord as he:
This faith each day deeper be my holding of,
Daily make me harder hope and dearer love.

O Thou our reminder of Christ crucified,
Living Bread the life of us for whom he died,
Lend this life to me then: feed and feast my mind,
There be thou the sweetness man was meant to find.

Bring the tender tale true of the Pelican;
Bathe me, Jesu Lord, in what thy bosom ran—
Blood that but one drop of has the world to win
All the world forgiveness of its world of sin.

Jesu, whom I look at shrouded here below,
I beseech thee send me what I thirst for so,
Some day to gaze on thee face to face in light,
And be blest for ever with thy glory's sight.

THOMAS AQUINAS (c. 1225–1274)

AQUINAS'S works may seem difficult for the average reader. After all, seminarians dabble in his writings, but why should a layperson be interested in them? One good reason for reading Aquinas is that he had many spiritual insights from which we can benefit. This poem is a good example of the spiritual riches found within his works.

Aquinas, like Christians throughout the ages, celebrated Communion. He, too, frequently heard the words, "Do this in remembrance of me." So in today's poem he melodiously prays, "Bring the tender tale true of the Pelican." This line alludes to Psalm 102:6, 10: "I am like a pelican of the wilderness: . . . Because of thine indignation and thy wrath: for thou hast lifted me up, and cast me down" (KJV). One way to interpret this passage is to see it as an expression of the loneliness and pain Christ experienced on the cross—forsaken by God and man. Though Christ's death was horrible, Aquinas pleads that the tale will be true for good reason. It was Christ's blood that purchased our redemption, the "blood that but one drop of has the world to win all the world forgiveness of its world of sin." If the tale were false, then we—as well as Aquinas—would be unforgiven.

The next time you partake of the Lord's Supper, think about the wonderful truths in this poem, and pray with Aquinas:

O Thou our reminder of Christ crucified,
Living Bread the life of us for whom he died,
Lend this life to me then: feed and feast my mind,
There be thou the sweetness man was meant to find.

This is what the Lord himself said, and I pass it on to you just as I received it. On the night when he was betrayed, the Lord Jesus took a loaf of bread, and when he had given thanks, he broke it and said, "This is my body, which is given for you. Do this in remembrance of me." 1 Corinthians 11:23-24

Good Friday, 1613. Riding Westward

PART ONE

Let man's soul be a sphere, and then, in this,
The intelligence that moves, devotion is,
And as the other spheres, by being grown
Subject to foreign motions, lose their own,
And being by others hurried every day,
Scarce in a year their natural form obey;
Pleasure or business, so, our souls admit
For their first mover, and are whirled by it.
Hence is't, that I am carried towards the West
This day, when my soul's form bends towards the East.
There I should see a sun, by rising, set,
And by that setting endless day beget:
But that Christ on this Cross did rise and fall,
Sin had eternally benighted all.
Yet dare I almost be glad I do not see
That spectacle, of too much weight for me.
Who sees God's face, that is self life, must die;
What a death were it then to see God die?
It made his own lieutenant[a] *nature, shrink;*
It made his footstool crack, and the sun wink.

(continued in next day's reading)

JOHN DONNE (1572–1631)

[a]The word *lieutenant* is formed from two Old French words: *lieu,* which means "place," and *tenant,* which means "hold." A lieutenant is a placeholder, that is, a person who takes the place of another.

JOHN DONNE was a consummate Christian thinker and a preeminent poet of seventeenth-century England. In "Good Friday, 1613. Riding Westward" we ride with him from his home on Drury Lane, London, along a road and enjoy the illumination of his brilliant mind. Perhaps he wanted to make that day's thoughts known to others and that is why he penned these lines. His vocabulary, marked by a faraway place and time, and the cadence of his couplets sound strange to our modern ears. Yet it shouldn't discourage us from discovering why he rode west when his soul would rather have gone east.

For Donne on this day, the sun rising in the east was symbolic of Christ rising on the cross to die. Ironically, Christ's death is the setting of that same sun, which simultaneously brings about the dawn of infinite day. What mystery! In describing this mystery, the poet reminds us that if Christ had not risen and fallen on the cross, everything would still be under the darkness of sin.

Donne then remarks profoundly about how glad he is not to have witnessed Christ's crucifixion. It wasn't that he became squeamish pondering the gruesome sight. Rather, he was overwhelmed by its paradox. Consider, says Donne, if seeing the living God's face brings death, what is it to see God die? Let us meditate on this question as we celebrate Good Friday.

My heart beats wildly, my strength fails, and I am going blind. My loved ones and friends stay away, fearing my disease. Even my own family stands at a distance. Psalm 38:10-11

Good Friday, 1613. Riding Westward

PART TWO

Could I behold those hands which span the poles,
And tune all spheres at once, pierced with those holes?
Could I behold that endless height which is
Zenith[a] *to us, and our Antipodes,*[b]
Humbled below us? Or that blood which is
The seat of all our souls, if not of His,
Make dirt of dust, or that flesh which was worn
By God, for his apparel, ragged and torn?
If on these things I durst not look, durst I
Upon his miserable mother cast mine eye,
Who was God's partner here, and furnished thus
Half of that sacrifice which ransomed us?
Though these things, as I ride, be from mine eye,
They are present yet unto my memory,
For that looks towards them; and thou lookst towards me,
O Savior, as thou hangst upon the tree.
I turn my back to Thee but to receive
Corrections, till thy mercies bid thee leave.
O think me worth thine anger; punish me;
Burn off my rusts, and my deformity,
Restore thine Image so much, by thy grace
That thou mayst know me, and I'll turn my face.

JOHN DONNE (1572–1631)

[a]the point directly overhead in the sky [b]any two places directly opposite each other

IS IT EASY to look upon Christ hanging on a cross, dead? John Donne thought not. The hands that tune the spheres—hold everything in balance—are pinned by spikes against a pole. The Zenith of the universe, he who is in every way our opposite, is humbled below us. Christ's blood, upon which every soul relies, becomes fertilizer, making barren dust into dirt. And God's human clothing, the likeness of the flesh of sin, is shredded.

Nor can the poet look at the Lord's mother, Mary, who is standing nearby—she who submitted to God's will and lent humanity to divinity so that we could have the perfect sacrifice for sin. So Donne rides west as he remembers these things. It is as if he can feel the eyes of the crucified Christ looking at his back, correcting his life in mercy and transforming him by grace.

Eventually we must leave our poetic companion and stand alone with our own searing memory of Christ's death. As you remember him and his death, may you pray, *You look toward me, O Savior, as you hang upon the tree. Burn off my rusts and my deformity; restore your image so much, by your grace, that you may know me.*

Some women were there, watching from a distance, including Mary Magdalene, Mary (the mother of James the younger and of Joseph), and Salome. Mark 15:40

Easter Hymn

Death and darkness get you packing,
Nothing now to man is lacking;
All your triumphs now are ended,
And what Adam marred is mended;
Graves are beds now for the weary,
Death a nap, to wake more merry;
Youth now, full of pious duty,
Seeks in thee for perfect beauty;
The weak and aged, tired with length
Of days, from thee look for new strength;
And infants with thy pangs contest
As pleasant, as if with the breast.
Then, unto Him, who thus hath thrown
Even to contempt thy kingdom down,
And by His blood did us advance
Unto His own inheritance,
To Him be glory, power, praise,
From this, unto the last of days!

HENRY VAUGHAN (1622–1695)

POETS are truly a blessing. They help us see the common, ordinary world around us from a fresh and vibrant perspective. Henry Vaughan is no exception. He wrote "Easter Hymn," not to the victorious, resurrected Jesus Christ but to defeated, old death. It takes a poet to be so creative.

"Death and darkness get you packing, nothing now to man is lacking," scolds the poet. If his subject wasn't so important, this could be the beginning of a jump-rope rhyme. But Vaughan sketches a different view of death. For the believer in Christ, death is no longer something to fear as a great, dim, unknown realm, where who-knows-what can happen. Instead, death is more like sleep. Hardly anyone is afraid to go to sleep at night, because there's nothing to fear. So, too, for the believer who has died. This is why Christians have hope at funerals. We know that those who have "fallen asleep" will awake when "the Lord himself [comes] down from heaven." Then "all the Christians who have died will rise from their graves" (1 Thessalonians 4:16). Paul says in 1 Corinthians 15:54-55: "'Death is swallowed up in victory. O death, where is your victory? O death, where is your sting?'"

Yes! Let's be as carefree as children on the playground. Christ has defeated death. Let's chant victoriously to the beaten foe: "All your triumphs now are ended, and what Adam marred is mended; graves are beds now for the weary, death a nap, to wake more merry."

So just as sin ruled over all people and brought them to death, now God's wonderful kindness rules instead, giving us right standing with God and resulting in eternal life through Jesus Christ our Lord.
Romans 5:21

The Descent from the Cross

Is this the Face that thrills with awe
Seraphs who veil their face above?
Is this the Face without a flaw,
The Face that is the Face of Love?
Yea, this defaced, a lifeless clod,
Hath all creation's love sufficed,
Hath satisfied the love of God,
This Face the Face of Jesus Christ.

CHRISTINA ROSSETTI (1830–1894)

IN ETERNITY the Son of God had a glorious face that the angels must have marveled at. But when the Son of God became a man—Jesus of Nazareth—he took on a human face. The Gospel writers tell us nothing about the physical appearance of the Lord Jesus. Legends and folklore such as the letter of P. Ientulus to the emperor Tiberius describing Jesus' appearance are spurious. The story of Jesus' portrait being sent to Abgar, king of Edessa, and his face being embroidered on Veronica's handkerchief is also without historical substance.

What we do know is that Jesus was an ordinary man with an ordinary face. Had he not been the very Son of God this wouldn't be remarkable. But this fact is startling—especially when we know that this face was eventually beaten and bloodied as Jesus suffered for the sins of the world, carrying out the will of his Father. We know this much from the prophet Isaiah, who predicted that the suffering Messiah's appearance would cause people to look away from him.

My servant grew up in the Lord's presence like a tender green shoot, sprouting from a root in dry and sterile ground. There was nothing beautiful or majestic about his appearance, nothing to attract us to him. He was despised and rejected—a man of sorrows, acquainted with bitterest grief. We turned our backs on him and looked the other way when he went by. He was despised, and we did not care. Isaiah 53:2-3

Sepulchre

O blessed body! Whither art thou thrown?
No lodging for thee, but a cold hard stone?
So many hearts on earth, and yet not one
Receive thee?

Sure there is room within our hearts good store;
For they can lodge transgressions by the score:
Thousands of toys dwell there, yet out of door
They leave thee.

But that which shows them large, shows them unfit.
Whatever sin did this pure rock commit,
Which holds thee now? Who hath indicted it
Of murder?

Where our hard hearts have took up stones to brain thee,
And missing this, most falsely did arraign thee;
Only these stones in quiet entertain thee,
And order.

And as of old, the law by heav'nly art
Was writ in stone; so thou, which also art
The letter of the word, find'st no fit heart
To hold thee.

Yet do we still persist as we began,
And so should perish, but that nothing can,
Though it be cold, hard, foul, from loving man
Withhold thee.

GEORGE HERBERT (1593–1633)

HERBERT'S most well-known volume of poetry is *The Temple* (1633), which was published two months after his death. Many of the poems in *The Temple* focus on an event in Christ's life—in this case, his burial.

As a metaphysical poet, Herbert often compared two objects not readily associated together to shock the reader. In this poem Herbert compares the stone sepulchre (tomb) that contained the body of Jesus to the stony hearts of people who have no room for Jesus. It was this stone-heartedness, this hard-heartedness, that caused the Jewish religious leaders to reject Jesus as their Messiah—even to the extent that they attempted to stone him to death. Jesus told these religious leaders, "I realize that you are descendants of Abraham. And yet some of you are trying to kill me because my message does not find a place in your hearts" (John 8:37).

Lest we find ourselves condemning the Jewish leaders, Herbert includes himself and all of humanity as having the same kind of heart toward Christ. May God help us to clean out the toys and transgressions in our heart so that Christ can make his home there.

I pray that Christ will be more and more at home in your hearts as you trust in him. May your roots go down deep into the soil of God's marvelous love. And may you have the power to understand, as all God's people should, how wide, how long, how high, and how deep his love really is. May you experience the love of Christ, though it is so great you will never fully understand it. Then you will be filled with the fullness of life and power that comes from God. Ephesians 3:17-19

Resurrection

Moist with one drop of thy blood, my dry soul
Shall (though she now be in extreme degree
Too stony hard, and yet too fleshly,) be
Freed by that drop, from being starved, hard, or foul,
And life, by this death abled, shall control
Death, whom thy death slew; nor shall to me
Fear of first or last death, bring misery,
If in thy little book my name thou enrol,
Flesh in that long sleep is not putrified,
But made that there, of which, and for which 'twas;
Nor can by other means be glorified.
May then sins sleep, and deaths soon from me pass,
That waked from both, I again risen may
Salute the last, and everlasting day.

JOHN DONNE (1572–1631)

JOHN DONNE wrote poetry for twenty years before he became an Anglican priest in 1615. Later that year he became a royal chaplain to the king. He attained eminence as a preacher, delivering some of the most brilliant and eloquent sermons of his time. In 1621 King James I appointed Donne dean of St. Paul's Cathedral, where Donne preached prolifically. In fact, a modern edition of his sermons fills ten volumes.

Today's poem, "Resurrection," shows that Donne could pack a lot of thought into a few words. He often accomplished this using a complex poetic image called a *conceit.* This is an extended figure of speech consisting of interwoven themes. The conceit in this poem is a drop of Christ's blood.

Consider with the poet the effect one drop of Christ's blood has had upon our souls. It freed us from being starved, hard, and foul. It brought to us the life that controls death and represents the death by which death itself is slain (Hebrews 2:14-15). This drop of blood is our release from the fear of the first and the second death (Revelation 2:11; 20:6, 14; 21:8). It inked our name into the Book of Life (Revelation 21:27; Philippians 4:3) and assured that our flesh will be glorified instead of putrefied (1 Corinthians 15:50-54).

With this in mind, let us join Donne in his prayer: *Dear God, may my sins sleep in death, and all deaths soon pass from me. And when you awaken me from sin and death and I arise with Jesus Christ, I will joyfully greet you that last and everlasting day.*

➺ *For the Lord himself will come down from heaven with a commanding shout, with the call of the archangel, and with the trumpet call of God. First, all the Christians who have died will rise from their graves. Then, together with them, we who are still alive and remain on the earth will be caught up in the clouds to meet the Lord in the air and remain wih him forever. So comfort and encourage each other with these words.* 1 Thessalonians 4:16-18

The Fountain PART ONE

There is a fountain filled with blood
Drawn from Immanuel's veins;
And sinners, plunged beneath that flood,
Lose all their guilty stains.

The dying thief rejoiced to see
That fountain in his day;
And there may I, as vile as he,
Wash all my sins away.

Dear dying Lamb, thy precious blood
Shall never lose its power,
Till all the ransomed church of God
Be saved,—to sin no more.

(continued in next day's reading)

WILLIAM COWPER (1731–1800)

THERE IS hardly a poem in the English language that can compare with "The Fountain" for its personal adoration of Jesus and the work he did on the cross.

Cowper drew the imagery for this poem from Zechariah 12:10; 13:1; John 19:36-37, and several verses in the book of Revelation. The prophet Zechariah predicted that Israel would look on the one whom they would pierce (12:10). He also predicted that a fountain would be opened up for the people of God—a fountain that would cleanse them from all their sins. When the Roman soldiers crucified Jesus, they fulfilled these two prophecies.

In his Gospel the apostle John recounts how these prophecies came to pass. The Jewish religious leaders asked Pilate to hurry up the death process for those who were crucified that day. Pilate complied and instructed the soldiers to break the legs of the crucified. After the soldiers broke the thieves' legs, they came to Jesus. Realizing that Christ had already died, one of the soldiers used a spear to pierce his side, from which blood and water flowed. John explicitly states that this fulfilled prophecy by quoting Zechariah 12:10: "They will look on him whom they pierced" (John 19:37).

Cowper, however, didn't just write this poem to retell the story of Christ's crucifixion. Identifying himself with the thief who believed, Cowper saw his own need to be cleansed with the blood that flowed from Jesus' side—that blessed fountain. May we, like Cowper, recognize our need for cleansing and come to the fountain that will wash away our sins.

On that day a fountain will be opened for the dynasty of David and for the people of Jerusalem, a fountain to cleanse them from all their sins and defilement. Zechariah 13:1

E'er since, by faith I saw the stream,
Thy flowing wounds supply,
Redeeming love has been my theme,
And shall be,—till I die.

Then in a nobler, sweeter song,
I'll sing thy power to save;
When this poor, lisping, faltering tongue
Lies silent in the grave.

Lord, I believe thou hast prepared
(Unworthy though I be)
For me a blood-bought free reward,
A golden harp for me!

'Tis strung, and tuned, for endless years,
And formed by power divine,
To sound in God the Father's ears
No other name but thine.

WILLIAM COWPER (1731–1800)

IN THIS portion of the poem Cowper acknowledges that he will always appreciate the flowing blood of Jesus. To him this was not just a onetime revelation but an ongoing unveiling. Even in eternity, after his death, the poet will sing praises to the Lamb, who shed his blood on Calvary:

Then in a nobler, sweeter song
I'll sing thy power to save;
When this poor, lisping, faltering tongue
Lies silent in the grave.

The apostle John wrote about this same eternal appreciation in the book of Revelation (1:3; 7:14; 22:14). Time and again he spoke of those blessed people who had washed their robes in the blood of the Lamb and thereby were entitled to enjoy paradise with Jesus forever. Read these verses from the last book of the Bible, and then get cleansed in the fountain of the blood of the Lamb.

"These are the ones coming out of the great tribulation. They washed their robes in the blood of the Lamb and made them white. That is why they are standing in front of the throne of God, serving him day and night in his Temple. And he who sits on the throne will live among them and shelter them. They will never again be hungry or thirsty, and they will be fully protected from the scorching noontime heat. For the Lamb who stands in front of the throne will be their Shepherd. He will lead them to the springs of life-giving water. And God will wipe away all their tears." . . . Blessed are those who wash their robes so they can enter through the gates of the city and eat the fruit from the tree of life. Revelation 7:14-17; 22:14

Split the Lark—and You'll Find the Music—

Split the Lark—and you'll find the Music—
Bulb after Bulb, in Silver rolled—
Scantily dealt to the Summer Morning
Saved for your Ear when Lutes be old.

Loose the Flood—you shall find it patent—
Gush after Gush, reserved for you—
Scarlet Experiment! Sceptic Thomas!
Now, do you doubt that your Bird was true?

EMILY DICKINSON (1830–1886)

"LET THIS Messiah, this king of Israel, come down from the cross so we can see it and believe him!" (Mark 15:32). The gawkers who came to see the spectacle of the triple crucifixion challenged Jesus to prove he was the Christ. They promised to believe in Jesus if he would perform some wondrous deed. To this day people try to strike deals with God—trying to trade faith for divine favor. If an innocent child says, "I'll believe in you, Jesus, if you'll let my puppy live," we may smile and hope his wish comes true. But Jesus wants mockers, doubters, and faithless people to test him. This is why Jesus asked Thomas to "put your hand into the wound in my side" (John 20:27).

A soldier had pierced Christ's side with a spear (19:34). Now Thomas thrust his hand into that wound (20:27). These men performed Dickinson's scarlet experiment—they split the lark—a procedure sure to destroy every bird but one. When Jesus' side was split, out flowed the music of redemption and eternal life.

The beginning of a person's faith in Christ is not always pretty. It can be bloody, meaning that we can make a mess of our life before or during the process of coming to Christ. Or, like Thomas, our faith may be incomplete and need an adjustment through a "scarlet experiment." But unless we experience the split lark—the bleeding Christ—we cannot truly sing, "There is a fountain filled with blood drawn from Immanuel's veins; and sinners, plunged beneath that flood, lose all their guilty stains."[a]

Here is where you learn that Christ is true—at the sin-cleansing gush reserved for you.

On that day a fountain will be opened for the dynasty of David and for the people of Jerusalem, a fountain to cleanse them from all their sins and defilement. Zechariah 13:1

[a] "The Fountain" by William Cowper

The Ribs and Terrors . . .

The ribs and terrors in the whale,
Arched over me a dismal gloom,
While all God's sun-lit waves rolled by,
And lift me to a deeper doom.

I saw the opening maw of hell,
With endless pains and sorrows there;
Which none but they that feel can tell—
Oh, I was plunging to despair.

In black distress, I called my God,
When I could scarce believe Him mine,
He bowed His ear to my complaints—
No more the whale did me confine.

With speed He flew to my relief,
As on a radiant dolphin borne;
Awful, yet bright, as lightning shone
The face of my Deliverer God.

My song for ever shall record
That terrible, that joyful hour;
I give the glory to my God,
His all the mercy and the power.

HERMAN MELVILLE (1819–1891)

HERMAN MELVILLE was one of America's greatest and most influential novelists. He was a major figure among the pre–Civil War writers known as the American Romantics. In "The Ribs and Terrors . . ." Melville wrote from the prophet Jonah's perspective.

The Lord wanted Jonah to go to Nineveh and preach repentance to that city. Jonah didn't want to and boarded a ship heading in the opposite direction. A storm arose, and the ship's sailors discovered that Jonah was to blame for it. So they tossed Jonah overboard, and a large fish swallowed him. Now the poem picks up the story. Inside the fish, Jonah prayed to God for deliverance. And God answered, delivering Jonah after he had spent three days inside the fish.

So why does Jonah's story appear here? What does it have to do with the Easter season? Although Jonah was a real person with a real story, he was also a sign pointing to Christ. Jesus made this clear when he predicted: "For as Jonah was in the belly of the great fish for three days and three nights, so I, the Son of Man, will be in the heart of the earth for three days and three nights" (Matthew 12:40). Thus, Jonah's experience symbolized Christ's resurrection.

How amazing our sovereign God is! Jonah could never have known that his time inside the fish would symbolize the Messiah's resurrection. Yet God—in his omniscience—used Jonah's disobedience for more than an opportunity to teach a wayward prophet a lesson. God is truly the great conductor of history. His thoughts and ways are far beyond anything we can imagine (Isaiah 55:8-9).

Then Jonah prayed to the Lord his God from inside the fish. He said, "I cried out to the Lord in my great trouble, and he answered me." . . . Then the Lord ordered the fish to spit up Jonah on the beach, and it did. Jonah 2:1, 10

One Crown That No One Seeks

One crown that no one seeks
And yet the highest head
Its isolation coveted
Its stigma deified

While Pontius Pilate lives
In whatsoever hell
That coronation pierces him
He recollects it well.

EMILY DICKINSON (1830–1886)

WHAT KIND of king doesn't wear the rare metals and jewels that adorn the heads of emperors and czars? A heavenly one. Christ's crown consisted of thorns—the very ones we chop, burn, or dump far away to rid our lives of. They are the weeds, brambles, and choking vines that return to our land year after year from the earth's wastelands, the tumbleweeds that line our fences and mock our vain efforts to eradicate them.

There was no need to dig deep into the earth to extract the materials for Christ's crown. His diadem is found on the surface of every human life. No refining, cutting, polishing—the work of an artisan wasn't necessary here. Since the long-ago night when a rude soldier laughingly crafted this crown, anyone can plait together the weeds of his or her life to decorate the brow of Christ.

"I have placed a curse on the ground," God told Adam and Eve. "It will grow thorns and thistles for you" (Genesis 3:17-18). Today we still live under this curse. Yet our curse became Christ's crown. Emily Dickinson says that Christ coveted its isolation and deified its stigma. The apostle Paul explains this: "When he was hung on the cross, he took upon himself the curse for our wrongdoing. For it is written in the Scriptures, 'Cursed is everyone who is hung on a tree'" (Galatians 3:13). Out of these thoughts Ernest C. Homburg composed this hymn:

Thou, O Son of God! wert bearing
Cruel mockings, hatred, scorn;
Thou, the King of glory, wearing,
For our sake, the crown of thorn.

You know how full of love and kindness our Lord Jesus Christ was. Though he was very rich, yet for your sakes he became poor, so that by his poverty he could make you rich. 2 Corinthians 8:9

Spring

Nothing is so beautiful as Spring—
When weeds, in wheels, shoot long and lovely and lush;
Thrush's eggs look little low heavens, and thrush
Through the echoing timber does so rinse and wring
The ear, it strikes like lightnings to hear him sing;
The glassy peartree leaves and blooms, they brush
The descending blue; that blue is all in a rush
With richness; the racing lambs too have fair their fling.

What is all this juice and all this joy?
A strain of the earth's sweet being in the beginning
In Eden garden. —Have, get, before it cloy,[a]
Before it cloud, Christ, lord, and sour with sinning,
Innocent mind and Mayday in girl and boy,
Most, O maid's child, thy choice and worthy the winning.

GERARD MANLEY HOPKINS (1844–1889)

[a]turning sickly sweet

GERARD MANLEY HOPKINS wrote some of the most ear-pleasing poetry of the nineteenth century. In his poetry Hopkins always tried to express the inner principle that gave a living object its delicate and surprising uniqueness. He sought to put into words the flow of the spirit's life that sweeps through the dull, dense world of matter and acts on the senses and, through them, makes the object alive to the beholder (or reader). Here that object is a woodsy marsh in spring.

Hopkins makes spring come alive to our senses by focusing on how the song of the thrush impacts the human ear—rinsing and wringing it, striking it like lightning. He also does the same with the color blue. This juicy and joyous spring is a "strain of the earth's sweet being in the beginning in Eden garden." But just as paradise didn't last long due to humanity's sin, so spring doesn't last long. Thus, Hopkins urges us to enjoy it before it cloys and clouds over.

At the same time he urges us by Christ's power to return to innocence. We can do this by ridding ourselves of this world's encumbrances and enjoying time alone with God in nature—by a stream, near the ocean, on a mountaintop, or in the woods. These creations of God still breathe with his creativity and remind us of life before sin corrupted the world.

Then the Lord God planted a garden in Eden, in the east, and there he placed the man he had created. And the Lord God planted all sorts of trees in the garden—beautiful trees that produced delicious fruit. At the center of the garden he placed the tree of life and the tree of the knowledge of good and evil. Genesis 2:8-9

from Meditations on the Six Days . . .

Lo here, within the waters liquid womb
The unborn Earth lay, as in native tomb;
Whilst she at first was buried in the deep,
And all her forms and seeds were fast asleep.
Th' Almighty word then spake, and straight was heard,
The Earth her head up from the waters reared.
The waters soon, as frighted, fled apace,
And all were swiftly gathered to one place.
See now the Earth, with life and verdue crowned,
Spring from her bed, gay, vigorous, and sound:
Her face ten thousand beauties now adorn,
With blessings numberless from plenty's horn.
Here, there, and every where they richly flow,
For us almighty bounty them does strow.
The hills and dales, the lawns and woods around,
God's wisdom, goodness, and his power resound.
Both far and near his wonders they proclaim.
How vilely then is wretched man to blame,
If he forget to praise that liberal hand,
Out-spread from sea to sea, from land to land?
Amen

THOMAS TRAHERNE (1637–1674)

THOMAS TRAHERNE, a Welshman, graduated from Brasenose College, Oxford, in 1656. He became a priest in 1660 and retired to a country parish near Hereford, where he remained until his death. During his lifetime he did not publish any of his poetry.

More than two hundred years later (in 1896) someone discovered his poems inside a manuscript in a London bookstall. The poems were initially attributed to Henry Vaughan, but the publisher identified them as Traherne's. Acclaim followed the publication of his *Poetical Works* in 1903, *The Centuries of Meditations* in 1908, and *Poems of Felicity* in 1910. The sanctity of childhood, the validity of intuition, the reality of spirit, and the immanence of God in nature are all prominent themes in his poems.

In this poem Traherne meditates on the third day of creation. The third day was a day of resurrection: the earth coming up out of the waters and the seeds springing forth into plants and trees. All was vibrant with life: "See now the Earth, with life and verdue crowned."

Today the earth and sea still exude this vibrancy and bounteous plenty. God has truly blessed us with his rich provision. Therefore, as we attend to the business of our day, let us make time to admire God's creation and to praise him liberally for the riches he has given us to enjoy.

And God said, "Let the waters beneath the sky be gathered into one place so dry ground may appear." And so it was. God named the dry ground "land" and the water "seas." And God saw that it was good. Then God said, "Let the land burst forth with every sort of grass and seed-bearing plant. And let there be trees that grow seed-bearing fruit. The seeds will then produce the kinds of plants and trees from which they came." And so it was. The land was filled with seed-bearing plants and trees, and their seeds produced plants and trees of like kind. And God saw that it was good. This all happened on the third day.
Genesis 1:9-13

Sweet Hour of Prayer

Sweet hour of prayer! sweet hour of prayer!
That calls me from a world of care,
And bids me at my Father's throne
Make all my wants and wishes known;
In seasons of distress and grief,
My soul has often found relief,
And oft escaped the tempter's snare,
By thy return, sweet hour of prayer!

Sweet hour of prayer! sweet hour of prayer!
The joys I feel, the bliss I share
Of those whose anxious spirits burn
With strong desires for thy return!
With such I hasten to the place
Where God my Savior shows His face,
And gladly take my station there,
And wait for thee, sweet hour of prayer!

Sweet hour of prayer! sweet hour of prayer!
Thy wings shall my petition bear
To Him whose truth and faithfulness
Engage the waiting soul to bless;
And since He bids me seek His face,
Believe His Word and trust His grace,
I'll cast on Him my every care,
And wait for thee, sweet hour of prayer!

WILLIAM W. WALFORD (1772–1850)

WILLIAM WALFORD was a blind preacher and shop owner in Coleshill, England, where he sold his own carvings of wood and ivory. He also composed poetry. As legend has it, Walford asked a local minister to write down this poem Walford had composed in his head. The minister gave the poem to a newspaper editor in the United States three years later. The editor published it, and eventually that poem was turned into a hymn.

This poem focuses our attention on the need to spend time with the Lord in prayer. In this prayerful time of communion we can unload our cares and worries on him, and in exchange receive refreshment and encouragement from his Spirit.

As this poem indicates, prayer also benefits other areas of our spiritual lives: (1) it helps us escape the "tempter's snare"; (2) it helps us look forward to Christ's return and even hasten it; (3) and it helps us "seek His face, believe His Word and trust His grace."

Let us do our best to follow this advice and spend time in prayer each day.

Then Jesus said, "Come to me, all of you who are weary and carry heavy burdens, and I will give you rest." Matthew 11:28

Prayer (I)

Prayer the Church's banquet, Angels' age,
God's breath in man returning to his birth,
The soul in paraphrase, heart in pilgrimage,
The Christian plummet sounding heav'n and earth;
Engine against th' Almighty, sinners' tower,
Reversed thunder, Christ-side-piercing spear,
The six-days world-transposing in an hour,
A kind of tune, which all things hear and fear;
Softness, and peace, and joy, and love, and bliss,
Exalted Manna, gladness of the best,
Heaven in ordinary, man well dressed,
The milky way, the bird of Paradise,
Church-bells beyond the stars heard, the soul's blood,
The land of spices; something understood.

GEORGE HERBERT (1593–1633)

HERBERT endured chronic illness during the last three years of his life. During this time, he came to value the potency of prayer, which is powerfully expressed in these lines. This poem is, in fact, one long definition of prayer—drawn from the poet's experience, the experiences of believers throughout the ages, and the Scriptures. This is what Herbert calls prayer (the bracketed words elucidate meaning):

the Church's banquet [a spiritual feast]
Angels' age [the period during which angels answer prayers]
God's breath in man returning to his birth [spirit communing with God who is Spirit]
soul in paraphrase [to express our heart]
heart in pilgrimage [free discourse with God]
Christian plummet [ball of lead] sounding heav'n and earth [as cymbals]
engine [war machine] against th' Almighty [to move God into action]
sinners' tower [for protection against evil]
reversed thunder [from earth to heaven]
Christ-side-piercing spear [to evoke the blood of Jesus]
the six-days world-transposing [as in music] in an hour . . .
exalted manna [the best spiritual food]
gladness of the best [the greatest joy]
heaven in ordinary [common words turned heavenly]
man well dressed [the best of human expressions]
the milky way [a glorious display]
the bird of Paradise [a symbol of Eden's purity] . . .
the soul's blood [the essence of life]
the land of spices [a symbol of paradise]
something understood

Let us pray!

Keep on praying. 1 Thessalonians 5:17

Prayer (II)

I know it is my sin, which locks thine ears,
And binds thy hands,
Out-crying my requests, drowning my tears;
Or else the chillness of my faint demands.

But as cold hands are angry[a] *with the fire,*
And mend it still;
So I do lay the want of my desire,
Not on my sins, or coldness, but thy will.

Yet hear, O God, only for his blood's sake
Which pleads for me:
For though sins plead too, yet like stones[b] *they make*
His blood's sweet current much more loud to be.

GEORGE HERBERT (1593–1633)

[a]impatient [b]as in a brook

THE SECOND part of Herbert's book of poems explores the aspirations and distresses that Christians experience when they try to commune with God. This poem is an eloquent expression of Herbert's frustration with unanswered prayer. As the poet makes clear, it is not his lack of fervency that keeps God from hearing his prayers. Rather, it is Herbert's inability to get at God's will. Therefore the poet prays, "So I do lay the want of my desire, not on my sins, or coldness, but thy will."

To strengthen his plea, Herbert asks God to listen for Christ's sake. Then, if Herbert's sins dissuaded God from answering, the blood of Jesus flowing like water over them (the "stones" in a brook) would make Herbert's requests louder and therefore heard by God.

Unanswered prayer can frustrate many a Christian, even the most devout believer. But it is important to keep in mind that God has a good reason for not answering, and sometimes that reason may be us. When it is, we have an advocate to plead our case. Christ's shed blood can bring us into the heart and mind of God. We should remember this the next time we struggle in our prayers.

My dear children, I am writing this to you so that you will not sin. But if you do sin, there is someone to plead for you before the Father. He is Jesus Christ, the one who pleases God completely. 1 John 2:1

The House of Prayer

Thy mansion is the christian's heart,
O Lord, thy dwelling-place secure!
Bid the unruly throng depart,
And leave the consecrated door.

Devoted as it is to thee,
A thievish swarm frequents the place;
They steal away my joys from me,
And rob my Savior of his praise.

There too a sharp designing trade
Sin, Satan, and the world maintain;
Nor cease to press me, and persuade,
To part with ease and purchase pain.

I know them, and I hate their din,
Am weary of the bustling crowd;
But while their voice is heard within,
I cannot serve thee as I would.

Oh! for the joy thy presence gives,
What peace shall reign when thou art here!
Thy presence makes this den of thieves,
A calm delightful house of prayer.

And if thou make thy temple shine,
Yet, self-abased, will I adore;
The gold and silver are not mine,
I give thee what was thine before.

WILLIAM COWPER (1731–1800)

SUPPOSE you go to church one Sunday and find someone selling tickets at the door. Puzzled, you pay the fee and enter the building. Inside you find strangers selling religious products—decorations, books, gifts. Others line up to use an automatic teller machine. The entire scene is completely unexpected. You have never seen people act like this in a church before. What would you do?

Would you do what Jesus did? He once saw merchants selling animals to sacrifice in the temple (John 2:14). There was even a currency exchange for foreign visitors! He "made a whip . . . and chased them all out of the Temple. He drove out the sheep and oxen, scattered the money changers' coins over the floor, and turned over their tables" (2:15).

It's doubtful that you would do this because you don't have the same authority over the church that Christ had over the temple. But you do have authority over your heart, which is God's present dwelling place. If you focus on this fact today, you might angrily cleanse your heart with the same authority that Jesus cleansed the temple.

Do you, like Cowper, ever grow weary of the "bustling crowd" buying and selling in your heart? The television advertisers, the enticing shops, your own appetites for possessions and the status they bring? The Lord said, "My house shall be called the house of prayer" (Matthew 21:13, KJV). But when it was turned into a place of commerce, he called it "a den of thieves."

Let's angrily drive out the merchants that have occupied our hearts! Join with Paul, who prayed "that Christ will be more and more at home in your hearts as you trust in him" (Ephesians 3:17).

Jesus entered the Temple and began to drive out the merchants and their customers. He knocked over the tables of the money changers and the stalls of those selling doves. Matthew 21:12

Take Ye Heed, Watch and Pray

Come suddenly, O Lord, or slowly come,
I wait Thy will, Thy servant ready is;
Thou hast prepared Thy follower a home,
The heaven in which Thou dwellest, too, is his.

Come in the morn, at noon, or midnight deep,
Come, for Thy servant still doth watch and pray
E'en when the world around is sunk in sleep,
I wake, and long to see Thy glorious day.

I would not fix the time, the day, nor hour,
When Thou with all Thine angels shalt appear;
When in Thy kingdom Thou shalt come with power,
E'en now, perhaps, the promised day is near!

For though, in slumber deep, the world may lie,
And e'en Thy church forget Thy great command;
Still year by year Thy coming draweth nigh,
And in its power Thy kingdom is at hand.

Not in some future world alone 't will be,
Beyond the grave, beyond the bounds of Time;
But on the earth Thy glory we shall see,
And share Thy triumph, peaceful, pure, sublime.

Lord! help me that I faint not, weary grow,
Nor at Thy coming slumber too, and sleep;
For Thou hast promised, and full well I know,
Thou wilt to us Thy word of promise keep.

JONES VERY (1813–1880)

JONES VERY was an American poet, clergyman, and religious mystic from Salem, Massachusetts. In most Christian circles these days the term *religious mystic* is likely to raise both eyebrows and questions. After all, isn't a mystic otherworldly, superspiritual, and impractical? Can't mysticism be involved with forbidden practices or mysterious cults? Yes, but this is not true of a *Christian* mystic. Our mysticism recognizes that despite all we know through the Bible, God is truly beyond human comprehension and his divine plan is mysterious and enigmatic. It has nothing to do with magic, obscure doctrines, special powers, or esoteric rites.

Our practice of eating and drinking at the Lord's Table—the Communion service—is actually quite mystical. We experience an unseen union with God while remembering the Lord's death, resurrection, and second coming. This fills a worshiper with wonder and awe.

This poem reminds us of the spiritual reality of Christ's second coming. When the poet proclaims, "E'en now, perhaps, the promised day is near," isn't he simply exercising a faith that is "the confident assurance that what we hope for is going to happen" (Hebrews 11:1)? And when Very prays, "Still year by year Thy coming draweth nigh, and in its power Thy kingdom is at hand," he draws upon the mystical "evidence of things we cannot yet see" (11:1).

If Christian mysticism involves comprehending something invisible or anticipating something impossible, let's all pray, *Lord, make us mystics like Jones Very, so we, too, can lay hold of the reality of the unseen things of your kingdom.*

However, no one knows the day or hour when these things will happen, not even the angels in heaven or the Son himself. Only the Father knows. And since you don't know when they will happen, stay alert and keep watch. Mark 13:32-33

Jesus Praying

He sought the mountain and the loneliest height,
For He would meet his Father all alone,
And there, with many a tear and many a groan,
He strove in prayer throughout the long, long night.
Why need He pray, who held by filial right,
O'er all the world alike of thought and sense,
The fullness of his Sire's omnipotence?
Why crave in prayer what was his own by might?
Vain is the question,—Christ was man in deed,
And being man, his duty was to pray.
The Son of God confessed the human need,
And doubtless asked a blessing every day,
Nor ceases yet for sinful man to plead,
Nor will, till heaven and earth shall pass away.

ERNEST HARTLEY COLERIDGE (1846–1920)

ERNEST HARTLEY COLERIDGE was the son of Derwen Coleridge, second son of the British poet Samuel Taylor Coleridge. In this poem, Coleridge poses a most logical question: If Jesus was God, why did he have to pray? After all, the New Testament says he is God (see Colossians 1:15). Christ is the one through whom God created everything in heaven and on earth. He made the things we can see and the things we can't see. He existed before everything else began, and he holds creation together.

But the Bible also says that God became human "and lived here on earth among us" (John 1:14). It is most important to understand that Jesus was truly human, or as today's poem says, "The Son of God confessed the human need." He ate and slept. He cried and experienced suffering and temptation. These experiences are unavoidable for us, so they were for him as well. In addition, Jesus prayed—an ordinary human act: "Christ was man in deed, and being man, his duty was to pray."

Then Jesus did something he couldn't do as God. He died to save the world. His death was powerful enough to redeem all of humanity and creation because he was a genuine human, a real creature. The Bible says, "God made Christ, who never sinned, to be the offering for our sin, so that we could be made right with God through Christ" (2 Corinthians 5:21).

In the end—when Jesus was dying on the cross in the most desperate, helpless place a man could be—what did he do? He prayed. First for others (Luke 23:34) and then for himself (Matthew 27:46). He knew even then that others needed God's help as did he.

➻ *One day soon afterward Jesus went to a mountain to pray, and he prayed to God all night.* Luke 6:12

The Prayer of Jabez

The prayer of Jabez, too, should be our prayer:
"Keep me from evil, that it may not grieve."
How hard the sight of wrong and ill to bear,
When we cannot the sufferers relieve!
The child of sorrow, he for others' woe,
As if it were his own, did deeply feel;
Though he had naught of riches to bestow,
Nor power their wrongs and miseries to heal.
God heard his prayer, and answered his request;
And by his sympathy did help impart
Unto the poor, the suffering, and oppressed,
That healed their wounds and robbed them of their smart;
Nor suffered cruel deeds, nor words unkind,
To grieve his heart, or rankle in his mind.

JONES VERY (1813–1880)

READING through the Bible is something like driving coast to coast. Crossing a state line *and* beginning a new book can be exciting. But if you've ever driven through Nebraska on I-80, you may understand why it can be similar to reading 1 Chronicles—they both seem interminable.

Nebraska has a reputation for being a boring place to travel. But this is undeserved. It's full of interesting surprises. Granted, they aren't like the Grand Canyon or the Rocky Mountains. They don't reach out and demand your attention, but at the same time, they aren't boring. The story of Jabez in 1 Chronicles 4 is something like one of these surprises. His story appears within a vast plain of genealogies. Although it's not extensive, what we learn about him is more than enough to hold our interest.

On the surface it's easy to understand what this interlude is about: Jabez prayed for something, and God gave it to him. But Very sees beyond the surface, focusing on the meaning of the name *Jabez*—similar to a Hebrew word for "distress" or "pain"—and connecting it with Christ's words in Matthew 5:4. With a poet's insight, he sees Jabez as a man who was distressed at the sight of wrong and suffering, yet he could do nothing to relieve these conditions. So Jabez prayed against the evil of the world and mourned. And this sympathy helped impart healing.

Very says, "The prayer of Jabez, too, should be our prayer." Even though we may be only one of a million of God's servants, we can participate in his divine plan as Jabez did, by praying and bringing comfort to those who mourn.

There was a man named Jabez who was more distinguished than any of his brothers. His mother named him Jabez because his birth had been so painful. He was the one who prayed to the God of Israel, "Oh, that you would bless me and extend my lands! Please be with me in all that I do, and keep me from all trouble and pain!" And God granted him his request. 1 Chronicles 4:9-10

The Hound of Heaven PART ONE

I fled Him, down the nights and down the days;
I fled Him, down the arches of the years;
I fled Him, down the labyrinthine ways
Of my own mind; and in the midst of tears
I hid from Him, and under running laughter.
Up vistaed hopes I sped;
And shot, precipitated,
Adown titanic glooms of chasméd fears,
From those strong feet that followed, followed after.
But with unhurrying chase,
And unperturbéd pace,
Deliberate speed, majestic instancy,
They beat—and a voice beat
More instant than the feet—
"All things betray thee, who betrayest Me."

(continued in next day's reading)

FRANCIS THOMPSON (1859–1907)

FRANCIS THOMPSON, the son of a British doctor, grew up in the Roman Catholic church. At one point in his life he thought about becoming a priest. Eventually, he rejected that idea and began to study medicine. But he was more interested in literature and, consequently, failed his medical examinations. Depressed, ill, and poor, he began to use opium, which reduced him to selling matches and papers. During this time, Thompson submitted two poems for publication to Wilfred Meynell, a London magazine editor. Meynell recognized Thompson's literary talent and published the poems, which won the commendation of Robert Browning.

"The Hound of Heaven," Thompson's best and most well-known poem, is one of the finest odes in English literature, in spite of its ornate language. In the poem a fugitive sinner seeks to escape God's relentless pursuit. The poem's cadence, heightened by the constant repetition of "the feet" hot on his trail, adds to its suspense. Will he escape his pursuer or be caught?

The divine love, however, is greater than the sinner, and eventually the hunted is captured. Along the way, the sinner discovers that nothing—other than God—can satisfy his soul: "All things betray thee, who betrayest Me." How true.

How many of us have tried to fill our life with anything or anyone but God, only to discover that what we thought would satisfy our heart left us feeling empty instead? This truth is part of the divine plan. The Hound of Heaven doesn't allow us to find peace and contentment in the things of this world apart from him. If he did, there would be no reason for him to pursue us, and there would be no reason for us to hope.

I could ask the darkness to hide me and the light around me to become night—but even in darkness I cannot hide from you. To you the night shines as bright as day. Darkness and light are both alike to you.
Psalm 139:11-12

The Hound of Heaven PART TWO

I pleaded, outlaw-wise,
By many a hearted casement, curtained red,
Trellised with intertwining charities
(For, though I knew His love Who followéd,
Yet was I sore adread
Lest, having Him, I must have naught beside);
But, if one little casement parted wide,
The gust of His approach would clash it to.
Fear wist[a] *not to evade, as Love wist to pursue.*
Across the margent[b] *of the world I fled,*
And troubled the gold gateways of the stars,
Smiting for shelter on their clangéd bars;
Fretted to dulcet jars
And silvern chatter the pale ports o' the moon.
I said to dawn: Be sudden; to eve, Be soon;
With thy young skiey blossoms heap me over
From this tremendous lover!
Float thy vague veil about me, lest He see!
I tempted all His servitors, but to find
My own betrayal in their constancy,
In faith to Him their fickleness to me,
Their traitorous trueness, and their loyal deceit.
To all swift things for swiftness did I sue;
Clung to the whistling mane of every wind,
But whether they swept, smoothly fleet,
The long savannahs of the blue;
Or whether thunder-driven
They clanged his chariot 'thwart a heaven
Plashy with flying lightnings round the spurn o' their feet:—
Fear wist not to evade as Love wist to pursue—
Still with unhurrying chase, . . .
Deliberate speed, majestic instancy,
Came on the following feet,
And a voice above their beat—
"Naught shelters thee, who wilt not shelter Me."

(continued in next day's reading)

FRANCIS THOMPSON (1859–1907)

[a]knew [b]margin

HERE the pursued tries to hide from the Lover (the Lord Jesus) because he thinks that he will have to give up everything if he gives in to his pursuer: "*For, though I knew His love Who followéd, yet was I sore adread lest, having Him, I must have naught beside.*"

The pursued attempted to hide behind everything that God had created—the sky, the sun, the moon, the ocean, the wind, becoming a kind of naturalist who sought meaning in nature. But all the elements of nature are God's servants, not humankind's. And so the pursued said, "I tempted all His servitors, but to find my own betrayal [of God] in their constancy."

Creation bears constant witness to the reality of God. To adore the creation and reject the Creator is a form of betrayal. Creation pointed the pursued to the Creator. He couldn't hide from the divine pursuer.

Still with unhurrying chase,
And unperturbéd pace,
Deliberate speed, majestic instancy,
Came on the following feet,
And a voice above their beat—
"Naught shelters thee, who wilt not shelter Me."

Nothing under the sun allowed the pursued one to stay hidden from God. They were all God's servants to bring the pursued to God. The writer of Ecclesiastes (perhaps Solomon) learned this. Having tried everything in this world to satisfy his deepest longings, he concluded that everything was empty. But this emptiness made him realize that it is God, and God alone, who can fill the void.

Everything is so weary and tiresome! No matter how much we see, we are never satisfied. No matter how much we hear, we are not content. History merely repeats itself. It has all been done before. Nothing under the sun is truly new. Ecclesiastes 1:8-9

The Hound of Heaven PART THREE

. . . I in their delicate fellowship was one—
Drew the bolts of Nature's secrecies.
I knew all the swift importings
On the willful face of skies;
I knew how the clouds arise
Spuméd of the wild sea-snortings;
All that's born or dies
Rose and drooped with—made the shapers
Of mine own moods, or wailful or divine—
With them joyed and was bereaven.[a]
I was heavy with the even,
When she lit her glimmering tapers[b]
Round the day's dead sanctities.
I laughed in the morning's eyes.
I triumphed and I saddened with all weather.
Heaven and I wept together.
And its sweet tears were salt with mortal mine;
Against the red throb of its sunset-heart
I laid my own to beat,
And share commingling heat;
But not by that, by that, was eased my human smart.
In vain my tears were wet on Heaven's grey cheek.
For ah! we know not what each other says,
These things and I; in sound I speak—
Their sound is but their stir, they speak by silences.
. . . Nigh and nigh draws the chase,
With unperturbéd pace,
Deliberate speed, majestic instancy;
And past those noiséd feet
A voice comes yet more fleet—
"Lo! naught contents thee, who content'st not Me."

(continued in next day's reading)

FRANCIS THOMPSON (1859–1907)

[a]bereaved [b]slender candles

As in yesterday's reading, the pursued explains how he tried to escape from God by finding contentment in all things God had created. But he discovered that there was a barrier between himself and the rest of creation; they could not communicate with each other. The poet cries, "We know not what each other says, these things and I." The poet tried in vain to commune with nature, when he should have been communing with God. Even though God created everything in nature, nature in and of itself cannot satisfy the deepest longings of the human soul, because God created humans to have a relationship with *him,* not the things he created.

Creation certainly doesn't deserve our heartfelt praise. Our worship belongs to the Creator alone. Only he is worthy of our praise. His creation serves to remind us of him, pointing us to the one who fills us with himself.

They exchanged the truth about God for a lie and worshiped and served the creature rather than the Creator, who is blessed forever! Amen. Romans 1:25, NRSV

The Hound of Heaven PART FOUR

Naked I wait Thy love's uplifted stroke!
My harness piece by piece Thou hast hewn from me,
And smitten me to my knee;
I am defenceless utterly.
I slept, methinks, and woke,
And, slowly gazing, find me stripped in sleep.
In the rash lustihead of my young powers,
I shook the pillaring hours
And pulled my life upon me; grimed with smears,
I stand amid the dust o' the mounded years—
My mangled youth lies dead beneath the heap.
My days have crackled and gone up in smoke,
Have puffed and burst as sun-starts on a stream.
Yea, faileth now even dream
The dreamer, and the lute the lutanist;
Even the linkéd fantasies, in whose blossomy twist
I swung the earth a trinket at my wrist,
Are yielding; cords of all too weak account
For earth with heavy griefs so overplussed.
Ah! is Thy love indeed
A weed, albeit an amaranthine[a] *weed,*
Suffering no flowers except its own to mount?
Ah! must—
Designer infinite!—
Ah! must Thou char the wood ere Thou canst limn[b]
My freshness spent its wavering shower i' the dust;
And now my heart is as a broken fount,
Wherein tear-droppings stagnate, spilt down ever
From the dank thoughts that shiver
Upon the sighful branches of my mind.
Such is; what is to be?
The pulp so bitter, how shall taste the rind?
I dimly guess what Time in mists confounds;
Yet ever and anon a trumpet sounds
From the hid battlements of Eternity;
Those shaken mists a space unsettle, then
Round the half-glimpséd turrets slowly wash again.

[a]a flower that never fades [b]draw, make an outline

But not ere him who summoneth
I first have seen, enwound
With glooming robes purpureal, cypress-crowned;
His name I know, and what his trumpet saith.
Whether man's heart or life it be which yields
Thee harvest, must Thy harvest fields
Be dunged with rotten death?

(continued in next day's reading)

FRANCIS THOMPSON (1859–1907)

IN THIS section the pursued lays his soul bare. He has been stripped of everything he thought would give his life meaning. He stands naked before God, with nothing to boast of or hold on to. He confesses that all his thoughts, dreams, and fantasies are void. His years have been a waste, and his life is worthless. It all tastes bitter and causes him great suffering. Like the writer of Ecclesiastes, he realizes that life is nothing but a chasing after the wind—a vexation of spirit and mind. He has nowhere left to go, nowhere left to hide. He fears that he might die in this condition and at the last trumpet be found without God.

Destitute, he glances at the Savior Jesus: the one in gloomy, purple robes, cypress-crowned. The pursued now knows Christ's name: He is the "King of kings and Lord of lords," as described by John in Revelation 19. This allusion helps us to understand the last lines of this section, for here we learn that the King of kings is coming to execute final judgment on this earth. It will be a gruesome scene—many people will die and rot on the fields of war. This reality terrified the pursued, as it should all who have yet to reconcile with God.

Then I saw heaven opened, and a white horse was standing there. And the one sitting on the horse was named Faithful and True. For he judges fairly and then goes to war. His eyes were bright like flames of fire, and on his head were many crowns. Revelation 19:11-12

The Hound of Heaven PART FIVE

Now of that long pursuit
Comes on at hand the bruit;[a]
That voice is round me like a bursting sea:
"And is thy earth so marred,
Shattered in shard on shard?
Lo, all things fly thee, for thou fliest Me!
Strange, piteous, futile thing!
Wherefore should any set thee love apart?
Seeing none but I makes much of naught"
(He said)
"And human love needs human meriting:
How hast thou merited—
Of all man's clotted clay the dingiest clot?[b]
Alack, thou knowest not
How little worthy of any love thou art!
Whom wilt thou find to love ignoble thee
Save Me, save only Me?
All which I took from thee I did but take,
Not for thy harms,
But just that thou might'st seek it in My arms.
All which thy child's mistake
Fancies as lost, I have stored for thee at home;
Rise, clasp My hand, and come!"
Halts by me that footfall:
Is my gloom, after all,
Shade of His hand, outstretched caressingly?
"Ah, fondest, blindest, weakest,
I am He whom thou seekest!
Thou dravest[c] *love from thee, who dravest Me."*

FRANCIS THOMPSON (1859–1907)

[a]noise, sound [b]lump [c]to drive away

WE COME to the climax of this dramatic poem. The pursued finally recognizes the Pursuer, the Hound of Heaven, to be kind and loving. Before, he had thought that the Lord was one who maliciously wanted to take away everything a man attached himself to. Now he realized that the Lord didn't take away things to be cruel. Rather, he allowed the pursued to experience the temporal nature of things: *"All which I took from thee I did but take, not for thy harms, but just that thou might'st seek it in My arms."*

Thus, the Lord lovingly allowed the pursued to find out how empty life is apart from God, so he could discover how much he needed the Lord and come to his arms. At the same time, the pursued realized that he was unworthy of God's love—for he had sinned trying to find satisfaction in this life. And so God says:

Alack, thou knowest not
How little worthy of any love thou art!
Whom wilt thou find to love ignoble thee
Save me, save only Me?

Nothing and no one satisfies but the Lord Jesus Christ. To push him away is to push away love and life. We all must realize that God is not vindictive and "out to get us." God pursues us because he loves us and wants us to experience his unconditional, everlasting love. The pursued realized Christ was not a hunter but a lover. The Hound was a Saint Bernard, not a pit bull. The sooner we surrender to the Hound of Heaven, the better. We need not waste an entire life running from him. Turn to him now, and discover his gracious love.

[David said to the Lord,] "Your unfailing love is better to me than life itself; how I praise you!" Psalm 63:3

May 13, 1657

As spring the winter doth succeed
And leaves the naked trees do dress,
The earth all black is clothed in green.
At sunshine each their joy express.

My sun's returned with healing wings,
My soul and body doth rejoice,
My heart exults and praises sings
To Him that heard my wailing voice.

My winter's past, my storms are gone,
And former clouds seem now all fled,
But if they must eclipse again,
I'll run where I was succored.

I have a shelter from the storm,
A shadow from the fainting heat,
I have access unto His throne,
Who is a God so wondrous great.

O hath Thou made my pilgrimage
Thus pleasant, fair, and good,
Blessed me in youth and elder age,
My Baca made a springing flood.

O studious am what I shall do
To show my duty with delight;
All I can give is but Thine own
And at the most a simple mite.

ANNE BRADSTREET (c. 1612–1672)

ANNE BRADSTREET, poet, mother, and wife, arrived in the New World in 1630. Eastern Massachusetts was wilderness, and its European settlers were the earliest of America's pioneers. This was not the New England of nostalgic postcards and calendars—white clapboard buildings and tall steeples on neat churches near stonewalled fields. Rather it was the hard edge of Western civilization. Twenty-seven years after her arrival, May 13, 1657, Anne Bradstreet likened this land to the Valley of Baca[a]—and this without a trace of bitterness.

America's first published poet had already written of her child's death, her own sickness, her husband's long absences, and the burning of her home in poems that weave together her faith and love for the God and Father of our Lord Jesus Christ. In fact, whatever in her pilgrimage was "pleasant, fair, and good" she attributed to the one who makes "rivers flow on barren heights, and springs within the valleys" (Isaiah 41:18, NIV). For Bradstreet, the New World had not been made livable by her own labors or those of her fellow pioneers. There, amidst hardship that we in modern America can never know, she found the King who reigns in righteousness to be like a "shelter . . . from the storm and the wind. He will refresh her as a river in the desert and as the cool shadow of a large rock in a hot and weary land" (Isaiah 32:2).

In the final verse Bradstreet may have alluded to a line from the Anglican *Book of Common Prayer,* which she had certainly found to be true: "All things come from thee, O Lord; and of thine own have we given thee."

When they walk through the Valley of Weeping, it will become a place of refreshing springs, where pools of blessing collect after the rains! Psalm 84:6

[a]Valley of Weeping, Psalm 84:6

Morning, Midday, and Evening Sacrifice

The dappled die-away
Cheek and the wimpled lip,
The gold-wisp, the airy-grey
Eye, all in fellowship—
This, all this beauty blooming,
This, all this freshness fuming,
Give God while worth consuming.

Both thought and thew[a] *now bolder*
And told by Nature: Tower;
Head, heart, hand, heel, and shoulder
That beat and breathe in power—
This pride of prime's enjoyment
Take as for tool, not toy meant
And hold at Christ's employment.
The vault and scope and schooling
And mastery in the mind,
In silk-ash kept from cooling,
And ripest under rind—
What death half lifts the latch of,
What hell hopes soon the snatch of,
Your offering, with despatch, of!

GERARD MANLEY HOPKINS (1844–1889)

[a]muscular power

IN THIS POEM Hopkins celebrates the idea that every living thing should be a living sacrifice to God. This especially applies to people in the prime of their lives—when they are most ripe. In the Old Testament the Israelites offered only the fruit that was ripe and sacrificed only the young animals who were without blemish and full of vigor to God. Thus it should be for Christians. They should offer themselves to God when their beauty is blooming and their freshness is fuming. They should offer the "pride of prime's enjoyment" and give it to Christ as a "tool" for his "employment." Hell should not get anything that was created by God. All that God created should give itself to him as a joyous, living sacrifice.

Hopkins wrote from experience. As a young, brilliant scholar, he dedicated himself to God's service by becoming a Jesuit priest. He had studied at Oxford and had taken a first-class honors degree in classics. But he then decided to become a Roman Catholic and entered the Novitiate of the Society of Jesus. Later he served as preacher or parish priest in London, Oxford, Liverpool, and Chesterfield. Many of his poems from these years, including this one, grew out of his experience as a priest. He practiced what he preached.

And so, dear brothers and sisters, I plead with you to give your bodies to God. Let them be a living and holy sacrifice—the kind he will accept. When you think of what he has done for you, is this too much to ask? Romans 12:1

Joy and Peace in Believing

Sometimes a light surprises
The Christian while he sings;
It is the Lord who rises
With healing in his wings:
When comforts are declining,
He grants the soul again
A season of clear shining
To cheer it after rain.

In holy contemplation,
We sweetly then pursue
The theme of God's salvation,
And find it ever new:
Set free from present sorrow,
We cheerfully can say,
E'en let th' unknown tomorrow
Bring with it what it may.

It can bring with it nothing
But he will bear us through;
Who gives the lilies clothing
Will clothe his people too:
Beneath the spreading heavens,
No creature but is fed;
And he who feeds the ravens
Will give his children bread.

Though vine, nor fig tree neither,
Their wonted fruit should bear,
Though all the fields should wither,
Nor flocks, nor herds, be there:
Yet God the same abiding,
His praise shall tune my voice;
For while in him confiding,
I cannot but rejoice.

WILLIAM COWPER (1731–1800)

COWPER spent years searching for healing from intermittent sieges of depression and insanity. In a private hospital he began reading the Bible and eventually converted to Christianity. Thereafter, he still struggled with depression, but he always kept his faith.

This poem is filled with biblical images that underscore one sublime truth: There is peace in believing in God. The Lord who "rises with healing in his wings" is "the Sun of righteousness" (Malachi 4:2)—Jesus Christ, who will come with swiftness to heal the wounds of his people. The lines "E'en let th' unknown tomorrow bring with it what it may!" are drawn from Jesus' Sermon on the Mount: "So don't worry about tomorrow, for tomorrow will bring its own worries. Today's trouble is enough for today" (Matthew 6:34). So are the lines "Who gives the lilies clothing will clothe his people too" (see Matthew 6:28-30).

These verses encourage people to trust God for their present and future needs, so they can be freed from anxiety. If God can use ravens to bring food to Elijah (1 Kings 17:4-6), he can supply "his children bread." But even if all the natural resources fail—vine, fig tree, fruit, flocks, and herd—God will not fail us, as promised in Habakkuk 3:17-19: "Even though the fig trees have no blossoms, and there are no grapes on the vine; even though the olive crop fails, and the fields lie empty and barren; even though the flocks die in the fields, and the cattle barns are empty, yet I will rejoice in the Lord! I will be joyful in the God of my salvation. The Sovereign Lord is my strength! He will make me as surefooted as a deer and bring me safely over the mountains."

But for you who fear my name, the Sun of Righteousness will rise with healing in his wings. And you will go free, leaping with joy like calves let out to pasture. Malachi 4:2

When I Consider How My Light Is Spent

When I consider how my light is spent
Ere half my days, in this dark world and wide,
And that one talent which is death to hide,
Lodged with me useless, though my soul more bent
To serve therewith my Maker, and present
My true account, lest he returning chide;
"Doth God exact day-labor, light denied?"
I fondly[a] *ask; but Patience to prevent*
That murmur, soon replies, "God doth not need
Either man's work or his own gifts; who best
Bear his mild yoke, they serve him best. His state
Is kingly. Thousands at his bidding speed
And post o'er land and ocean without rest:
They also serve who only stand and wait."

JOHN MILTON (1608–1674)

[a]foolishly

JOHN MILTON was blind when he wrote this poem (1652). Years of extensive study had taken their toll on his eyes. He had trained to go into the ministry but decided instead to serve God through writing. He accomplished much for the Puritan cause in England by writing revolutionary pamphlets, and he demonstrated his Christian devotion, undergirded by his classical learning, in such poems as "Lycidas"—a pastoral elegy commemorating the death of his friend, Edward King. Yet he had not written his greatest works, *Paradise Lost and Paradise Regained.*

As he wrote "When I Consider How My Light Is Spent," Milton wrestled with how he could serve God now that he was blind. He agonized over whether or not he had hidden his "one talent" in the ground—as did the servant in Jesus' parable recorded in Matthew 25:14-30. And what would happen to that servant with one bag of gold? Jesus said he would be thrown into outer darkness for his slothfulness. Milton wondered if this would be his fate as well. Would God require a full day's labor (that is, a full life's labor) from him if God denied Milton his eyesight halfway through his life? But then Milton realized he didn't need to do active things to serve God because God had many servants to perform those tasks. Milton could serve God just by standing near him and waiting on him.

A few years after this revelation, Milton received the inspiration to write *Paradise Lost,* which he dictated to his daughters over the course of several years. Unquestionably, this is one of the greatest poems to have graced the English language. It was written by a blind man, a Christian, who understood that truly serving the Lord begins by waiting on him.

Those who wait on the Lord will find new strength. They will fly high on wings like eagles. They will run and not grow weary. They will walk and not faint. Isaiah 40:31

On the Late Massacre in Piedmont

Avenge, O Lord, thy slaughtered saints, whose bones
Lie scattered on the Alpine mountains cold,
Even them who kept thy truth so pure of old
When all our fathers worshiped stocks and stones,
Forget not: in thy book record their groans
Who were thy sheep and in their ancient fold
Slain by the bloody Piemontese that rolled
Mother with infant down the rocks. Their moans
The vales redoubled to the hills, and they
To Heaven. Their martyred blood and ashes sow
O'er all th' Italian fields where still doth sway
The triple tyrant: that from these may grow
A hundredfold, who having learnt thy way
Early may fly the Babylonian woe.

JOHN MILTON (1608–1674)

IN THIS POEM Milton decries the killing of several Christians known as the Waldensians. This sect had lived in the Italian Alps since the twelfth century. They supposedly had religious liberty. But in 1655 the Roman Catholic ruler of the Piedmont trampled their freedom by sending troops to slaughter many of their members.

At this time in history there was tremendous tension between Roman Catholics and Protestants. Milton, a leading Protestant in England, voiced his protest against this slaughter. Speaking for his countrymen, Milton confessed that the English (in the twelfth century) had still been Roman Catholics who worshiped wooden and stone statues, while the Waldensians carried on the true faith. Now (in the seventeenth century) as Protestants, the English were free from "the triple tyrant" (the pope, who supposedly had authority over heaven, earth, and hell). The irony is that the Waldensians, who had come under the pope's sword, were martyrs liberated to heaven—way above his control.

In the last lines Milton prays that the martyrs' seed will multiply a hundredfold, producing many more new believers, who will know the truth and thereby escape "the Babylonian woe." That woe is the destruction of Babylon as depicted in Revelation 18, which Protestants in Milton's day understood to mean the destruction of Rome.

From this sad scene in Christian history, depicted so poignantly by Milton, let us learn tolerance for other Christians—especially those who are most different from us.

When the Lamb broke the fifth seal, I saw under the altar the souls of all who had been martyred for the word of God and for being faithful in their witness. They called loudly to the Lord and said, "O Sovereign Lord, holy and true, how long will it be before you judge the people who belong to this world for what they have done to us? When will you avenge our blood against these people?" Revelation 6:9-10

Wonder PART ONE

How like an angel came I down!
How bright are all things here!
When first among his works I did appear,
O how their glory did me crown!
The world resembled his eternity,
In which my soul did walk,
And everything that I did see
Did with me talk.

The skies in their magnificence,
The lively, lovely air;
O how divine, how soft, how sweet, how fair!
The stars did entertain my sense,
And all the works of God so bright and pure,
So rich and great did seem,
As if they ever must endure,
In my esteem.

A native health and innocence
Within my bones did grow,
And while my God did all his glories show,
I felt a vigor in my sense
That was all SPIRIT. I within did flow
With seas of life like wine;
I nothing in the world did know
But 'twas divine.

Harsh ragged objects were concealed,
Oppression's tears and cries,
Sins, griefs, complaints, dissensions, weeping eyes,
Were hid; and only things revealed
Which heavenly spirits and the angels prize.
The state of innocence
And bliss, not trades and poverties,
Did fill my sense.

(continued in next day's reading)

THOMAS TRAHERNE (1637–1674)

IN THIS POEM, as in many of his other works, Traherne celebrates the innocence of nativity. He compares a newborn to an angel, a pure spirit, who comes into a God-created world that beams with untarnished beauty. The newborn enjoys the divine qualities of the universe. God speaks to the newborn in everything, and everything speaks of divinity. All the evils of this world are not yet seen or known by the newborn. God shelters the infant from "sins, griefs, complaints, dissensions, weeping eyes"—and therein is the reason for the babe's bliss.

Not one adult can truly see the world this way. This is a gift given only to the newborn. But God has given something unique and special to adults—and older children—who have been born again by his Spirit. He has given us a new existence, cleansing us of our sin and filling us with new life. And even though we are still painfully aware of sin and its consequences, we do have an advantage over the newborn in this respect: We have the Spirit of life within us as a foretaste and guarantee of the new, eternal life to come.

What this means is that those who become Christians become new persons. They are not the same anymore, for the old life is gone. A new life has begun! 2 Corinthians 5:17

Wonder PART TWO

The streets were paved with golden stones,
The boys and girls were mine,
O how did all their lovely faces shine!
The sons of men were holy ones.
In joy and beauty then appeared to me
And everything which here I found
While like an angel I did see,
Adorned the ground.

Rich diamond and pearl and gold
In every place was seen;
Rare splendors, yellow, blue, red, white, and green,
Mine eyes did everywhere behold.
Great wonders clothed with glory did appear,
Amazement was my bliss.
That and my wealth was everywhere:
No joy to this!

Cursed and devised proprieties, With envy, avarice,
And fraud, those fiends that spoil even paradise,
Fled from the splendor of mine eyes.
And so did hedges, ditches, limits, bounds,
I dreamed not aught of those,
But wandered over all men's grounds,
And found repose.

Proprieties themselves were mine,
And hedges ornaments;
Walls, boxes, coffers, and their rich contents
Did not divide my joys, but all combine.
Clothes, ribbons, jewels, laces, I esteemed
My joys by others worn;
For me they all to wear them seemed
When I was born.

THOMAS TRAHERNE (1637–1674)

TRAHERNE sees the world in a dreamlike vision, as it should have been before it was corrupted by the Fall. In effect, he was seeing the new earth and the new heaven wherein dwell righteousness and perfection. That world, though envisioned in our mind, has not yet come to reality. But it is our hope.

We have this hope because the prophets foretold the day when there would be a new heaven and a new earth. God, speaking through Isaiah said, "As surely as my new heavens and earth will remain, so will you always be my people, with a name that will never disappear" (Isaiah 66:22). Peter also spoke of our hope for the new heavens and new earth: "We are looking forward to the new heavens and new earth he has promised, a world where everyone is right with God" (2 Peter 3:13). John foresaw the final outcome, too: "Then I saw a new heaven and a new earth, for the old heaven and the old earth had disappeared. And the sea was also gone. And I saw the holy city, the new Jerusalem, coming down from God out of heaven like a beautiful bride prepared for her husband" (Revelation 21:1-2).

In that new age, when all the universe is regenerated, we will enjoy a world of immaculate glory. At the center of that world will be the embodiment of perfection, truth, righteousness, and beauty—God the Father and his Son. What a magnificent sight to behold! What an incredible presence to experience! May our heart swell with excitement as we anticipate the day when we will enter God's glory forever.

I heard a loud shout from the throne, saying, "Look, the home of God is now among his people! He will live with them, and they will be his people. God himself will be with them. He will remove all of their sorrows, and there will be no more death or sorrow or crying or pain. For the old world and its evils are gone forever." Revelation 21:3-4

Lord Jesus, Think on Me

Lord Jesus, think on me,
And purge away my sin;
From earthborn passions set me free,
And make me pure within.

Lord Jesus, think on me,
With care and woe oppressed;
Let me Thy loving servant be,
And taste Thy promised rest.

Lord Jesus, think on me,
Nor let me go astray;
Through darkness and perplexity
Point Thou the heav'nly way.

Lord Jesus, think on me,
That, when the flood is past,
I may th' eternal brightness see,
And share Thy joy at last.

SYNESIUS OF CYRENE (c. 375–430)
Translated by Allen W. Chatfield (1808–1896)

SYNESIUS, from Cyrene in northern Africa, was a philosopher who eventually became a Christian bishop. When he was thirty-three, Synesius married a Christian woman who helped him understand the gospel. But even after he embraced Christianty, he struggled to reconcile his philosophy with Christian doctrine.

In this poem Synesius expresses his desire for the Lord to enlighten him and guide him into the truth:

Lord Jesus, think on me,
Nor let me go astray;
Through darkness and perplexity
Point Thou the heav'nly way.

Any philosophy, no matter how good, can distract people from Christ. This is why Paul said, "See to it that no one takes you captive through philosophy and empty deceit, according to human tradition . . . and not according to Christ" (Colossians 2:8, NRSV). Philosophies help people think about ways to view their life, but philosophies cannot give life or light. Life and light are found only in Jesus Christ. We need him to illumine our spirits and fill us with his divine wisdom.

In the beginning the Word already existed. He was with God, and he was God. . . . Life itself was in him, and this life gives light to everyone. The light shines through the darkness, and the darkness can never extinguish it. John 1:1, 4-5

The Kingdom of God

"In No Strange Land"

O world invisible, we view thee,
O world intangible, we touch thee,
O world unknowable, we know thee,
Inapprehensible, we clutch thee!

Does the fish soar to find the ocean,
The eagle plunge to find the air—
That we ask of the stars in motion
If they have rumour of thee there?

Not where the wheeling systems darken,
And our benumbed conceiving soars!—
The drift of pinions, would we harken,
Beats at our own clay-shuttered doors.

The angels keep their ancient places;—
Turn but a stone and start a wing!
'Tis ye, 'tis your estrangèd faces,
That miss the many-splendoured thing.

But (when so sad thou canst not sadder)
Cry,—and upon thy so sore loss
Shall shine the traffic of Jacob's ladder
Pitched betwixt Heaven and Charing Cross.

Yea, in the night, my Soul, my daughter,
Cry—clinging Heaven by the hems;
And lo, Christ walking on the water
Not of Gennesareth, but Thames!

FRANCIS THOMPSON (1859–1907)

FRANCIS THOMPSON spent many years searching for his calling. Ironically, he found it at the lowest point in his life. Addicted to opium and selling matches and papers for a living, Thompson submitted two of his poems to a magazine editor named Wilfred Meynell, who agreed to publish them. The warm reception given to Thompson's work encouraged him to publish more. His first volume, *Poems* (1893), was also favorably received. He dedicated his second volume, *Sister Songs* (1895), to Meynell's children. *New Poems,* his last volume, appeared in 1897.

In this poem Thompson proclaims the astounding truth that Christ's kingdom and presence have come to us. We don't need to seek Christ and his dominion in a "strange" land. As fish don't soar through the air to find the ocean or eagles plunge into the sea to discover air, we need not look beyond the stars in search of Christ. For Christ has established his kingdom in our midst. Christ, like Jacob's ladder connecting heaven to earth and earth to heaven, has brought heaven to earth. Since his ascension, we can find Christ's Spirit present on earth. Wherever we are, he is there also. Thus Thompson, a resident of London (where the river Thames flows), concludes: "And lo, Christ walking on the water not of Gennesareth, but Thames!"

As believers, we don't need to travel to the Sea of Galilee (also known as Gennesaret) to see Christ walk on water. Christ's presence is with us—right here, right now. Heaven's "hems" are within our grasp. Take a hold!

One day the Pharisees asked Jesus, "When will the Kingdom of God come?" Jesus replied, "The Kingdom of God isn't ushered in with visible signs. You won't be able to say, 'Here it is!' or 'It's over there!' For the Kingdom of God is among you." Luke 17:20-21

The Created

There is naught for thee by thy haste to gain;
'Tis not the swift with Me that win the race;
Through long endurance of delaying pain,
Thine opened eye shall see thy Father's face;
Nor here nor there, where now thy feet would turn,
Thou wilt find Him who ever seeks for thee;
But let obedience quench desires that burn,
And where thou art, thy Father, too, will be.
Behold! as day by day the spirit grows,
Thou see'st by inward light things hid before;
Till what God is, thyself, his image shows;
And thou dost wear the robe that first thou wore,
When bright with radiance from his forming hand,
He saw thee Lord of all his creatures stand.

JONES VERY (1813–1880)

VERY wrote this poem on the theme that God wants to restore his pure image in men and women. In the beginning God created Adam and Eve in his image, making humanity unique and special among all his creation (Genesis 1:26). But the Fall marred and ruined his image in human beings. Instead of expressing God, Adam and Eve expressed "self" and "sin." But God has never relinquished his desire to have many sons and daughters who reflect the glorious image of his Son.

But how can God restore his image in us? The only way is by transformation. Second Corinthians 3:18 says: "But we all, with unveiled face beholding as in a mirror the glory of the Lord, are being transformed into the same image from glory to glory, just as from the Lord, the Spirit" (NASB). The Lord is the Spirit who is near to us, as near as a turn of our heart. When we turn our heart to him, he "unveils" our face so that we can reflect his image. And as we mirror him, he gradually transforms us into the image we behold.

It seems that we need an entire lifetime of transformation to grow into mature children of God. The Bible often depicts this process of maturation as a pathway that every believer must travel until he or she reaches the goal: conformation to the glorious image of God's Son. This is the goal toward which we press daily and the goal on which we fix our thoughts. In the end we will be like him—and we will see him as he is.

For those whom he foreknew he also predestined to be conformed to the image of his Son, in order that he might be the firstborn within a large family. Romans 8:29, NRSV

We Cover Thee—Sweet Face—

We Cover Thee—Sweet Face—
Not that We tire of Thee—
But that Thyself fatigue of Us—
Remember—as Thou go—
We follow Thee until
Thou notice Us—no more—
And then—reluctant—turn away
To Con Thee o'er and o'er—

And blame the scanty love
We were Content to show—
Augmented—Sweet—a Hundred fold—
If Thou would'st take it—now—

EMILY DICKINSON (1830–1886)

FROM the late 1850s through the early 1860s was Dickinson's most productive period. During this time she began earnestly writing poems, often on scraps of paper. Dickinson was fascinated by the subject of death, and her poetry reflected this interest. Death, eternity, God, and the afterlife are common topics in her writing. By 1866 Dickinson had written the majority of her poems. Only seven of her 1,775 poems appeared in print while she was alive, and those were published anonymously.

In this poem she addresses a deceased friend or relative and expresses her remorse. But this remorse is not for the person's death—after all, he or she had gone to a better place. Dickinson's remorse is for the fact that she and others had failed to love this person fully while he or she was alive. How many of us feel the same about our friends and relatives who have gone on to the next life?

Let us learn from Mary, the sister of Lazarus, for she expressed her love to Jesus before he died. She poured upon his feet an extremely costly perfume during a dinner party six days before his crucifixion (John 12:1-8). Possibly Mary alone (of all Jesus' followers) perceived his imminent death, or perhaps she just sensed that this evening would be her last with him. Jesus was so touched by Mary's outpouring of love that he declared her act would always accompany the testimony of the gospel (Mark 14:9).

May we, like Mary, realize how precious our loved ones are—to have them with us is the best we can ask for in life. Let us seize the opportunities to show them our love.

A dinner was prepared in Jesus' honor. Martha served, and Lazarus sat at the table with him. Then Mary took a twelve-ounce jar of expensive perfume made from essence of nard, and she anointed Jesus' feet with it and wiped his feet with her hair. John 12:2-3

Ascension Eve

O Lord Almighty, Who hast formed us weak,
With us whom Thou hast formed deal fatherly;
Be found of us whom Thou has deigned to seek,
Be found that we the more may seek for Thee;
Lord, speak and grant us ears to hear Thee speak;
Lord, come to us and grant us eyes to see;

Lord, make us meek, for Thou Thyself art meek;
Lord, Thou art Love, fill us with charity.
O Thou the Life of living and of dead,
Who givest more the more Thyself hast given,
Suffice us as Thy saints Thou hast sufficed;
That beautified, replenished, comforted,
Still gazing off from earth and up at heaven
We may pursue Thy steps, Lord Jesus Christ.

CHRISTINA ROSSETTI (1830–1894)

THROUGHOUT this poem the poet asks the Lord to make her more like him. The climax comes in the last two lines: "Still gazing off from earth and up at heaven we may pursue Thy steps, Lord Jesus Christ." As Paul said, "We are citizens of heaven, where the Lord Jesus Christ lives. And we are eagerly waiting for him to return as our Savior. He will take these weak mortal bodies of ours and change them into glorious bodies like his own, using the same mighty power that he will use to conquer everything, everywhere" (Philippians 3:20-21).

When Christ returns, he will come not only as our Savior (3:20) but also as our transfigurer, giving us new physical bodies. Following the pattern of his own resurrection, our identities will not change, but our form and mode of existence certainly will (see 1 Corinthians 15:51). Christ, as life-giving Spirit (1 Corinthians 15:45) indwelling us, will instantly change our bodies to be like his. This is the easy part of becoming like Christ.

As Rossetti's poem illustrates, it's the transformation of our soul that is the hard part. This transformation takes a lifetime, while the transfiguration "will happen in a moment, in the blinking of an eye" (1 Corinthians 15:52). But when the transfiguration takes place—when we become completely like Jesus in mind, body, and spirit—that is when we will fully realize our heavenly citizenship.

Yes, dear friends, we are already God's children, and we can't even imagine what we will be like when Christ returns. But we do know that when he comes we will be like him, for we will see him as he really is.
1 John 3:2

Ascension Day

"A Cloud received Him out of their sight."

When Christ went up to Heaven the Apostles stayed
Gazing at Heaven with souls and wills on fire,
Their hearts on flight along the track He made,
Winged by desire.

Their silence spake: "Lord, why not follow Thee?
Home is not home without Thy Blessed Face,
Life is not life. Remember, Lord, and see,
Look back, embrace.

"Earth is one desert waste of banishment,
Life is one long-drawn anguish of decay.
Where Thou wert wont to go we also went:
Why not today?"

Nevertheless a cloud cut off their gaze:
They tarry to build up Jerusalem,
Watching for Him, while thro' the appointed days
He watches them.

They do His Will, and doing it rejoice,
Patiently glad to spend and to be spent:
Still He speaks to them, still they hear His Voice
And are content.

For as a cloud received Him from their sight,
So with a cloud will He return ere long:
Therefore they stand on guard by day, by night,
Strenuous and strong.

They do, they dare, they beyond seven times seven
Forgive, they cry God's mighty word aloud:
Yet sometimes haply lift tired eyes to Heaven—
"Is that His cloud?"

CHRISTINA ROSSETTI (1830–1894)

IN THIS POEM Rossetti recounts the day of Christ's ascension. As his disciples looked on, Jesus ascended into heaven. They remained there—even after he disappeared—amazed at what they had seen and straining to see him still. At this point, the angels appeared to them and said, "Men of Galilee, why are you standing here staring at the sky? Jesus has been taken away from you into heaven. And someday, just as you saw him go, he will return!" (Acts 1:11).

Although they desired to go with Christ, he left them behind to work, "to build up Jerusalem." And they did. As a result of their obedience, Christ's disciples grew in number from a few hundred to thousands. The Good News spread from Palestine to Asia Minor to Europe.

Since then, millions of people throughout history have come to know Christ as Savior, and believers have preached the gospel in almost every nation. But even with Christ's return more imminent than ever, there is still much work to be done. We must serve others, stand for truth, and forgive those who have hurt us. At times we may tire of our work. But we must continue to build Christ's kingdom, while anxiously awaiting his return. Until then, we may from time to time longingly ask, "Is that His cloud?"

Set your minds on things that are above, not on things that are on earth, for you have died, and your life is hidden with Christ in God. When Christ who is your life is revealed, then you also will be revealed with him in glory. Colossians 3:2-4, NRSV

from The Eternal Goodness

I know not what the future hath
Of marvel or surprise,
Assured alone that life and death
His mercy underlies.

And if my heart and flesh are weak
To bear an untried pain,
The bruisèd reed he will not break,
But strengthen and sustain.

No offering of my own I have,
Nor works my faith to prove;
I can but give the gifts he gave,
And plead his love for love.

And so beside the silent sea
I wait the muffled oar;
No harm from him can come to me
On ocean or on shore.

I know not where his islands lift
Their fronded palms in air;
I only know I cannot drift
Beyond his love and care.

JOHN GREENLEAF WHITTIER (1807–1892)

JOHN GREENLEAF WHITTIER grew up on a farm near Haverhill, Massachusetts. His parents were poor in possessions but rich in faith, and Whittier benefited from his Quaker and Puritan ancestry. At a young age he exhibited excellent writing skills and, later on in life, became editor of a weekly newspaper in Boston. His first published volume, including poetry and prose, drew largely from his local New England experience and was entitled *Legends of New England* (1831).

The height of his fame came in the 1880s, when student readers studied his writings because they were easy to understand. This earned Whittier the distinction of being a "schoolroom poet." But students weren't the only ones who enjoyed his poetry. People from all walks of life admired Whittier's poetry for its piety, compassion, and commendation of goodness. Whittier's most admired poem is "Snow-Bound" (1866). Well known also are "Maud Muller," "Ichabod," and "The Brewing of Soma."

In this poem Whittier expresses his assurance that God would be with him in all of life's circumstances. Though he couldn't predict his future, he had faith that God would protect him no matter what happened. He affirms this in the last two stanzas: "No harm from him can come to me on ocean or on shore"; and "I only know I cannot drift beyond his love and care."

Paul declares in Romans that nothing can separate us from God's love. Like Whittier, we cannot drift beyond God's love and care. Let us praise him for this assurance.

Whether we are high above the sky or in the deepest ocean, nothing in all creation will ever be able to separate us from the love of God that is revealed in Christ Jesus our Lord. Romans 8:39

Santa Teresa's Book-Mark

Let nothing disturb thee,
Nothing affright thee;
All things are passing;
God never changeth;
Patient endurance
Attaineth to all things;
Who God possesseth
In nothing is wanting;
Alone God sufficeth.

SANTA TERESA DE AVILA (1515–1582)
Translated by William Wordsworth

A TRUE appreciation of this poem comes from understanding the person who penned these words, originally in Spanish. This poem succinctly expresses the desires of one who aspired to live in God's presence one day at a time.

Santa Teresa de Avila called herself Teresa of Jesus. She became a nun at sixteen and found solace in deep contemplation, even though she suffered both emotionally and physically in the convent. At the age of forty she experienced a trance in which she had a vision of Christ for the first time. This increased her spiritual sensitivity and eventually prompted her to found a new, reformed order.

She accomplished this, against protests, in 1562. From the new convent of St. Joseph in Avila, Teresa, a semi-invalid, traveled incessantly throughout Spain, founding and administering seventeen convents. All of the nuns who lived in her convents followed the Carmelite rule, which emphasized strict enclosure, discipline, and mental prayer. Teresa herself was a model of rigorous discipline, wearing a hair shirt and often scourging herself.

In all of her writings she emphasized the mystical way. She wrote *Autobiography* (1562), *Way of Perfection, Book of Foundations,* and *Interior Castle.* These works eventually earned her the title Doctor (teacher) of the church. Forty years after her death, the Roman Catholic church canonized Teresa for her saintliness and the miracles attributed to her.

The short poem cited here teaches us two great truths about God. First, God never changes. The world does and we do, but God is constant. Second, God is all sufficient. Those who belong to him have everything they need, for he alone sustains life and provides for those who are his. These profound truths should be the "bookmarks" for our life.

➼ *How do you benefit if you gain the whole world but lose your own soul in the process? Is anything worth more than your soul?*
Matthew 16:26

Sons PART ONE

Father, Thy name our souls would bless
As children taught by grace,
Lift up our hearts in righteousness
And joy before Thy face.

Sweet is the confidence Thou giv'st,
Though high above our praise;
Our hearts resort to where Thou liv'st
In heaven's unclouded rays.

There in the purpose of Thy love
Our place is now prepared,
As sons with Him who is above,
Who all our sorrows shared.

Eternal ages shall declare
The riches of Thy grace,
To those who with Thy Son shall share
A son's eternal place.

Absent as yet, we rest in hope,
Treading the desert path,
Waiting for Him who takes us up
Beyond the power of death.

(continued in next day's reading)

JOHN NELSON DARBY (1800–1882)

THIS POEM celebrates God's desire and plan to have many "sons" (male and female believers), who would be like his beloved Son. This theme is emphasized in the New Testament, especially in the opening verses in the book of Ephesians: God's heart's desire is to obtain many children in and through his Son. These children, in union with the unique Son, would bring great glory and satisfaction to the Father.

In Ephesians 1:5, 9, 11 Paul used a Greek word that conveys the idea of desire, even heart's desire. The word usually translates as "will" or "the will of God." But the English word *will* sublimates the primary meaning. The Greek word *(thelema)* is primarily an emotional word and secondarily volitional. "God's will" is not so much "God's intention" as it is "God's heart's desire." God does have an intention, a purpose, a plan. It is called *prothesis* in Greek (see Ephesians 1:11), and it literally means "a laying out beforehand" (like a blueprint). God's counsel created this plan. But behind the plan and the counsel was not just a mastermind but a heart, a heart of love and good pleasure. Paul talks about "the good pleasure of God's heart's desire" (1:5, author paraphrase). Paul also says, "He made known to us the mystery of his heart's desire, according to his good pleasure which he purposed in him" (1:9, author paraphrase).

How blessed we are to be "those who with [God's] Son shall share a son's eternal place." This is our glorious destiny!

In love He predestined us to adoption as sons through Jesus Christ to Himself, according to the kind intention of His will. Ephesians 1:4-5, NASB

Unchanging glory fills the place
Where Jesus dwells on high;
But brighter joy our spirits trace
With Him, for ever nigh!

We joy in Thee; Thy holy love
Our endless portion is—
Like Thine own Son, with Him above,
In brightest heavenly bliss.

His Father Thou, and ours thro' grace,
We taste the same delight—
Blest in the brightness of Thy face,
In heaven's unclouded light.

Father! Thy love my portion is,
As son, like Christ, with Thee;
Oh, who can tell of love like this,
So sov'reign, full, and free!

O Holy Father, keep us here
In that blest name of Love,
Walking before Thee without fear,
Till all be joy above.

JOHN NELSON DARBY (1800–1882)

AS EXPLAINED in the previous day's reading, the impetus of God's eternal purpose came from his heart's desire to have many children like his only Son. In love, he predestined many people to participate in this "sonship"—not by their own merits but by virtue of being in the Son (Ephesians 1:4-5). Notice how often in Ephesians 1 Paul speaks of the believers' position "in him." Outside of him (the Son), no one can be a son or daughter of God, and no one can be pleasing to the Father. God's sons and daughters owe all their divine privileges to the beloved Son, as ones graced in him (Ephesians 1:6). In fact, if it were not for God's satisfaction in his beloved Son, there would not have been the inspiration for the creation of humanity in the first place. Humans exist because God wanted to obtain many more children, each bearing the image of his unique Son.

We please God and bring him satisfaction by being united to the one who has always satisfied him. Apart from the Son, we have no access, no right to sonship. He is our unique way to the Father.

Thank God that it was his good pleasure to include us in his Son. As the poem so often states, we have been given this privilege because of God's love for us. His love is our portion. And so we join the poet "in that blest name of Love."

God is faithful; by him you were called into the fellowship of his Son, Jesus Christ our Lord. 1 Corinthians 1:9, NRSV

from *Religio Laici*

Thus Man by his own strength to Heaven would soar:
And would not be obliged to God for more.
Vain, wretched creature, how art thou misled
To think thy Wit these God-like notions bred!
These truths are not the product of thy mind,
But dropped from Heaven, and of a nobler kind.
Revealed religion first informed thy sight,
And Reason saw not till Faith sprung the light.
Hence all thy Natural Worship takes the source:
'Tis Revelation what thou thinkst Discourse.

But if there be a Power too just and strong
To wink at crimes and bear unpunished wrong,
Look humbly upward, see his will disclose
The forfeit first, and then the fine impose,
A mulct[a] *thy poverty could never pay*
Had not eternal wisdom found the way
And with celestial wealth supplied thy store;
His justice makes the fine, his mercy quits the score.
See God descending in thy human frame;
The offended, suffering in the offender's name.
All thy misdeeds to Him imputed see,
And all His righteousness devolved[b] *on thee.*

JOHN DRYDEN (1631–1700)

[a]fine, penalty [b]to pass on powers from one person to another

EDUCATED at Trinity College, Cambridge, Dryden was the most eminent literary figure in England during the last four decades of the seventeenth century. His life and work reflected most of the major trends of his time. In politics he was staunchly Royalist; in religion he was first Anglican, then Roman Catholic; in philosophy he was cautiously rationalistic. His work eventually earned him the title poet laureate.

In 1682 Dryden published *Religio Laici (A Layman's Faith)*. In this poem, he examined his religious convictions and supported Anglicanism as the middle way between rationalism and Roman Catholicism. The poem's prologue (printed above) presents the central theme of the Protestant movement: A person is justified by faith, not by works. This was the clarion call of the Reformation.

His poem also attacks rationalism, which views reason as the basis for establishing religious truth. Dryden believed that people must receive divine revelation to become believers. Wit—reason—doesn't save people. In fact, reason relies on faith to understand salvation: "And *Reason* saw not till *Faith* sprung the light." As Dryden makes poignantly clear, the truths of faith were "not the product of [man's] mind," but they were "dropped from Heaven, and of a nobler kind." Thus, humanity is vain and misled to think that reason produces religious truth.

To receive the revelation that leads to salvation, we must "look humbly upward." For God opposes the proud (James 4:6) and will not disclose his will to those who mistake revelation for human reason.

But now God has shown us a different way of being right in his sight—not by obeying the law but by the way promised in the Scriptures long ago. We are made right in God's sight when we trust in Jesus Christ to take away our sins. And we all can be saved in this same way, no matter who we are or what we have done. Romans 3:21-22

A Better Resurrection

I have no wit, no words, no tears;
My heart within me like a stone
Is numbed too much for hopes or fears;
Look right, look left, I dwell alone;
I lift mine eyes, but dimmed with grief
No everlasting hills I see;
My life is in the falling leaf:
O Jesus, quicken me.

My life is like a faded leaf,
My harvest dwindled to a husk;
Truly my life is void and brief
And tedious in the barren dusk;
My life is like a frozen thing,
No bud or greenness can I see:
Yet rise it shall—the sap of Spring;
O Jesus, rise in me.

My life is like a broken bowl,
A broken bowl that cannot hold
One drop of water for my soul
Or cordial in the searching cold;
Cast in the fire the perished thing,
Melt and remould it, till it be
A royal cup for Him my King:
O Jesus, drink of me.

CHRISTINA ROSSETTI (1830–1894)

IN THIS POEM Christina Rossetti expresses her desire for the Lord to enliven her flagging spiritual condition in a triple plea: "O Jesus, quicken me. . . . O Jesus, rise in me. . . . O Jesus, drink of me."

Several biblical allusions appear in these stanzas. In the first stanza she complains, "I lift mine eyes, but dimmed with grief no everlasting hills I see." This alludes to Psalm 121:1, where the psalmist (returning to Jerusalem from a journey) says, "I lift up my eyes to the hills" (NIV). This expresses desire (cf. Psalms 25:1; 123:1) mingled with expectation that God is able to protect and sustain him.

In the second stanza Rossetti complains of her lifelessness through images that are akin to those recorded in Job: "Their roots will dry up, and their branches will wither" (18:16). The image of a broken bowl in stanza three is similar to what we find in Jeremiah 2:13 concerning broken cisterns. God told the Israelites that they had forsaken him, the fountain of living waters, for broken cisterns that could hold no water.

We, like the poet, have seasons of spiritual dryness. As we weather these times, we should cry out to Christ for rejuvenation. He will not only infuse new life into us but in the process will use our dryness for his divine purpose, remolding us for a more noble use.

Even though the fig trees have no blossoms, and there are no grapes on the vine; even though the olive crop fails, and the fields lie empty and barren; even though the flocks die in the fields, and the cattle barns are empty, yet I will rejoice in the Lord! I will be joyful in the God of my salvation. The Sovereign Lord is my strength! Habakkuk 3:17-19a

Sin (I)

Lord, with what care hast thou begirt us round!
Parents first season us: then schoolmasters
Deliver us to laws; they send us bound
To rules of reason, holy messengers,
Pulpits and Sundays, sorrow dogging sin,
Afflictions sorted, anguish of all sizes,
Fine nets and stratagems to catch us in,
Bibles laid open, millions of surprises,
Blessings beforehand, ties of gratefulness,
The sound of glory ringing in our ears:
Without, our shame; within, our consciences;
Angels and grace, eternal hopes and fears.
Yet all these fences and their whole array
One cunning bosom-sin blows quite away.

GEORGE HERBERT (1593–1633)

EVEN though George Herbert was a minister, he wasn't immune to the average struggles of a Christian. Sin was one such struggle he not only faced but wrote about in several poems. Here Herbert reveals just how easy it is for believers to transgress into sin, even when God has given them so many barriers of protection against it.

Think of what God has given us to keep us from sinning: training from parents and teachers, laws, rules, reason, messages from the pulpit, sorrowful reminders and regrets of sins past, public shame, guilty conscience, the Word of God, countless blessings, ties of gratitude, thoughts of the coming glory, angels, God's grace, eternal hopes and fears. And yet we still "blow it" and, in so doing, blow away all this protection God has provided.

The only way to escape sin is to live in the Spirit because the Spirit is stronger than the flesh and can produce righteousness in us. May God grant us the desire to live our life completely in his Spirit.

So I advise you to live according to your new life in the Holy Spirit. Then you won't be doing what your sinful nature craves. The old sinful nature loves to do evil, which is just opposite from what the Holy Spirit wants. And the Spirit gives us desires that are opposite from what the sinful nature desires. These two forces are constantly fighting each other, and your choices are never free from this conflict. But when you are directed by the Holy Spirit, you are no longer subject to the law.
Galatians 5:16-18

Holy Baptism (I)

As he that sees a dark and shady grove,
Stays not, but looks beyond it on the sky;
So when I view my sins, mine eyes remove
More backward still, and to that water fly,
Which is above the heav'ns, whose spring and rent
Is in my dear Redeemer's pierced side.
O blessed streams! either ye do prevent
And stop our sins from growing thick and wide,
Or else give tears to drown them, as they grow.
In you Redemption measures all my time,
And spreads the plaster equal to the crime:
You taught the Book of Life my name, that so
Whatever future sins should me miscall,
Your first acquaintance might discredit all.

GEORGE HERBERT (1593–1633)

ALMOST all of Herbert's poetry is contained in *The Temple* (1633), which was published two months after his death. Shortly before he died, Herbert sent this manuscript to Nicholas Ferrar, head of the Anglican community at Little Gidding, with instructions that "if he can think it may turn to the advantage of any dejected poor soul, let it be made public; if not, let him burn it, for I and it are the least of God's mercies." Thankfully, his poems weren't burned, for they have helped many a dejected soul.

Many of the poems from the first half of *The Temple* deal with such subjects as sacraments, rituals, and events from Christ's life. In this poem, the subject is the ritual of baptism. As Herbert looks back to his baptism, he sees it as the point where he first met Christ and was washed from all his sins. No matter what sins he committed thereafter, he could look back to this time and be assured that this was when his name was written in the Book of Life forever.

What assurance our baptism gives us! It is the seal of our salvation, guaranteeing that we belong to the Savior and have eternal life.

➻ *Baptism . . . now saves you by the power of Jesus Christ's resurrection.* 1 Peter 3:20

Thou Art Indeed Just, Lord

Thou art indeed just, Lord, if I contend
With thee; but, sir, so what I plead is just.
Why do sinners' ways prosper? and why must
Disappointment all I endeavour end?

Wert thou my enemy, O thou my friend,
How wouldst thou worse, I wonder, than thou dost
Defeat, thwart me? Oh, the sots and thralls of lust
Do in spare hours more thrive than I that spend,

Sir, life upon thy cause. See, banks and brakes
Now, leavèd how thick! lacèd they are again
With fretty chervil, look, and fresh wind shakes

Them; birds build—but not I build; no, but strain,
Time's eunuch, and not breed one work that wakes.
Mine, O thou lord of life, send my roots rain.

GERARD MANLEY HOPKINS (1844–1889)

HOPKINS studied at Oxford, where he converted from Anglicanism to Roman Catholicism. Later he became a Jesuit priest. In so doing, he decided to never again write poetry. But Hopkins soon felt compelled to write. In 1875 he composed his first great poem, "The Wreck of the Deutschland," a lament for the death of four nuns, in which he explored the issue of God's sovereignty. During his last years he wrote other excellent poems that reflect his faith through trials.

In this poem Hopkins asks the age-old question: Why do saints suffer, while sinners prosper? Perhaps what prompted his question is also found in the poem. It seemed to Hopkins that all his labor was for nothing. Birds could build nests that withstood the wind, but he was "time's eunuch" and couldn't produce anything substantial or lasting. All he endeavored ended in disappointment. If God was Hopkins's friend, why didn't he help him succeed? It seemed, instead, that God was his enemy: "Wert thou my enemy, O thou my friend, how wouldst thou worse, I wonder, than thou dost defeat, thwart me?" Through all of this, Hopkins's spirit withered, so he prayed, "Mine, O thou lord of life, send my roots rain."

Most people don't question God like this when life is fine. Suffering provokes these interrogatories to heaven. But as Christians we must realize and accept the fact that we are called to suffer because it conforms us to the image of Christ. Though suffering is never enjoyable, it is also never in vain. We know that God works through all things in the lives of those who love him and are called according to his purpose (Romans 8:28). In the end, we have the most to gain through suffering.

We know that all things work together for good for those who love God, who are called according to his purpose. For those whom he foreknew he also predestined to be conformed to the image of his Son.
Romans 8:28-29, NRSV

The Windows

Lord, how can man preach thy eternal word?
He is a brittle crazy glass:
Yet in thy temple thou dost him afford
This glorious and transcendent place,
To be a window, through thy grace.

But when thou dost anneal[a] *in glass thy story,*
Making thy life to shine within
The holy Preacher's; then the light and glory
More rev'rend grows, and more doth win:
Which else shows wat'rish, bleak, and thin.

Doctrine and life, colours and light, in one
When they combine and mingle, bring
A strong regard and awe: but speech alone
Doth vanish like a flaring thing,
And in the ear, not conscience ring.

GEORGE HERBERT (1593–1633)

[a] to burn in colors upon glass, as in stained glass

HERBERT'S book of poetry, *The Temple* (1633), is an architectural metaphor. It has associations with the Old Testament temple as well as with the Greek and Roman temples. But these associations give way to the New Testament view of the human heart as a temple—the dwelling place of the Spirit of God.

In true metaphysical style (in which a physical object is a metaphor for a spiritual truth), Herbert makes the stained-glass windows in a church a metaphor for the believer. It is important to note that most stained-glass windows depict stories in the Bible. In medieval times, when most people didn't read, they learned about Christ and the Bible from oral and visual storytelling, through a priest and the stained-glass windows, respectively.

Knowing this background, we can understand how Herbert wanted his actual life to become a living picture that displayed God's glory. To use the metaphor, he wanted to become a window for God. But he didn't want to be one that was "wat'rish, bleak, and thin." He desired to be a window full of color and light. He wanted to be permanently "annealed"—that is, to have the colors burned into his very being as an artisan burns colors into glass. In this way, the poet himself—not just his words—would be a permanent story of God's glory. May we have the same aspiration!

Yes, dear friends, we are already God's children, and we can't even imagine what we will be like when Christ returns. But we do know that when he comes we will be like him, for we will see him as he really is. And all who believe this will keep themselves pure, just as Christ is pure. 1 John 3:2-3

As Kingfishers Catch Fire

As kingfishers catch fire, dragonflies draw flame;
As tumbled over rim in roundy wells
Stones ring; like each tucked string tells, each hung bell's
Bow swung finds tongue to fling out broad its name;
Each mortal thing does one thing and the same:
Deals out that being indoors each one dwells;
Selves—goes itself; myself it speaks and spells,
Crying What I do is me: for that I came.

Í say more: the just man justices;
Keeps gráce: thát keeps all his goings graces;
Acts in God's eye what in God's eye he is—
Chríst. For Christ plays in ten thousand places,
Lovely in limbs, and lovely in eyes not his
To the Father through the features of men's faces.

GERARD MANLEY HOPKINS (1844–1889)

HOPKINS'S poetry is a study of the inner nature of living beings as expressed by their outward appearance. To communicate this concept, he coined the word *inscape* for that individually distinctive form that makes up the essential nature of each being. Hopkins wasn't content to study living beings and their nature for study's sake. He desired to find the one unique characteristic of each creature that would tell him more about God and his character. As Hopkins himself put it, when speaking of a bluebell: "I know the beauty of our Lord by it."

"As Kingfishers Catch Fire" is an excellent example of Hopkins's philosophy. Here he focuses on the revelation that aspects of Christ's nature can be seen in animals and humans. "As kingfishers catch fire, dragonflies draw flame" is a fluid description of these creatures' movements—as if one caught a glimpse of them in quick flight. The kingfisher, a brightly colored bird, looks like it's on fire as it flashes by. So also the dragonfly. Hopkins doesn't make explicit what aspect of Christ's nature he saw in these beings. Perhaps he thought again of the beauty of the Lord or how God as Spirit might look as he moves. Whatever the case may be, the most important thought comes in the second stanza. Hopkins says that we should see Christ in justified humans (that is, Christians). Thus, redeemed humans are a kind of ongoing incarnation, giving great enjoyment to the Father: *"Christ plays in ten thousand places, lovely in limbs, and lovely in eyes not his to the Father through the features of men's faces."*

➻ *According to my earnest expectation and my hope, that in nothing I shall be ashamed, but that with all boldness, as always, so now also Christ shall be magnified in my body, whether it be by life, or by death.* Philippians 1:20, KJV

Epithalamium

The voice that breathed o'er Eden,
That earliest wedding-day,
The primal marriage blessing,
It hath not passed away.

Still in the pure espousal
Of Christian man and maid
The Holy Three are with us,
The threefold grace is said,

For dower of blessed children,
For love and faith's sweet sake,
For high mysterious union
Which naught on earth may break.

Be present, Holy Father,
To give away this bride,
As Eve Thou gav'st to Adam
Out of his piercèd side.

Be present, Holy Jesus,
To join their loving hands,
As Thou didst bind two natures
In Thine eternal bands.

Be present, Holy Spirit,
To bless them as they kneel,
As Thou for Christ the Bridegroom
The heavenly spouse dost seal.

O spread Thy pure wings o'er them!
Let no ill power find place,
When onward through life's journey
The hallowed path they trace,

To cast their crowns before Thee,
In perfect sacrifice,
Till to the home of gladness
With Christ's own bride they rise.

JOHN KEBLE (1792–1866)

JOHN KEBLE, a notable Oxford scholar, was a leading figure in the Oxford movement of 1833, in which several young men strongly criticized the Church of England for doctrinal indifference. Keble's participation in the movement cost him a professorship. Keble spent the rest of his life in rural ministries, chiefly in the parish of Hursley. His personal devotional life, faithful visitation, teaching of the parishioners, and attentiveness to the church services provided a model of the Oxford movement's principles.

During these years he wrote many poems. This one celebrates God's presence at a Christian wedding. The title "Epithalamium" denotes a song or poem composed for a bride and bridegroom. Keble blesses three "marriages" in this poem: the first man and woman (Adam and Eve), who received God's blessings; the Christian marriage; and the marriage of Christ and his bride, the church. God's presence is alive in them all.

The poet also invokes the Holy Trinity—Father, Son, and Spirit—to bless the marriage from its inception to its consummation. As the triune God will show himself faithful to them, so they should be faithful to each other and to the Lord. For those who are about to get married or who are already married, this is a perfect "epithalamium."

You husbands must love your wives with the same love Christ showed the church. He gave up his life for her. Ephesians 5:25

Consider the Lilies of the Field

Flowers preach to us if we will hear:—
The rose saith in the dewy morn:
I am most fair;
Yet all my loveliness is born
Upon a thorn.
The poppy saith amid the corn:
Let but my scarlet head appear
And I am held in scorn;
Yet juice of subtle virtue lies
Within my cup of curious dyes.
The lilies say: Behold how we
Preach without words of purity.
The violets whisper from the shade
Which their own leaves have made:
Men scent our fragrance on the air,
Yet take no heed
Of humble lessons we would read.

But not alone the fairest flowers:
The merest grass
Along the roadside where we pass,
Lichen and moss and sturdy weed,
Tell of His love who sends the dew,
The rain and sunshine too,
To nourish one small seed.

CHRISTINA ROSSETTI (1830–1894)

THIS POEM praises the God of creation, who gives rain and sunshine to everything. From the rose, poppy, and lily to the lichen, moss, and weed—God cares for them all.

Of course, we are familiar with Jesus' words about the lilies: "Why worry about your clothes? Look at the lilies and how they grow. They don't work or make their clothing, yet Solomon in all his glory was not dressed as beautifully as they are. And if God cares so wonderfully for flowers that are here today and gone tomorrow, won't he more surely care for you? You have so little faith!" (Matthew 6:28-30). These words apply not only to lilies but to every single seed on earth.

We may wonder—with all the things to care about throughout the universe—why God concerns himself with the welfare of flowers. The answer is found in Genesis 1, where we read six times, "And God saw that it was good" (vv. 4, 10, 12, 18, 21, 25). From this we can surmise that God took delight in what he created. The apex of his creation was humanity. Therefore, if he cares about the flowers, providing "rain and sunshine . . . to nourish one small seed," he most certainly cares about us.

Your heavenly Father already knows all your needs, and he will give you all you need from day to day if you live for him and make the Kingdom of God your primary concern. Matthew 6:32b-33

The Reflection PART ONE

Lord, art thou at the table head above
Meat, med'cine, sweetness, sparkling beauties, to
Enamor souls with flaming flakes of love,
And not my trencher, nor my cup o'erflow?
Ben't I a bidden guest? Oh! sweat mine eye:
O'erflow with tears: Oh! draw thy fountains dry.

Shall I not smell thy sweet, oh! Sharon's rose?
Shall not mine eye salute thy beauty? Why?
Shall thy sweet leaves their beauteous sweets upclose?
As half ashamed my sight should on them lie?
Woe's me! For this my sighs shall be in grain,
Offered on sorrow's altar for the same.

Had not my soul's, thy conduit, pipes stopped been
With mud, what ravishment would'st thou convey?

Let grace's golden spade dig till the spring
Of tears arise, and clears this filth away.
Lord, let thy spirit raise my sighings till
These pipes my soul do with thy sweetness fill.

(continued in next day's reading)

EDWARD TAYLOR (1642–1729)

EDWARD TAYLOR was a metaphysical poet who wrote in the tradition of George Herbert. He was also the first American poet, but this recognition did not come until the twentieth century, when someone discovered his poetry in the Yale University library. His most well-known volume is *Preparatory Meditations,* a collection of more than two hundred spiritual meditations written in preparation for the Lord's Supper. "The Reflection" is one of those poems.

As a metaphysical poet, Taylor used physical objects to depict spiritual realities. In this section the poet laments that he can't partake of any of the Lord's gracious riches because he (the poet) has no capacity for them. It is not that he doesn't want the "meat, med'cine, sweetness, [and] sparkling beauties" the Lord has to offer, but that he is full of sin and therefore can't receive anything from the Lord: "Had not my soul's, thy conduit, pipes stopped been with mud, what ravishment would'st thou convey?"

Consequently, the poet calls upon the Lord to be his "trencher"—to dig away all the filth so his conduits can fill with God's rich, sweet graces:

Let grace's golden spade dig till the spring
Of tears arise, and clears this filth away.
Lord, let thy spirit raise my sighings till
These pipes my soul do with thy sweetness fill.

Though this language may be unfamiliar to us, the experience isn't. Often we come to the Lord and cannot receive from him because we are "clogged up" with sin or self-absorption. A good, cleansing "cry" in the presence of the Lord clears away the filth and allows us to enjoy his sweet graces.

For [the Lord] satisfies the thirsty, and fills the hungry with good things. Psalm 107:9

Earth once was paradise of heaven below,
Till ink-faced sin had it with poison stocked;
And chased this paradise away into
Heaven's upmost loft, and it in glory locked.
But thou, sweet Lord, has with thy golden key
Unlocked the door, and made a golden day.

Once at thy feast, I saw the pearl-like stand
'Tween heaven and earth, where heaven's bright glory all
In streams fell on thee, as a floodgate and
Like sunbeams through thee on the world to fall.
Oh! Sugar-sweet then! My dear sweet Lord, I see
Saints' heaven-lost happiness restored by thee.

Shall heaven and earth's bright glory all up lie,
Like sunbeams bundled in the sun in thee?
Dost thou sit rose at table head, where I
Do sit, and carv'st no morsel sweet for me?
So much before, so little now! Sprindge,[a] *Lord,*
Thy rosy leaves, and me their glee afford.

Shall not thy rose my garden fresh perfume?
Shall not thy beauty my dull heart assail?
Shall not thy golden gleams run through this gloom?
Shall my black velvet mask thy fair face veil?
Pass o'er my faults: shine forth, bright sun; arise!
Enthrone thy rosy self within mine eyes.

EDWARD TAYLOR (1642–1729)

[a]to spring

IN THIS POEM Taylor draws upon several images that center around the feast of the coming kingdom, when paradise will be restored. At this time the believers will enjoy the Lord as the divine perfume, divine radiance, and glorious host at the feast. According to Taylor's theology, when humans sinned, paradise left earth and returned to heaven locked away from humanity. Only Christ has the key, and in the coming kingdom, he will open paradise so we can enjoy him forever.

The greatest joy we have to look forward to is that we will be transformed completely into the image of Christ. John said: "We will be like him, for we will see him as he really is" (1 John 3:2). For now, we look at our reflections and see ourselves as sinners—our black velvet mask veils his fair face. But one day all our faults will be taken care of, and we will see Jesus as we look at our reflections: "Pass o'er my faults: shine forth, bright sun; arise! Enthrone thy rosy self within mine eyes."

➻ *[Jesus said,] "Anyone who is willing to hear should listen to the Spirit and understand what the Spirit is saying to the churches. Everyone who is victorious will eat from the tree of life in the paradise of God."* Revelation 2:7

On Jacob's Purchase

How poor was Jacob's motion, and how strange
His offer! How unequal was th' exchange!
A mess of porridge for inheritance?
Why could not hungry Esau strive t' enhance
His price a little? So much underfoot?
Well might he give him bread and drink to boot:
An easy price! The case is even our own;
For toys we often sell our Heaven, our Crown.

FRANCIS QUARLES (1592–1644)

THERE seems to be no end of Bible stories in which someone does something stupid. For example, Abraham sold Sarah; Sarah laughed at God; the sons of Israel sold Joseph. In today's poem Quarles focuses on one such story, in essence asking, "How could Esau be so stupid?"

Genesis 25:27-34 tells us that one day Esau returned home from hunting, tired and hungry. He noticed that his brother, Jacob, was cooking stew and demanded a bowl of it. Jacob, whose name means "he grasps the heel," agreed to give him one for a price—that price was Esau's birthright.

In ancient times a birthright was of great importance. It belonged to the firstborn son and meant that he would become the head of the family and receive a double portion of his parents' possessions when they passed on. For Esau to sell such a right wasn't smart. Quarles sums up this transaction succinctly: "How unequal was th' exchange! A mess of porridge for inheritance?"

Lest we think we are smarter than Esau and wouldn't make such a foolish choice, Quarles concludes his poem arguing, "The case is even our own; for toys we often sell our Heaven, our Crown." How often do we as Christians try to trade our birthright as children of God for the temporary things of this world? How often do we allow immediate needs or desires to entice us to sell what is most valuable? As Jesus said, "People need more than bread for their life; they must feed on every word of God" (Matthew 4:4). "You cannot serve both God and money" (Matthew 6:24). What toys do you value more than your crown? What toys do you need to sell for heaven?

Then Jacob gave Esau some bread and lentil stew. Esau ate and drank and went on about his business, indifferent to the fact that he had given up his birthright. Genesis 25:34

The Bunch of Grapes

Joy, I did lock thee up: but some bad man
Hath let thee out again:
And now, me thinks, I am where I began
Seven years ago: one vogue and vain,
One air of thoughts usurps my brain.
I did toward Canaan draw; but now I am
Brought back to the Red sea, the sea of shame.

For as the Jews of old by God's command
Traveled, and saw no town:
So now each Christian hath his journeys spanned:
Their story pens and sets us down.
A single deed is small renown.
God's works are wide, and let in future times;
His ancient justice overflows our crimes.

Then have we too our guardian fires and clouds;
Our Scripture-dew drops fast:
We have our sands and serpents, tents and shrouds;
Alas! our murmurings come not last.
But where's the cluster? where's the taste
Of mine inheritance? Lord, if I must borrow,
Let me as well take up their joy, as sorrow.

But can he want the grape, who hath the wine?
I have their fruit and more.
Blessed be God, who prospered Noah's vine,
And made it bring forth grapes good store.
But much more him I must adore,
Who of the law's sour juice sweet wine did make,
Even God himself, being pressed for my sake.

GEORGE HERBERT (1593–1633)

PAUL was at the end of his life's journey and wrote to Timothy: "I have fought a good fight, I have finished the race, and I have remained faithful" (2 Timothy 4:7). We all will arrive there someday. As Herbert says in today's poem, this is a journey not unlike Israel's exodus across Sinai. But instead of pillars of cloud and fire to guide us, we have Scripture and the Spirit; in place of manna we have the Word of God; sand and serpents vex us in the common troubles and ills of life; and life seems as temporary as a tent. And yes, like Israel, we murmur almost from beginning to end.

Have you ever asked, "OK, Lord, where is the reward? What is in this for me? You gave Israel that huge cluster of grapes as an incentive to continue the journey into the Promised Land. How about giving *me* something like that?" This is not uncommon. At such times it is prudent to remember that you are not living in Old Testament times. Since the advent, death, and resurrection of Jesus Christ, believers' rewards are not physical.

This is why Herbert makes a distinction between the grapes and the wine. God was "pressed" on the cross in the person of Jesus Christ. Our reward in this age is the sweet taste of that which Jesus accomplished there. The human journey today is much the same as in past millennia. The difference is that we may enjoy the ineffable effects of redemption.

So they went up and explored the land from the wilderness of Zin as far as Rehob, near Lebo-hamath. . . . When they came to what is now known as the valley of Eshcol, they cut down a cluster of grapes so large that it took two of them to carry it on a pole between them! They also took samples of the pomegranates and figs. Numbers 13:21, 23

Give Ear, O Heavens, . . .

Give ear, O heavens, to that which I declare;
And hear, O earth, what my mouth's sayings are.

Drop down as doth the rain shall my doctrine;
Distill as dew so shall my speech divine,

As on the tender herb the small rain pours,
And as upon the grass the greater showers,

For I Jehovah's name proclaim abroad;
O give ye greatness unto him our God.

Do ye Jehovah in this wise regard,
O foolish folk, and wanting wise regard?

Thy Father, that hath brought thee, is not he?
Hath he not made thee and established thee?

Remember thou the days that were of old;
Mind ye the years of ages manifold;

Ask thou thy Father, and thee show will he;
Thine elders ask, and they will tell it thee.

HENRY AINSWORTH (1571–1622)

HENRY AINSWORTH was an English Separatist clergyman and scholar. He moved to Amsterdam in 1593, where he taught a Separatist congregation and drew up a confession of faith for the Separatist (Puritan) movement (1596). Ainsworth was a noted Hebrew scholar and author of *Annotations* on several Old Testament books.

Today's poem is Ainsworth's version of Deuteronomy 32:1-7—the beginning phrases of the Song of Moses (32:1-43). It is a poetic recitation of the history and future of Israel.

Before you read Moses' song, review its preface in 32:24-29. Scripture says that Moses wrote the entire law in a book. He then placed that book by the ark of the covenant as a witness against the people. Notice that the law is not a witness *for* Israel. It does not tell what they have done right. Nor was it in the tabernacle as an instruction book on living by biblical principals. These are not God's intentions for the law.

The law is a witness *against* us in the court of God's justice. Over and over again the law says: "All have sinned; all fall short of God's glorious standard" (Romans 3:23).

The tragic mistake of Christians through the centuries is to assume that they could live in a manner pleasing to God. Are you trying to do this? Well, listen to the good news: "The law of Moses could not save us, because of our sinful nature. . . . God destroyed sin's control over us by giving his Son as a sacrifice for our sins. *He did this so that the requirement of the law would be fully accomplished for us*" (Romans 8:3-4, italics added). This is why we believe in Christ. This is what our Father has shown us.

Listen, O heavens, and I will speak! Hear, O earth, the words that I say! My teaching will fall on you like rain; my speech will settle like dew. My words will fall like rain on tender grass, like gentle showers on young plants. Deuteronomy 32:1-2

The Call of the Christian PART ONE

Not always as the whirlwind's rush
On Horeb's mount of fear,
Not always as the burning bush
To Midian's shepherd seer,
Nor as the awful voice which came
To Israel's prophet bards,
Nor as the tongues of cloven flame,
Nor gift of fearful words,—

Not always thus, with outward sign
Of fire or voice from Heaven,
The message of a truth divine,
The call of God is given!
Awaking in the human heart
Love for the true and right,—
Zeal for the Christian's better part,
Strength for the Christian's fight.

Nor unto manhood's heart alone
The holy influence steals:
Warm with a rapture not its own,
The heart of woman feels!
As she who by Samaria's wall
The Saviour's errand sought,—
As those who with the fervent Paul
And meek Aquila wrought:

Or those meek ones whose martyrdom
Rome's gathered grandeur saw:
Or those who in their Alpine home
Braved the Crusader's war,
When the green Vaudois, trembling, heard,
Through all its vales of death,
The martyr's song of triumph poured
From woman's failing breath.

(continued in next day's reading)

JOHN GREENLEAF WHITTIER (1807–1892)

WHITTIER'S poetry often reflects his Christian piety in the tradition of the Quakers. One of the Quakers' more prominent traditions is receiving God's call, which comes to them in times of silence and meditation.

In this poem Whittier explores the many ways God calls people to his service. This call has come in extraordinary ways: in a whirlwind on Mt. Horeb to the Israelites, in a burning bush to Moses, in an awe-inspiring voice to the prophets, and in flaming tongues to those assembled on the day of Pentecost. But these are the unusual manifestations of God's call—as Whittier puts it in the second stanza:

Not always thus, with outward sign
Of fire or voice from Heaven,
The message of a truth divine,
The call of God is given!

The more common way God calls people is simply to awaken the human heart and thereby enliven the person with "love for the true and right,—zeal for the Christian's better part, strength for the Christian's fight."

The "holy influence" (divine call) doesn't come just to men. The poet speaks of the Samaritan woman, who told her whole town about Jesus the Savior (see John 4), and of Priscilla (wife of Aquila), who was Paul's coworker in spreading the gospel. The poet also includes the female martyrs among the Waldensians, who were slaughtered along with the men for their Protestant-like faith (see "On the Late Massacre in Piedmont," May 17).

Whether God calls to us from a whirlwind or with a tug on our heart, we need to listen and obey. When we hear his voice, we can answer the call to serve him, no matter where he leads us or what we experience as the result.

God loves you dearly, and he has called you to be his very own people. Romans 1:7

And gently, by a thousand things
Which o'er our spirits pass,
Like breezes o'er the harp's fine strings,
Or vapors o'er a glass,
Leaving their token strange and new
Of music or of shade,
The summons to the right and true
And merciful is made.

Oh, then, if gleams of truth and light
Flash o'er thy waiting mind,
Unfolding to thy mental sight
The wants of human-kind;
If, brooding over human grief,
The earnest wish is known
To soothe and gladden with relief
An anguish not thine own;

Though heralded with naught of fear,
Or outward sign or show;
Though only to the inward ear
It whispers soft and low;
Though dropping, as the manna fell,
Unseen, yet from above,
Noiseless as dew-fall, heed it well,—
Thy Father's call of love!

JOHN GREENLEAF WHITTIER (1807–1892)

THE SECOND part of this poem continues the theme of how God calls people. But it also endeavors to proclaim why God calls us.

God's call touches the hearts of people in a thousand different ways because God relates to each person individually. But the call usually comes "gently," not forcefully—God never forces anyone to serve him. It stirs the human spirit like a breeze moving on the strings of a harp. It comes like the invisible dew (or vapors) of the morning, leaving its covering (or shade) upon everything it touches. This touch of the Spirit produces music in the heart that cannot be ignored. Those who hear it will respond.

This call upon the soul is also an illumination, an enlightenment that gives the receiver insight concerning the needs of humanity:

Oh, then, if gleams of truth and light
Flash o'er thy waiting mind,
Unfolding to thy mental sight
The wants of human-kind.

Whittier also points out that the call doesn't just enlighten those who hear it. It motivates people to action. It moves people outside themselves to see the hurts and needs of others and to offer them relief.

May we hear God's call—even when it comes to us softly and lowly—and "heed it well." For it is the "Father's call of love." How could we dare ignore it?

Therefore I [Paul], a prisoner for serving the Lord, beg you to lead a life worthy of your calling, for you have been called by God. Be humble and gentle. Be patient with each other, making allowance for each other's faults because of your love. Always keep yourselves united in the Holy Spirit, and bind yourselves together with peace. Ephesians 4:1-3

Expectation

Lord Jesus, source of every grace,
Glorious in light divine,
Soon shall we see Thee face to face,
And in that glory shine;

Be ever with Thee, hear Thy voice,
Unhindered then shall taste
The love which doth our hearts rejoice,
Though absent in this waste.

In peaceful wonder we adore
The thoughts of Love divine,
Which in that world for evermore
Our lot with Thine entwine!

JOHN NELSON DARBY (1800–1882)

DARBY was a gifted leader of the Brethren movement and a prolific writer. In this poem he expresses his anticipation of being with Christ in glory. After Jesus entered into glory, he didn't just wait around for his followers to arrive. Instead, he came back to earth in the Spirit to be with those who love him and to lead them into glory.

Hebrews 2:10-12 tells us that Jesus is in the midst of the church, dwelling with those whom he unashamedly calls his brothers and sisters. It's impossible for our finite minds to comprehend how Jesus can be both in heaven and in the midst of the church simultaneously. But it is the truth—verified by Scripture and by our experience. Before Jesus left this world to return to the Father, he repeatedly told the disciples that he would be with them (see Matthew 18:20; 28:20; John 14:18). He also promised that his followers would share in his glory: "Father, I want these whom you've given me to be with me, so they can see my glory. You gave me the glory because you loved me even before the world began!" (John 17:24).

Jesus, the one in our midst, leads us to where he has already gone—into the glorious presence of the Father. The path to that glorious destiny is the one the Lord himself traveled. He left a pattern for us to follow, a mold for us to conform to. Each believer, if he or she is to grow and mature, must become more like Christ. The Father wills it because he desires that all his children reach maturity and so bear the image of his beloved Son.

It was only right that God—who made everything and for whom everything was made—should bring his many children into glory. Through the suffering of Jesus, God made him a perfect leader, one fit to bring them into their salvation. Hebrews 2:10

The Rapture

Sweet infancy!
O fire of Heaven! O sacred light!
How fair and bright!
How great am I,
Whom all the world doth magnify!

O heavenly joy!
O great and sacred blessedness,
Which I possess!
So great a joy
Who did into my arms convey!

From God above
Being sent, the Heavens me enflame,
To praise his Name.
The stars do move!
The burning sun doth show his love.

O how divine
Am I! To all this sacred wealth,
This life and health,
Who raised? Who mine
Did make the same? What hand divine!

THOMAS TRAHERNE (1637–1674)

TRAHERNE'S excitement about the Rapture overflows in this celebratory and vibrant poem. Because the poet uses vague language, we can read this poem as either a celebration of Christ's rapture or of the Christian's rapture. It's probably a mingling of both, for it is because of Christ's rapture into heaven (his ascension) that Christians will also ascend just as he did. As such, the "I" of this poem could be Christ speaking or the poet, representing all others who hope for the Rapture.

The concept of the Rapture comes from the apostle Paul's writings, especially his epistles to the Thessalonians. There Paul proclaimed that all believers—both dead and living—would experience the Rapture. Christians who have died await the Resurrection and Rapture, when they will be taken up from earth to be with the Lord forever. Though their spirits are with the Lord now, they are waiting for new, glorified bodies, which they will receive just before they are raptured. Those Christians who are alive at the time of Christ's return will receive new, transfigured bodies and ascend to the Lord in the air.

When you think about it, it's nearly unbelievable. However, since this happened to Jesus, it will also happen to us who believe in him and hope for his return.

The Lord himself will come down from heaven with a commanding shout, with the call of the archangel, and with the trumpet call of God. First, all the Christians who have died will rise from their graves. Then, together with them, we who are still alive and remain on the earth will be caught up in the clouds to meet the Lord in the air and remain with him forever. 1 Thessalonians 4:16-17

The Collar

I struck the board, and cried, No more.
I will abroad.
What? shall I ever sigh and pine?
My lines and life are free; free as the road,
Loose as the wind, as large as store.
Shall I be still in suit?
Have I no harvest but a thorn
To let me blood, and not restore
What I have lost with cordial fruit?
Sure there was wine
Before my sighs did dry it; there was corn
Before my tears did drown it.
Is the year only lost to me?
Have I no bays[a] *to crown it,*
No flowers, no garlands gay? All blasted?
All wasted?
Not so, my heart: but there is fruit,
And thou hast hands.
Recover all thy sigh-blown age
On double pleasures: leave thy cold dispute
Of what is fit, and not. Forsake thy cage,
Thy rope of sands,
Which petty thoughts have made, and made to thee
Good cable, to enforce and draw,
And be thy law,
While thou dost wink and wouldst not see.
Away; take heed:
I will abroad.
Call in thy death's head there: tie up thy fears.
He that forbears
To suit and serve his need,
Deserves his load.
But as I raved and grew more fierce and wild
At every word,
Me thoughts I heard one calling, Child:
And I replied, My Lord.

GEORGE HERBERT (1593–1633)

[a]laurel, as in a crown given to a victorious athlete

COUNTRY minister wasn't George Herbert's first choice of profession. He had held positions in public office until his benefactors—including King James I—died. In 1630 he became the minister of a village parish at Bemerton. His small book on the duties of his new life, *A Priest to the Temple,* or *The Country Prison* (1652), testifies to the earnestness and uneasiness with which he embraced his new role. In chronic bad health, Herbert spent his final three years at Bemerton performing pastoral duties, while writing and revising his poems.

Nearly all of Herbert's poetry is included in *The Temple* (1633). The second section of the book, called "The Church," explores the relationship between Christ and man. This is where "The Collar" is found. It is a personal unveiling of a minister's frustration with his position—wherein the minister wants to rebel and throw off his "collar" (a dual symbol of clergy and bondage) but ultimately submits once again to Jesus, calling him "my Lord."

Throughout the poem images depict freedom from bondage. The poet felt trapped in a cage, tied to his ecclesiastical rope and collar. He knew he could give it up and use his hands and mind to make a living for himself rather than live in poverty and dependence on his congregation. Yet this desire for freedom was only temporary. Ultimately, he knew that servitude to Christ is true liberty. Interestingly enough, the poet felt at liberty to make this full complaint out loud to the Lord, who listened all the while and then calmed his child.

[Jesus said] "Take my yoke upon you. Let me teach you, because I am humble and gentle, and you will find rest for your souls. For my yoke fits perfectly, and the burden I give you is light." Matthew 11:29-30

Self-Acquaintance

Dear Lord! accept a sinful heart,
Which of itself complains,
And mourns, with much and frequent smart,
The evil it contains.

There fiery seeds of anger lurk,
Which often hurt my frame;
And wait but for the tempter's work
To fan them to a flame.

Legality holds out a bribe
To purchase life from Thee;
And discontent would fain prescribe
How Thou shalt deal with me.

While unbelief withstands thy grace,
And puts the mercy by,
Presumption, with a brow of bass,
Says, 'Give me, or I die!'

How eager are my thoughts to roam
In quest of what they love!
But ah! when duty calls them home,
How heavily they move!

Oh, cleanse me in a Saviour's blood,
Transform me by thy power,
And make me Thy belov'd abode,
And let me roam no more.

WILLIAM COWPER (1731–1800)

COWPER'S *Poems* (1782) consists chiefly of delicate satire and didactic works. Titles in that volume include "Charity," which shows what humanity has made out of God's creation; "Truth," a sermon on grace; and "Expostulation," which exhorts the English to avoid the downfall that had overtaken God's "chosen people." The publication of *The Task* (1785) established Cowper's reputation as a poet. He was considered for the laureateship in 1788 but declined the honor.

"Self-Acquaintance" is an honest confession of one who strongly desired to be a dwelling place for the Lord's presence. He knew himself—his weaknesses, his faults, and his sins. So he asked for cleansing, renewal, and transformation so the Lord could dwell in him without any hindrance.

May we strive to know ourselves this well and confess all of our weaknesses to Christ, who can cleanse and renew us.

[Jesus said] "Those who obey my commandments are the ones who love me. And because they love me, my Father will love them, and I will love them. And I will reveal myself to each one of them. . . . All those who love me will do what I say. My Father will love them, and we will come to them and live with them." John 14:21, 23

Church Lock-and-Key

Give me my captive soul, or take
My body also thither.
Another lift like this will make
Them both to be together.

Before that sin turned flesh to stone,
And all our lump to leaven,
A fervent sigh might well have blown
Our innocent earth to heaven.

For sure when Adam did not know
To sin, or sin to smother,
He might to heav'n from Paradise go,
As from one room t'another.

Thou hast restored us to this ease
By this thy heav'nly blood,
Which I can go to, when I please,
And leave th'earth to their food.

George Herbert (1593–1633)

WHAT was life like before Adam and Eve sinned? Perfect? Peaceful? Fulfilling? While we can dream up many ideas of what Paradise might have been like, we will undoubtedly miss much of what it really was. In this poem, found in the second section of *The Temple,* Herbert discusses an interesting idea about this pre-Fall state.

"Church Lock-and-Key" is essentially about two transports that Herbert looks forward to—the first of his soul to heaven, the next of his body. However, he speculates that the two transports may never have been necessary if Adam hadn't sinned. Herbert surmises that Adam could have gone body and soul from Paradise to heaven "as from one room t'another." And "Before that sin turned flesh to stone, . . . a fervent sigh might well have blown our innocent earth to heaven."

Despite this loss, Herbert still had access to heaven *now* because of the shed blood of Jesus. This is the same spiritual access that all believers enjoy today—that is, those who worship God in spirit. But the two transports remain. So when we die, our soul will enter Christ's presence, as our body awaits the Resurrection.

Every human being has an earthly body just like Adam's, but our heavenly bodies will be just like Christ's. Just as we are now like Adam, the man of the earth, so we will someday be like Christ, the man from heaven. 1 Corinthians 15:48-49

Carrion Comfort

Not, I'll not, carrion comfort, Despair, not feast on thee,
Not untwist—slack they may be—these last strands of man
In me ór, most weary, cry I can no more. I can;
Can something, hope, wish day come, not choose not to be.

But ah, but O thou terrible, why wouldst thou rude on me
Thy wring-world[a] *right foot rock? lay a lionlimb against me? scan*
With darksome devouring eyes my bruisèd bones? and fan,
O in turns of tempest, me heaped there; me frantic to avoid thee and flee?

Why? That my chaff might fly; my grain lie, sheer and clear.
Nay in all that toil, that coil, since (seems) I kissed the rod,
Hand rather, my heart lo! lapped strength, stole joy, would laugh, chéer.
Cheer whom though? The Hero whose heaven-handling flung me, fóot tród[b]
Me? or me that fought him? O which one? is it each one? That night, that year
Of now done darkness I wretch lay wrestling with (my God!) my God.

GERARD MANLEY HOPKINS (1844–1889)

[a]The poet asks God why he is kicking him. [b]The poet claims that God has walked over him.

HOPKINS showed his poetic talent in 1875, when he composed his first great poem, "The Wreck of the Deutschland." During his last years he wrote many more excellent poems, including "Carrion Comfort," which reflects Hopkins's faith as a powerful source of comfort in times of trial.

Leaning on this comfort, Hopkins refuses to give in to despair. "I'll not, carrion comfort"; that is, he will not devour God's comfort like a scavenger consumes a carcass. Even though he feels himself unraveling like a strand of thread or rope, he will not allow himself to fall apart completely. Instead, he will hope and wish for the day when his trial comes to an end.

Then Hopkins—in great irony—questions God. He believes that God has given him more than he can handle and shockingly concludes that his trial has been a wrestling match with God himself. But he refuses to give in, as he wrestles with a God whom he needs and yet tries to flee (as in the story of Jacob in Genesis 32:22-32). What a paradox!

How often are we tempted to give up in the midst of trials? How often do we run from God—believing he has given us more than we can handle—while at the same time seeking his comfort? Let us not be fickle in our devotion to God, accepting his comfort but not his correction.

You can be sure that the more we suffer for Christ, the more God will shower us with his comfort through Christ. 2 Corinthians 1:5

Preface to *Pilgrim's Progress* PART ONE

When at the first I took my pen in hand,
Thus for to write, I did not understand
That I at all should make a little book
In such a mode; nay, I had undertook
To make another, which when almost done,
Before I was aware, I this begun.
And thus it was: I writing of the way
And race of saints in this our Gospel-day,
Fell suddenly into an allegory
About their journey, and the way to glory,
In more than twenty things, which I set down;
This done, I twenty more had in my crown,
And they again began to multiply,
Like sparks that from the coals of fire do fly.
Nay, then, thought I, if that you breed so fast,
I'll put you by yourselves, lest you at last
Should prove ad infinitum, and eat out
The book that I already am about.
Well, so I did; but yet I did not think
To show to all the world my pen and ink
In such a mode; I only thought to make
I knew not what, nor did I undertake
Thereby to please my neighbour; no, not I,
I did it mine own self to gratify.
Neither did I but vacant seasons spend
In this my scribble, nor did I intend
But to divert myself in doing this,
From worser thoughts which make me do amiss.
Thus I set pen to paper with delight,
And quickly had my thoughts in black and white.
For having now my method by the end,
Still as I pulled it came, and so I penned
It down, until it came at last to be
For length and breadth the bigness which you see.

(continued in next day's reading)

JOHN BUNYAN (1628–1688)

THE MAN who penned *Pilgrim's Progress* has a tale worth telling. Born in Bedfordshire, England, Bunyan was a tinker—a mender of household utensils. Shortly after his marriage, he became a zealous Christian and began preaching the gospel. News that the once-blaspheming tinker had turned preacher drew large crowds. But in 1660 the government outlawed Nonconformist congregations, closing meeting houses and requiring believers to attend their parish church. Bunyan defied the law and continued to preach in barns, private homes, the countryside, or church. He was arrested in November of that same year, while on his way to conduct a religious service near Bedford, and imprisoned for several years.

During his imprisonment, Bunyan wrote several books; the most noteworthy are *Grace Abounding to the Chief of Sinners* (1666) and *Pilgrim's Progress* (1678). He introduced *Pilgrim's Progress* with a long poetical preface, in which he explains how and why he wrote this work. Bunyan tells his readers that he did not originally intend to write an allegory about the saints' "journey, and the way to glory." But as he began to write about the "race of saints in this our Gospel-day," it suddenly came to him that he should present this "race" as an allegory. All at once, a hundred ideas filled his head, which he hurried to write down. These came to him "like sparks that from the coals of fire do fly." Writing at a furious pace as a man divinely inspired, he created one of the greatest Christian classics—*Pilgrim's Progress.*

Jesus told him, "I am the way, the truth, and the life. No one can come to the Father except through me." John 14:6

Preface to *Pilgrim's Progress* PART TWO

Well, when I had thus put mine ends together,
I show'd them others that I might see whether
They would condemn them, or them justify:
And some said, 'let them live'; some, 'let them die':
Some said, 'John, print it'; others said, 'not so':
Some said, 'it might do good'; others said, 'no'.
Now was I in a strait, and did not see
Which was the best thing to be done by me:
At last I thought, since you are thus divided,
I print it will, and so the case decided.
For, thought I, some I see would have it done,
Though others in that channel do not run.
To prove then who advised for the best,
Thus I thought fit to put it to the test.
I further thought, if now I did deny
Those that would have it thus, to gratify,
I did not know, but hinder them I might,
Of that which would to them be great delight.
For those that were not for its coming forth,
I said to them, offend you I am loth;
Yet since your brethren pleased with it be,
Forbear to judge, till you do further see.
If that thou wilt not read, let it alone;
Some love the meat, some love to pick the bone:
Yea, that I might them better palliate,
I did too with them thus expostulate.

(continued in next day's reading)

JOHN BUNYAN (1628–1688)

IN THIS part of the preface Bunyan addresses his critics. Any writer who has suffered criticism will appreciate this line: "Some love the meat, some love to pick the bone." There is no escape from criticism! All a writer can do is provide the best meal for his readers. Those who are fed by it enjoy "the meat," while those who aren't simply pick the bones.

As Bunyan points out in his preface, readers will hail or condemn written works, depending on their point of view. When Bunyan showed his work to various people, he received mixed responses. Some said that the work should be "printed" because "it might do good." Others condemned it and said, "let them [the words] die."

Authors must have a good deal of boldness and courage when they put something into print, because critics will either crown the work or crucify it. Very few authors can separate acclaim or criticism of their work from their person. It is only natural for an author to feel personally attacked when someone criticizes his or her work.

If we are honest with ourselves, we will admit that we feel this way about anything we do. We prefer praise to criticism. When we receive the latter, we need grace to respond appropriately. Fortunately, God will provide the grace we need to act in a way that pleases him (Hebrews 4:15-16).

The next time someone criticizes your work, say to yourself, "It is my work that is being criticized, not me. My work can benefit from the criticism." Then ask God to grant you the grace to improve what is lacking and to respond appropriately.

Now this is an allegory: these women are two covenants. One woman, in fact, is Hagar, from Mount Sinai, bearing children for slavery. Now Hagar is Mount Sinai in Arabia and corresponds to the present Jerusalem, for she is in slavery with her children. But the other woman corresponds to the Jerusalem above; she is free, and she is our mother. Galatians 4:24-26, NRSV

May I not write in such a style as this?
In such a method too, and yet not miss
Mine end, thy good? why may it not be done?
Dark clouds bring waters, when the bright bring none;
Yea, dark, or bright, if they their silver drops
Cause to descend, the earth by yielding crops
Gives praise to both, and carpeth not at either,
But treasures up the fruit they yield together:
Yea, so commixes both, that in her fruit
None can distinguish this from that, they suit
Her well when hungry, but if she be full
She spews out both, and makes their blessing null. . . .
'Well, yet I am not fully satisfied,
That this your book will stand, when soundly tried.'
Why, what's the matter? 'It is dark', What tho'?
'But it is feigned', What of that I trow?
Some men by feigning words as dark as mine,
Make truth to spangle, and its rays to shine.
'But they want solidness.' Speak man thy mind.
'They drowned the weak; metaphors make us blind.'
Solidity, indeed becomes the pen
Of him that writeth things divine to men:
But must I needs want solidness, because
By metaphors I speak; was not God's laws,
His Gospel-laws in olden time held forth
By types, shadows and metaphors? Yet loth
Will any sober man be to find fault
With them, lest he be found for to assault
The highest wisdom. No, he rather stoops,
And seeks to find out what by pins and loops,
By calves, and sheep, by heifers, and by rams,
By birds and herbs, and by the blood of lambs
God speaketh to him: and happy is he
That finds the light, and grace that in them be.
Be not too forward therefore to conclude
That I want solidness, that I am rude:
All things solid in show not solid be;
All things in parables despise not we
Lest things most hurtful lightly we receive;

And things that good are, of our souls bereave.
My dark and cloudy words they do but hold
The truth, as cabinets enclose the gold.

(continued in next day's reading)

JOHN BUNYAN (1628–1688)

BUNYAN'S first work to use allegory was a book on the parable of the rich man and Lazarus, *Sighs from Hell,* or *The Groans of a Damned Soul* (1658). He produced other allegorical works while he was in prison. One such work, *The Holy City* (1665), interprets the symbolism of Revelation. Following this book, he wrote the allegory that he is best known for—*Pilgrim's Progress* (1672). *Pilgrim's Progress* has been translated into hundreds of dialects and languages and has captured the imaginations of readers all around the world. Who can forget the pilgrim, the burden, the monsters, the road with its sloughs and bypaths, the guides true and false, the resting places, and the final goal of the heavenly city?

Bunyan's defense of the allegorical method continues in this section of the preface. He knew that his critics wanted straightforward prose about spiritual truths—what they called "solid" writing. They complained that his allegorical writing was too "dark" and enigmatic. Bunyan defended his position by stating that God himself speaks through allegories and metaphors: "God speaketh to him: and happy is he that finds the light, and grace that in them be." Even Jesus' followers once asked Jesus why he used parables when he taught, and he replied in kind.

Then the disciples came and asked him, "Why do you speak to them in parables?" . . . "The reason I speak to them in parables is that 'seeing they do not perceive, and hearing they do not listen, nor do they understand.'" Matthew 13:10, 13, NRSV

The prophets used much by metaphors
To set forth truth; yea, who so considers
Christ, his Apostles too, shall plainly see,
That truths to this day in such mantles be.
Am I afraid to say that Holy Writ,
Which for its style and phrase puts down all wit,
Is everywhere so full of all these things,
(Dark figures, allegories), yet there springs
From that same book that lustre and those rays
Of light that turns our darkest nights to days.
Come, let my carper[a] *to his life now look,*
And find there darker lines than in my book
He findeth any. Yea, and let him know
That in his best things there are worse lines too.
May we but stand before impartial men,
To his poor one, I durst adventure ten
That they will take my meaning in these lines
Far better than his lies in silver shrines.
Come, truth, although in swaddling-clouts, I find
Informs the judgement, rectifies the mind,
Pleases the understanding, makes the will
Submit; the memory too it doth fill
With what doth our imagination please,
Likewise, it tends our troubles to appease.
Sound words I know Timothy is to use, . . .
But yet grave Paul him nowhere doth forbid
The use of parables; in which lay hid
That gold, those pearls, and precious stones that were
Worth digging for, and that with greatest care. . . .
I find that Holy Writ in many places
Hath semblance with this method, where the cases
Doth call for one thing to set forth another:
Use it I may then, and yet nothing smother
Truth's golden beams, nay, by this method may
Make it cast forth its rays as light as day.

(continued in next day's reading)

JOHN BUNYAN (1628–1688)

[a]carper—critic

BUNYAN continues to defend his use of allegories, metaphors, and parables in *Pilgrim's Progress* on the basis that the Bible itself contains these forms of writing to communicate divine truths. Jesus himself was the master of parables. In fact, he used parables in more than a third of all his teachings.

The early Christian church respected these forms of writing. Later, allegorization lost its credibility because Christian writers abused it. Augustine (354–430), a fourth-century scholar, is a good example. His interpretation of the parable of the Good Samaritan views Christ as the Good Samaritan, the oil as the comfort of good hope, the animal as the flesh of the incarnation, the inn as the church, and the innkeeper as the apostle Paul. Obviously, this interpretation has nothing in common with Jesus' intended meaning because the interpreter read his preconceived ideas into it. While this approach may sound good theologically, it actually is a hindrance because it prohibits the hearing of God's Word.

Bunyan's approach to allegory was different from Augustine's. While Augustine created unintended meaning in his interpretations of Scripture, Bunyan used biblical truth as the foundation for his creative writing. As Bunyan wrote, "The prophets used much by metaphors to set forth truth; yea, who so considers Christ, his Apostles too, shall plainly see, that truths to this day in such mantles be." *Pilgrim's Progress* is Bunyan's attempt to communicate truths too difficult to explain in prose.

As Bunyan's example teaches us, we must be true to God's truth whenever and however we attempt to communicate it.

When we tell you this, we do not use words of human wisdom. We speak words given to us by the Spirit, using the Spirit's words to explain spiritual truths. 1 Corinthians 2:13

Preface to *Pilgrim's Progess*

And now, before I do put up my pen,
I'll show the profit of my book, and then
Commit both thee, and it unto that hand
That pulls the strong down, and makes weak ones stand.
This book it chalketh out before thine eyes
The man that seeks the everlasting prize:
It shows you whence he comes, whither he goes,
What he leaves undone, also what he does:
It also shows you how he runs, and runs,
Till he unto the Gate of Glory comes.
It shows too who sets out for life amain,
As if the lasting crown they would attain:
Here also you may see the reason why
They lose their labour, and like fools do die.
This book will make a traveller of thee,
If by its counsel thou wilt ruled be;
It will direct thee to the Holy Land,
If thou wilt its directions understand:
Yea, it will make the slothful active be,
The blind also delightful things to see.
Art thou for something rare, and profitable?
Would'st thou see a truth within a fable?
Art thou forgetful? Wouldest thou remember
From New Year's Day to the last of December?
Then read my fancies, they will stick like burrs,
And may be to the helpless, comforters.
This book is writ in such a dialect
As may the minds of listless men affect:
It seems a novelty, and yet contains
Nothing but sound and honest gospel-strains.
Would'st thou divert thyself from melancholy?
Would'st thou be pleasant, yet be far from folly?
Would'st thou read riddles and their explanation,
Or else be drowned in thy contemplation? . . .
O then come hither,
And lay my book, thy head and heart together.

JOHN BUNYAN (1628–1688)

EARLY in the Christian tradition, *pilgrimage* represented the journey through life or the progress of human life to a state of blessedness. In *Pilgrim's Progress,* the pilgrim seeks God's grace, and the pilgrimage is the progress of a human soul in quest of peace with God.

Bunyan himself had a long pilgrimage. The once-blaspheming tinker became a believer and then a preacher. When it became illegal to conduct worship services apart from the Anglican church, Bunyan contined to preach without the church's authority and was arrested and imprisoned.

While in prison Bunyan wrote *Grace Abounding to the Chief of Sinners* (1666). Hailed as the greatest Puritan spiritual autobiography, it was patterned after the Christian account of human history with its two climaxes: (1) the fall of man through the original sin of Adam and (2) the redemption of man through the sacrifice of Christ. Bunyan revealed the doubts, struggles, temptations, fears, and hopes in his own growth from condemnation to salvation. He also began *Pilgrim's Progress* while in prison.

After his release, he continued to preach. On one of his journeys to London in August 1688, Bunyan went out of his way to help settle a quarrel between a father and son. After riding through heavy rain, he arrived at the home of a London friend. He preached the following Sunday but in a few days developed a violent fever, which led to his death. His pilgrimage was over, and he found lasting peace with God.

Because of our faith, Christ has brought us into this place of highest privilege where we now stand, and we confidently and joyfully look forward to sharing God's glory. Romans 5:2

The Over-Heart PART ONE

Above, below, in sky and sod,
In leaf and spar, in star and man,
Well might the wise Athenian scan
The geometric signs of God,
The measured order of His plan.

And India's mystics sang aright,
Of the one life pervading all,—
One being's tidal rise and fall
In soul and form, in sound and sight,—
Eternal outflow and recall.

God is: and man in guilt and fear
The central fact of nature owns;
Kneels, trembling by his altar stones,
And darkly dreams the ghastly smear
Of blood appeases and atones.

Guilt shapes the terror: deep within
The human heart the secret lies
Of all the hideous deities;
And, painted on a ground of sin,
The fabled gods of torment rise!

(continued in next day's reading)

JOHN GREENLEAF WHITTIER (1807–1892)

WHITTIER'S poetry depicts his Christian piety and compassion. In this poem, he proclaims the superiority of Christianity over every other religion. Whittier also acknowledges that there are universal truths other religions share with Christianity. For example, in the first stanza he states that the Greeks ("the wise Athenian") could discern God's plan by studying the design of the stars. In other words, the stars exist to point people to God. Romans 1:20 affirms this clearly: "From the time the world was created, people have seen the earth and sky and all that God made. They can clearly see his invisible qualities—his eternal power and divine nature."

In the second stanza Whittier affirms the Hindus' ("India's mystics") belief that everything lives because of God. Scripture also confirms this: "For of Him and through Him and to Him are all things, to whom be glory forever" (Romans 11:36, NKJV).

This is not to say that everything is God. While he gives life to everything and sustains everything, he retains his own identity outside of creation. But, as the next stanzas make clear, other religions lead people to worship "hideous deities." This is the unfortunate tragedy: people worshiping created things instead of the Creator. May God keep us from such horrible idolatry.

They exchanged the truth about God for a lie and worshiped and served the creature rather than the Creator, who is blessed forever! Amen. Romans 1:25, NRSV

The Over-Heart PART TWO

And what is He? The ripe grain nods,
The sweet dews fall, the sweet flowers blow;
But darker signs His presence show:
The earthquake and the storm are God's,
And good and evil interflow.

O hearts of love! O souls that turn
Like sunflowers to the pure and best!
To you the truth is manifest:
For they the mind of Christ discern
Who lean like John upon His breast!

In him of whom the sybil[a] *told,*
For whom the prophet's harp was toned,
Whose need the sage and magian[b] *owned,*
The loving heart of God behold,
The hope for which the ages groaned!

Fade, pomp of dreadful imagery
Wherewith mankind have deified
Their hate, and selfishness, and pride!
Let the scared dreamer wake to see
The Christ of Nazareth at his side!

(continued in next day's reading)

JOHN GREENLEAF WHITTIER (1807–1892)

[a]prophetess [b]magician

THE POEM now turns to the question of where the true seeker can find God. How has God manifested himself? Whittier again points to nature. God can be seen in the pleasant aspects (ripe grain, sweet dews, sweet flowers) as well as the dreadful (earthquakes, storms). But the poet doesn't stop there. To see God only in nature is an incomplete revelation of him.

Those who truly seek God will find him in Jesus Christ, and that is where the full revelation of God resides. As Whittier says about the seeker: "The scared dreamer [will] wake to see the Christ of Nazareth at his side!"

How good God is to reveal Jesus to those who are seeking truth! No matter where a person originates the search—whether he or she begins as a Hindu, a Buddhist, a pantheist, a naturalist, or even an honest agnostic—if that person honestly seeks ultimate truth, God will lead him or her to Jesus Christ. For he is truth.

Jesus told him, "I am the way, the truth, and the life. No one can come to the Father except through me." John 14:6

What doth that holy Guide require?
No rite of pain, nor gift of blood,
But man a kindly brotherhood,
Looking, where duty is desire,
To Him, the beautiful and good.

Gone be the faithlessness of fear,
And let the pitying heaven's sweet rain
Wash out the altar's bloody stain;
The law of hatred disappear,
The law of love alone remain.

How fall the idols false and grim!
And lo! their hideous wreck above
The emblems of the Lamb and Dove!
Man turns from God, not God from him;
And guilt, in suffering, whispers Love!

The world sits at the feet of Christ,
Unknowing, blind, and unconsoled;
It yet shall touch his garment's fold,
And feel the heavenly alchemist
Transform its very dust to gold.

The theme befitting angel tongues
Beyond a mortal's scope has grown.
O heart of mine! with reverence own
The fulness which to it belongs,
And trust the unknown for the known.

JOHN GREENLEAF WHITTIER (1807–1892)

WITH a full heart Whittier sings of the glorious grace that has come to him because he knows Christ. And this grace is available to all who will come to God. Unfortunately, many don't. As Whittier put it so well: "Man turns from God, not God from him."

But those who do turn to God discover how much better he is than any idol. Christ doesn't require people to make sacrifices in order to assuage their guilt. He has already paid the price for their sin. The recipients of his grace can show their gratitude to him by loving others. This is the highest expression of thanks: "The law of hatred disappear, the law of love alone remain."

Sadly, most of the world is blind to these wonderful, spiritual realities: "The world sits at the feet of Christ, unknowing, blind, and unconsoled." All they have to do is reach out to him, and the "heavenly alchemist," who can change lives with his supernatural power, will heal them.

Whittier knew firsthand the transforming touch of Christ. So he praised his Savior for the fullness he had received and for the reality that he had come to "trust the unknown for the known." May we with Whittier sing Christ's praises for the transforming work he does in our lives.

You love him [Jesus Christ] even though you have never seen him. Though you do not see him, you trust him; and even now you are happy with a glorious, inexpressible joy. Your reward for trusting him will be the salvation of your souls. 1 Peter 1:8-9

Peace

When will you ever, Peace, wild wooddove, shy wings shut,
Your round me roaming end, and under be my boughs?
When, when, Peace, will you, Peace? I'll not play hypocrite
To own my heart: I yield you do come sometimes; but
That piecemeal peace is poor peace. What pure peace allows
Alarms of wars, the daunting wars, the death of it?

O surely, reaving[a] *Peace, my Lord should leave in lieu*
Some good! And so he does leave Patience exquisite,
That plumes[b] *to Peace thereafter. And when Peace here does house*
He comes with work to do, he does not come to coo,[c]
He comes to brood and sit.

GERARD MANLEY HOPKINS (1844–1889)

[a]robbing, plundering, seizing [b]flourishes [c]low, soft cry of dove or pigeon

GERARD MANLEY HOPKINS was one of the greatest Christian poets of the nineteenth century. His poems are potent in message and form. In many of his works, Hopkins shares his insights about how Christ is revealed in nature.

The poet compares the peace of Christ to the wild wood-dove. The dove has been a symbol of peace since biblical times. Christians also use the dove as a symbol of the Holy Spirit because the Spirit descended on Jesus in the form of a dove when he was baptized (see Luke 3:21-22). In Hopkins's experience, the peace of Christ often came and went just like a wild wooddove. In other words, he did not feel like he had the constant presence of Christ's peace through the Holy Spirit. Wouldn't all Christians say the same?

Hopkins looked forward to the day when Christ would come to earth permanently and begin his reign of peace. This is the final image of the poem: The dove of peace will come "to brood and sit." This is an allusion to the activity of the Holy Spirit in creation (Genesis 1:2). The new creation will begin in similar fashion. The Spirit of peace will dwell on earth and in the hearts of people.

For a child is born to us, a son is given to us. And the government will rest on his shoulders. These will be his royal titles: Wonderful Counselor, Mighty God, Everlasting Father, Prince of Peace. His ever expanding, peaceful government will never end. Isaiah 9:6-7a

The Salutation

These little limbs,
These eyes and hands which here I find,
These rosy cheeks wherewith my life begins,
Where have ye been? Behind
What curtain were ye from me hid so long!
Where was, in what abyss, my speaking tongue.

When silent I,
So many thousand thousand years,
Beneath the dust did in a chaos lie,
How could I smiles or tears,
Or lips or hands or eyes or ears perceive?
Welcome ye treasures which I now receive.

I that so long
Was nothing from eternity,
Did little think such joys as ear or tongue,
To celebrate or see:
Such sounds to hear, such hands to feel, such feet,
Beneath the skies, on such a ground to meet.

New burnisht joys!
Which yellow gold and pearl excell!
Such sacred treasures are the limbs in boys,
In which a soul doth dwell;
Their organized joints, and azure veins
More wealth include, than all the world contains.

From dust I rise,
And out of nothing now awake,
These brighter regions which salute mine eyes,
A gift from God I take
The earth, the seas, the light, the day, the skies,
The sun and stars are mine; if those I prize.

Long time before
I in my mother's womb was born,
A God preparing did this glorious store,
The world for me adorn.
Into this Eden so divine and fair,
So wide and bright, I come his son and heir.

A stranger here
Strange things doth meet, strange glories see;
Strange treasures lodged in this fair world appear,
Strange all, and new to me.
But that they mine should be, who nothing was,
That strangest is of all, yet brought to pass.

THOMAS TRAHERNE (1637–1674)

TRAHERNE'S perception of a divinely directed cosmos surrounding individuals and active within them was common in the early seventeenth century. In this poem Traherne marvels—as one newly born—at the world created for him long before he came into being. This is a wonderful thought, one definitely worth pondering. When God made this world, he had us in mind. He didn't make it just for his own pleasure but for ours as well.

Genesis 2:8-9 says that "the Lord God planted a garden in Eden" and there "put the man whom he had formed. . . . God made to grow every tree that is pleasant to the sight and good for food" (NRSV). God purposely made the world for our enjoyment. As Traherne put it: "Into this Eden so divine and fair, so wide and bright, I come his son and heir."

May we remember to thank God for making a wonderful world for us to inhabit and enjoy. Let us also remember to praise him for the heavenly home his Son is preparing for us right now.

Since everything God created is good, we should not reject any of it. We may receive it gladly, with thankful hearts. 1 Timothy 4:4

This World Is Not Conclusion

This World is not Conclusion.
A Species stands beyond—
Invisible, as Music—
But positive, as Sound—
It beckons, and it baffles—
Philosophy—don't know—
And through a Riddle, at the last—
Sagacity, must go—
To guess it, puzzles scholars—
To gain it, Men have borne
Contempt of Generations
And Crucifixion, shown—
Faith slips—and laughs, and rallies—
Blushes, if any see—
Plucks at a twig of Evidence—
And asks a Vane, the way—
Much Gesture, from the Pulpit—
Strong Hallelujahs roll—
Narcotics cannot still the Tooth
That nibbles at the soul—

EMILY DICKINSON (1830–1886)

THE AFTERLIFE fascinated Emily Dickinson; many of her poems reflect her thoughts and feelings about it. Here Dickinson eloquently affirms her faith in the afterlife: "This World is not Conclusion." Life continues in the beyond—what many call heaven.

Though invisible, the afterlife is as real as music and sound. We hear its call, but it baffles us at the same time. We want to experience it, but we don't know what to expect and are afraid of what we might find. Philosophy tries to explain this riddle but can't. It puzzles even the most sagacious.

Nonetheless, believers have endured much to gain this life, bearing the contempt of generations and even suffering crucifixion to live beyond this world. These believers had bold faith and trusted God to grant them eternal life. The writer of Hebrews lists such people in chapter 11. Noteworthy among them are the martyrs. They "trusted God and were tortured, preferring to die rather than turn from God and be free. They placed their hope in the resurrection to a better life" (11:35). They couldn't still the "tooth" of eternity that nibbled at their souls.

May we also feel afterlife's nibble and respond by putting our trust in "Christ Jesus, our Savior, who broke the power of death and showed us the way to everlasting life" (2 Timothy 1:10).

What is faith? It is the confident assurance that what we hope for is going to happen. It is the evidence of things we cannot yet see.
Hebrews 11:1

On the Spirit Adulterated by the Flesh

How do I spin my time away
In caring how to get
Ungodly wealth, and fret
My self to sweat,
As if thou Lord hadst meant this clay
No after life, no reckoning day.

What graceless fool would love his earth
So, as with all his might
To pamper with delight
The same 'gainst right,
Forgetting his divine soul's birth
Was nobler, and of greater worth?

Thou Lord didst frame this soul of mine
Only to honor thee,
Not basely fond to be
Of vanity,
Unflesh it then, and so refine
It Lord it may be all divine.

Quicken my dull-drooping spirit
That it may praise thy name,
Cleanse it from sin and blame,
Take from it shame.
Grant that by my Savior's merit
Eternity it may inherit.

Let it not grovelling lie pressed down
With earth, but mount, and gain
An everlasting reign,
Let it retain
No dross, and when it shall have thrown
Its cover off, grant it a crown.

HENRY COLMAN (fl. 1640)

HAVE YOU ever prayed like Henry Colman does in today's poem? This is actually a common prayer, but Colman has composed it in an uncommonly artistic way. Isn't this the job of the artist? To help the world see itself through fresh eyes?

An average person might have prayed this prayer:

> Lord Jesus, I've been all wrapped up in my job and my worries. It's as if there is no other purpose for my life and I'd forgotten that I have eternal life. I'd have to be really stupid to love the world so much and work so hard for its comforts and forget that I've been born again for your kingdom.
>
> Dear God, you made me for your glory—not for this world and its pleasures. Take away my taste for these things and make me more like your Son.
>
> I feel dead inside, Lord. Make my spirit alive again so I can praise you. I'm sorry for my sins. I pray that you will cleanse me. I believe in Jesus—he died for my sins so that I can have eternal life!
>
> Don't let my soul be held down by the cares of this world. Let me live knowing that your kingdom is on its way. Make me clean and pure, O Lord, so when that day comes I can enjoy your glory.

Colman was a fine poet who contributed to the rich heritage of Christian literature. Thank God for this heritage! We can see in it new definitions of our experience in these old-fashioned words: "Thou Lord didst frame this soul of mine only to honor thee, not basely fond to be of vanity."

The thorny ground represents those who hear and accept the Good News, but all too quickly the message is crowded out by the cares of this life and the lure of wealth, so no crop is produced. Matthew 13:22

Composed upon Westminster Bridge

Earth has not anything to show more fair:
Dull would he be of soul who could pass by
A sight so touching in its majesty;
This City now doth, like a garment, wear
The beauty of the morning; silent, bare,
Ships, towers, domes, theaters, and temples lie
Open unto the fields, and to the sky;
All bright and glittering in the smokeless air.
Never did sun more beautifully steep
In his first splendor, valley, rock, or hill;
Ne'er saw I, never felt, a calm so deep!
The river glideth at his own sweet will:
Dear God! the very houses seem asleep;
And all that mighty heart is lying still!

WILLIAM WORDSWORTH (1770–1850)

WORDSWORTH was born in the beautiful Lake District of northwest England. The setting of his home deeply affected his personality, ideas, and poetry. A prolific writer throughout his long life, Wordsworth produced his best poetry between 1797 and 1808. His verse reveals a strong reliance on feeling and emotion, an awareness of mystical insights, a fervent devotion to nature, a love of solitude, and a rejection of materialism. Some of his best poems are "Tintern Abbey," "Intimations of Immortality," "The Solitary Reaper," "Michael," "The Prelude," and the Lucy Poems.

In this poem (called a sonnet), Wordsworth calls our attention to the divinity inherent in creation. Astutely aware of God's presence in nature, he was tuned in to those moments—those epiphanies—where God reveals himself in creation. Here he paints a scene of a city in the sleepy hours of early morning: "This City now doth, like a garment, wear the beauty of the morning; silent, bare." As the sun rises, Wordsworth—overwhelmed with such tranquil peace—exclaims, "Ne'er saw I, never felt, a calm so deep!" For Wordsworth the scene was "so touching in its majesty" that he believed anyone who could pass by it and not be affected was dull of soul.

God has truly blessed humanity with the sublime beauty of creation and the innate ability to recognize and enjoy it. From open fields to blue skies to glorious sunrises, the beauty of creation abounds, testifying to the glory of God. When we ignore this beauty or take it for granted, our soul can become dull to the Creator. But if we allow creation to stir our soul, we will desire to worship and praise the one who made everything. May God save us all from dullness so we can perceive his glory in creation.

The earth is the Lord's, and everything in it. The world and all its people belong to him. Psalm 24:1

Lines Written under the Influence . . .

composed while under the care of Dr. Cotton, at St. Albans

Hatred and vengeance,—my eternal portion
Scarce can endure delay of execution,—
Wait with impatient readiness to seize my
Soul in a moment.

Damned below Judas; more abhorred than he was,
Who for a few pence sold his holy Master!
Twice betrayed, Jesus me, the last delinquent,
Deems the profanest.

Man disavows, and Deity disowns me,
Hell might afford my miseries a shelter;
Therefore, Hell keeps her ever-hungry mouths all
Bolted against me.

Hard lot! encompassed with a thousand dangers;
Weary, faint, trembling with a thousand terrors,
I'm called, if vanquished, to receive a sentence
Worse than Abiram's.

Him the vindictive rod of angry Justice
Sent quick and howling to the centre headlong;
I fed with judgment, in a fleshy tomb, am
Buried above ground.

WILLIAM COWPER (1731–1800)

WILLIAM COWPER was related to the great seventeenth-century poet and preacher John Donne. Cowper suffered from mental illness throughout his life; this poem describes his inner condition shortly after he attempted suicide. The contents hardly seem fit for a daily meditation. But consider this: Have you ever felt that you betrayed the Lord?

Cowper believed that he had, and because he betrayed Jesus after Judas did, he also believed that his condemnation should be greater than that of the man who sold his master. In this respect, Cowper was like Paul, who called himself the foremost sinner (1 Timothy 1:15). Cowper felt like a refugee, disavowed by earth, disowned by heaven, and locked out of hell.

In stanza 4 Cowper reveals his belief that he will receive a sentence worse than Abiram, whom God caused the earth to swallow up for his rebellion with Korah against Moses (Numbers 16). The hard lot these lines describe should remind us that we "were [once] without Christ . . . strangers from the covenants of promise, having no hope and without God in the world" (Ephesians 2:12, NKJV). The poet makes his final declaration of despair in the last stanza, describing his life as a living death, buried above ground in a fleshly tomb.

This is a hymn to the fall of humanity written by a man hospitalized for mental illness. But in that hospital William Cowper began to read the Bible. He found faith in Christ and became an influential hymn writer. With his friend John Newton, Cowper published *Olney Hymns* (1779). Among his many inspirational works are "O for a Closer Walk with God!" "The Fountain," and "God Moves in a Mysterious Way." He certainly does.

Oh, what a miserable person I am! Who will free me from this life that is dominated by sin? Thank God! The answer is in Jesus Christ our Lord. Romans 7:24-25

Meditation 8 PART ONE

I kenning[a] through astronomy divine
The world's bright battlement,[b] wherein I spy
A golden path my pencil cannot line
From that bright throne unto my threshold lie.
And while my puzzled thoughts about it pore
I find the bread of life in't at my door.

When that this bird of paradise[c] put in
This wicker cage (my corpse) to tweedle praise
Had pecked the fruit forbade: and so did fling
Away its food; and lost its golden days;
It fell into celestial famine sore:
And never could attain a morsel more.

Alas! alas! poore bird, what wilt thou do?
The creatures' field no food for souls e'er gave.
And if thou knock at angels' doors they show
An empty barrel: they no soul bread have.
Alas! poor bird, the world's white loaf is done.
And cannot yield thee here the smallest crumb.

In this sad state, God's tender bowels[d] run
Out streams of grace: and He to end all strife
The purest wheat in heaven, His dear-dear son
Grinds, and kneads up into this bread of life.
Which bread of life from Heaven down came and stands
Dished on thy table up by Angels' hands.

(continued in next day's reading)

EDWARD TAYLOR (1642–1729)

[a]seeing, knowing [b]a parapet with open spaces [c]soul [d]heart

EDWARD TAYLOR was a metaphysical poet who wrote in the tradition of George Herbert. He was not as polished and refined as Herbert or the other great metaphysical poets such as Donne and Crashaw. Nonetheless, he contributed to our American heritage of Christian poetry and was recognized as the first American poet. This recognition did not come until the twentieth century, when someone discovered his poetry in the Yale University library. One of his volumes, *Preparatory Meditations,* is a collection of over two hundred spiritual meditations written in preparation for the Lord's Supper.

The poet meditates on one aspect of the Lord's Supper: the bread. In the opening stanzas Taylor bemoans that he, in his sinful, fallen condition, has no life. Likening himself to the bird of paradise—that once had access to the tree of life—he decries the fact that he threw away the bread of life and that heaven had no more bread to give. But God was merciful. He prepared his Son to be the bread of life come in human form so people could eat of him and partake of eternal life.

This comes from John 6:51; Jesus declares, "I am the living bread that came down out of heaven." Jesus was the bread of God, who came to be the ever-present, life-giving supply. Jesus told the people that he had come to give his flesh for the life of the world (that is, he had come to sacrifice his life so the world could have eternal life). Jesus surrendered his body to death on the cross so that by his death the world could have life.

[Jesus said,] "I am the bread of life. No one who comes to me will ever be hungry again. . . . I am the living bread that came down out of heaven. Anyone who eats this bread will live forever; this bread is my flesh, offered so the world may live." John 6:35, 51

Meditation 8 PART TWO

Did God mold up this bread in heaven, and bake,
Which from His table came, and to thine goeth?
Doth He bespeak thee thus, this soul bread take.
Come eat thy fill of this thy God's white loaf?
It's food too fine for angels, yet come, take
And eat thy fill. It's heaven's sugar cake.

What grace is this knead in this loaf? This thing
Souls are but petty things it to admire.
Ye angels, help: This fill would to the brim
Heav'ns whelmed-down crystal meal bowl, yea and higher.
This bread of life dropped in thy mouth, doth cry.
Eat, eat me, Soul, and thou shalt never die.

EDWARD TAYLOR (1642–1729)

EDWARD TAYLOR wrote most of his poems as spiritual meditations in preparation for the Lord's Table or Communion, which he administered to his congregation. Here he marvels at God's gracious act of giving his Son as the bread of life for all to partake of. He exclaims that this is food "too fine for angels" and too full and rich for human beings. Yet God gives it to humans and invites them to eat of it freely.

This entire line of thinking comes from John 6. The Jews told Jesus that their forefathers had eaten manna in the wilderness for forty years. They expected Jesus—if he was the Messiah—to reenact this miracle. But Jesus told them that manna doesn't give eternal life. The Israelites who ate it died in the wilderness. If God had given the Jews in Jesus' day manna, they, too, would have died. But God had something better to give; he gave his Son from heaven as the bread of life! Whoever would eat of that bread would not die—that is, would not experience spiritual death but, instead, would participate in the resurrection and have eternal life.

In becoming a man and dying on the cross, the Son of God was "prepared" and "baked" as bread. What a thought! What must we do to thank God for this bread of life? Open our heart and soul to Jesus. Let him into our life. God is asking us to do this: "This bread of life dropped in thy mouth, doth cry. Eat, eat me, Soul, and thou shalt never die."

This is the bread that comes down from heaven, so that one may eat of it and not die. John 6:50, NRSV

Old Testament Gospel

Israel, in ancient days
Not only had a view
Of Sinai in a blaze,
But learned the Gospel too;
The types and figures were a glass
In which they saw a Savior's face.

The paschal sacrifice
And blood-besprinkled door,
Seen with enlightened eyes,
And once applied with power,
Would teach the need of other blood,
To reconcile an angry God.

The Lamb, the Dove, set forth
His perfect innocence,
Whose blood of matchless worth
Should be the soul's defence;
For he who can for sin atone,
Must have no failings of his own.

The scape-goat on his head
The people's trespass bore,
And, to the desert led,
Was to be seen no more:
In him our surety seemed to say,
"Behold, I bear your sins away."

Dipped in his fellow's blood,
The living bird went free;
The type, well understood,
Expressed the sinner's plea;
Described a guilty soul enlarged,
And by a Savior's death discharged.

Jesus, I love to trace,
Throughout the sacred page,
The footsteps of thy grace,
The same in every age!
O grant that I may faithful be
To clearer light vouchsafed to me!

WILLIAM COWPER (1731–1800)

THE CHILDREN of Israel witnessed many miraculous events and symbolic ceremonies that foreshadowed God's plan for salvation. In light of the New Testament, we can view these occurrences as the footsteps of grace. Cowper mentions a few: the Passover lamb (Exodus 12:3; 1 Corinthians 5:7); the blood on the doorposts in Egypt (Exodus 12:7; Acts 16:30-31); the countless innocent lambs and doves sacrificed (Hebrews 9:23-26); the scapegoat disappearing into the wilderness (Leviticus 16:10; 1 John 2:2); and the flight of the blood-soaked dove (Leviticus 14:6-7, 51-53; Acts 1:9). These "types and figures were a glass [mirror] in which they [Israel] saw a Savior's face."

Paul once confessed that he could see Christ only dimly as in a mirror (1 Corinthians 13:12). So Old Testament Jews would have needed remarkable vision to see the death of the Messiah foreshadowed by the animal sacrifices. This doesn't mean they didn't have faith. Surely there were thousands who believed in the effectiveness of the sacrifices. But God's plan is not always clearly seen in the present. Believers born after the time of Christ have the distinct advantage of looking back through history to see how God's plan unfolded.

"Faith is the assurance of things hoped for, the conviction of things not seen" (Hebrews 11:1, NASB), and "hope that is seen is not hope" (Romans 8:24, NASB). Today we are in a situation similar to that of the Israelites. God is still unfolding his plan, which we have a glimpse of in Revelation. But we aren't quite sure how it will work out. Therefore, we need to follow Paul's advice and live by faith, not by sight (2 Corinthians 5:7), praying, "O grant that I may faithful be to clearer light vouchsafed to me!"

So be on your guard, not asleep like the others. Stay alert and be sober. 1 Thessalonians 5:6

For the Magdalene

These eyes (dear Lord) once brandons[a] *of desire,*
Frail scouts betraying what they had to keep,
Which their own heart, then others set on fire,
Their traitorous black before thee here out-weep:
These locks, of blushing deeds the fair attire,
Smooth-frizzled waves, sad shelfs which shadow deep,
Soul-stinging serpents in gilt curls which creep,
To touch thy sacred feet do now aspire.
In seas of care behold a sinking bark,[b]
By winds of sharp remorse unto thee driven,
O let me not exposed be ruin's mark,
My faults confessed (Lord) say they are forgiven.
Thus sighed to Jesus the Bethanian fair,
His tear-wet feet still drying with her hair.

WILLIAM DRUMMOND OF HAWTHORNDEN (1585–1649)

[a]torches [b]a small sailing boat

AS YOU READ, can't you hear the voice of Mary the Magdalene—her repentance overflowing in tears as she wipes Christ's feet with her hair? What love she had for him! Then there is the voice of the Pharisee—despising both Mary and Jesus. "That gluttonous drunkard is no prophet. Why, he makes friends with sinners! Look at that woman—that sinner. He's letting her touch his feet!" (See Luke 7:34, 39.)

Jesus took this occasion to instruct Simon the Pharisee about forgiveness and love. Through a parable Jesus made it clear that Mary was not the only sinner present in the house. Mary's sinfulness seemed more apparent than the Pharisee's. Nonetheless, both needed forgiveness. The question is, why was Mary on her knees weeping and anointing Christ's feet? Was it because she knew her sinfulness and sought forgiveness? Or was she overwhelmed with love because she knew Christ had already forgiven her? We must be careful not to think like the Pharisee, who justified himself because he was a good man. Good or bad, everyone needs God's forgiveness, and no one can earn it.

We don't know whether Simon asked for and received forgiveness for his sin. His lack of faith at that time certainly exposed his indifference to the Lord as well as his ignorance of just how sinful he really was. In contrast, Mary the Magdalene was acutely aware that Jesus had wiped her sinful slate clean. So she fell to her knees in loving gratitude (Luke 7:38). Love was the expression of her faith. This is why Jesus said to her, "Your faith has saved you; go in peace" (7:50).

Oh, what joy for those whose rebellion is forgiven, whose sin is put out of sight! Yes, what joy for those whose record the Lord has cleared of sin, whose lives are lived in complete honesty! Psalm 32:1-2

Love III

Love bade me welcome yet my soul drew back,
Guilty of dust and sin.
But quick-eyed Love, observing me grow slack
From my first entrance in,
Drew nearer to me, sweetly questioning,
If I lacked any thing.

A guest, I answered, worthy to be here:
Love said, You shall be he.
I the unkind, ungrateful? Ah my dear,
I cannot look on thee.
Love took my hand, and smiling did reply,
Who made the eyes but I?

Truth Lord, but I have marred them: let my shame
Go where it doth deserve.
And know you not, says Love, who bore the blame?
My dear, then I will serve.
You must sit down, says Love, and taste my meat:
So I did sit and eat.

GEORGE HERBERT (1593–1633)

HERE is a lovely conversation between the poet and the Lord. George Herbert is candid about himself, his feelings, and his motives toward God. Can you see yourself here?

Love welcomed Herbert, perhaps with these words: "Let the thirsty ones come—anyone who wants to. Let them come and drink the water of life without charge" (Revelation 22:17). Yet Herbert's awareness of his sin caused him to draw back. So Love drew nearer. The poet describes himself as unkind and ungrateful, unworthy to be Love's guest. He is shameful that he has so damaged the eyes God gave him that he cannot look at Love. He wishes Love would cast him out instead of inviting him in.

This poem describes a typical human reaction to God's invitation to eternal life. We think that we must be worthy, sinless, to be a guest of the loving creator. But Love reminds us that he has borne the blame for our sin. It is natural to feel unworthy, but faith in Jesus Christ can alleviate this feeling.

The poet introduces another human misconception that intrudes upon God's love. Herbert says in the last stanza: "My dear, then I will serve." He means: Lord, since you have done so much for me, I must serve you with all I have. In a sense the poet, like many of us, concludes that he is righteous enough to do good for God. Love, sounding like a doting aunt, corrects him: "You must sit down . . . and taste my meat." Persuaded by Love, the poet "did sit and eat."

May we never forget that "human hands can't serve his needs—for he has no needs. He himself gives life and breath to everything, and he satisfies every need there is" (Acts 17:25).

There will be special favor for those who are ready and waiting for his return. I tell you, he himself will seat them, put on an apron, and serve them as they sit and eat! Luke 12:37

Neutrality Loathesome

God will have all, or none; serve Him, or fall
Down before Baal, Bel, or Belial:
Either be hot, or cold: God doth despise,
Abhor, and spew out all Neutralities.

Robert Herrick (1591–1674)

CLERGYMAN Robert Herrick was a Cavalier poet, part of a group of seventeenth-century English lyric poets associated with the Royalists. Their poems are generally brief, have a correct and polished form, show restrained emotion, and deal with loyalty, beauty, and love. Herrick's only published work is *Hesperides,* or *The Works Both Human and Divine of Robert Herrick, Esq.* (1648). This volume of more than fourteen hundred poems was named for the mythological garden of golden apples. Bound into this book, with a separate title page, is a group of religious poems titled *His Noble Numbers* (1647).

In "Neutrality Loathesome" Herrick's verse is so concise that it carries us all the way from Exodus 20:5 ("I, the Lord your God, am a jealous God who will not share your affection with any other god!") to Revelation 3:16 ("But since you are like lukewarm water, I will spit you out of my mouth!") in just four lines. These sobering words reveal a part of God's character that we would rather forget. Here we see God despise and abhor, spit and spew. Hardly a flattering image of the God we prefer to think of as love (John 1:14). But if we believe God loves, then we must also acknowledge that he possesses the entire range of emotions that accompany love—anger, compassion, dejection, disappointment, fondness, hurt, loneliness, modesty, and sadness. God, in essence, is *the* perfect personality.

So we must add to the above list *jealousy.* God is jealous for your love. As Herrick boldly and rightly says, God abhors neutrality. Love him or leave him. Clearly, God and money have agreed on this: They are unwilling to share your affection.

➻ *No one can serve two masters. For you will hate one and love the other, or be devoted to one and despise the other. You cannot serve both God and money.* Matthew 6:24

To His Conscience

Can I not sin, but thou wilt be
My private Protonotary?[a]
Can I not woo thee to pass by
A short and sweet iniquity?
I'll cast a mist and cloud, upon
My delicate transgression,
So utter dark, as that no eye
Shall see the hugged impiety:
Gifts blind the wise,[b] *and bribes do please,*
And wind all other witnesses:
And wilt not thou, with gold, be tied
To lay thy pen and ink aside?
That in the murk and tongueless night,
Wanton I may, and thou not write?
It will not be: And, therefore, now,
For times to come, I'll make this vow,
From aberrations to live free;
So I'll not fear the Judge, or thee.

ROBERT HERRICK (1591–1674)

[a]a rarely used word indicating the chief clerk in a law court. [b]Deuteronomy 16:19 (KJV)

ROBERT HERRICK personifies his conscience and casts it as a character in a courtroom drama. In his day, the protonotary recorded the court's activities. But we know from watching *Perry Mason* and *Matlock* that a court stenographer serves this function today. The stenographer taps the keys of her machine and chronicles everything that is said and done before the judge. Herrick shows and experience proves that our conscience cannot be bribed. It is a tenacious witness to our conduct. The apostle Paul wrote of this: "I speak with utter truthfulness—I do not lie—and my conscience and the Holy Spirit confirm that what I am saying is true" (Romans 9:1).

The Greek word for conscience in the New Testament means "co-knowledge"—a knowledge within oneself. Your conscience is a personal witness to your life—the stenographer of your heart. It bears witness to the requirements of the law (Romans 2:15), works in union with the Holy Spirit (Romans 9:1) to make you conscious of sin (Hebrews 10:2), and controls your actions (Romans 13:5). Paul used his conscience to live rightly before God and man (Acts 23:1; 24:16) and to serve God (2 Timothy 1:3). The conscience is a key to the condition of our faith (1 Timothy 1:19).

How sobering to know that "some people have deliberately violated their consciences; as a result, their faith has been shipwrecked" (1 Timothy 1:19). Let's heed Paul's admonition to Timothy: "Hold fast to the mystery of the faith with a clear conscience" (1 Timothy 3:9, NRSV) and pray, *Lord, sensitize my conscience. I repent that I let it become callous and unfeeling. May it always be my guide to your living law in my heart and a strong guardian of the mystery of the faith.*

We can say with confidence and a clear conscience that we have been honest and sincere in all our dealings. We have depended on God's grace, not on our own earthly wisdom. That is how we have acted toward everyone, and especially toward you. 2 Corinthians 1:12

At His Execution

THE MANNER OF MEN

I am made all things to all men—
Hebrew, Roman, and Greek—
In each one's tongue I speak,
Suiting to each my word,
That some may be drawn to the Lord!

I am made all things to all men—
In city or wilderness
Praising the crafts they profess
That some may be drawn to the Lord—
By any means to my Lord!

Since I was overcome
By that great Light and Word,
I have forgot or forgone
The self men call their own
(Being made all things to all men)
So that I might save some
At such small price, to the Lord,
As being all things to all men.

I was made all things to all men,
But now my course is done—
And now is my reward . . .
Ah, Christ, when I stand at Thy Throne
With those I have drawn to the Lord,
Restore me my self again!

RUDYARD KIPLING (1865–1936)

IN THE FINAL stanza of this poem Kipling sees the apostle Paul standing at the throne of God. Paul had fought a good fight; he had finished the race; he had remained faithful (2 Timothy 4:7). The poet imagines Paul asking God to "restore me my self again." If God were to do this, what would he restore? For example, here is how Paul describes himself before his conversion: "You know what I was like when I followed the Jewish religion—how I violently persecuted the Christians. I did my best to get rid of them. I was one of the most religious Jews of my own age, and I tried as hard as possible to follow all the old traditions of my religion" (Galatians 1:13-14). We can safely say that Paul wouldn't want this person restored.

So what did Kipling mean? Perhaps he had in mind Paul's redeemed self as described in Galatians 2:19-20: "I have been crucified with Christ. I myself no longer live, but Christ lives in me." How did Paul become such a person? "God poured out his special favor on" Paul so he could accomplish all that God desired to do through him (1 Corinthians 15:10).

Paul's request, as presented by Kipling, was to be made complete in the image of Christ. This concept is found in John's first epistle: "Yes, dear friends, we are already God's children, and we can't even imagine what we will be like when Christ returns. But we do know that when he comes we will be like him, for we will see him as he really is" (1 John 3:2). May we, like Paul, long for the day when God will fulfill this promise.

Yes, I try to find common ground with everyone so that I might bring them to Christ. I do all this to spread the Good News, and in doing so I enjoy its blessings. 1 Corinthians 9:22-23

The Warning

Beware! The Israelite of old, who tore
The lion in his path,—when, poor and blind,
He saw the blessed light of heaven no more
Shorn of his noble strength and forced to grind
In prison, and at last led forth to be
A pander[a] *to Philistine revelry,—*

Upon the pillars of the temple laid
His desperate hands, and in its overthrow
Destroyed himself, and with him those who made
A cruel mockery of his sightless woe;
The poor, blind slave, the scoff and jest of all,
Expired, and thousands perished in the fall!

There is a poor, blind Samson in this land,
Shorn of his strength and bound in bonds of steel,
Who may, in some grim revel, raise his hand,
And shake the pillars of this Commonweal,[b]
Till the vast temple of our liberties
A shapeless mass of wreck and rubbish lies.

HENRY WADSWORTH LONGFELLOW (1807–1882)

[a]a person who provides the means of helping to satisfy the degraded ambitions, desires, or vices of another [b]a commonwealth; the common good

HENRY WADSWORTH LONGFELLOW was one of the most widely read American poets of the nineteenth century. His best-known poems include "The Song of Hiawatha," "Paul Revere's Ride," and "The Wreck of the Hesperus." Some consider Longfellow's poetry sentimental or didactic. Indeed, today's poem, "The Warning" is sermonic, but it is a warning we need to hear again and again.

Longfellow warns: "There is a poor, blind Samson in this land." Who or what could this be—something "shorn of his strength and bound in bonds of steel"? Longfellow gives no hint of what he thought was threatening "the vast temple of our liberties." In Longfellow's day this Samson that rose up and shook "the pillars of this Commonweal" could have been the Civil War, which nearly made our nation "a shapeless mass of wreck and rubbish lies."

What about our country's social and civic life today? Aren't bigotry, racism, and intolerance still here—poor and blind and grinding? Let's take his poem as a prophecy and warning for ourselves and our own time. Have we, like the Philistines, forsaken righteousness for revelry? Have we willingly overlooked injustice for personal prosperity? The consequences of our actions may be within our land at this very moment, poised to bring the pillars of our society down around us.

For this reason, we must pray for ourselves and our country that such narrow-mindedness will not become a catalyst to destruction.

Then Samson put his hands on the center pillars of the temple and pushed against them with all his might. "Let me die with the Philistines," he prayed. And the temple crashed down on the Philistine leaders and all the people. So he killed more people when he died than he had during his entire lifetime. Judges 16:29-30

On the Holy Scriptures

Why did our blessed Savior please to break
His sacred thoughts in parables; and speak
In dark enigmas? Whosoe'er thou be
That findst them so, they were not spoke to thee:
In what a case is he, that haps to run
Against a post, and cries, How dark's the sun?
Or he, in summer, that complains of frost?
The Gospel's hid to none, but who are lost:
The Scripture is a ford, wherein, 'tis said,
An elephant shall swim; a lamb may wade.

FRANCIS QUARLES (1592–1644)

HAVE you ever felt like an elephant struggling to swim in the swift stream of Scripture? At times all Bible readers feel like a character in Quarles's poem— bumping into a post in broad daylight, frostbitten in midsummer. It is then that the Lord's saying, "People see what I do, but they don't really see. They hear what I say, but they don't really hear, and they don't understand" (Matthew 13:13) can cause a real fright. So here is another saying that may help: "The only foolish question is the one you don't ask."

Take, for example, the Philippian jailer. His life was falling down around him, but he asked the most important and intelligent question of all, "What must I do to be saved?" (Acts 16:30).

Another man who knew the value of a good question was Nicodemus. He was the first to contend with the idea that "you must be born again." So he asked, "How can an old man . . . be born again?" (see John 3:1-10).

Thomas truly wanted to follow Jesus when he asked, "How can we know the way?" This was the cue for Jesus to set up a guidepost for all eternity, saying, "I am the way" (John 14:5-6).

These men were all standing at a seemingly impossible crossing along the river of truth. But they were like children willing to ask anything because they were hungry to learn. And their questions turned them from swimming elephants to wading lambs.

Jesus once prayed, "I thank you Father, . . . because you have hidden these things from the wise and the intelligent [elephants] and have revealed them to little infants [lambs]" (Matthew 11:25, NRSV). May we have a child's desire to learn and, therefore, ask the questions that will lead us to the truth of God's Word.

But I am using these stories to conceal everything about it from outsiders." Mark 4:11

The Woman and the Angel

A angel was tired of heaven, as he lounged in the golden street;
His halo was tilted side-ways, and his harp lay mute at his feet;
So the Master stooped in His pity, and gave him a pass to go,
For the space of a moon,[a] *to the earth-world, to mix with the men below. . . .*

Never was seen such an angel—eyes of heavenly blue,
Features that shamed Apollo, hair of a golden hue;
The women simply adored him; his lips were like Cupid's bow;
But he never ventured to use them—and so they voted him slow.

Till at last there came One Woman, a marvel of loveliness,
And she whispered to him: "Do you love me?" And he answered that woman, "Yes."
And she said: "Put your arms around me, and kiss me, and hold me—so—"
But fiercely he drew back, saying: "This thing is wrong, and I know."

Then sweetly she mocked his scruples, and softly she him beguiled:
"You, who are verily man among men, speak with the tongue of a child.
We have outlived the old standards; we have burst, like an over-tight thong,
The ancient, outworn, Puritanic traditions of Right and Wrong."

Then the Master feared for His angel, and called him again to His side,
For oh, the woman was wondrous, and oh, the angel was tried!
And deep in his hell sang the Devil, and this was the strain of his song:
"The ancient, outworn, Puritanic traditions of Right and Wrong."

ROBERT SERVICE (1874–1958)

[a]one month

CANADIAN Robert Service wrote ballads depicting the life of gold prospectors published in *The Spell of the Yukon and Other Verses* (1907). Service's "The Shooting of Dan McGrew" appears regularly in anthologies.

"The Woman and the Angel" is also a ballad—a song or poem that tells a fanciful story. Heavenly halos, harps, and streets of gold are make-believe, as are Peter at the golden gates and imps pattering on the red-hot pavement of hell.

But the meaning of the story isn't whimsical. Change the woman's statement in stanza 5 to a question, and ask yourself, Have I outlived the old standards—"the ancient, outworn, Puritanic traditions of Right and Wrong"? An honest answer to this question requires careful, prayerful thought.

Next consider this. Was the angel puritanical when he said, "This thing is wrong, and I know"? What does Service mean by *puritanic?* Service most likely did not mean the hyper self-righteousness and illiberal law-keeping associated with the Puritans of New England. The angel conformed to a standard of right and wrong older than that of our Puritan forebears. This standard came from God himself, of which the angel's clear conscience allowed him to bear witness. As Paul wrote to Timothy: "The purpose of my instruction is that all the Christians there would be filled with love that comes from a pure heart, a clear conscience, and sincere faith" (1 Timothy 1:5).

Let us hold to God's standard of right and wrong, purifying our heart through prayer and making our faith sincere through the reading of Scripture.

Instead, you must worship Christ as Lord of your life. And if you are asked about your Christian hope, always be ready to explain it. But you must do this in a gentle and respectful way. Keep your conscience clear. Then if people speak evil against you, they will be ashamed when they see what a good life you live because you belong to Christ. 1 Peter 3:15-16

Taste

O guide my judgment and my taste,
Sweet Spirit, author of the book
Of wonders, told in language chaste
And plainness, not to be mistook.

O let me muse, and yet at sight
The page admire, the page believe;
'Let there be light, and there was light,
Let there be Paradise and Eve!'

Who his soul's rapture can refrain?
At Joseph's ever-pleasing tale,
Of marvels, the prodigious train,
To Sinai's hill from Goshen's vale.

The Psalmist and proverbial Seer,
And all the prophets' sons of song,
Make all things precious, all things dear,
And bear the brilliant word along.

O take the book from off the shelf,
And con[a] *it meekly on thy knees;*
Best panegyric[b] *on itself,*

And self-avouched[c] *to teach and please. Respect,*
adore it heart and mind.
How greatly sweet, how sweetly grand,
Who reads the most, is most refined,
And polished by the Master's hand.

CHRISTOPHER SMART (1722–1771)

[a]to carefully study; fix in the memory [b]a formal speech or piece of writing praising a person or event [c]guaranteed

THE ENGLISH poet Christopher Smart published his *Poems on Several Occasions* in 1752. Thereafter, he suffered from mental illness that led to his confinement in an asylum. There he produced his most original and powerful poem, *A Song to David* (1763). Many people may have difficulty respecting someone committed to a psychiatric ward. But who among us could write something as beautiful as Smart's poem "Taste"?

Smart leads us on a brisk walk through Scripture. No doubt he often lovingly held the Bible, carefully studied it, and fixed it in his memory. He allows the Bible to speak its own "panegyric." This, he recognizes, is the best way to know it. "Indeed, the word of God is living and active" (Hebrews 4:12, NRSV); Moses "received living oracles to give to us" (Acts 7:38, NRSV); and our very life source is "the eternal, living word of God" (1 Peter 1:23). Smart knew that these verses were not merely slogans for preachers, so he proclaims to his readers: "O take the book from off the shelf, and con it meekly on thy knees."

Jeremiah predicted the coming of a new covenant: "'But this is the new covenant I will make with the people of Israel on that day,' says the Lord. 'I will put my laws in their minds, and I will write them on their hearts' " (Jeremiah 31:33). You are a beneficiary of this covenant, and the words God has written on your heart complement those on the pages of your Bible. Allow them to speak to and teach you.

You have been taught the holy Scriptures from childhood, and they have given you the wisdom to receive the salvation that comes by trusting in Christ Jesus. All Scripture is inspired by God and is useful to teach us what is true and to make us realize what is wrong in our lives. It straightens us out and teaches us to do what is right. It is God's way of preparing us in every way, fully equipped for every good thing God wants us to do. 2 Timothy 3:15-17

On the Bible

When thou dost take this sacred book into thy hand
Think not that thou the included sense dost
understand.

It is a sign thou wantest sound intelligence
If that thou think thyself to understand the sense.

Be not deceived thou then on it in vain mayst gaze;
The way is intricate that leads into a maze.

Here's naught but what's mysterious to an
understanding eye;
Where reverence alone stands ope,[a] *and sense*
stands by.

THOMAS TRAHERNE (1637–1674)

[a]open

THOMAS TRAHERNE was an English poet and religious writer. He was one of the English metaphysical poets, which included Richard Crashaw, John Donne, George Herbert, Andrew Marvell, and Henry Vaughan. Traherne's verse has a musical quality and contains original imagery. His important prose works are *Christian Ethicks* (1675) and the visionary *Centuries of Meditations* (1908).

After reading this poem, we might mistakenly think the poet is saying that we aren't smart enough to understand the Bible. In reality, Traherne gives good advice about how we should approach the sacred Word.

We could paraphrase Traherne's "On the Bible" like this: When you read the Bible, don't immediately assume that you understand it. If you do, you probably aren't as smart as you think you are. If you have the attitude that you already understand the Bible, your study is a waste of time and will lead to confusion. The truth of the Bible is an absolute mystery to the natural understanding of the human mind. Set your sense aside and come to the Scriptures with prayerful humility and reverent awe, and allow it to teach you its spiritual mysteries in its own perfect way.

This approach to the Christian understanding of the truth is in keeping with Traherne's tendency toward mysticism. And it is an approach that, with patience, actually works to reveal God's truth to a believer. Such was Peter's experience at Caesarea Philippi when Jesus said to him, "You are blessed, Simon son of John, because my Father in heaven has revealed this to you. You did not learn this from any human being" (Matthew 16:17).

➻ *Your words were found, and I ate them, and your words became to me a joy and the delight of my heart; for I am called by your name, O Lord, God of hosts.* Jeremiah 15:16, NRSV

H. Scriptures

Welcome dear book, soul's joy, and food! The feast
Of Spirits, Heaven extracted lies in thee;
Thou art life's charter, the dove's spotless nest
Where souls are hatched unto Eternity.

In thee the hidden stone, the manna lies,
Thou art the great elixir, rare, and choice;
The key that opens to all mysteries,
The Word in characters, God in the voice.

O that I had deep cut in my hard heart
Each line in thee! Then would I plead in groans
Of my Lord's penning, and by sweetest art
Return upon himself the Law, and stones.
Read here, my faults are thine. This book, and I
Will tell thee so; Sweet Savior thou didst die!

HENRY VAUGHAN (1622–1695)

LOVE POEMS are usually written *in* books. But here is one that is written *to* a book. But what a book! Henry Vaughan loved the Bible, and the first two stanzas of this poem catalog twelve exquisite things the Bible is to him, such as the soul's joy, life's charter, and the great elixir.

Then Vaughn pleads: "O that I had deep cut in my hard heart each line in thee!" This plea is the very promise of the new covenant: " 'But this is the new covenant I will make with the people of Israel on that day,' says the Lord: 'I will put my laws in their minds so they will understand them, and I will write them on their hearts so they will obey them. I will be their God, and they will be my people' " (Hebrews 8:10).

How has God written the law on our heart? "Clearly, you are a letter from Christ prepared by us," wrote the apostle Paul. "It is written not with pen and ink, but with the Spirit of the living God. It is carved not on stone, but on human hearts" (2 Corinthians 3:3). The Spirit of God brings the law into our heart when we believe in Jesus Christ. In fact, the Spirit *is* God's law in our heart because in Romans 8:2 Paul spoke of "the law of the Spirit of life in Christ Jesus" (NRSV). Knowing this, it is easier to understand Proverbs 4:23: "Above all else, guard your heart, for it affects everything you do." Whatever is in our heart spontaneously controls our life. Thus, Vaughan aspired to "plead in groans of my Lord's penning."

Put on salvation as your helmet, and take the sword of the Spirit, which is the Word of God. Pray at all times and on every occasion in the power of the Holy Spirit. Stay alert and be persistent in your prayers for all Christians everywhere. Ephesians 6:17-18

My People Are Destroyed . . .

For lack of knowledge do my people die!
No fell diseases in our land abound,
No pestilential vapors fill the sky,
No drought or barrenness has cursed the ground;
The harvest-fields are white on every side,
For God has given to all with liberal hand;
To none His sun and rain has He denied,
But with abundance blesses our fruitful land.
But Him who gives to all, they have not known!
His truth, His mercy, and unfailing love;
Who sends not on one favored race alone
His gifts and mercies from the heavens above;—
Therefore the land doth mourn; and, day by day,
War wastes our fields and doth the people slay!

JONES VERY (1813–1880)

ALTHOUGH Very derived today's poem from Hosea 4:1-7, he might as well have described modern-day America. Certainly we have problems with diseases, such as cancer and AIDS. But "no fell diseases in our land *abound.*" Yes, we have air pollution, but "no pestilential vapors *fill* the sky." The land isn't cursed with drought or barrenness. In fact, our harvests are so abundant we feed much of the world. Of all the nations on this earth, we must admit that here "God has given to all with liberal hand . . . [and] with abundance blesses our fruitful land."

Much of Very's poem could serve as an outline for the president's State of the Union address. But the chief executive probably wouldn't mention the plague that afflicts this and all nations: "Him who gives to all, they have not known!" This is not to say that most people aren't good, hardworking, and honest. But the basic problem is that we are dead and dying—not physically, but spiritually. So Hosea spoke for God when he said, "My people are being destroyed because they don't know me" (4:6).

Anyone could argue why this is by quoting the Bible: "No one has ever seen God" (John 1:18). Yet this verse continues: "But his only Son, who is himself God, is near to the Father's heart; he has told us about him." Elsewhere Christ said, "This is the way to have eternal life—to know you, the only true God, and Jesus Christ, the one you sent to earth" (John 17:3). Eternal life is found in the unknowable God who is knowable through Christ.

Tell this to your friends! Tell it to yourself! And when you do, use the words of Jesus Christ: "For it is my Father's will that all who see his Son and believe in him should have eternal life" (John 6:40).

Yes, everything else is worthless when compared with the priceless gain of knowing Christ Jesus my Lord. I have discarded everything else, counting it all as garbage, so that I may have Christ. Philippians 3:8

The Cities of the Plain

"Get ye up from the wrath of God's terrible day!
Ungirded, unsandalled, arise and away!
'Tis the vintage of blood, 'tis the fulness of time,
And vengeance shall gather the harvest of crime!"

The warning was spoken—the righteous had gone,
And the proud ones of Sodom were feasting alone;
All gay was the banquet—the revel was long,
With the pouring of wine and the breathing of song.

'Twas an evening of beauty; the air was perfume,
The earth was all greenness, the trees were all bloom;
And softly the delicate viol was heard,
Like the murmur of love or the notes of a bird.

And beautiful maidens moved down in the dance,
With the magic of motion and sunshine of glance;
And white arms wreathed lightly, and tresses fell free
As the plumage of birds in some tropical tree.

Where the shrines of foul idols were lighted on high,
And wantonness tempted the lust of the eye;
Midst rites of obsceneness, strange, loathsome, abhorred,
The blasphemer scoffed at the name of the Lord.

Hark! the growl of the thunder,—the quaking of earth!
Woe, woe to the worship, and woe to the mirth!
The black sky has opened; there's flame in the air;
The red arm of vengeance is lifted and bare!

Then the shriek of the dying rose wild where the song
And the low tone of love had been whispered along;
For the fierce flames went lightly o'er palace and bower,
Like the red tongues of demons, to blast and devour!

Down, down on the fallen the red ruin rained,
And the reveller sank with his wine-cup undrained;
The foot of the dancer, the music's loved thrill,
And the shout and the laughter grew suddenly still.

The last throb of anguish was fearfully given;
The last eye glared forth in its madness on Heaven!
The last groan of horror rose wildly and vain,
And death brooded over the pride of the Plain!

JOHN GREENLEAF WHITTIER (1807–1892)

THE LORD appeared to Abraham by the oaks of Mamre (Genesis 18:1). Abraham learned that God was considering the destruction of Sodom and Gomorrah because of their wickedness. "I am going down to see whether or not these reports are true," God told Abraham. "Then I will know" (18:20-21). God was not quick to judge these cities. He checked the facts himself. What a relief to know that God is so merciful!

Abraham bargains with God to spare these cities (18:23-33), arguing that there may be righteous people living there. In fact, Abraham's nephew, Lot, and his family, were the only righteous ones. So two angels extract Lot's family out of harm's way. At this point Whittier begins today's poem. The story is familiar. There is no need to dwell on the evil and sin of this place. Instead, let's consider who escaped.

"God rescued Lot out of Sodom because he was a [righteous] man" (2 Peter 2:7). Lot learned righteousness from his uncle Abraham, who "believed the Lord, and the Lord declared him righteous because of his faith" (Genesis 15:6). Lot was righteous, not because of what he did but because of whom he believed. Likewise, "we are made right in God's sight when we trust in Jesus Christ to take away our sins. And we all can be saved in this same way, no matter who we are or what we have done" (Romans 3:22). Give thanks that "Christ, who never sinned, [was made] the offering for our sin, so that we could be made right with God through Christ" (2 Corinthians 5:21).

The sun was rising as Lot reached the village. Then the Lord rained down fire and burning sulfur from the heavens on Sodom and Gomorrah. He utterly destroyed them, along with the other cities and villages of the plain, eliminating all life—people, plants, and animals alike. Genesis 19:23-25

Songs of Experience: Introduction

PART ONE

Hear the voice of the Bard!
Who Present, Past, and Future, sees;
Whose ears have heard
The Holy Word
That walked among the ancient trees,

Calling the lapsed Soul,
And weeping in the evening dew;
That might control
The starry pole,
And fallen, fallen light renew!

(continued in next day's reading)

WILLIAM BLAKE (1757–1827)

WILLIAM BLAKE was an English poet, artist, and engraver. He illustrated his own work and engraved and printed it as well. He also illustrated the book of Job, Gray's *Poems,* Chaucer's *Canterbury Tales,* and Dante's *Divine Comedy.*

Blake was a Christian mystic and visionary. In today's poem he calls us to hear the sound of God walking among the trees in the Garden of Eden. Adam and Eve knew this sound well because God walked there often. "The Holy Word . . . walked among the ancient trees." Perhaps this was God's habit just as we might enjoy a daily walk in the evening breeze.

But the day recorded in Genesis 3 wasn't just any other day in Paradise. It was a day so momentous that others of its magnitude wouldn't arrive until Christ's death and resurrection. This was the day humanity fell.

Surely God knew what had occurred. Did he just happen to walk by as the deceived pair donned their fig leaves? Not likely. Did God know that the man was hiding among the trees? Yes. Can you, like the bard, hear God calling the lapsed soul? To Blake this is so poignant that he envisions God weeping in the falling dew.

Could this be true? Did God weep? There is no record that this happened, though the Bible often reveals God's emotions—anger, jealousy, joy. The New Testament says that Jesus wept (John 11:35). If God wept in the Garden, the tears fell for the same reason Jesus wept by Lazarus's grave: humanity's unbelief. In the Garden the couple ignored God's command and partook of death. In Bethany the people focused on the dead Lazarus instead of the divine embodiment of life—Jesus Christ. In this way they perpetuated the tragedy of the fall. How often do we do the same?

Toward evening they heard the Lord God walking about in the garden, so they hid themselves among the trees. The Lord God called to Adam, "Where are you?" Genesis 3:8-9

Songs of Experience: Introduction

PART TWO

"O Earth, O Earth, return!
"Arise from out the dewy grass:
"Night is worn,
"And the morn
"Rises from the slumberous mass.

"Turn away no more;
"Why wilt thou turn away?
"The starry floor,
"The watery shore,
"Is given thee till the break of day."

WILLIAM BLAKE (1757–1827)

IN GENESIS 3:9-11 God asked Adam three questions. But why was this necessary since God already knew the answers? One of the primary functions of Scripture is to reveal the nature and character of God. The divine hand could have swatted Adam like a bug. Instead of dew, fire could have fallen that evening.

But in the tragedy of the Fall, God demonstrates his love and mercy and grace. Through these questions the Creator entered into a dialogue with his creatures and established a new relationship with them. Yes, a curse did come upon the couple and is still with us today (3:14-19). But humanity was and still is precious to God, and we are loved in spite of our failure and curse.

In this light, notice that God didn't angrily demand that Adam and Eve cover their own nakedness. Nothing we do can hide our sin from God. Instead, the God of love and mercy and grace sacrificed an animal and made clothes for the couple (3:21). Perhaps this is the moment when Blake imagined God weeping—cruel death came into the perfect creation when this animal died. This first death anticipates the time when God would walk among us as " 'the Lamb of God who takes away the sin of the world!' " (John 1:29, NRSV).

Then Adam named his wife Eve, because she would be the mother of all people everywhere. And the Lord God made clothing from animal skins for Adam and his wife. Genesis 3:20-21

To My Dear and Loving Husband

If ever two were one, then surely we.
If ever man were loved by wife, then thee;
If ever wife was happy in a man,
Compare with me ye women if you can.
I prize thy love more than whole mines of gold,
Or all the riches that the East doth hold.
My love is such that rivers cannot quench,
Nor ought but love from thee give recompense.
Thy love is such I can no way repay;
The heavens reward thee manifold, I pray.
Then while we live, in love let's so persever,
That when we live no more we may live ever.

ANNE BRADSTREET (c. 1612–1672)

KEEP in mind the popular image of the staid Puritan. Now imagine a mid-seventeenth-century housewife as she sits to write a poem to her husband. Does she write of love that "flashes like fire, the brightest kind of flame" and is so powerful that floods cannot quench it (Song of Solomon 8:6-7)? Not likely. But could anyone today write a love poem so intimate, so passionate as "To My Dear and Loving Husband"? Maybe so. But surely our modern expressions are no substitute for the rare honesty and innocence that reveal Bradstreet's deep relationship with her husband.

It's difficult not to envy a marriage of such love and devotion. It is as if Bradstreet's marriage came out the Song of Songs. It could even be seen as a model of Christ's relationship to the church from Ephesians 5, where Paul first verbalized God's standard for the marital relationship. In Paul's day polygamy was common, and wives were akin to slaves without civil rights. When Paul wrote, "Husbands must love your wives" (5:25), he initiated a social revolution.

Returning to the popular image of a Puritan, would you say that our New England housewife was filled with the Spirit? Based on this poem, we could answer yes. This is because the secret to the relationship described in Ephesians 5:22-29 is found earlier in verses 15-21, which depicts a rather puritan way of life: wise, hardworking, spurning foolishness, not given to excess, circumspect in speech, giving thanks to God, and submitting to one another. We cannot separate these characteristics from the exhortation, "Be filled with the Spirit." With these qualities marital "love [can be] strong as death, passion fierce as the grave" (Song of Solomon 8:6, NRSV).

And further, you will submit to one another out of reverence for Christ. You wives will submit to your husbands as you do to the Lord. . . . And you husbands must love your wives with the same love Christ showed the church. Ephesians 5:21-22, 25

Christ's Triumph after Death STANZA 30

Here let my Lord hang up his conquering lance,
And bloody armor with late slaughter warm,
And looking down on his weak militants,
Behold his saints, midst of their hot alarm,
Hang all their golden hopes upon his arm.
And in this lower field dispacing[a] *wide,*
Through windy thoughts, that would their sails misguide,
Anchor their fleshly ships fast in his wounded side.

(continued in next day's reading)

GILES FLETCHER (c. 1585–1623)

[a]roaming

THIS POEM starts with the word *here.* The context of the entire work gives us good reason to say that the poet has cast us forward to the new Jerusalem of Revelation 21–22. It has been a bloody journey through the previous twenty chapters, and now we are "here." Only here at the end are peace and a peaceful place for Christ to "hang up his conquering lance, and bloody armor." He has no more need for it.

The poet shows us Christ, who looks out over all the people gathered together as a city. Then they proceed to hang their hopes upon Christ's arm—his strength. They have no more need of hope. The new Jerusalem is its fulfillment.

It's true—we're not there yet. Fletcher says we are in a "lower field dispacing wide," where there are still "windy thoughts, that would [our] sails misguide." This is a reminder of the charge in Ephesians 4:14: "That we henceforth be no more children, tossed to and fro, and carried about with every wind of doctrine" (KJV).

How can believers stop such winds from filling their sails? They can "anchor their fleshly ships fast in his wounded side." Wonderful! "His wounded side" represents the redemptive death of Jesus Christ. The "fleshly ships" are our frail bodies, which contain our souls. But what is the anchor? Scripture answers: "God has given us both his promise and his oath. . . . Therefore, we who have fled to him for refuge can take new courage, for we can hold on to his promise with confidence. *This confidence is like a strong and trustworthy anchor for our souls*" (Hebrews 6:18-19, italics added).

Then I saw a new heaven and a new earth, for the old heaven and the old earth had disappeared. And the sea was also gone. And I saw the holy city, the new Jerusalem, coming down from God out of heaven like a beautiful bride prepared for her husband. Revelation 21:1-2

Full, yet without satiety,[a] *of that*
Which whets,[b] *and quiets greedy appetite,*
Where never sun did rise, nor ever sat,
But one eternal day, and endless light
Gives time to those, whose time is infinite,
  Speaking with thought, obtaining without fee,
  Beholding him, whom never eye could see,
And magnifying him, that cannot greater be.

(continued in next day's reading)

GILES FLETCHER (c. 1585–1623)

[a]gratified beyond capacity [b]stimulates

THERE are many things and people in life that we get more than our fill of. But Christ is not one of them. Today's poem says that Christ satisfies and stimulates our soul's appetite at the same time. He fills us, yet we never feel stuffed. We have him, yet we want more of him.

Long ago a psalmist caught a glimpse of this idea and wrote, "Great is the Lord, and greatly to be praised; and his greatness is unsearchable" (Psalm 145:3, KJV). Paul knew this to be true and expressed it in his many letters. For example, "Unto me, who am less than the least of all saints, is this grace given, that I should preach among the Gentiles the unsearchable riches of Christ" (Ephesians 3:8, KJV). Elsewhere he wrote, "O the depth of the riches both of the wisdom and knowledge of God! how unsearchable are his judgments, and his ways past finding out!" (Romans 11:33, KJV). Paul discovered that since Christ is unsearchable, he is inexpressible.

But that doesn't mean we cannot know Christ. Again Paul wrote: "I can really know Christ and experience the mighty power that raised him from the dead. . . . I don't mean to say that I have already achieved these things or that I have already reached perfection!" (Philippians 3:10-12). Though he knew Christ, Paul also knew that there was more of Christ to know.

As Fletcher's poem reveals, we have an eternity to get to know Christ more fully. The poet describes this time as "one eternal day, and endless light" that "gives time to those, whose time is infinite" that they can behold "him, whom never eye could see."

Today let us praise and thank God that our hope, our destiny, is to dwell with him in eternity, "magnifying him, that cannot greater be."

Jesus replied, "I am the bread of life. No one who comes to me will ever be hungry again. Those who believe in me will never thirst." John 6:35

Christ's Triumph after Death STANZA 33

How can such joy as this want words to speak?
And yet what words can speak such joy as this?
Far from the world, that might their quiet break,
Here the glad souls the face of beauty kiss,
Poured out in pleasure, on their beds of bliss.
And drunk with nectar torrents, ever hold
Their eyes on him, whose graces manifold,
The more they do behold, the more they would behold.

(continued in next day's reading)

GILES FLETCHER (c. 1585–1623)

IT IS DIFFICULT to trace in the Bible the idea of heaven as a destination. Most Christians, familiar with Christ's words in John 14:2—"I am going to prepare a place for you"—take them literally. Presumably, the place to which Jesus refers is heaven. But when Thomas complained, "We haven't any idea where you are going, so how can we know the way?" (14:5), Jesus revealed that he was going to the Father (14:12). It is well known that the Father is in heaven. So Jesus *was* going to heaven. Yet he was going much deeper (or higher) than this—he was going to prepare a place for us in God! So Giles Fletcher sings, as should we all, "How can such joy as this want words to speak? And yet what words can speak such joy as this?"

The Bible does describe what may be called heaven. Yet it refers to this place as the new Jerusalem (Revelation 21–22). This city exists outside of time in eternity, and we have no idea if it is an actual place, though it is certainly real. Scripture describes this city as the aggregate of God's people throughout the ages.

Today's poem describes this city's inhabitants as "Far from the world, that might their quiet break, here the glad souls the face of beauty kiss, poured out in pleasure, on their beds of bliss." Call it what you will, but this sounds heavenly! Unquestionably, this is the place Christ prepared for us when he returned to the Father. If you long for this, you are in good company. As C. S. Lewis wrote, "If I find in myself a desire which no experience in this world can satisfy, the most probable explanation is that I was made for another world."[a]

The Spirit and the bride say, "Come." Let each one who hears them say, "Come." Let the thirsty ones come—anyone who wants to. Let them come and drink the water of life without charge. Revelation 22:17

[a] *Mere Christianity* (New York: Macmillan, 1952), 120.

No sorrow now hangs clouding on their brow,
No bloodless malady empales their face,
No age drops on their hairs his silver snow,
No nakedness their bodies doth embase,
No poverty themselves, and theirs disgrace,
  No fear of death the joy of life devours.
  No unchaste sleep their precious time deflowers,
No loss, no grief, no change wait on their winged hours.

GILES FLETCHER (c. 1585–1623)

COULD this be true, or is Fletcher dreaming? Did this Elizabethan man think that things would improve as time passed? or that knowledge and technology would free humanity from physical decay, raise it up from poverty, and even free it from the need for sleep? No. The dream of evolutionary improvement would not arrive for another 150 years. Fletcher was not in a futuristic reverie. The conditions he describes exist in the new Jerusalem of Revelation 21–22.

Yet God's Word mentions these utopian conditions long before the book of Revelation. They are the hope of everyone who believes in the God of Abraham, Isaac, and Jacob—the Father of our Lord Jesus Christ. And it makes sense that Scripture would conclude with the fulfillment of humanity's highest hopes.

What would you have thought had you lived near Jerusalem during the eighth century B.C. and heard Isaiah say, "In that day he will remove the cloud of gloom, the shadow of death that hangs over the earth. He will swallow up death forever! The Sovereign Lord will wipe away all tears" (Isaiah 25:7-8)? And how would you respond to this: "Those who have been ransomed by the Lord will return to Jerusalem, singing songs of everlasting joy. Sorrow and mourning will disappear, and they will be overcome with joy and gladness" (35:10)? Maybe you would have scoffed, as some did. But there is another universal reply to such prophecy—words that have always echoed in the human heart: "I hope so."

God will fulfill these hopes when he throws death and the grave into the lake of fire and brings forth the new Jerusalem prepared as a bride adorned for her husband (Revelation 20:14; 21:2).

➻ *He will remove all of their sorrows, and there will be no more death or sorrow or crying or pain. For the old world and its evils are gone forever.* Revelation 21:4

Another to Urania PART ONE

On the Death of Her First and Only Child

Attend, ye mournful parents, while
I sing, a Mother in Israel;
The famed, the gracious Shunammite,
Whose beauteous story would invite
A saint to yield her only one,
Almost without a tear or groan.
A wondrous son she did embrace,
Heaven's signal work, and special grace;
Nor long embraced, but on her knees
Arrested by a fierce disease,
Scarce could he cry, My Head, My Head!
E're the dear parent saw him dead:
She laid him breathless on the bed.
Deep was her anguish, yet her peace
She held, and went to God for ease.
No signs of grief distort her face,
Nor cloud its wonted beams of grace.
No moans, no shrieks, no piercing cries;
No wringed hands, or flowing eyes
Distressed the house in that surprise.

(continued in next day's reading)

BENJAMIN COLMAN (1673–1747)

POETRY can be difficult to understand because its message is not always explicit. But the beauty of poetry lies not only in its patterns but also its meanings. Think of the words of a poem as a rugged path. The going may be rough at first, but if you stay with it, you will come to a pool of insight that will refresh you with understanding.

The path in this poem begins with its title, "Another to Urania." Urania was a name occasionally used for Aphrodite, the Greek goddess of beauty and love. Urania personified spiritual love, so we may conclude that this poem is about love. As we follow this path farther, we see a relationship of love between a believer and her intercessor—in this case, between the Shunammite woman and the prophet Elisha.

A Shunammite woman was hospitable to Elisha. Moved by her generosity, he wanted to show her his appreciation. When he found out she didn't have a son, he told the woman she would have one within a year. Sometime later this promised son suddenly collapsed and died. Colman picks up the story here.

How does love enter the scene? Despite her heart-wrenching loss, the Shunammite woman "went to God for ease." To do so, she had to visit her intercessor, Elisha. He would go to God on her behalf. Here is love: Two people not romantically involved caring for one another's needs. Because the woman cared for the prophet, she knew that she could go to him in her time of need. She knew he would care for her. In their relationship, they fulfilled the second most important command: Love your neighbor as yourself (Leviticus 19:18).

But when she came to the man of God at the mountain, she fell to the ground before him and caught hold of his feet. Gehazi began to push her away, but the man of God said, "Leave her alone. Something is troubling her deeply, and the Lord has not told me what it is."
2 Kings 4:27

Another to Urania PART TWO

On the Death of Her First and Only Child

She hastes her to the Man of God,
Hastes to the place of his abode:
Mildly denies the cause to tell
To her dear spouse; all would be well
She trusts: so did her faith excel.
Elisha, with a tender fear,
Saw his illustrious friend draw near:
'Twas not one of the Holy Days
Sacred to public prayer and praise;
Why then the Shunammite from home?
On what great errand was she come?
Her speed bespoke some weighty care,
Which generous friendship longed to share.
It struck him, something had befell
The husband, child,—All was not well—
Go, run Gehazi, said the Seer,
Enquire, with earnestness sincere;
"Say, generous host, if all be well?—
"All's well; my Lord! she said, and fell
At her great intercessor's feet:
There vents her grief in accents sweet,
Mild in her anguish, in her plaints discreet.
Such dear Urania, you to me!
O might I be but such to thee!
Mind, gracious friend, the word she said,
All well, and yet the child was dead.
What God ordains is well and best.
Well 'tis with ours, when gone to rest.
It's well with us, who stay behind,
If more from earth and sense refined
We're patient, prayerful, meek, resigned.

BENJAMIN COLMAN (1673–1747)

THE POET distills into one sentence the essence of spiritual love as seen in the Shunammite woman's prayer: "There vents her grief in accents sweet, mild in her anguish, in her plaints discreet." Colman says this is the Lord's attitude toward him, and he longs to respond with similar love. And what of us? Shall we take this as instruction on how to pray—sweet, mild, and discreet? No. This is not a poem about a woman who has been taught how to pray. Rather, she has been refined from earthly, selfish desires and so lives in love.

Do you look for rules, laws, and biblical principles clearly delineated in Scripture, hoping they will instruct you on how to live with God? Could you say, "If only Moses' two tablets were still here, I could easily read those words etched in stone." Wait a minute! The New Testament says "that old system of law etched in stone led to death" (2 Corinthians 3:7). Today we do not labor under the killing letter of the Jewish law, but we have the letter of Christian biblical principals that can be just as deadly.

The gospel of Jesus Christ begins this way: "The law indeed was given through Moses; grace and truth came through Jesus Christ" (John 1:17, MRSV). Jesus said, "I came that they may have life" (John 10:10). The entire New Testament can be understood in the light of this phrase: "The letter kills, but the Spirit gives life" (2 Corinthians 3:6, NIV).

The list of the attributes of love in 1 Corinthians 13:4-7 describes life that has been given to the believers of Jesus Christ. And the story of the Shunammite woman is a glimpse of how this life is lived out.

When Elisha arrived, the child was indeed dead, lying there on the prophet's bed. He went in alone and shut the door behind him and prayed to the Lord. 2 Kings 4:32-33

from Cain: A Mystery PART ONE

Act iii, Scene i, ll. 528–536

Cain. *Oh! thou dead*
And everlasting witness! whose unsinking
Blood darkens earth and heaven! what thou now art
I know not! but if thou seest what I am,
I think thou wilt forgive him, whom his God
Can ne'er forgive, nor his own soul. —Farewell!
I must not, dare not touch what I have made thee.
I, who sprung from the same womb as thee, drained
The same breast, clasped thee often to my own.

(continued in next day's reading)

LORD BYRON (1788–1824)

DESPITE Cain's horrendous crime, he was not a monster. He was still a man made in the image of God. Here Byron enriches our understanding of this first felon, where he sensitively colorizes the story in hues of grief and love.

What brought about this tragedy? An offering to God: "At harvest time Cain brought to the Lord a gift of his farm produce, while Abel brought several choice lambs" (Genesis 4:3-4). But God "did not accept Cain's. This made Cain very angry and dejected" (4:5).

There was nothing intrinsically wrong with Cain's farm produce. In fact, later in Israel's history, God required grain offerings from his people (Leviticus 2). So God didn't reject Cain's produce. Rather, he rejected Cain's motivation. This was the difference between Cain and Abel.

But this poem is not so much about motivation as it is about grief, self-condemnation, and self-pity. Byron imagines that Cain cannot forgive himself for this despicable act. Cain even believes that God won't forgive him. Thus, he laments, "But if thou seest what I am, I think thou wilt forgive him, whom his God can ne'er forgive, nor his own soul." But Cain is wrong. As Scripture shows us in the same chapter as the murder, God spares Cain's life, demonstrating his divine love and forgiveness: "Then the Lord put a mark on Cain to warn anyone who might try to kill him" (4:15). Though Cain suffered the consequences of his sin, God still cared for him, protecting Cain from the very crime he committed. In this, we see God's justice and mercy, which leave no room for self-condemnation nor self-pity.

At harvest time Cain brought to the Lord a gift of his farm produce, while Abel brought several choice lambs from the best of his flock. The Lord accepted Abel's offering, but he did not accept Cain's. This made Cain very angry and dejected. Genesis 4:3-5

from Cain: A Mystery

Act iii, Scene i, ll. 537–544

In fondness brotherly and boyish, I
Can never meet thee more, nor even dare
To do that for thee, which thou shouldst have done
For me—compose thy limbs into their grave—
The first grave yet dug for mortality.
But who hath dug that grave? Oh, earth! Oh, earth!
For all the fruits thou hast rendered to me, I
Give thee back this. Now for the wilderness.

LORD BYRON (1788–1824)

WHEN we meet Cain and Abel in Genesis 4, they are fully grown. Byron poetically helps us consider them as children when they shared a "fondness brotherly and boyish." The poet imagines a bitterly regretful Cain unable to do that which Abel would have done for him—arrange his body in the grave. Sadly, Cain realizes that he has repaid the faithful earth—which has yielded him fruit—with the blood of Abel.

It's too bad Cain didn't simply ask, "Why did the Lord accept Abel and his offering, but reject me and my offering?" Perhaps the answer is found in one of Paul's letters: "God saved you by grace when you believed. So you can't take credit for this; it is a gift from God. Salvation is not a reward for the good work we have done, so none of us can boast about it" (Ephesians 2:8-9, paraphrase). Just as the Lamb of God came as a sacrifice for our sins, so the lambs Abel offered came to him through no effort of his own. But Cain, the farmer, worked hard to bring forth the fruit for his offering—clearing land, tilling, watering, weeding, harvesting, and carrying the produce to the Lord. Thus, Cain attempted to gain God's favor through hard work.

Aren't you sometimes pleased (maybe even proud) when you accomplish something good in God's service? Fine. But don't make Cain's mistake and think that your work will buy God's favor. Instead, give thanks to God that "Christ . . . died for our sins once for all time. . . . He died for sinners that he might bring us safely home to God" (1 Peter 3:18). His Son is a "gift too wonderful for words!" (2 Corinthians 9:15).

But the Lord said, "What have you done? Listen—your brother's blood cries out to me from the ground! You are hereby banished from the ground you have defiled with your brother's blood. No longer will it yield abundant crops for you, no matter how hard you work!" Genesis 4:10-12

Sardis

"Write to Sardis," saith the Lord,
And write what he declares,
He whose Spirit and whose word,
Upholds the seven stars:
"All thy works and ways I search,
Find thy zeal and love decayed:
Thou art called a living church,
But thou art cold and dead.

"Watch, remember, seek, and strive,
Exert thy former pains;
Let thy timely care revive,
And strengthen what remains:
Cleanse thine heart, thy works amend,
Former times to mind recall,
Lest my sudden stroke descend,
And smite thee once for all.

"Yet I number now in thee
A few that are upright:
These my Father's face shall see,
And walk with me in white,
When in judgment I appear,
They for mine shall be confessed;
Let my faithful servants hear,
And woe be to the rest!"

WILLIAM COWPER (1731–1800)

IN THE mid to late first century, the church began to stray from God's way. Some apostles wrote several epistles (for example, 2 Timothy, 2 Peter, and Jude) to address this problem. Christ's seven letters to the churches in Revelation 2–3 were also meant to adjust the church's course as it veered from God's way. In these letters Christ delivered the most severe warnings to God's people since he rebuked the Pharisees (Matthew 23:13-29). This poem focuses on the letter to the church in Sardis.

The church in Sardis appeared spiritually alive, but in reality it was dead. Surrounded by a pagan culture, the believers had lost their zeal for God and compromised their faith. They lived at peace with their culture, tolerating—perhaps even condoning—immorality. In essence, they had lost their flavor as salt, and their light was dim (Matthew 5:13-16). Thus, Christ warns them to remember what they had received and heard, obey it, and repent. Otherwise, they would reap his judgment: "Former times to mind recall, lest my sudden stroke descend, and smite thee once for all."

Sadly, the condition of today's church in some parts of the world is no different from that of Sardis. Many believers have fallen asleep and become "cold and dead." They have compromised with the ungodly, immoral culture that surrounds them. We should take Christ's words in Revelation 3:1-6 personally and ask ourselves, "Do I appear to have a living faith yet am actually dead?" If the answer is yes, then let us "watch, remember, seek, and strive" to strengthen the faith that remains and repent of our errant ways. Enduring the world's persecution is far easier than bearing God's judgment.

I know all the things you do, and that you have a reputation for being alive—but you are dead. Now wake up! Strengthen what little remains, for even what is left is at the point of death. Revelation 3:1-2

Holy Sonnet XIX

Oh, to vex me, two contraries meet in one:
Inconstancy unnaturally hath begot
A constant habit, that when I would not
I change in vows, and in devotion.
As humorous is my contrition
As my profane love, and as soon forgot:
As ridingly distempered, cold and hot,
As praying, as mute; as infinite, as none.
I durst not view heaven yesterday; and today
In prayers, and flattering speeches, I court God:
Tomorrow I quake with true fear of his rod.
So my devout fits come and go away
Like a fantastic ague:[a] *save that here*
Those are my best days, when I shake with fear.

JOHN DONNE (1572–1631)

[a] a malarial fever marked by regularly recurring chills

TODAY it is popular to equate emotion with faith. Intense expressions of love, exulting joy, and gushing gratitude are often seen in worship. But in this poem Donne pinpoints a common Christian experience—the vexation we feel when two "contraries" meet within us. The apostle Paul was the pioneer of such self-condemnation. "I don't understand myself at all," he wrote, "for I really want to do what is right, but I don't do it. Instead, I do the very thing I hate" (Romans 7:15). Likewise, Donne calls his contrition humorous, his love profane, and his praying mute because of his constant habit: "I change in vows, and in devotion." His wavering, inconsistent faith in and devotion to God disturbed Donne deeply. Does this sound familiar to you?

You may protest, "This is wrong, I shouldn't feel this way." Perhaps not, but honesty is the best policy. Have you ever felt Donne's "devout fits" that come and go "like a fantasic ague"? Anyone who wants to live in the New Testament pattern must slog through the swamp of Romans 7 at least once. There we suffer the chill of verse 24: "Oh, what a miserable person I am! Who will free me from this life that is dominated by sin?" The poet calls these his best days, "when I shake with fear." But read on, trembling Christian! Find warmth and solid ground in Romans 8:1: "Now there is no condemnation for those who belong to Christ Jesus."

I know I am rotten through and through so far as my old sinful nature is concerned. No matter which way I turn, I can't make myself do right. I want to, but I can't. When I want to do good, I don't. And when I try not to do wrong, I do it anyway. Romans 7:18-19

The Jewish Cemetery at Newport PART ONE

How strange it seems! These Hebrews in their graves,
Close by the street of this fair seaport town,
Silent beside the never-silent waves,
At rest in all this moving up and down!

The trees are white with dust, that o'er their sleep
Wave their broad curtains in the southwind's breath,
While underneath these leafy tents they keep
The long, mysterious Exodus of Death.

And these sepulchral stones, so old and brown,
That pave with level flags their burial-place,
Seem like the tablets of the Law, thrown down
And broken by Moses at the mountain's base.

The very names recorded here are strange,
Of foreign accent, and of different climes;
Alvares and Rivera interchange
With Abraham and Jacob of old times.

"Blessed be God! for he created Death!"
The mourners said, "and Death is rest and peace;"
Then added, in the certainty of faith,
"And giveth Life that nevermore shall cease."

Closed are the portals of their Synagogue,
No Psalms of David now the silence break,
No Rabbi reads the ancient Decalogue[a]
In the grand dialect the Prophets spake.

Gone are the living, but the dead remain,
And not neglected, for a hand unseen,
Scattering its bounty, like a summer rain,
Still keeps their graves and their remembrance green.

(continued in next day's reading)

HENRY WADSWORTH LONGFELLOW (1807–1882)

[a]the Ten Commandments

THE HISTORY of Newport, Rhode Island, is fascinating. Settlers fleeing religious intolerance in Massachusetts established this town at the mouth of Narragansett Bay in 1639. Longfellow, a popular and influential American poet of the nineteenth century, was familiar with Newport's history. He had seen it become a fashionable resort for the rich after the Civil War. But for Longfellow, the most interesting or unique aspect of this seaside settlement was a small, Jewish cemetery—a seemingly unlikely find in Anglo-Saxon New England. But bear in mind that Newport is the home of Touro Synagogue (1763), the oldest synagogue in the United States.

In this cemetery the poet sees the history of God's chosen race. The trees remind him of the tents of the Exodus. The smooth gravestones are like the broken tablets of the Law. The names inscribed recall foreign lands and an ancient people. Here they rest in death, never again to pass through the synagogue doors to hear a Rabbi read the Torah.

Longfellow calls this "the long, mysterious Exodus of Death." He pictures these people still traveling, as their forebears have from the days of Abraham. Through this image Longfellow conveys a truth that a modern poet has pronounced more plainly: "Just remember that death is not the end."

Longfellow once said that the purpose of the imagination was not "to devise what has no existence, but rather to perceive what really exists, not creation but insight." With his imagination the poet sees God's faithfulness in "a hand unseen . . . [that] still keeps their graves and their remembrance green."

But Moses told the people, "Don't be afraid. Just stand where you are and watch the Lord rescue you. The Egyptians that you see today will never be seen again. The Lord himself will fight for you. You won't have to lift a finger in your defense!" Exodus 14:13-14

The Jewish Cemetery at Newport

How came they here? What burst of Christian hate,
What persecution, merciless and blind,
Drove o'er the sea—that desert desolate—
These Ishmaels and Hagars of mankind?

They lived in narrow streets and lanes obscure,
Ghetto and Judenstrass,[a] *in mirk and mire;*
Taught in the school of patience to endure
The life of anguish and the death of fire.

All their lives long, with the unleavened bread
And bitter herbs of exile and its fears,
The wasting famine of the heart they fed,
And slaked its thirst with marah[b] *of their tears.*

Anathema maranatha![c] *was the cry*
That rang from town to town, from street to street;
At every gate the accursed Mordecai[d]
Was mocked and jeered, and spurned by Christian feet.

Pride and humiliation hand in hand
Walked with them through the world where'er they went;
Trampled and beaten were they as the sand
And yet unshaken as the continent.

For in the background figures vague and vast
Of patriarchs and of prophets rose sublime,
And all the great traditions of the Past
They saw reflected in the coming time.

And thus forever with reverted look
The mystic volume of the world they read,
Spelling it backward, like a Hebrew book,
Till life became a Legend of the Dead.

But ah! what once has been shall be no more!
The groaning earth in travail and in pain
Brings forth its races, but does not restore,
And the dead nations never rise again.

HENRY WADSWORTH LONGFELLOW (1807–1882)

[a]Jew's Street [b]bitterness [c]1 Corinthians 16:22, KJV [d]Esther 2:5; 3:1-2

THE SECOND half of this poem causes one to wonder: *What would Longfellow have written about the Holocaust?* Here, a century before that atrocity, the poet tells of the hate that drove this race over the sea to escape "persecution, merciless and blind."

Just as the "never-silent waves" pound the shore, the Gentile nations have beaten upon the Jews for centuries. Yet here is this burial ground in Newport—a silent witness to a race as "unshaken as the continent." How can a persecuted race be unshaken? Longfellow's answer: The Jews see their history reflected "in the coming time" and gain encouragement from it. That is to say, the hope promised to the patriarchs, the words of the prophets, and the great traditions of the past bring them hope for the future. Although they appear to move away from the past, they actually revert back to it as though they were reading a book in Hebrew from right to left, from end to beginning.

Hebrews 11:13-16 expresses this idea: "All these faithful ones died without receiving what God had promised them, but they saw it all from a distance and welcomed the promises of God. They agreed that they were no more than foreigners and nomads here on earth. . . . They were looking for a better place, a heavenly homeland. That is why God is not ashamed to be called their God, for he has prepared a heavenly city for them."

In the last stanza Longfellow expresses the hope that sustains both messianic Jew and Christian alike: "What once has been shall be no more!" God's people will live forever in the new Jerusalem (Revelation 21:1-4). The travail and pain of life shall end, and those who persecuted God's people will "never rise again."

I saw the dead, both great and small, standing before God's throne. And the books were opened, including the Book of Life. Revelation 20:12

Blind Bartimæus

Blind Bartimæus at the gates
Of Jericho in darkness waits;
He hears the crowd—he hears a breath
Say, "It is Christ of Nazareth!"
And calls, in tones of agony,
"Jesus, have mercy now on me!"

The thronging multitudes increase;
Blind Bartimæus, hold thy peace!
But still, above the noisy crowd,
The beggar's cry is shrill and loud;
Until they say, "He calleth thee!"
"Fear not, arise, He calleth thee!"

Then saith the Christ, as silent stands
The crowd, "What wilt thou at my hands?"
And he replies, "O give me light!
Rabbi, restore the blind man's sight!"
And Jesus answers, "Go in peace,
Thy faith from blindness gives release!"

Ye that have eyes, yet cannot see,
In darkness and in misery,
Recall those mighty Voices Three,
"Jesus, have mercy now on me!
Fear not, arise, and go in peace!
Thy faith from blindness gives release!"

HENRY WADSWORTH LONGFELLOW (1807–1882)

FROM the hundreds of Bible stories, Longfellow chose to write of Bartiæmus. Longfellow witnessed nineteenth-century America and recorded its spirit in poetry. Yet here he does not compose an epic similar to his other works; he tells a simple story told time and again in children's Sunday school. But Scripture hints that this story is not so elementary.

Although the blind man created a ruckus, it wasn't the noise that caught the Lord's attention. It was the title "Son of David" that Bartiæmus used that caused Jesus to stop. Why? Because Bartiæmus understood who Jesus is and believed. He knew that Jesus was not only human but divine. Believing in Christ, Bartiæmus presented the Savior with a request: He wanted his vision restored.

Bartima{e}us was unique. Though blind, he could see what really mattered. While the crowds could see, many were blind to the truth that would set them free. Unfortunately, many people today are as blind as those in the crowd. Even some who attend church and say and do the right things are unaware of Christ's true identity. They think they only need a little of the Savior's power to make them better. They believe they can live in a way that pleases God and thus redeem themselves. This is what it means to be spiritually blind, to be self-righteous like the Pharisees (Matthew 15:12-14). It is an affliction we can call "the cloak of Bartiæmus"[a] (see Mark 10:50, NRSV). Let us all throw it off—if we haven't done so yet—to follow Jesus unencumbered!

As he and his disciples and a large crowd were leaving Jericho, Bartimaeus son of Timaeus, a blind beggar, was sitting by the roadside. When he heard that it was Jesus of Nazareth, he began to shout out and say, "Jesus, Son of David, have mercy on me!" Mark 10:46-47, NRSV

[a]something to cast off to come to the Lord without hindrance

On the Babel-Builders

Sure, if those Babel-builders had thought good
To raise their heaven-high tower before the flood,
The wiser sort of people might deride
Their folly, and that folly had salved their pride;
Or had their faiths but enterprised that plot,
Their hearts had finished what their hands could
not;
'Twas not for love of heaven: nor did they aim
So much to raise a building, as a name:
They that by works shall seek to make intrusion
To heaven, find nothing but their own confusion.

FRANCIS QUARLES (1592–1644)

IN THE beginning God took dirt and made Adam (Genesis 2:7). Later the people of Babel took dirt and made bricks, which they used to build a tower to heaven that would stand as a monument to their greatness as a people (11:3-4).

Millennia later, teachers preaching a distorted gospel visited Christian churches throughout Galatia. They convinced the Galatians that salvation came through obeying the Jewish law. The apostle Paul, who brought the gospel to this region, said God's curse would fall on these teachers for their lies (Galatians 1:8-9). The truth is, salvation comes through faith in Jesus Christ alone, not by obeying any system of religious law (2:16).

This brings us back to Babel. Could those ancient builders have reached heaven with their tower? How far would they have had to build? Their endless effort of manufacturing and piling brick upon brick to reach heaven is the same as the Galatians' attempts to become perfect by keeping law after law. Paul warned the Galatians of the terrible consequences of this false gospel: "If you are trying to make yourselves right with God by keeping the law, you have been cut off from Christ! You have fallen away from God's grace" (5:4).

And what about the false teachers? They plied their trade for the same reason Babel's masons built the tower—to make a name for themselves (6:13). The end result for the builders and the teachers is the same: "They that by works shall seek to make intrusion to heaven, find nothing but their own confusion."

As the people migrated eastward, they found a plain in the land of Babylonia and settled there. They began to talk about construction projects. "Come," they said, "let's make great piles of burnt brick and collect natural asphalt to use as mortar. Let's build a great city with a tower that reaches to the skies—a monument to our greatness! This will bring us together and keep us from scattering all over the world."
Genesis 11:2-4

The Sower

Ye sons of earth prepare the plough,
Break up your fallow ground!
The Sower is gone forth to sow,
And scatter blessings round.

The seed that finds a stony soil,
Shoots forth a hasty blade;
But ill repays the sower's toil,
Soon withered, scorched, and dead.

The thorny ground is sure to balk
All hopes of harvest there;
We find a tall and sickly stalk,
But not the fruitful ear.

The beaten path and high-way side
Receive the trust in vain;
The watchful birds the spoil divide,
And pick up all the grain.

But where the Lord of grace and power
Has blessed the happy field;
How plenteous is the golden store
The deep-wrought furrows yield!

Father of mercies we have need
Of thy preparing grace;
Let the same hand that gives the seed,
Provide a fruitful place.

WILLIAM COWPER (1731–1800)

OUR HEART, the hearts of our family members, and those of our friends, colleagues, and neighbors are all like the soil in a farmer's field. Paul says, "You are God's field" (1 Corinthians 3:9), and elsewhere Jesus says, "My Father is the gardener" (John 15:1). So we have some soil, a farmer, and seed, which is God's message. Here, in the parable of the sower, vital action occurs: The farmer sows the seed, and the seed falls on the soil. Then the seed grows. Finally the soil bears fruit. This shows the simplicity of God's way. But other things are happening as well: Feet trample, birds eat, and thorns grow. These kill the seed.

Picture a garden—perhaps it is your own. What is the soil doing? Nothing. It lays there waiting for you, its gardener, to make it into a productive plot by tilling, sifting, fertilizing, planting, weeding, watering, etc. The soil functions in one way. It provides a place for your seeds to grow. But unless you do the work, the soil is helpless to produce fruit. If it had any awareness, it would trust you to do what is best.

At times we are God's field, not his farmhand. God does the work, the seed does the growing, and we—the soil—provide one thing: patient endurance. The growing season on God's farm lasts our whole life. All too soon the wonderful day of harvest comes. As we patiently await that day, enduring our share of tramping feet, pecking birds, and annoying thorns, let us pray with William Cowper, "Father of mercies we have need of thy preparing grace; let the same hand that gives the seed, provide a fruitful place."

But the good soil represents honest, good-hearted people who hear God's message, cling to it, and steadily produce a huge harvest.
Luke 8:15

Aaron

Holiness on the head,
Light and perfections on the breast,
Harmonious bells below, raising the dead
To lead them unto life and rest.
Thus are true Aarons dressed.

Profaneness in my head,
Defects and darkness in my breast,
A noise of passions ringing me for dead
Unto a place where is no rest.
Poor priest thus am I dressed.

Only another head
I have, another heart and breast,
Another music, making live not dead,
Without whom I could have no rest:
In him I am well dressed.

Christ is my only head,
My alone only heart and breast,
My only music, striking me even dead;
That to the old man I may rest,
And be in him new dressed.

So holy in my head,
Perfect and light in my dear breast,
My doctrine tuned by Christ, (who is not dead,
But lives in me while I do rest)
Come people; Aaron's dressed.

GEORGE HERBERT (1593–1633)

GEORGE HERBERT expressed many of his struggles as a Christian and a parish priest in his poetry. Herbert compares himself to the first true priest, Aaron. Herbert admits his shortcomings; he is the exact opposite of Aaron. Instead of "holiness on the head," Herbert has "profaneness in [his] head." In place of "light and perfections on the breast," he has "defects and darkness in [his] breast."

But all is not lost because Herbert has Christ, who lives in him. Christ renews Herbert's mind and cleanses his heart. And in Christ, Herbert is appropriately dressed to minister to God's people. Thus Herbert concludes, "Come people; Aaron's dressed."

Whether or not we are a pastor, minister, or priest, what Herbert says is true of us too. We have profaneness in our head and defects and darkness in our breast. But this is what we were *in ourself,* without Christ. And because this is what we were, we believed in Jesus, our Savior. The apostle Paul wrote, "The death [Christ] died, he died to sin, once for all; but the life he lives, he lives to God. So you also must consider yourselves dead to sin and alive to God *in Christ Jesus*" (Romans 6:10-11, NRSV; italics added). Herbert said, "That to the old man I may rest, and be in [Christ] new dressed." When we clothe ourselves with Christ, we die to sin. He put to death the old man—our old nature—making us a new creature (2 Corinthians 5:17). Now in Christ we are well dressed; perfection and light reside in our breast.

They are to make a chestpiece, an ephod, a robe, an embroidered tunic, a turban, and a sash. They will also make special garments for Aaron's sons to wear when they serve as priests before me. These items must be made of fine linen cloth and embroidered with gold thread and blue, purple, and scarlet yarn. Exodus 28:4-5

John

What went ye out to see? a shaken reed?
In him whose voice proclaims "prepare the way;"
Behold the oak that stormy centuries feed!
Though but the buried acorn of My day;
What went ye out to see? a kingly man?
In the soft garments clothed that ye have worn;
Behold a servant whom the hot suns tan,
His raiment from the rough-haired camel torn;
Ye seek ye know not what; blind children all,
Who each his idle fancy will demand;
Nor heed my true-sent prophet's warning call,
That you may learn of me the new command,
And see the Light that cometh down from heaven,
Repent! and see, while yet its light is given.

JONES VERY (1813–1880)

"WHO is John the Baptist?" Jesus asked the crowd that gathered around him. Judging from Luke 7:24-28, the Jewish people held various opinions about John's identity. Perhaps some thought he was weak like a reed bent by the wind. Others may have thought he was rich and dressed in regal attire. Still others believed he was a prophet (7:26). But what does a prophet look like?

The Old Testament foretold John's coming but didn't describe his appearance (Malachi 3:1). Was he a reed or an oak? rich or rough? regal or wild? At that time who knew? A prophet could have been all, or some, or none of these things. John lived in the wilderness and wore the rough hide of the unclean camel. Very describes John's strength as "the oak that stormy centuries feed!"

Perhaps the Pharisees and experts in religious law misjudged John's identity because of his appearance. When they looked at him they saw a man who didn't drink wine and fasted often, and they concluded, "He's demon possessed" (Luke 7:33). They had "rejected God's plan for them, for they had refused John's baptism" (7:30). They also misjudged Jesus. When they saw Jesus feasting and drinking, they said, "He's a glutton and a drunkard, and a friend of the worst sort of sinners!" (7:34).

Imagine their arrogance, judging John and Jesus only on appearances. As the Pharisees' actions showed, they failed to heed the warning God gave Samuel centuries earlier: "Don't judge by his appearance" (1 Samuel 16:7). In the end, they missed the message and the Messiah. Let's not make the same mistake.

➻ *Who is this man in the wilderness that you went out to see? Did you find him weak as a reed, moved by every breath of wind? Or were you expecting to see a man dressed in expensive clothes? . . . Were you looking for a prophet? Yes, and he is more than a prophet.* Luke 7:24-26

Oh! Weep for Those

Oh! weep for those that wept by Babel's stream,
Whose shrines are desolate, whose land a dream;
Weep for the harp of Judah's broken shell;
Mourn—where their god hath dwelt the godless
dwell!

And where shall Israel lave[a] *her bleeding feet?*
And when shall Zion's songs again seem sweet?
And Judah's melody once more rejoice
The hearts that leaped before its heavenly voice?

Tribes of the wandering foot and weary breast,
How shall ye flee away and be at rest!
The wild-dove hath her nest, the fox his cave,
Mankind their country—Israel but the grave!

LORD BYRON (1788–1824)

[a]to wash or bathe

In 586 B.C. "the Lord brought the king of Babylon against [Jerusalem]. The Babylonians killed Judah's young men, even chasing after them into the Temple. They had no pity on the people, killing both young and old, men and women, healthy and sick. God handed them all over to Nebuchadnezzar" (2 Chronicles 36:17). Jerusalem—the city of God—was no more.

Roughly two thousand years later, the English poet Lord Byron wept for "those that wept by Babel's stream." Jerusalem had been "trampled down by the Gentiles" (Luke 21:24). But all the poet's insight could not tell him that in the next century, our century, a man more brutal than Nebuchadnezzar would enkindle an incomprehensible holocaust upon the people whom God had enjoyed like "fresh grapes in the desert" and the "first ripe figs of the season" (Hosea 9:10). Only sixty years ago, a man named Hitler attempted to wipe out God's grapevines and fig trees. He stripped their bark and left their branches white and bare (Joel 1:7).

One day Jesus sat on the slopes of the Mount of Olives. His disciples asked him, "Will there be any sign ahead of time to signal your return and the end of the world?" (Matthew 24:3). Jesus answered, "Now learn a lesson from the fig tree. When its buds become tender and its leaves begin to sprout, you know without being told that summer is near" (24:32-33). This saying may have been cryptic then, but our generation has witnessed this event. The nation of Israel has risen out of the ashes of World War II. Its buds are tender, its leaves have begun to sprout, and the summer of the Lord's return is near. May we be ready.

The few who survived were taken away to Babylon, and they became servants to the king and his sons until the kingdom of Persia came to power. So the message of the Lord spoken through Jeremiah was fulfilled. The land finally enjoyed its Sabbath rest, lying desolate for seventy years, just as the prophet had said. 2 Chronicles 36:20-21

"All Is Vanity, Saith the Preacher"

Fame, wisdom, love, and power were mine,
And health and youth possessed me;
My goblets blushed from every vine,
And lovely forms caressed me;
I sunned my heart in beauty's eyes,
And felt my soul grow tender;
All earth can give, or mortal prize,
Was mine of regal splendour.

I strive to number o'er what days
Remembrance can discover,
Which all that life or earth displays
Would lure me to live over.
There rose no day, there rolled no hour
Of pleasure unembittered;
And not a trapping decked my power
That galled not while it glittered.

The serpent of the field, by art
And spells, is won from harming;
But that which coils around the heart,
Oh! who hath power of charming?
It will not list[a] *to wisdom's lore,*
Nor music's voice can lure it;
But there it stings for evermore
The soul that must endure it.

LORD BYRON (1788–1824)

[a]to listen to

THE BOOK of Ecclesiastes begins and ends with the same words: "All is meaningless," says the Teacher, "utterly meaningless!" (1:2; 12:8). It would hardly be a best-seller on the self-help list these days! But Lord Byron seems to have read it.

In literature there is a character type known as the Byronic hero—an emotional young man who shuns human company and wanders through life weighed down by a sense of guilt for mysterious past transgressions. The hero of Byron's poem "Childe Harold" is the first example of such a character and is to some extent patterned after the poet himself. So Byron surely knew what he was talking about when he described the serpent "which coils around the heart," continually stinging its victim with the venom of life's meaninglessness—emptiness that a world of snake charmers with their music and wisdom cannot subdue.

We don't know if Byron ever found relief through Christ from life's vanity. Only the day of the Lord will tell. Ironically, the inner turmoil Byron expressed here isn't an accurate portrayal of his thirty-six short years on earth. He was quite successful, becoming one of the most important and versatile writers of the English romantic movement. He also served as the commander in chief of English forces who fought the Turks in Greece. Still there is little doubt that he knew "everything under the sun is meaningless, like chasing the wind" (Ecclesiastes 1:14). And if Byron didn't live for Christ, then all he accomplished is meaningless in the light of eternity.

May the message of Ecclesiastes—and Byron's poem—constantly remind us of the temporal nature of this world and the importance of living for Christ and for eternity.

Don't let the excitement of youth cause you to forget your Creator. Honor him in your youth before you grow old and no longer enjoy living. Ecclesiastes 12:1

I Took My Power in My Hand—

I took my Power in my Hand—
And went against the World—
'Twas not so much as David—had—
But I—was twice as bold—

I aimed my Pebble—but Myself
Was all the one that fell—
Was it Goliath—was too large—
Or was myself—too small?

EMILY DICKINSON (1830–1886)

EMILY DICKINSON asks a good question: Did she fail to slay the giant because he was too large or because she was too small? In the eyes of Saul and the army of Israel, Goliath was so much bigger than they. Terrified and greatly shaken by the sight of the Philistine champion, the Israelites refused to fight him (1 Samuel 17:11). After all, they were too small. But David saw things differently. He compared the strength of Goliath to the power of God. Which is smaller?

In the valley of Elah the two stood exchanging insults—little David and giant Goliath. The boy warned the man of his impending defeat: "Everyone will know that the Lord does not need weapons to rescue his people," said David. "It is his battle, not ours. The Lord will give you to us!" (17:47).

These days we face gigantic opponents of our soul. False religion is one such opponent, serving the appetites of its adherents rather than the purposes of God. Rampant consumerism is another, enticing people into an endless cycle of earning and spending spurred on by advertising. Still another is the breakdown of communities, generating distrust and suspicion between neighbors that leaves people isolated and lonely.

Dickinson said, "I took my Power in my Hand—And went against the World—." No wonder she fell. Our own power is an encumbrance, just as Saul's armor would have been for David. David didn't stumble into battle under its weight. That would have been faithless. Instead, David trusted God for the victory, and God was faithful. How are you trusting in your own power to overcome the world today? What armor do you need to leave behind? God will overcome the world for us if we are weak enough to let him.

Then Goliath, a Philistine champion from Gath, came out of the Philistine ranks to face the forces of Israel. He was a giant of a man, measuring over nine feet tall! 1 Samuel 17:4

Holy Sonnet VII

At the round Earth's imagined corners, blow
Your trumpets, Angels, and arise, arise
From death, you numberless infinities
Of souls, and to your scattered bodies go,
All whom the flood did, and fire shall o'erthrow,
All whom war, dearth, age, agues, tyrannies,
Despair, law, chance, hath slain, and you whose eyes,
Shall behold God, and never taste death's woe.
But let them sleep, Lord, and me mourn a space,
For, if above all these, my sins abound,
'Tis late to ask abundance of thy grace,
When we are there; here on this lowly ground,
Teach me how to repent; for that's as good
As if thou hadst sealed my pardon, with thy blood.

JOHN DONNE (1572–1631)

JOHN DONNE'S poetry embraces a wide range of secular and religious subjects. He wrote cynical verse, love poems, satires, hymns, and holy sonnets—which depicted his own spiritual struggles. Some analysts have assumed that Donne's poetry reflects his personal growth from a libertine into the somber dean of St. Paul's. Thus they attribute Donne's sensual love poetry to his youth and his religious sonnets to his maturity. But most of Donne's poems were published posthumously and cannot be dated. Moreover, they display a unity of literary technique.

In "Holy Sonnet VII" Donne pictures the end of the world and the resurrection of "numberless infinities of souls" to judgment. The poet's response to this sight is to pray for more time. "Let them sleep," he asks, "and [let] me mourn a space." Perhaps Donne desired more time so that more people could come to faith in Christ. But most likely, he wanted time to repent thoroughly. He suggests that his sins are more plentiful than those of all these souls and states a fact that must sober every Christian: "'Tis late to ask abundance of thy grace, when we are there" at the judgment. John the apostle wrote that a time will come when "God will wait no longer. . . . God's mysterious plan will be fulfilled . . . just as he announced it to his servants the prophets" (Revelation 10:6-7).

Painfully aware of this day, the poet prays, "Here on this lowly ground, teach me how to repent; for that's as good as if thou hadst sealed my pardon, with thy blood." May we, like Donne, remember that the day of judgment is fast approaching. May this reality also help to keep us humble and mournful before our God.

But God showed his great love for us by sending Christ to die for us while we were still sinners. And since we have been made right in God's sight by the blood of Christ, he will certainly save us from God's judgment. Romans 5:8-9

Hope

Ah! Hannah, why shouldst thou despair,
Quick to the tabernacle speed;
There on thy knees prefer thy prayer,
And there thy cause to mercy plead.

Her pious breathings now ascend,
As from her heart the sighs she heaves;
And angels to her suit attend,
Till strong in hope she now conceives.

Then Samuel soon was brought to light
To serve the Lord, as yet a child—
O what a heart-reviving sight!
Sure cherubims and seraphs smiled.

CHRISTOPHER SMART (1722–1771)

THE BOOK of 1 Samuel paints a bleak portrait of Israel's spiritual condition. In those days, messages and visions from the Lord were rare. Apparently, the people's hearts were far from the Lord. Worse yet, the high priest's sons defiled offerings to the Lord and sinned in the Tabernacle. With a corrupt people and priesthood, Israel's need for restoration seemed hopeless.

At this same time there lived a devout woman named Hannah, who couldn't conceive. Her husband's other wife, Peninnah, made fun of her because she was barren. Yet Hannah didn't give up hope. She did the only thing she could—poured her heart out to the Lord (1 Samuel 1:15). He heard her prayer and blessed her with a son, whom she later gave up for the Lord's service. Through this child, Samuel, the Lord would restore his priesthood, and through the priesthood, Israel: "Then I will raise up a faithful priest who will serve me and do what I tell him to do. I will bless his descendants, and his family will be priests to my anointed kings forever" (2:35).

It is quite amazing how God uses people for his glorious purposes. Through one woman's prayer, God raised up a little boy who would one day become the trustworthy prophet of the Lord (3:20) and anoint Israel's greatest king—David.

When all seems hopeless, we can place our hope in God. He will bring us through life's difficulties and trials at just the right time.

➭ *Once when they were at Shiloh, Hannah went over to the Tabernacle after supper to pray to the Lord. Eli the priest was sitting at his customary place beside the entrance. Hannah was in deep anguish, crying bitterly as she prayed to the Lord. And she made this vow: "O Lord Almighty, if you will look down upon my sorrow and answer my prayer and give me a son, then I will give him back to you. He will be yours for his entire lifetime, and as a sign that he has been dedicated to the Lord, his hair will never be cut."* 1 Samuel 1:9-11

Enoch

I looked to find a man who walked with God,
Like the translated patriarch of old;—
Though gladdened millions on his footstool trod,
Yet none like him did such sweet converse hold;
I heard the wind in low complaint go by
That none its melodies like him could hear;
Day unto day spoke wisdom from on high,
Yet none like David turned a willing ear;
God walked alone unhonored through the earth;
For him no heart-built temple open stood,
The soul forgetful of her nobler birth
Had hewn him lofty shrines of stone and wood,
And left unfinished and in ruins still
The only temple he delights to fill.

JONES VERY (1813–1880)

IN THIS poem Jones Very draws our attention to Genesis 5:23-24: "Enoch walked with God." The expression "walked with" was a common phrase in Eastern countries, denoting constant fellowship. Enoch had close fellowship with God—so much so that God took him straight to heaven one day before he died.

God has always looked for people with whom he could have close fellowship. But most people have closed hearts and/or have turned to other gods—the idols of stone and wood. However, throughout history, God has found various individuals with whom he has had close fellowship: David, Daniel, Paul, Peter, and John—to name a few. These people opened their hearts to God, so they became his temple, a place for him to dwell and live and make his home—for human beings are "the only temple he delights to fill."

Paul once wrote to the church in Corinth: "You are . . . God's building" (1 Corinthians 3:9), and to the church in Ephesus: "We who believe are carefully joined together, becoming a holy temple for the Lord. Through him you Gentiles are also joined together as part of this dwelling where God lives by his Spirit" (Ephesians 2:21-22).

May God grant each one of us the same grace: to walk with him and to allow him to live in us.

Jesus [said], "All those who love me will do what I say. My Father will love them, and we will come to them and live with them." John 14:23

from The Cry of a Stone

Therefore John read how that thou wouldst
the earth again restore.
None shall hinder them from those thrones
which John there did declare:
Oh a sea of glass there crystal was
which none could it compare:
But oh your standing on the earth,
on glass that brittle is,
Which shall crumble under your feet
when that there comes forth this,
This sea of glass which is indeed,
that where thine thee behold:
Oh they may look up unto thee,
and thorough it extol
Thy love that did a book write sweet,
and many things there in store
Of royalties which should come out,
and be given more and more,
Unto those that deny thy foes,
and Antichrist also,
They that go forth to strike at him,
thou wilt upon them blow,
Thy spirit upon them shall come forth
and Antichrist shall fall
Both in person, and also too,
in his coming principal.
Oh it is Lord, then sweet surely,
to read of such things here,
And John he mourned abundantly,
that th' mystery might draw near,
That new Jerusalem above,
might come down here below,
And that they might see their High,
when that forth he doth go.

ANNA TRAPNELL (c. 1622–1654)

IMAGINE the grief of John, this old apostle. He had been with Christ from the beginning. Called from his fishing boat on the sea of Galilee, he witnessed the ministry of the Savior of Israel and stood nearby when he died on the cross. He personally met the risen Christ, witnessed his ascension, and received the baptism of the Holy Spirit on Pentecost. He also labored to establish the early churches, wrote the Gospel and the epistles that bear his name, and endured exile on an island for keeping the faith. On that island John received a vision, a revelation of Jesus Christ, which is recorded in the book of Revelation and is the subject of today's poem.

John sees a scroll containing all the answers to the mystery of God. "But no one in heaven or on earth or under the earth was able to open the scroll and read it" (Revelation 5:3). Overwhelmed, John began to weep. But then he saw Jesus, who looked like "a Lamb that had been killed" (5:6). Jesus took the scroll and unrolled it, revealing the mystery of God.

Here in Revelation is the end of the gospel, and Jesus is still the Lamb of God because he is our redemptive sacrifice for sin. Even in eternity Christ's redemptive work stands for us before God because there the throne belongs to God *and* the Lamb (22:3).

Therefore, let's be ready to "rejoice and honor him." For the time of the wedding feast for the Lamb and his bride is coming soon (19:7).

Then I saw thrones, and the people sitting on them had been given the authority to judge. And I saw the souls of those who had been beheaded for their testimony about Jesus, for proclaiming the word of God. And I saw the souls of those who had not worshiped the beast or his statue, nor accepted his mark on their forehead or their hands. They came to life again, and they reigned with Christ for a thousand years.
Revelation 20:4

To God

Do with me, God! as Thou didst deal with John,
(Who writ that heavenly Revelation)
Let me (like him) first cracks of thunder hear;
Then let the harp's enchantments strike mine ear;
Here give me thorns; there, in thy Kingdom, set
Upon my head the golden coronet;[a]
There give me day; but here my dreadful night:
My sackcloth here; but there my stole of white.

ROBERT HERRICK (1591–1674)

[a] a small crown worn by princes and others of high rank

WHILE exiled on the island of Patmos for preaching the word of God, John received visions that God instructed him to write down (Revelation 1:9-11). He did this, and as a result we have the book of Revelation.

Unlike John, no one in the West today lives in exile for his or her faith. In addition, none of us had to endure the frightening experience of receiving God's final revelation. Yet Robert Herrick prays in today's poem, "Do with me, God! as Thou didst deal with John." Why would he pray this? Was he actually asking to suffer? In all likelihood that is what he prayed. But why would anyone ask for that? Perhaps Herrick knew the benefits of suffering. As Peter wrote in his first epistle, suffering strengthens and purifies our faith. It also helps us to identify with Christ and share in his glory. Suffering here on earth also produces another benefit—it causes us to long for our heavenly home where suffering will be absent.

Earthly lives of leisure create little motivation to desire Christ's kingdom and presence. Therefore, let us live boldly for Christ, braving the criticism and suffering that may come. May we pray as Herrick did: "Here give me thorns; there, in thy Kingdom, set upon my head the golden coronet."

➼ *This is a revelation from Jesus Christ, which God gave him concerning the events that will happen soon. An angel was sent to God's servant John so that John could share the revelation with God's other servants. John faithfully reported the word of God and the testimony of Jesus Christ—everything he saw.* Revelation 1:1-2

The Resurrection PART ONE

Not winds to voyagers at sea,
Not showers to earth more necessary be,
(Heavens vital seed cast on the womb of earth
To give the fruitful year a birth)
Than verse to virtue, which can do
The midwife's office, and the nurse's too;
It feeds it strongly, and it clothes it gay,
And when it dies, with comely pride
Embalms it, and erects a pyramid
That never will decay
Till Heaven itself shall melt away,
And nought behind it stay.

Begin the song, and strike the living lyre;
Low how the years to come, a numerous and well-fitted choir,
All hand in hand do decently advance,
And to my song with smooth and equal measures dance.
Whilst the dance lasts, how long so e'er it be,
My music's voice shall bear it company.
Till all gentle notes be drowned
In the last Trumpet's dreadful sound.
That to the spheres themselves shall silence bring,
Untune the universal string.
Then all the wide extended sky,
And all th' harmonious worlds on high,
And Virgil's[a] *sacred work*[b] *shall die.*
And he himself shall see in one fire shine
Rich nature's ancient Troy,[c] *though built by hands divine.*

(continued in next day's reading)

ABRAHAM COWLEY (1618–1667)

[a]Roman poet (70–19 B.C.) [b]*The Aeneid,* an epic poem about the wanderings of Aeneas
[c]ancient city located in northwest Turkey and site of the Trojan wars

ABRAHAM COWLEY was one of England's metaphysical poets. He was also a Royalist spy, botanist, essayist, and founder of the Royal Society. Cowley published his first volume of poetry at age fifteen.

These first two verses of "The Resurrection" are challenging. The poet makes some grandiose claims. What is more necessary than wind to a sailor or rain to the earth? His answer: Verse—that is, poetry. It is necessary for virtue, for general moral excellence, right action and thinking, goodness or morality. To Cowley, poetry is a midwife at the birth of virtue and a wet nurse through its infancy. Poetry is virtue's food and clothing in life, its embalming fluid and monument in death. Poetry certainly is not all these things to everyone. Cowley probes into unseen realities and uses verse as a metaphor for the resurrection of the dead, undoubtedly the most mysterious topic other than God. In verse 2 a song begins—it is the poet's life. A choir sings the poet's song to accompany the dance of his life. But one musical note ends it all—the sound of the last trumpet silences the music of the entire universe.

As Paul wrote, this event "will happen in a moment, in the blinking of an eye, when the last trumpet is blown. For when the trumpet sounds, the Christians who have died will be raised with transformed bodies" (1 Corinthians 15:52). On that great day we will see the fulfillment of our hope—eternal life in the presence of our Savior—and enter that ancient city "built by divine hands."

Then I saw a new heaven and a new earth, for the old heaven and the old earth had disappeared. And the sea was also gone. And I saw the holy city, the new Jerusalem, coming down from God out of heaven like a beautiful bride prepared for her husband. Revelation 21:1-2

Whom thunders dismal noise,
And all that Prophets and Apostles louder spake,
And all the creatures plain conspiring voice,
Could not whilst they lived, awake,
This mightier sound shall make
When dead t'arise,
And open tombs, and open eyes
To the long sluggards of five thousand years.
This mightier sound shall make its hearers ears.

Then shall the scattered atoms crowding come
Back to their ancient home, . . .
And where th'attending soul naked, and shivering stands,
Meet, salute, and join their hands.
As dispersed soldiers at the trumpet's call,
Haste to their colors all.
Unhappy most, like tortured men,
Their joints new set, to be new racked again.
To mountains they for shelter pray,
The mountains shake, and run about no less confused than they.

Stop, stop, my Muse, allay thy vigorous heat,
Kindled at a hint so great.
Hold thy Pindaric[a] *Pegasus*[b] *closely in,*
Which does to rage begin,
And this steep hill would gallop up with violent course,
'Tis an unruly, and a hard-mouthed horse,
Fierce, and unbroken yet,
Impatient of the spur or bit.
Now prances stately, and anon flies o'er the place,
Disdains the servile law of any settled pace,
Conscious and proud of his own natural force.
'Twill no unskillful touch endure,
But flings writer, and reader too, that sits not sure.

ABRAHAM COWLEY (1618–1667)

[a]Pindar, Greek lyric poet of the third and fourth centuries B.C., who created the Pindaric ode, an elaborate poem of loose or irregular verses [b]the winged horse of classical mythology

HERE COWLEY pictures the resurrection of the dead. First, he sees those who, while alive, could not hear the Word of God, whether it was spoken by the Old Testament prophets, the New Testament apostles, or creation itself. But the trumpet of the resurrection is loud enough to wake them. Next, he sees atoms gathering from everywhere to form resurrected bodies for the souls of humanity assembled before the throne of God's judgment.

Finally, he cries out, "Stop, stop, my Muse!" This is all too much even for the metaphysicist. He feels like he is riding a runaway horse of prosody. He concludes abruptly with a warning that this vision of the resurrection will, like a runaway horse, throw anyone who is not secure in the saddle.

How can we be secure in the saddle and ride out the tumultuous end of time when the dead are resurrected? Here's the good news: Christ "saved us, not because of the good things we did, but because of his mercy. He washed away our sins and gave us a new life through the Holy Spirit. . . . And now we know that we will inherit eternal life" (Titus 3:5-7). This is the simple secret.

We shouldn't believe in our own accomplishments—our good works—or entrust our salvation to the rightness of the denomination we prefer or to the eloquence of its leaders. We don't have to build a knowledge of the Scripture to impress God. We simply believe in the one he sent to save us. Jesus said, "You trust God, now *trust in me*" (John 14:1, italics added). This is how to sit "sure" in the saddle.

Remember, each of us will stand personally before the judgment seat of God. For the Scriptures say, "'As surely as I live,' says the Lord, 'every knee will bow to me and every tongue will confess allegiance to God.'" Yes, each of us will have to give a personal account to God.
Romans 14:10-12

To Heaven

Open thy gates
To him, who weeping waits
And might come in,
But that held back by sin.
Let mercy be
So kind, to set me free,
And I will strait
Come in, or force the gate.

ROBERT HERRICK (1591–1674)

IS IT possible to force open the narrow door of salvation? Herrick may cause us to wonder. In today's poem he appears so desperate for God that he claims he would even force open the gate of heaven if that were possible. Herrick causes us to consider what use human effort may be in attaining salvation. After all, Jesus advised that we "strive to enter through the narrow door" (Luke 13:24, NRSV). This certainly indicates the need for some effort.

Elsewhere Jesus says, "Keep on asking, and you will be given what you ask for. Keep on looking, and you will find. Keep on knocking, and the door will be opened" (Matthew 7:7). This does not convey the image of someone sitting outside, passively waiting for God to let him in. We can say, in a preliminary way, that to enter into God's salvation, one must be actively seeking it. It is true that we don't gain salvation through strength, ability, or effort. But we do need the desire—the aspiration—to know the truth.

We also need to have compassion for those who are still seeking, especially those who question Christianity and challenge our understanding of God. Let's not look down on them, even when they ridicule God's only way to salvation, because they may honestly desire to know the truth. Instead, let's remember that only God knows their heart, and our job is to pray for them as they strive to enter the narrow door, knocking but sometimes violently kicking at it. Such eager people eventually find the way. But don't worry. They can't *widen* the door by force. They can only rush in when God opens it to them.

Jesus went through one town and village after another, teaching as he made his way to Jerusalem. Someone asked him, "Lord, will only a few be saved?" He said to them, "Strive to enter through the narrow door; for many, I tell you, will try to enter and will not be able. Luke 13:22-24, NRSV

I Never Saw a Moor—

I never saw a Moor—
I never saw the Sea—
Yet know I how the Heather looks
And what a Billow be.

I never spoke with God
Nor visited in Heaven—
Yet certain am I of the spot
As if the Checks were given—

EMILY DICKINSON (1830–1886)

DICKINSON spent much of her earthly life contemplating the next. As a result, she filled her poems with images of eternal expectations and intimations of immortality.

In this poem she expresses her faith in God and her belief in heaven and uses an interesting argument to support her beliefs. Basically, Dickinson says that she doesn't have to see something to know that it exists. Living a sequestered life, she most likely never saw a moor—a boggy area of grasses and sedges—or the sea. But that didn't mean she denied their existence or was ignorant or unaware of their characteristics—such as, heather and billows. In fact, her knowledge of heather and billows may have been proof to her of the moors and the sea. Evidence of one proves the existence of the other. Likewise, Dickinson knew that heaven existed even though she had never been there. She had evidence of its existence "as if the Checks were given."

Hebrews 11:1 says, "What is faith? It is the confident assurance that what we hope for is going to happen. It is the evidence of things we cannot yet see." It is safe to say that none of us have seen God or heaven. Yet we have evidence of their existence. The Bible is one proof and the Holy Spirit another (2 Corinthians 5:5; Ephesians 1:13-14). Thus we believe he exists and is preparing a place for us to dwell with him forever (John 14:2-3). This is our hope, our "confident assurance." We need not doubt like Thomas, who demanded physical proof of Christ's resurrection before he would believe. Instead, we can patiently trust our Lord and Savior to take us home someday.

Lord, through all the generations you have been our home! Before the mountains were created, before you made the earth and the world, you are God, without beginning or end. Psalm 90:1-2

Forbearance

Gently I took that which ungently came,
And without scorn forgave:—Do thou the same.
A wrong done to thee think a cat's eye spark
Thou wouldst not see, were not thine own heart
dark.
Thine own keen sense of wrong that thirsts for sin,
Fear that—the spark self-kindled from within,
Which blown upon will blind thee with its glare,
Or smothered stifle thee with noisome air.
Clap on the extinguisher, pull up the blinds,
And soon the ventilated spirit finds
Its natural daylight. If a foe have kenned,[a]
Or worse than foe, an alienated friend,
A rib of dry rot in thy ship's stout side,
Think it God's message, and in humble pride
With heart of oak replace it;—thine the gains—
Give him the rotten timber for his pains!

SAMUEL TAYLOR COLERIDGE (1772–1834)

[a]Scottish for "to know"

COLERIDGE throws light on the problem of being offended by other's actions. Quite simply, the problem is that we harbor a "keen sense of wrong"—the poet calls this a thirst for sin—a deep desire to point out others' misdeeds. This attitude magnifies the slightest spark of a mistake so that it lights up this dark temperament, exposes it, and blinds us with the glare. So the real source of our anger, hurt feelings, and offense is not the other person's deed but our own dark heart. We find two examples of this in the Gospels.

Judas Iscariot is one case. He once criticized a woman for anointing Jesus with expensive, fragrant oils: "That perfume was worth a small fortune. It should have been sold and the money given to the poor" (John 12:5). But Scripture notes his real motivation, "Not that he cared for the poor—he was a thief who was in charge of the disciples' funds, and he often took some for his own use" (12:6). His greed blinded him to the preciousness of Christ. The Lord told him, "You will always have the poor among you, but I will not be here with you much longer" (12:8).

Simon the Pharisee was another. When a prostitute, overwhelmed with gratitude for the forgiveness Christ offered her, washed Jesus' feet with her tears, Simon said to himself, "This proves that Jesus is no prophet. If God had really sent him, he would know what kind of woman is touching him. She's a sinner!" (Luke 7:39). In the darkness of his self-righteousness, Simon did not see that he too was a sinner, though his sins were less obvious than hers.

Today's poem informs us that offenses come to us with this message from God: Examine your own heart, find the weak and rotten parts, and with gratitude make the repairs.

[Love] is never glad about injustice but rejoices whenever the truth wins out. Love never gives up, never loses faith, is always hopeful, and endures through every circumstance. 1 Corinthians 13:6-7

Church-Monuments

While that my soul repairs to her devotion,
Here I intomb my flesh, that it betimes
May take acquaintance of this heap of dust;
To which the blast of death's incessant motion,
Fed with the exhalation of our crimes,
Drives all at last. Therefore I gladly trust

My body to this school, that it may learn
To spell his elements, and find his birth
Written in dusty heraldry and lines:
Which dissolution sure doth best discern,
Comparing dust with dust, and earth with earth.
These laugh at Jet and Marble put for signs,

To sever the good fellowship of dust,
And spoil the meeting. What shall point out them,
When they shall bow, and kneel, and fall down flat
To kiss those heaps, which now they have in trust?
Dear flesh, while I do pray, learn here thy stem
And true descent; that when thou shalt grow fat,

And wanton in thy cravings, thou mayst know,
That flesh is but the glass,[a] *which holds the dust*
That measures all our time; which also shall
Be crumbled into dust. Mark here below
How tame these ashes are, how free from lust,
That thou mayst fit thyself against thy fall.

GEORGE HERBERT (1593–1633)

[a]hourglass

MANY literary types consider George Herbert one of the greatest metaphysical poets. Though his life was short, he wrote a great deal of poetry that is not only eloquent in style but deeply spiritual. Herbert's entire poetical works are in *The Temple* (1633).

In the second section of this book, called "The Church," Herbert explores the essence of the relationship between Christ and man. In these poems the tone of the speaker ranges from the rebellious, colloquial language of "The Collar" (see June 17) to the highly formal praise of "Antiphon (I)" and "Antiphon (II)" to the meditations of "Church-Monuments."

In this poem Herbert compares the church monuments in a graveyard to the flesh of a human being. The monuments remind him that his flesh is entombed—that is, dead and destined to become dust, even as a church monument attests to the fact that a deceased person (over which it stands) is also dust returned to dust. Herbert laughs at the pretense of the monuments to be eternal (with their "jet and marble"). He knows that each of our bodies is like an hourglass (the "glass") with a certain amount of sand falling each minute, from the top cylinder to the bottom, thereby measuring the falling away of our lives. This is what Herbert means when he says that we should meditate on this truth as proper preparation "against thy fall" (into death). Paradoxically, it is the contemplation of this "fall" that should arm us against falling into sin.

Lord, remind me how brief my time on earth will be. Remind me that my days are numbered, and that my life is fleeing away. My life is no longer than the width of my hand. An entire lifetime is just a moment to you; human existence is but a breath. Psalm 39:4-5

Belshazzar Had a Letter—

Belshazzar had a Letter—
He never had but one—
Belshazzar's Correspondent
Concluded and begun
In that immortal Copy
The Conscience of us all
Can read without its Glasses
On Revelation's Wall—

EMILY DICKINSON (1830–1886)

EMILY DICKINSON was an eighth-generation New Englander born into a severely religious, puritanical family. She attended what is now Mount Holyoke College—America's first college for women. Although she was known as a high-spirited and active young woman, Dickinson later withdrew entirely from society; her only contact with friends was through whimsical and epigrammatic letters. Her friends knew that she wrote poetry and some urged her to publish it. After her death in 1886, two thousand poems and fragments of poems were found among her papers.

In Dickinson's writings we find universal themes expressed with intense personal feeling, mystical directness, acute observation of nature, and thought that is as playful and witty as it is metaphysical. Despite her family's puritanical life, she did not include subjective religious condemnation in her poems.

This is not to say that she did not have an active conscience; we can detect severe pangs of conscience in her writings. A healthy conscience is vital to a Christian. Dickinson read the handwriting on the wall: "You have been weighed on the balances and have failed the test" (Daniel 5:27). We all must come to this realization, and not by religious browbeating. Rather, we must read the message on "revelation's wall." This revelation of our own failure to please God will come hand in hand with the understanding that our faith in Jesus Christ *does* please the Father. In this way your conscience sweetly knows why the voice from heaven said, "This is my beloved Son, and I am fully pleased with him" (Matthew 3:17).

For you have defied the Lord of heaven and have had these cups from his Temple brought before you. You and your nobles and your wives and concubines have been drinking wine from them while praising gods of silver, gold, bronze, iron, wood, and stone. . . . But you have not honored the God who gives you the breath of life and controls your destiny! Daniel 5:23

Holy Sonnet V

I am a little world made cunningly
Of elements, and an angelic sprite,
But black sin hath betrayed to endless night
My world's both parts, and (oh) both parts must die.
You which beyond that heaven which was most high
Have found new spheres, and of new lands can write,
Pour new seas in my eyes, that so I might
Drown my world with my weeping earnestly,
Or wash it if it must be drowned no more:
But oh it must be burnt! alas the fire
Of lust and envy have burnt it heretofore,
And made it fouler; Let their flames retire
And burn me ô Lord, with a fiery zeal
Of thee and thy house, which doth in eating heal.

JOHN DONNE (1572–1631)

JOHN DONNE'S early poetry, represented best in his *Songs and Sonnets and Elegies,* is remarkable for its vivid language, startling and often exaggerated imagery, and frequent use of paradox. The Divine Poems, many of them splendid sonnets, are products of Donne's later years and reveal an intensity of feeling and depth of insight rarely equaled in English poetry.

Here Donne compares himself to the earth (or world) in need of God's twofold purging—by water and by fire. God's judgment on the earth first came by water—the flood during Noah's time. The final judgment will come by fire—at the end of time (see 2 Peter 3:6-10). Donne, believing in the life hereafter ("that heaven which was most high" and "new spheres"), asks God to bring judgment to him now so he can be washed and burned in purification. Then he would be free from "black sin" and "lust and envy."

In the last two lines Donne draws on an image from the Gospel of John's depiction of Jesus cleansing the temple: "Jesus made a whip from some ropes and chased them all out of the Temple. He drove out the sheep and oxen, scattered the money changers' coins over the floor, and turned over their tables. Then, going over to the people who sold doves, he told them, 'Get these things out of here. Don't turn my Father's house into a marketplace!' Then his disciples remembered this prophecy from the Scriptures: 'Passion for God's house burns within me'" (John 2:15-17).

How we all need our "temples" washed, purged, and cleansed so the holy God can live within us!

Then [God] used the water to destroy the world with a mighty flood. And God has also commanded that the heavens and the earth will be consumed by fire on the day of judgment, when ungodly people will perish. . . . Since everything around us is going to melt away, what holy, godly lives you should be living! 2 Peter 3:6-7, 11

Moses in Infancy

How! Canst thou see the basket wherein lay
The infant Moses by the river's side,
And her who stood and watched it on the tide;
Will Time bring back to thee that early day?
And canst thou to the distant Nile be near,
Where lived that mother, tossed with hope and fear
Yet more than was her infant by the wave?
No: Time will not his dark domain unbar;
Himself he cannot from oblivion save,
Nor canst thou make come nearer what is far;
But thou hast human sympathies to feel
What eye, nor ear, nor sense can e'er reveal;
Hope too is thine, that past the ocean sails,
And Memory, that over Time himself prevails!

JONES VERY (1813–1880)

DESPITE its title, this poem is not about Moses. It's about hope. Jones Very, the American poet, clergyman, and contemporary of Emerson, was quite spiritual. One belief he emphasizes in this poem is that Christians shouldn't long for the past. The time of Moses is as out of reach to us today as the time of Jesus is. "Nor canst thou make come nearer what is far," says Very.

Hope, on the other hand, is as near to us as our most cherished memories, and it redirects our thoughts and desires to the future—in particular to God's coming kingdom.

"That is what the Scriptures mean when they say, 'No eye has seen, no ear has heard, and no mind has imagined what God has prepared for those who love him'" (1 Corinthians 2:9). We hope for what God has prepared for us. Not that we can see or explain it. But hope is a sense, a "human sympathy," which, as Very says, sails past the ocean of memory and prevails over time. So Paul wrote, "If we have hope in Christ only for this life, we are the most miserable people in the world" (1 Corinthians 15:19).

So what are we to do? There is no going back. It's vain to think longingly of the past. But built into our faith is hope. With this we can follow the apostle Paul, who fought a good fight, finished the race, and remained faithful: "And now the prize awaits me—the crown of righteousness that the Lord, the righteous Judge, will give me on that great day of his return. And the prize is not just for me but for all who eagerly look forward to his glorious return" (2 Timothy 4:8).

But when she could no longer hide him, she got a little basket made of papyrus reeds and waterproofed it with tar and pitch. She put the baby in the basket and laid it among the reeds along the edge of the Nile River. The baby's sister then stood at a distance, watching to see what would happen to him. Exodus 2:3-4

Hath the Rain a Father?

We say, "It rains." An unbelieving age!
Its very words its unbelief doth show;
Forgot the lessons of the sacred page,
Spoken by men of faith so long ago!
No farther than they see men's faith extends;
The mighty changes of the earth and sky
To them are causeless all, where Science ends;
And Unseen Cause they know not or deny.
They hear not in the whirlwind, or the storm,
The mighty Voice which spake to man of old;
They see not in the clouds of heaven His form,
Nor in His ceaseless works his power behold;
Who maketh small the countless drops of rain,
And sendeth showers upon the springing grain.

JONES VERY (1813–1880)

"Surely I spoke of things I did not understand, things too wonderful for me to know" (Job 42:3, NIV), said Job after the Lord answered him from the whirlwind.

Jones Very points to a simple figure of speech that reveals how much we are like Job: "It rains." Today we have detailed, accurate, scientific explanations for why it rains. In Very's day people did not have this advantage. Some of them, instead of being scientific, were superstitious and believed that the positions of stars or the phases of the moon or tokens and good luck controlled the environment. We must not mistakenly equate science with superstition. Yet both are pierced by the barb of God's word: "Does the rain have a father?" (Job 38:28). Yes! Beyond evaporation and condensation, far past astrology, is the Creator of the rain and all things, whom we cannot understand and is too wonderful to know.

Rain is not the only mystery we explain away scientifically. In Job 38–41, God questions Job about several other mysteries that he could ask us as well. "Have [we] ever commanded the morning to appear and caused the dawn to rise in the east? . . . Have [we] explored the springs from which the seas come? . . . Have [we] given the horse its strength or clothed its neck with a flowing mane? . . . Are [we] the one who makes the hawk soar and spread its wings to the south?" (Job 38:12, 16; 39:19, 26).

The answers are obvious. But God's point may not be: We humans are finite, but God is infinite. So recall the wisdom of God when you observe the mysteries of his creation and do not forget "the lessons of the sacred page, spoken by men of faith so long ago!"

Then the Lord answered Job from the whirlwind: . . . Does the rain have a father? Where does dew come from? Who is the mother of the ice? Who gives birth to the frost from the heavens? For the water turns to ice as hard as rock, and the surface of the water freezes. Job 38:1, 28-30

O Grant . . .

O grant that like to Peter I
May like to Peter B,
And tell me, lovely Jesus, Y
This Peter went to C.

O grant me like to Peter I
May like to Peter B,
And tell me, lovely Jesus, Y
Old Jonah went to C.

JOHN KEATS (1795–1821)

JOHN KEATS'S life was short and tragic. He was orphaned as a child and died of tuberculosis at age twenty-five. Yet during his life Keats wrote poems of such power that many literary critics consider his verse some of the greatest English literature ever written.

Keats didn't write on biblical themes often. But in today's whimsical verse he makes an interesting observation about two evangelists, Peter and Jonah. One went to *see,* and the other went to *sea.* One wanted to get close to the Lord; the other wanted to get away from God.

When Simon went with his brother Andrew to meet Jesus, the Lord told him, "'You are Simon, the son of John—but you will be called Cephas' (which means Peter)" (John 1:42). Since *Cephas* means "rock" in Aramaic, and *Peter* means "rock" in Greek, we can interpret Jesus' statement this way: "You, Peter, are going to change into someone solid for God." And, indeed, Peter did change!

What about Jonah? He ran from the Lord, was thrown into the Mediterranean Sea and swallowed by a large fish. "Then Jonah prayed to the Lord his God from inside the fish" (Jonah 2:1). What an eloquent prayer this was (2:2-9)! When the fish vomited Jonah out onto the shore, Jonah set out to do exactly what he had refused to do in the first place—go to Nineveh to preach repentance (1:1-2; 3:1-3).

While Peter's and Jonah's experiences were vastly different, Keats's poem helps us draw one lesson from their lives: You can run from the Lord, or you can run to the Lord. Either way, if you belong to God, he will change you.

As Jesus walked by, John looked at him and then declared, "Look! There is the Lamb of God!" Then John's two disciples turned and followed Jesus. . . . Andrew, Simon Peter's brother, was one of these men who had heard what John said and then followed Jesus. The first thing Andrew did was to find his brother, Simon, and tell him, "We have found the Messiah" (which means the Christ). John 1:36-37, 40-41

The Bottle

Thou bearst the bottle, I the bag (oh Lord)
Which daily I do carry at my back,
So stuffed with sin, that ready 'tis to crack:
I have no unfeigned nectar for thy gourd,
Mine eyes will no such precious drink afford:
Yet both my heart, and eyes, are deserts dry,
Even Lybian sands, where serpents crawl and fly.

Yea the two extreme zones took up my heart,
For unto good, a cold as ice, I am;
But unto evil, like an Ætna[a] *flame:*
I paralytical seem in each part,
One utterly deprived of strength, and art,
When I should execute my master's will,
But active am as fire, t'accomplish ill.

I bear the bag like Judas: (Lord) do Thou,
From this unwieldy burden me dismiss,
And this bag empty, which so heavy is:
Then shall my tears into thy bottle flow;
Not only tears, which do from sorrow grow,
But cooler drops, which do from joy distill,
And to the brim, these shall thy bottle fill.

RALPH KNEVET (1601–1671)

[a]Mount Etna, a volcanic mountain in eastern Sicily

KNEVET'S poem is full of biblical allusions. The lines "I paralytical seem in each part, . . . when I should execute my master's will, but active am as fire, t'accomplish ill" sound much like part of an epistle Paul wrote: "No matter which way I turn, I can't make myself do right. I want to, but I can't. When I want to do good, I don't. And when I try not to do wrong, I do it anyway" (Romans 7:18-19).

It seems that both these men knew that *trying* to be good is not good enough. They were also honest enough to admit that, despite all good intentions, they tended toward wrong or evil. How about you? Is your behavior good enough to meet God's standards? Be honest, and remember, good intentions do not count.

Jesus once said, "Why do you call me good? . . . Only God is truly good" (Mark 10:18). So, if only God is good, why try? Knevet said, "Daily I do carry at my back, [a bag] so stuffed with sin, that ready 'tis to crack." In other words, he was trying to bear his own sin and it was breaking his back.

None of us are good enough to redeem ourselves from sin. This is not to say that we should not do our utmost to live an upright life. But we must understand that if we try to *please God* through our conduct, we must obey the entire law of Moses (Galatians 5:3). And the New Testament practically screams out that the law cannot save us because of our sinful *nature.* It is of this nature that Knevet and Paul write.

But rejoice! "God put into effect a different plan to save us. He sent his own Son in a human body like ours, except that ours are sinful. God destroyed sin's control over us by giving his Son as a sacrifice for our sins" (Romans 8:3).

This he said, not that he cared for the poor; but because he was a thief, and had the bag, and bare what was put therein. John 12:6, KJV

Hymn

Thou art my God, sole object of my love;
Not for hope of endless joys above;
Not for the fear of endless pains below,
Which they who love thee must not undergo.
For me, and such as me, thou deignst to bear
An ignominious cross, the nails, the spear:
A thorny crown transpierced thy sacred brow,
While bloody sweats from every member flow.
For me in tortures thou resignst thy breath,
Embraced me on the cross, and saved me by death.
And can these sufferings fail my heart to move?
Such as then was, and is, thy love to me,
Such is, and shall be still, my love to thee—
To thee, Redeemer! mercy's sacred spring!
My God, my Father, Maker, and my King!

ALEXANDER POPE (1688–1744)

ALEXANDER POPE was a sixteenth-century English poet and satirist. Two of his better-known works are *An Essay on Criticism* and *The Rape of the Lock.* In today's poem, which clearly shows his love for God, Pope first tells why he does *not* love God: Not because he hopes to go to heaven, and not because he fears going to hell. In other words, we should not love God for selfish reasons.

So what is the proper motivation for loving God? Quite simply it is Christ's love for us. Christ bore "cross, the nails, the spear" for us. He wore the crown of thorns and sweat drops of blood on our behalf. As Pope wrote, "For me in tortures thou resignst thy breath, embraced me on the cross, and saved me by death." The apostle John wrote, "We love because he first loved us" (1 John 4:19, NIV). This is why Pope loves the Lord. But that is not his only reason. He also loves the Lord because he is Redeemer, God, Father, Maker, and King. Here are the right reasons to love and obey Christ.

We should not love the Lord for what we can get from him or what we can become through him. These are things that come to us *out of* his love, not *because of* ours. Thus, we are free to simply love God for who he is and what Christ did on the cross.

Then Jesus shouted, "Father, I entrust my spirit into your hands!" And with those words he breathed his last. Luke 23:46

On the Life of Man

A thousand years, with God (the Scriptures say)
Are reckoned but a day;
By which account, this measured life of ours
Exceeds not much an hour;
The half whereof nature does claim and keep
As her own debt for sleep:
A full sixth part of what remains, we riot
In more than needful diet:
Our infancy, our childhood, and the most
Of our green youth is lost:
The little that is left, we thus divide;
One part to clothe our pride,
An other share we lavishly deboise[a]
To vain, or sinful joys;
If then, at most, the measured life of man
Be counted but a span,
Being halved and quartered, and disquartered thus,
What, what remains for us?
Lord, if the total of our days do come
To so-so poor a sum;
And if our shares so small, so nothing be,
Out of that nothing, what remains to Thee?

FRANCIS QUARLES (1592–1644)

[a]to debauch or squander

FRANCIS QUARLES figures that since one thousand years is like one day to God, a human lifetime must last a little more than one hour of that day. Let's do the math.

• Twenty-four hours multiplied by 60 minutes per hour equals 1440 minutes in a day.

• Divide 1440 by 1000 to find out how many minutes equals a year according to 2 Peter 3:8. (The answer is 1.44 minutes.)

• Next divide 60 minutes by 1.44 to find out what Quarles considered a lifetime. The answer is about 42 years—an average life span for a seventeenth-century English male.

Next, Quarles tells how we use our allotted hour:

• One-half we spend asleep (30 minutes). This may not be the case today. But in Quarles's time, before electric lights, people did sleep more than we do.

• One-sixth of the hour that is left (that is, 10 minutes) we spend in unnecessary indulgences. For example, what would our poet think of television?

• Subtract our infancy, childhood, and youth from the time that is left. Let's allow 15 years total for these three developmental stages. Fifteen multiplied by 1.44 minutes equals about 22 minutes, which gives us a total of 62 minutes so far.

So there are maybe 5 minutes left, according to Francis Quarles's accounting. What becomes of this time?

• Half of it we use to "clothe our pride," as Quarles says, which, when we think about it, is correct. We spend much of our lives protecting and embellishing our ego.

• The other half we give to vain or sinful joys.

Let's conclude this arithmetical exercise with two questions: "What, what remains for us?" . . . "Out of that nothing, what remains to [God]?" Your answers?

But you must not forget, dear friends, that a day is like a thousand years to the Lord, and a thousand years is like a day. 2 Peter 3:8

On the Cards, and Dice

Before the sixth day of the next new year,
Strange wonders in this kingdom shall appear.
Four kings shall be assembled in this Isle,
Where they shall keep great tumult for a while.[a]
Many men then shall have an end of crosses,
And many likewise shall sustain great losses.
Many that now full joyful are and glad,
Shall at that time be sorrowful and sad.
Full many a Christian's heart shall quake for fear,
The dreadful sound of trump when he shall hear.
Dead bones shall then be tumbled up and down,
In every city, and in every town.
By day or night this tumult shall not cease,
Until an herald shall proclaim a peace,
An herald strange, the like was never born
Whose very beard is flesh, and mouth is horn.

SIR WALTER RALEIGH (c. 1552–1618)

[a]Daniel 7:17-23

IN OLD England, "tables" was the name for backgammon because the board looked like two tables. Like cards, backgammon was a game of gambling. One rule of this complicated game allowed a player to double the stakes in certain situations and physically turn the tables. The winning player suddenly begins to lose. By this we understand the saying, "The tables are turned."

In this poem Raleigh draws on Daniel's prophecy of the final days but titles it for the instruments of gambling. Why did the poet use gambling as a metaphor for the end times? The Bible contains many stories about people who gambled with their eternal destiny and lost. The stories of the flood, Sodom and Gomorrah, the ten plagues, and Korah's rebellion come to mind—not to forget the entire book of Judges. In each instance, those who lost did not take God's warnings seriously. They gambled with their life and paid the price.

So, too, with the end times and the return of Christ. Every day, everywhere, people who refuse to accept Christ as their Savior gamble that it will not be their last day. They go about their business oblivious to the eternal misery that awaits them. Luke says: "In those days before the flood, the people enjoyed banquets and parties and weddings right up to the time Noah entered his boat and the flood came to destroy them all. . . . Yes, it will be 'business as usual' right up to the hour when the Son of Man returns" (Luke 17:27, 30). On this day "dead bones shall then be tumbled up and down, in every city, and in every town." The time will have come, the tables will have turned, and those who don't know Christ will be lost forever. Let us not gamble with their destiny but make the most of every opportunity to share our faith in Christ.

However, no one knows the day or the hour when these things will happen, not even the angels in heaven or the Son himself. Matthew 24:36

The Wind

Who has seen the wind?
Neither I nor you.
But when the leaves hang trembling,
The wind is passing through.
Who has seen the wind?
Neither you nor I.
But when the trees bow their heads,
The wind is passing by.

CHRISTINA ROSSETTI (1830–1894)

HAS ANYONE ever asked you, "Are you born again?" or "When were you saved?" Some people can answer such questions succinctly with a firm yes or a definite date. Other believers may not be familiar with the term *born again* or may have experienced a gradual conversion to faith in Christ. Some people welcome the opportunity to talk about their faith. Others are shy about it, private, reserved. Unfortunately, some believers are quick to question the authenticity of a shy brother's or sister's faith.

In today's poem Christina Rossetti reminds us of Christ's words to Nicodemus. Jesus told this Jewish teacher that explaining how people are born of the Spirit is like trying to follow the wind. We can hear it, but we don't know where it came from or where it is going. Thus, Rossetti wrote, "Who has seen the wind? Neither you nor I."

The experience of new birth cannot always be pinned down. That is not to say, however, that we don't have evidence of it. Christ said we can hear wind, and Rossetti says we can see its effects: "But when the leaves hang trembling, the wind is passing through." What are these effects, the evidence, of being born again? The apostle Paul referred to them as fruit: "But when the Holy Spirit controls our lives, he will produce this kind of fruit in us: love, joy, peace, patience, kindness, goodness, faithfulness, gentleness, and self-control" (Galatians 5:22-23).

The evidence of rebirth is not when it happened, how it happened, or how outspoken we are about it. The evidence is the fruit God's Spirit produces in our life.

Do not be astonished that I said to you, "You must be born from above." The wind blows where it chooses, and you hear the sound of it, but you do not know where it comes from or where it goes. So it is with everyone who is born of the Spirit. John 3:7-8, NRSV

Upon Stephen Stoned

Under this heap of stones interred lies
No holocaust, but stoned sacrifice
Burnt not by altar-coals, but by the fire
    Of Jewish ire,
Whose softest words in their hard hearts alone
    Congealed to stone,
Not piercing them recoiled in him again,
    Who being slain
As not forgetful, whence they once did come,
Now being stones he found them in a tomb.

SIR JOHN SUCKLING (1609–1642)

STONING was the method of execution used in Israel to punish capital offenses. One of the few legal executions mentioned in Scripture is found in Joshua 7:25: "And all the Israelites stoned Achan and his family and burned their bodies." But careful judicial examination preceded this execution.

Most stonings in Scripture were unjustified. Israelites stoned Adoniram as an act of rebellion against Rehoboam (1 Kings 12:17-19); Jezebel had Naboth stoned so her husband could have Naboth's vineyard (21:1-14); mobs threatened both Moses and Jesus with stoning (Exodus 17:4; John 8:59; 10:31); and angry crowds stoned Paul and left him for dead at Lystra (Acts 14:8-20; 2 Corinthians 11:25).

The stoning of Stephen was also unjustified. Authorities hauled Stephen before the Jewish council where "lying witnesses said, 'This man is always speaking against the Temple and against the law of Moses' " (Acts 6:13). Then, for the final time in Scripture, God's servant—in this case, Stephen—recites the history of the Jewish people—this time in light of Christ's death and resurrection. These are the "softest words" mentioned in today's poem. As Suckling says, these words congealed to stone in the hard hearts of Stephen's accusers and recoiled upon the prophet.

Enraged, the court and the mob dragged Stephen out of the city and stoned him to death. This was entirely illegal according to both Jewish and Roman laws. But it fulfilled Stephen's own words: "Name one prophet your ancestors didn't persecute! They even killed the ones who predicted the coming of the Righteous One—the Messiah whom you betrayed and murdered" (7:52).

As they stoned him, Stephen prayed, "Lord Jesus, receive my spirit." And he fell to his knees, shouting, "Lord, don't charge them with this sin!" And with that, he died. Acts 7:59-60

The World PART ONE

I saw Eternity the other night
Like a great ring of pure and endless light,
All calm, as it was bright,
And round beneath it, time in hours, days, years
Driven by the spheres
Like a vast shadow moved, in which the world
And all her train were hurled;
The doting lover in his quaintest strain
Did there complain,
Near him, his lute, his fancy, and his flights,
Wit's sour delights,
With gloves, and knots the silly snares of pleasure
Yet his dear treasure
All scattered lay, while he his eyes did pour
Upon a flower.

The darksome statesman hung with weights and woe
Like a thick midnight-fog moved there so slow
He did nor stay, nor go;
Condemning thoughts (like sad eclipses) scowl
Upon his soul,
And clouds of crying witnesses without
Pursued him with one shout.
Yet digged the mole, and lest his ways be found
Worked under ground,
Where he did clutch his prey, but one did see
That policy,
Churches and altars fed him, perjuries
Were gnats and flies,
It rained about him blood and tears, but he
Drank them as free.

(continued in next day's reading)

HENRY VAUGHAN (1622–1695)

TODAY'S portion of Henry Vaughan's "The World" begins far away, beyond time, in eternity. But it quickly focuses on the realm of time that "like a vast shadow moved, in which the world and all her train were hurled."

Here in time the poet sketches the world and details the seedy underside of humanity. Vaughan begins with the doting lover, who really loves no one but himself. Then he turns to the "darksome statesman"—a politician who is a subterranean mole clutching his prey, surrounded by the buzzing gnats and flies of perjury. The scene is bleak, grotesque, as Vaughan lifts the smooth veneer of humanity off, exposing the true condition of the human heart.

The poet makes these observations from the vantage point of eternity. We glimpse that view in John's first epistle. In the wisdom of the Spirit John wrote, "The world around us is under the power and control of the evil one" (1 John 5:19). "The world offers only the lust for physical pleasure, the lust for everything we see, and pride in our possessions. . . . And this world is fading away, along with everything it craves" (2:16-17). Vaughan certainly attests to this.

Fortunately, those who love goodness and righteousness are not without hope. For this world has a Redeemer who lives in the "pure and endless light" of eternity. Jesus Christ has made a way for those who no longer love this dark world but desire to live in his light.

Jesus said to the people, "I am the light of the world. If you follow me, you won't be stumbling through the darkness, because you will have the light that leads to life." John 8:12

The World PART TWO

The fearful miser on a heap of rust
Sat pining all his life there, did scarce trust
His own hands with the dust,
Yet would not place one piece above, but lives
In fear of thieves.
Thousands there were as frantic as himself
And hugged each one his pelf,[a]
The down-right epicure[b] *placed heaven in sense*
And scorned pretence
While others slipped into a wide excess
Said little less;
The weaker sort slight, trivial wares enslave
Who think them brave,
And poor, despised truth sat counting by
Their victory.

Yet some, who all this while did weep and sing,
And sing, and weep, soared up into the ring,
But most would use no wing.
O fools (said I,) thus to prefer dark night
Before true light,
To live in grots, and caves, and hate the day
Because it shows the way,
The way which from this dead and dark abode
Leads up to God,
A way where you might tread the sun, and be
More bright than he.
But as I did their madness so discuss
One whispered thus,
This ring the Bride-groom did for none provide
But for his bride.

HENRY VAUGHAN (1622–1695)

[a]money or wealth [b]a person who enjoys fine foods and drinks

THE POEM continues to catalog the inhabitants of the world: A fearful miser on a heap of rust, who gives nothing to God, and the downright epicure whose heaven is his senses. Vaughan briefly mentions others who, weeping and singing, choose to live in the light and soar into the ring of eternity.

The poet grumbles about the world's madness in preferring darkness to light. How could they choose to live in grottoes and caves instead of rising up in the light of God's brightness? But suddenly a voice interrupts Vaughan, whispering, *"This ring the Bride-groom did for none provide but for his bride."* What a wonderful yet sad truth! Like a doting groom, Christ favors his bride above all else, presenting her (the church) with a ring of eternal commitment. But many choose not to participate in the most wonderful wedding ceremony of all, even though Christ invites everyone. Vaughan reminds us that this sad fact should not be our focus. We should celebrate our inclusion in this exclusive ceremony.

The next time you attend a wedding ceremony, think about Ephesians 5:25-33: "And you husbands must love your wives with the same love Christ showed the church. . . . This is a great mystery, but it is an illustration of the way Christ and the church are one" (5:25, 32). Then thank God that you will not only witness but be part of that glorious wedding feast of the Lamb.

Let us be glad and rejoice and honor him. For the time has come for the wedding feast of the Lamb, and his bride has prepared herself.
Revelation 19:7

On Saul and David

Sure, Saul as little looked to be a king,
As I: and David dreamed of such a thing,
As much as he; when both alike did keep,
The one his father's asses; t'other, sheep:
Saul must forsake his whip: And David flings
His crook aside; and they must both be kings:
Saul had no sword; and David, then, no spear;
There was none conquered, nor no conqueror there;
There was no sweat; there was no blood, to shed:
The unsought crown besought the wearer's head;
There was no stratagem; no opposition;
No taking parts; no jealous competition:
There needs no art; there needs no sword to bring,
And place the crown, where God appoints the king.

FRANCIS QUARLES (1592–1644)

THE MESSAGE of today's poem is simple, yet people throughout the centuries have either missed or rejected it. The message is this: We should accept those whom God appoints as rulers. There is no need to oppose God's appointed. But that is exactly what has happened throughout history even to this day. Although many modern kings are just figureheads, there is one king who is all-powerful and reigns on high. Who is he? Jesus Christ. We know that the world does not acknowledge his kingship. But this does not mean that Christ is not the supreme ruler of all. It means that people have chosen to ignore or oppose him.

When Jesus Christ died on the cross and redeemed humanity for God, he also destroyed the power of the only pretender to the throne of the universe—Satan. When you think about it, it's ridiculous to devise some stratagem to oppose Christ's kingship: "There was no stratagem; no opposition; no taking parts; no jealous competition" for Saul's or David's throne. Just as it was fact that David was king of ancient Israel, so today God is king.

Yes, there are horrendous blasphemies against God in this world. And there are times when we must speak up in the face of impiety. But God is the judge. He will protect his divine honor. We are privileged to wait in peace for the day when the seventh angel will blow his trumpet and loud voices will shout, "The whole world has now become the kingdom of our Lord and of his Christ, and he will reign forever and ever" (Revelation 11:15).

[The Lord told Samuel,] "About this time tomorrow I will send you a man from the land of Benjamin. Anoint him to be the leader of my people, Israel." . . . Then Samuel took a flask of olive oil and poured it over Saul's head. He kissed Saul on the cheek and said, "I am doing this because the Lord has appointed you to be the leader of his people Israel." 1 Samuel 9:16; 10:1

He Shook Off the Beast

Our Christian savages expect
That by the hellish viper stung
We soon shall feel the dire effect,
The poison of a slanderous tongue,
And gasp our last infected breath,
And die the everlasting death.

But lo, the tooth of calumny[a]
Calm and unmoved we still abide,
From nature's fretful passion free,
Hasty revenge and swelling pride;
Men cannot their own spirit impart,
Or taint a pure, believing heart.

Ourselves with Jesus' mind we arm,
And our envenomed foes confound,
Defy their sharpest words to harm,
Or once inflict the slightest wound
While all the power of faith we prove
In meek invulnerable love.

Let Satan still their tongues employ,
The vipers fastened on our fame,
The deadly things can not annoy,
Shook off at last into the flame:
But O, they never can expire,
The worms in that infernal fire!

CHARLES WESLEY (1707–1788)

[a] a false and malicious statement meant to hurt someone's reputation

CHARLES WESLEY needs no introduction. He is at the top of any list of great writers of Christian hymns.

This poem draws a lesson from Paul's experience of being bitten by a snake. We Christians do not have to be snake handlers to experience the venom of vipers. The "tooth of calumny" can fasten onto our flesh at any time. Read the biographies of John and Charles Wesley. These men often endured the poison of sharp, critical words injected by slanderous tongues. Wesley's advice for this circumstance: "Men cannot their own spirit impart, or taint a pure, believing heart."

A poisonous spirit infects people who criticize and slander others. Paul wrote, "Nothing is pure to those who are corrupt and unbelieving, because their minds and consciences are defiled" (Titus 1:15). In other words, nothing you do will be pure in their eyes. But remember, that "everything is pure to those whose hearts are pure" (1:15).

With the lines "Ourselves with Jesus' mind we arm, and our envenomed foes confound," Wesley invokes the words of another ancient Christian hymnist whom Paul quoted. It is perhaps the best advice ever given: "Your attitude should be the same that Christ Jesus had. Though he was God, he did not demand and cling to his rights as God. He made himself nothing; he took the humble position of a slave and appeared in human form. And in human form he obediently humbled himself even further by dying a criminal's death on a cross" (Philippians 2:5-8). May we model Christ's humility when critics and slanderers assault us with their deadly words.

As Paul gathered an armful of sticks and was laying them on the fire, a poisonous snake, driven out by the heat, fastened itself onto his hand. The people of the island saw it hanging there and said to each other, "A murderer, no doubt! . . . justice will not permit him to live." But Paul shook off the snake into the fire and was unharmed. Acts 28:3-5

And Did Those Feet

And did those feet in ancient time
Walk upon England's mountains green?
And was the holy Lamb of God
On England's pleasant pastures seen?

And did the Countenance Divine
Shine forth upon our clouded hills?
And was Jerusalem builded here
Among these dark Satanic Mills?

Bring me my bow of burning gold:
Bring me my Arrows of desire:
Bring me my Spear: O clouds unfold!
Bring me my Chariot of fire.

I will not cease from Mental Fight,
Nor shall my Sword sleep in my hand
Till we have built Jerusalem
In England's green and pleasant Land.

"Would to God that all the Lord's people were Prophets."

Numbers, xi. ch., 29 v.

WILLIAM BLAKE (1757–1827)

WILLIAM BLAKE was passionate in his desire to see the kingdom come. But the fourth stanza of this poem shows that he was also realistic. He was willing to work for the realization of his hope. He was like Nehemiah, who wept and mourned for the ruined Jerusalem and prayed and repented for the entire nation of Israel (Nehemiah 1:4-11). In the midst of his prayer, he planned to do something with his passion. As the book of Nehemiah unfolds, we see his passion take action.

Those who built the wall of Jerusalem "labored on the work with one hand and with the other held a weapon" (4:17, NRSV). Under Nehemiah's leadership, the Israelites successfully rebuilt Jerusalem's walls (around 450 B.C.). Two millennia later William Blake wrote: "I will not cease from Mental Fight nor shall my Sword sleep in my hand till we have built Jerusalem in England's green and pleasant Land." Although Blake surely did his part to bring the kingdom of God to England, he did not live to see this occur. Today we pray precisely the prayer that rose from Blake's lips: "Your kingdom come."

But what of our sword? Does it sleep in our hand? Our struggle to build the church is unlike that of Nehemiah's generation because "our struggle is not against enemies of blood and flesh" (Ephesians 6:12, NRSV). We do not walk around cutting off the ears of God's enemies. No, we are up against "the cosmic powers of this present darkness." We have been given an appropriate weapon: the sword of the Spirit, which is the Word of God (6:17). So let's rephrase Blake's words to be our exhortation and rebuke: *Do not cease from the good fight or allow the Word of God to sleep in your hand!*

➺ *When our enemies heard that we knew of their plans and that God had frustrated them, we all returned to our work on the wall. But from then on, only half my men worked while the other half stood guard with spears, shields, bows, and coats of mail.* Nehemiah 4:15-16

The Conversion of S. Paul

A blessed conversion, and a strange
Was that, when Saul a Paul became:
And, Lord, for making such a change,
We praise and glorify thy name.
For whilst he went from place to place,
To persecute thy truth and thee;
(And running to perdition was)
By powerful grace called back was he.

When from thy truth we go astray,
(Or wrong it through our blinded zeal)
Oh come, and stop us in the way,
And then thy will to us reveal;
That brightness show us from above
Which proves the sensual eyesight blind:
And from our eyes those scales remove,
That hinder us the way to find.

And as thy blessed servant Paul,
When he a convert once became,
Exceeded thy Apostles all,
In painful preaching of thy name:
So grant that those who have in sin
Exceeded others heretofore,
The start of them in faith may win,
Love, serve, and honor thee the more.

GEORGE WITHER (1588–1667)

LIKE the poet George Wither, we can say in hindsight that Paul exceeded the other apostles in spreading the gospel. But Paul himself said, "I am the least of all the apostles, and I am not worthy to be called an apostle after the way I persecuted the church of God" (1 Corinthians 15:9). He did not think more highly of himself than he should have (Romans 12:3). But consider this: Paul also said, "Christ Jesus came into the world to save sinners—of whom I am the foremost" (1 Timothy 1:15, NRSV). In his own estimation Paul was the least of apostles *and* the foremost of sinners. Yet we still call him Saint Paul.

Do you know believers who "have in sin exceeded others heretofore"? Maybe you are such a believer yourself. If so, Paul is your example. He had no trouble serving God despite his sinful background. He could easily say, "I serve [God] with a clear conscience" (2 Timothy 1:3).

In the church former sinners are saints serving God freely. What has made this possible? It is not *what;* it is *who.* Christ has made this possible. His death satisfied God's righteousness. So we can "go right into the presence of God, with true hearts fully trusting him. For our evil consciences have been sprinkled with Christ's blood to make us clean" (Hebrews 10:22).

Perhaps Paul was zealous in his service because he understood how effective the blood of Christ is to wash away sin's dark stains. In this way he was like the prostitute who boldly washed the Lord's feet (see Luke 7:36-38, 44-47). Jesus said, "Her sins—and they are many—have been forgiven, so she has shown me much love. But a person who is forgiven little shows only little love" (7:47).

So Ananias went and found Saul. He laid his hands on him and said, "Brother Saul, the Lord Jesus, who appeared to you on the road, has sent me so that you may get your sight back and be filled with the Holy Spirit." Acts 9:17

Neither Durst Any Man . . .

Midst all the dark and knotty snares,
Black wit or malice can or dares,
Thy glorious wisdom breaks the nets,
And treads with uncontrolled steps.
Thy quelled foes are not only now
Thy triumphs, but thy trophies too:
They, both at once thy conquests be,
And thy conquests' memory.
Stony amazement makes them stand
Waiting on thy victorious hand,
Like statues fixed to the fame
Of thy renown, and their own shame.
As if they only meant to breath,
To be the Life of their own Death.
'Twas time to hold their peace when they,
Had ne'er another word to say:
Yet is their silence unto thee,
The full sound of thy victory.
Their silence speaks aloud, and is
Thy well pronounced Panegyris.[a]
While they speak nothing, they speak all
Their share, in thy memorial.
While they speak nothing, they proclaim
Thee, with the shrillest trump of fame.
To hold their peace is all the ways,
These wretches have to speak thy praise.

RICHARD CRASHAW (c. 1613–1649)

[a]the Greek form of the English *panegyric,* a formal speech or piece of writing praising a person or event

BEHIND today's poem is a question Jesus asked the Pharisees in Matthew 22:42: "What do you think about the Messiah? Whose son is he?" The Pharisees answered correctly: "He is the son of David." But their answer was incomplete. So Jesus asked these teachers of the law why David called the Messiah his Lord (22:43-45). They didn't know the answer "and after that, no one dared to ask him any more questions" (22:46).

Jesus had already asked a similar question to his disciples: "Who do people say that the Son of Man is?" (16:13). The disciples answered, "'Some say John the Baptist, some say Elijah, and others say Jeremiah or one of the other prophets'" (16:14). But then Simon Peter answered, "You are . . . the Son of the living God" (16:16). This is the answer Jesus wanted from the Pharisees.

How did the fisherman Peter know that Jesus was the Son of God, yet the eminent teachers of Israel did not? Jesus tells us: "You are blessed, Simon son of John, because my Father in heaven has revealed this to you. You did not learn this from any human being" (16:17). Peter understood by revelation that which is unique to all Christians.

Christians differ in many ways—church organization, worship styles, ways of baptism, understanding of miraculous gifts. These and many other things have divided the church. But there is one thing that unites us, and this must always be emphasized. Like Peter, we have received a unique revelation from God that cannot be taught by the greatest of teachers: Jesus Christ the Savior is the Son of the living God.

Jesus responded, "Then why does David, speaking under the inspiration of the Holy Spirit, call him Lord? For David said, 'The Lord said to my Lord, Sit in honor at my right hand until I humble your enemies beneath your feet.' Since David called him Lord, how can he be his son at the same time?" No one could answer him. And after that, no one dared to ask him any more questions. Matthew 22:43-46

Christ, My Beloved

Christ, my Beloved which still doth feed
Among the flowers, having delight
Among his faithful lilies,
Doth take great care for me indeed,
And I again with all my might
Will do what so his will is.

My Love in me and I in him,
Conjoined by love, will still abide
Among the faithful lilies
Till day do break, and truth do dim
All shadows dark and cause them slide,
According as his will is.

WILLIAM BALDWIN (fl. 1547–1549)

How intense is the love between Christ and his believers! William Baldwin describes it: "My Love in me and I in him, conjoined by love." This is not some old-time poet's wistful fantasy. Jesus Christ himself said, "When I am raised to life again, you will know that I am in my Father, and you are in me, and I am in you" (John 14:20). This verse describes what theologians call "mutual indwelling": The Son (Jesus Christ) is in the Father, we (the believers) are in the Son, and the Son is in us.

Jesus described this relationship in a different way in John 15:1, 4: "I am the true vine. . . . Remain in me, and I will remain in you." To understand this concept, picture a grapevine as the resurrected Christ. Now see the branches on that vine? That's us. Are the vine and the branches separate? No. Are they independent? No. The vine depends on the farmer (the Father), and the branches depend on the vine. They are, as Baldwin says, "conjoined."

The flowing sap from the vine of a plant maintains life in the branches. Likewise, our relationship with Christ is in the divine life we received when we believed. Ours is not a business connection or a working association with God. We share with Christ the intimacy of divine life.

Yes, this is deep. It is, as Paul says, a great mystery (Ephesians 5:32). But one day the dawn will come. Christ will return and the shadows will flee. Then we will know God fully, even as we are known (1 Corinthians 13:12), and we will understand the mysteries of Christ. Until that day let us continue to abide in the true vine.

My lover is mine, and I am his. He feeds among the lilies! Before the dawn comes and the shadows flee away, come back to me, my love. Run like a gazelle or a young stag on the rugged mountains. Song of Songs 2:16-17

Contrition

My heart is broken (oh my God)
Break me not like a potters vessel,
Bruise me not with an iron rod,
But form me by thy holy chisel,
That I a statue may become,
Fit to adorn thy heavenly room.

The fig tree yields a fruit that's sweet,
Yet is unprofitable wood;
For sculptor's art it is unmeet,
And neither serves for saint, or rood:[a]
For Vulcan's[b] *use it is unfit,*
His bellows do no good on it.

But I that wretched tree am, which
The hunger of my Christ deceives,
He fruit expects, but I am rich
In nothing but vain spreading leaves,
Nor am I wood so fit, and apt
That of me can a saint be shaped.

Yea, I am that same fig tree vain,
Which in Christ's vineyard planted was,
Dressed many years with care, and pain,
Yet only serve to fill a place:
I therefore fear the axes wound,
Because I cumber[c] *but the ground.*

(Lord) in me repair (by thy grace)
The image Thou didst first create:
Though Adam's sin did it deface,
Yet mine, did it more vitiate:[d]
Vouchsafe t'amend it with thy hand,
Then in thy gallery it may stand.

RALPH KNEVET (1601–1671)

[a]a cross as used in crucifixion [b]Roman god of fire and metalworking [c]to trouble or harass [d]to make impure or faulty

KNEVET expresses a keen sense of his sin and uselessness to God. Drawing on biblical imagery, he compares himself to the fig tree Jesus cursed (Matthew 21:18-22) and the fig tree Jesus used in a parable (Luke 13:6-9). Human weaknesses and failure in ourselves and others may be hard to accept, but it is necessary to do so in the light of the gospel. Romans 5:12 says: "Sin came into the world through one man, and death came through sin, and so death spread to all because all have sinned" (NRSV). This is a gloomy statement, but it is a necessary part of the gospel. Unless we understand that we have failed God, we will not appreciate the work of Jesus Christ.

Romans continues: "For if the many died through the one man's trespass, much more surely have the grace of God and the free gift in the grace of the one man, Jesus Christ, abounded for the many" (5:15, NRSV). Thus Knevet prays, "(Lord) in me repair (by thy grace) the image Thou didst first create: though Adam's sin did it deface." Knevet believed that grace would return him to a right standing before God. "Just as sin exercised dominion in death, so grace might also exercise dominion through justification leading to eternal life through Jesus Christ our Lord" (Romans 5:21, NRSV).

➺ *Then Jesus used this illustration: "A man planted a fig tree in his garden and came again and again to see if there was any fruit on it, but he was always disappointed. Finally, he said to his gardener, 'I've waited three years, and there hasn't been a single fig! Cut it down. It's taking up space we can use for something else.' The gardener answered, 'Give it one more chance. Leave it another year, and I'll give it special attention and plenty of fertilizer. If we get figs next year, fine. If not, you can cut it down.'"* Luke 13:6-9

Abide with Me

Abide with me; fast falls the eventide;
The darkness deepens; Lord, with me abide!
When other helpers fail, and comforts flee,
Help of the helpless, O abide with me.

Swift to its close ebbs out life's little day;
Earth's joys grow dim, its glories pass away;
Change and decay in all around I see;
O Thou who changest not, abide with me.

I need Thy presence every passing hour;
What but Thy grace can foil the tempter's power?
Who, like Thyself, my guide and stay can be?
Through cloud and sunshine, Lord, abide with me.

I fear no foe, with Thee at hand to bless;
Ills have no weight, and tears no bitterness.
Where is death's sting? where, grave, thy victory?
I triumph still, if Thou abide with me.

Hold Thou Thy cross before my closing eyes;
Shine through the gloom, and point me to the skies;
Heaven's morning breaks, and earth's vain shadows flee;
In life, in death, O Lord, abide with me.

HENRY LYTE (1793–1847)

HENRY LYTE was born in Scotland and educated at Trinity College in Dublin. Upon graduation, he entered the ministry of the Church of Ireland. Plagued by ill health, he made frequent trips to Europe in search of sunshine and cures. Because of his dependence on God through his constant illness, Lyte wrote out of deep spiritual experience. His daughter published his work *Remains* (1850)—which contains poems, letters, sermons, and a brief biography—after he died.

Shortly before Lyte passed away, he penned this hymn, which often appears in anthologies of Christian poetry. The words of the two disciples on the road to Emmaus were its inspiration: "Abide with us; for it is toward evening, and the day is far spent" (Luke 24:29, KJV). As Lyte wrote these lines, he was dying of tuberculosis. His "evening" had come, and he felt lonely. So he asked the Lord to stay with him through the dark nights—the darkest of which is death.

Not many of us long to die, even though we may long to be with the Lord. That may be because death remains a mystery, despite all we know about it. But God has blessed us in this respect: He has promised to be with us even as we walk through the valley of the shadow of death. Thus Lyte could write: "Hold Thou Thy cross before my closing eyes; shine through the gloom, and point me to the skies; . . . In life, in death, O Lord, abide with me."

And be sure of this: I am with you always, even to the end of the age. Matthew 28:20

Ode: The Dying Christian to His Soul

Vital spark of heavenly flame!
Quit, oh quit this mortal frame:
  Trembling, hoping, lingering, flying,
  Oh the pain, the bliss of dying!
Cease, fond nature, cease thy strife,
And let me languish into life.

Hark! they whisper; Angels say,
Sister Spirit, come away.
  What is this absorbs me quite?
  Steals my senses, shuts my sight,
Drowns my spirits, draws my breath?
Tell me, my soul, can this be death?

The world recedes; it disappears!
Heaven opens on my eyes! my ears
  With sounds seraphic ring:
Lend, lend your wings! I mount! I fly!
O grave! where is thy victory?
  O death! where is thy sting?

ALEXANDER POPE (1688–1744)

DEATH is not an event that many people—even Christians—look forward to. But in this poem, Pope seems to welcome it. Why? Pope had a biblical view of death. He knew it wasn't an end in itself but the beginning of something far more wonderful.

The apostle Paul's view of death most likely influenced Pope's. Death and the afterlife were topics Paul addressed in several of his epistles. He even admitted that he longed to leave this world so he could be with Christ (Philippians 1:23). To be with Christ meant that Paul had to die, but that wasn't something he was afraid to do. He had faced death many times as he preached the gospel (2 Corinthians 11:22-27), knowing that at any moment he could be in the presence of Christ, the giver of eternal life. Pope counseled his soul to "cease thy strife, and let me languish into life."

Despite Pope's positive view of death, he wasn't naive about it. He acknowledged death's dark side—"the pain"—and imagined it to be somewhat like drowning: "What is this absorbs me quite? Steals my senses, shuts my sight, drowns my spirits, draws my breath?" But he didn't let the pain and fear of passing away cloud his perspective. He knew that joy awaited him on the other side: "The world recedes; it disappears! Heaven opens on my eyes! my ears with sounds seraphic ring: Lend, lend your wings! I mount! I fly!"

Here is the paradox of death. What is the end of life on earth is the beginning of life in heaven. For those of us who believe in Christ, death is something we need not fear. Christ has defeated the grave, and death no longer has the power to harm us. We can remember this truth when our appointed time comes and we pass from this life into the next in peace.

➾ *Death is swallowed up in victory. O death, where is your victory? O death, where is your sting* 1 Corinthians 15:54-55

On a Feast

The Lord of Heaven and Earth has made a feast,
And every soul is an invited guest:
The Word's the food; the Levites are the cooks;
The Fathers' Writings are their diet-books;
But seldom used; for 'tis a fashion grown,
To recommend made dishes of their own:
What they should boil, they bake; what roast, they broil,
Their luscious salads are too sweet with oil:
In brief, 'tis nowadays too great a fault,
T'have too much pepper, and too little salt.

FRANCIS QUARLES (1592–1644)

A STORY in Matthew begins this way: "When the disciples reached the other side, they had forgotten to bring any bread. Jesus said to them. 'Watch out, and beware of the yeast of the Pharisees and Sadducees.' They said to one another, 'It is because we have brought no bread' " (Matthew 16:5-7, NRSV).

But Jesus wasn't speaking of physical bread. "How could you fail to perceive that I was not speaking about bread? Beware of the yeast of the Pharisees and Sadducees!" (16:11, NRSV). Then the disciples began to understand that Jesus wasn't warning them about yeast but about the ideas, the teachings of the Pharisees and Sadducees (16:8-12).

In today's poem God's chosen ministers—the Levites—are preparing a feast. The poet points out that the cooks have discarded the recipes in God's Word to follow their own. While the meal they prepare looks beautiful and tastes good, it doesn't satisfy the diners. That is, it doesn't lead to eternal life and therefore is not the feast God intends for anyone to eat.

Quarles's poem reminds us of the importance of correct, biblical teaching. The Pharisees and Sadducees had strayed from God's Word, substituting human teachings for divine truth. It's no wonder Jesus said, "You crush people beneath impossible religious demands, and you never lift a finger to help ease the burden" (Luke 11:46). Whether we teach Sunday school, lead a Bible study, or give devotions in our home, let us strive to teach accurately what God has said in his Word. May our teaching never "have too much pepper, and too little salt."

➻ *Get rid of the old yeast that you may be a new batch without yeast—as you really are. For Christ, our Passover lamb, has been sacrificed. Therefore let us keep the Festival, not with the old yeast, the yeast of malice and wickedness, but with bread without yeast, the bread of sincerity and truth.* 1 Corinthians 5:7-8, NIV

The Night PART ONE

Through that pure Virgin-shrine,
That sacred veil drawn o'er thy glorious noon
That men might look and live as glow-worms shine,
And face the moon:
Wise Nicodemus saw such light
As made him know his God by night.

Most blessed believer he!
Who in that land of darkness and blind eyes
Thy long expected healing wings could see,
When thou didst rise,
And what more can be done,
Did at midnight speak with the sun!

O who will tell me, where
He found thee at that dead and silent hour!
What hallowed solitary ground did bear
So rare a flower
Within whose sacred leafs did lie
The fulness of the Deity.

No mercy-seat of gold,
No dead and dusty cherub, nor carved stone,
But his own living works did my Lord hold
And lodge alone;
Where trees and herbs did watch and peep
And wonder, while the Jews did sleep.

(continued in next day's reading)

HENRY VAUGHAN (1622–1695)

"WISE NICODEMUS saw such light as made him know his God by night," wrote Henry Vaughan. When you think about it, everyone comes to know the Lord at night. Jesus was born into a dark world; "In him was life, and the life was the light of all people [who] . . . shines in the darkness, and the darkness did not overcome it" (John 1:4-5, NRSV).

Many events in the life of Jesus occurred at night:

• "Joseph left for Egypt with the child and Mary, his mother" during the night (Matthew 2:14).

• One night the disciples were "rowing hard and struggling against the wind and waves. About three o'clock in the morning [Jesus] came to them, walking on the water" (Mark 6:48).

• Jesus "prayed to God all night" (Luke 6:12).

• Judas betrayed Christ at night (Luke 22:47-48).

• The disciples deserted Jesus at night (Matthew 26:31).

• Peter denied Jesus during the night of Jesus' trial (Matthew 26:34, 70-74).

• When Christ was crucified, "darkness came over the whole land until three in the afternoon" (Matthew 27:45, NRSV).

• "He may [return] in the middle of the night" (Luke 12:38).

Vaughan uses night as a metaphor for spiritual blindness or apathy. Nicodemus sought "the sun" at midnight, meaning that he was spiritually awake, not asleep like the other Jews, as Vaughan poetically implies. Because Nicodemus was awake, he could see what others couldn't. Therefore Vaughan calls him "Most blessed believer he!" How true. Those who find Christ are most blessed, for they have found the light of the world (John 8:12).

After dark one evening, a Jewish religious leader named Nicodemus, a Pharisee, came to speak with Jesus. "Teacher," he said, "we all know that God has sent you to teach us. Your miraculous signs are proof enough that God is with you." John 3:1-2

The Night PART TWO

Dear night! this world's defeat;
The stop to busy fools; cares check and curb;
The day of spirits; my soul's calm retreat
Which none disturb!
Christ's[a] *progress, and his prayer time;*
The hours to which high Heaven doth chime.

God's silent, searching flight:
When my Lord's head is filled with dew, and all
His locks are wet with the clear drops of night;
His still, soft call;
His knocking time; The soul's dumb watch,
When spirits their fair kindred catch.

Were all my loud, evil days
Calm and unhaunted as is thy dark tent,
Whose peace but by some angel's wing or voice
Is seldom rent;
Then I in Heaven all the long year
Would keep, and never wander here.

But living where the sun
Doth all things wake, and where all mix and tire
Themselves and others, I consent and run
To every mire,
And by this world's ill-guiding light,
Err more than I can do by night.

There is in God (some say)
A deep, but dazzling darkness; As men here
Say it is late and dusky, because they
See not all clear;
O for that night! where I in him
Might live invisible and dim.

HENRY VAUGHAN (1622–1695)

[a]Mark, chap. 1.35. S. Luke, chap. 21. 37. [Vaughan's note]

IN THIS portion of "The Night" Vaughan turns to another kind of night, which he calls the "deep, but dazzling darkness" that is in God. He longs to hide in that dusky invisibility—to take refuge from the tiresome, running world and its ill-guiding light and to rest in the quiet comfort of God's darkened tent.

As a child it wasn't too difficult to find such a place in this world. Perhaps you found it in the family tent out back. You may remember the warmth of the summer day the tent retained in the quiet dusk and silent air, permeated by the odor of canvas. As you lay in this secret place, it was almost spiritual, if only for a few moments.

But now we are grown up and "living where the sun doth all things wake, and where all mix and tire themselves and others." But there is a verse—thank God there is always a verse—that can help us locate the calm and unhaunted tent of God "whose peace but by some angel's wing or voice is seldom rent."

"In the morning, while it was still very dark, he got up and went out to a deserted place, and there he prayed" (Mark 1:35, NRSV). In the morning, in the deserted living room or the wilderness of the cellar, before anything begins to move and mix and tire—the traffic in the street, the family in the house, the anxiety in the mind—kneel and pray. Do this daily and soon you will find "that night! where I in him might live invisible and dim."

He created everything there is. Nothing exists that he didn't make. Life itself was in him, and this life gives light to everyone. The light shines through the darkness, and the darkness can never extinguish it. John 1:3-5

Ezekiel EPILOGUE

And thus, O Prophet-bard of old,
Hast thou thy tale of sorrow told!
The same which earth's unwelcome seers
Have felt in all succeeding years.
Sport of the changeful multitude,
Nor calmly heard nor understood,
Their song has seemed a trick of art,
Their warnings but the actor's part.
With bonds, and scorn, and evil will,
The world requites[a] *its prophets still.*

So was it when the Holy One
The garments of the flesh put on!
Men followed where the Highest led
For common gifts of daily bread,
And gross of ear, of vision dim,
Owned not the Godlike power of Him.
Vain as a dreamer's words to them
His wail above Jerusalem,
And meaningless the watch He kept
Through which His weak disciples slept.

Yet shrink not thou, whoe'er thou art,
For God's great purpose set apart,
Before whose far-discerning eyes,
The Future as the Present lies!
Beyond a narrow-bounded age
Stretches thy prophet-heritage,
Through Heaven's vast spaces angel-trod.
And through the eternal years of God!
Thy audience, worlds!—all things to be
The witness of the Truth in thee!

JOHN GREENLEAF WHITTIER (1807–1892)

[a]pays

THESE are the final verses of Whittier's poem "Ezekiel." The first nine verses are written in the voice of the prophet himself. They briefly tell of Israel's captivity in Babylon, their forsaking God, Ezekiel's call as a prophet, the visions he saw, and his audiences' response to his message.

In the first verse of the epilogue the poet tells Ezekiel that today's world deals with its prophets in the same manner as he was treated. The second verse illustrates that Jesus Christ was given identical treatment as the prophets. In the last verse Whittier speaks directly to anyone who is set apart for the purpose of God—today's prophets. Whittier, a Quaker, speaks of "the witness of the Truth in thee." This fundamental Quaker belief states that divine revelation is immediate and individual. All persons may perceive the Word of God in their soul and should endeavor to heed it. Such revelation is called the "inward light" or the "Christ within."

The New Testament gives us reason to think that all believers are prophets: "You can all prophesy one by one, so that all may learn and all be encouraged" (1 Corinthians 14:31, NRSV). This does not mean that we can foretell the future. But we can speak of God according to the truth of the gospel—according to the witness of the truth within us as it corresponds to Scripture. When we do so, we function as prophets.

With this understanding, let us not shrink from the purpose for which God has called us, even if the world repays us with scorn and ill will. Whittier says we have a "prophet-heritage" that stretches beyond our age. We can draw encouragement from the examples of others' faithfulness under fire.

O Jerusalem, Jerusalem, the city that kills the prophets and stones God's messengers! How often I have wanted to gather your children together as a hen protects her chicks beneath her wings, but you wouldn't let me. And now look, your house is left to you, empty and desolate. Matthew 23:37-38

Worship PART ONE

The Pagan's myths through marble lips are spoken,
And ghosts of old Beliefs still flit and moan
Round fane[a] *and altar overthrown and broken,*
O'er tree-grown barrow and gray ring of stone.

Blind faith had martyrs in those old high places,
The Syrian hill grove and the Druid's[b] *wood,*
With mothers offering, to the Fiend's embraces,
Bone of their bone, and blood of their own blood.

Red altars, kindling through that night of error,
Smoked with warm blood beneath the cruel eye
Of lawless power and sanguinary[c] *terror,*
Throned on the circle of a pitiless sky;

Beneath whose baleful shadow, over-casting
All heaven above, and blighting earth below,
The scourge grew red, the lip grew pale with fasting,
And man's oblation[d] *was his fear and woe!*

Then through great temples swelled the dismal moaning
Of dirge-like music and sepulchral prayer;
Pale wizard priests, o'er occult symbols droning,
Swung their white censers in the burdened air:

As if the pomp of rituals, and the savor
Of gums and spices could the Unseen One please;
As if His ear could bend, with childish favor,
To the poor flattery of the organ keys!

Feet red from war-fields trod the church aisles holy,
With trembling reverence: and the oppressor there,
Kneeling before his priest, abased and lowly,
Crushed human hearts beneath his knee of prayer.

(continued in next day's reading)

JOHN GREENLEAF WHITTIER (1807–1892)

[a]a temple or church [b]ancient Celtic priest [c]flowing with blood [d]an offering in worship

IN THE first half of Whittier's poem on worship he describes the dark side of pagan worship. We see stone idols and secret places, human sacrifice, and blood sacrifices to a pitiless, bloodthirsty god. Next, the worshipers, whipped bloody and sick with fasting, can only offer fear and distress to their deity. Verses five and six show the laughable vanity of occult rituals—contrived music and prayers and secret symbols shrouded with smoky incense. Finally, we see the harvest of this worship—crushed human hearts.

Fear dominates these verses—fear of some god, but more specifically, fear of angering this god. How could one anger the god? By doing something wrong, by breaking a rule, by forgetting some aspect of the ritual and worship.

Needless to say, Christians do not participate in such sickening, superstitious cruelty. Still, let us take Whittier's words as a warning. Our worship must not involve fear.

We often invoke Numbers 6:24-26: "May the Lord bless you and protect you. May the Lord smile on you and be gracious to you. May the Lord show you his favor and give you his peace." How can we know God's blessing and protection, his gracious smile, his peaceful favor? By doing everything right and making no mistakes? No. There was only one person who never made a mistake—the sinless one, Jesus Christ. We need do but one right deed—believe in him. In this way we become the worshipers God seeks.

But the time is coming and is already here when true worshipers will worship the Father in spirit and in truth. The Father is looking for anyone who will worship him that way. For God is Spirit, so those who worship him must worship in spirit and in truth. John 4:23-24

Worship PART TWO

Not such the service the benignant Father
Requireth at His earthly children's hands:
Not the poor offering of vain rites, but rather
The simple duty man from man demands.

For Earth he asks it: the full joy of heaven
Knoweth no change of waning or increase;
The great heart of the Infinite beats even,
Untroubled flows the river of His peace.

He asks no taper lights, on high surrounding
The priestly altar and the saintly grave,
Not dolorous chant nor organ music sounding,
Nor incense clouding up the twilight nave.

For he whom Jesus loved hath truly spoken:
The holier worship which he deigns to bless
Restores the lost, and binds the spirit broken,
And feeds the widow and the fatherless!

Types of our human weakness and our sorrow!
Who lives unhaunted by his loved ones dead?
Who, with vain longing, seeketh not to borrow
From stranger eyes the home lights which have fled?

O brother man! fold to thy heart thy brother;
Where pity dwells, the peace of God is there;
To worship rightly is to love each other,
Each smile a hymn, each kindly deed a prayer.

Follow with reverent steps the great example
Of Him whose holy work was 'doing good';
So shall the wide earth seem our Father's temple,
Each loving life a psalm of gratitude.

Then shall all shackles fall; the stormy clangor
Of wild war music o'er the earth shall cease;
Love shall tread out the baleful fire of anger,
And in its ashes plant the tree of peace!

JOHN GREENLEAF WHITTIER (1807–1892)

HOW broad is the range of styles in Christian worship? It sweeps from the sinner's tears to the ecstatic joy of the forgiven; from kneeling prayers to dancing in the aisles. The New Testament says this about true worship: "But the time is coming and is already here when true worshipers will worship the Father in spirit and in truth. The Father is looking for anyone who will worship him that way" (John 4:23).

Whittier, a Quaker, considered worship as a way of life: "The holier worship which he deigns to bless . . . feeds the widow and the fatherless!" The concept of worship as a way of life came out of Jewish law and festivals. God specifically commanded his people to care for the poor, the helpless, and the foreigners (Deuteronomy 14:28-29; 24:19). Certain festivals were an extension of this command. During the Festival of Firstfruits, for example, the Israelites brought "the priest some grain from the first portion of [their] grain harvest" (Leviticus 23:10). In that way, they worshiped God by providing for the needs of those set aside to minister to him.

We also see this view in the New Testament. Consider Galatians 6:9-10: "Don't get tired of doing what is good. Don't get discouraged and give up, for we will reap a harvest of blessing at the appropriate time. Whenever we have the opportunity, we should do good to everyone." In Romans 12:1 Paul wrote, "offer your bodies as living sacrifices, holy and pleasing to God—this is your spiritual act of worship" (NIV).

We don't have to limit our worship of God to the traditional church setting. We can live each minute of each day in worship by doing what God requires of us.

➻ *And those who are peacemakers will plant seeds of peace and reap a harvest of goodness.* James 3:18

Crossing the Bar

Sunset and evening star,
And one clear call for me!
And may there be no moaning of the bar,
When I put out to sea,

But such a tide as moving seems asleep,
Too full for sound and foam,
When that which drew from out the boundless deep
Turns again home.

Twilight and evening bell,
And after that the dark!
And may there be no sadness of farewell,
When I embark;

For though from out our bourn[a] *of Time and Place*
The flood may bear me far,
I hope to see my Pilot face to face
When I have crossed the bar.

ALFRED, LORD TENNYSON (1809–1892)

[a]boundary; limit

LISTEN to the sounds in this poem and enjoy the sights the poet describes. Do you see the wash of color over a clear sky shortly after sunset and the evening star in the midst of it? Now remember how the sea silently moves in its tidal flow and lets the color of the sky reflect upon the outgoing flood. A ship rides the rising current and clears the sandbar that blocks the harbor, quietly returning home from the boundless deep of God's mystery. Now walk back upon the shore in the ineffable twilight. A bell begins to ring—not a church bell announcing a death but the usual evening bell.

So Tennyson describes his death. Silent, remarkable only in the light of the setting sun and rising star. Not signaled by a bell of mourning but by that which marks the passing of time. An unexceptional embarkation without the sadness of farewell.

"I am about to go the way of all the earth" (1 Kings 2:2, NRSV). This is how David—a man after God's own heart—described his death. "Then David died and was buried in the City of David" (1 Kings 2:10). That is all—no memorials, no account of one shed tear. Instead, "Solomon succeeded him as king" (1 Kings 2:12). Life went on.

Death is not remarkable. It is the way of the earth. Tennyson's swelling tide carried him across the bar (death) just like a thousand ships (lives) before him. But here is the extraordinary part of this common event, the unique seal set upon every believer's death: Tennyson sailed far away from this region of time and space where all we know is partial and imperfect. In death he embarked toward God and the complete knowledge that now only God possesses.

Now we see things imperfectly as in a poor mirror, but then we will see everything with perfect clarity. All that I know now is partial and incomplete, but then I will know everything completely, just as God knows me now. 1 Corinthians 13:12

Mock On, Mock On Voltaire, Rousseau

Mock on, Mock on Voltaire, Rousseau:
Mock on, Mock on: 'tis all in vain!
You throw the sand against the wind,
And the wind blows it back again.

And every sand becomes a Gem
Reflected in the beams divine;
Blown back they blind the mocking Eye,
But still in Israel's paths they shine.

The Atoms of Democritus
And Newton's Particles of light
Are sands upon the Red sea shore,
Where Israel's tents do shine so bright.

WILLIAM BLAKE (1757–1827)

TO UNDERSTAND this poem we must know a little about Voltaire and Rousseau. They were deists in the latter half of the eighteenth century. Deists believed in natural religion—a body of religious knowledge that could be acquired through reason. They believed in a creator but denied his ongoing involvement in creation.

Around the time Blake wrote this poem, deists were becoming more militant, attacking orthodox Christianity as intolerant, corrupt, and unenlightened. Blake responded with this simple yet elegant warning to those who would mock God. Blake likens this mockery to throwing "sand against the wind." It's vain, fruitless folly that only hurts the perpetrator because the wind blows the sand back into "the mocking Eye."

With great irony, Blake then alludes to two scientific theories that support the deists' views of an ordered universe operating by rational, natural rules. The first is "The Atoms of Democritus." The Greek philosopher Democritus (c. 460–370 B.C.) developed the atomic theory of the universe: All things are composed of minute, indestructible particles, which move about eternally in infinite empty space. Democritus viewed the creation of worlds as the natural consequence of the ceaseless whirling motion of atoms.

The second theory is Sir Isaac Newton's (1642–1727) "Particles of light." Newton described light as an emission of particles, which is partially true. Light is actually a transport of energy both in particulate flow and in waves, or *rays.*

As important as these theories are to our understanding of the universe, Blake reminds us of a far more important truth. Rational, natural rules and scientific theories "are sands upon the Red sea shore, where Israel's tents do shine so bright." That is, order and science are subservient to the ever-present God, who can use these truths to accomplish his purposes.

Do not be deceived: God cannot be mocked. Galatians 6:7, NIV

In Memoriam L (Stanza 50)

Bear near me when my light is low,
When the blood creeps, and the nerves prick
And tingle; and the heart is sick,
And all the wheels of being slow.

Be near me when the sensuous frame
Is racked with pangs that conquer trust;
And Time, a maniac scattering dust,
And Life, a Fury slinging flame.

Be near me when my faith is dry,
And men the flies of latter spring,
That lay their eggs, and sting and sing
And weave their petty cells and die.

Be near me when I fade away,
To point the term of human strife,
And on the low dark verge of life
The twilight of eternal day.

ALFRED, LORD TENNYSON (1809–1892)

THE STORY behind *In Memoriam* begins during Tennyson's university days. At Cambridge he developed a close friendship with Arthur Henry Hallam. Hallam later became engaged to Tennyson's sister but died suddenly in Vienna at the age of twenty-two. Tennyson, greatly affected by Hallam's death, published a long sequence of elegies in tribute to his friend. Completed in 1850, *In Memoriam* is Tennyson's finest work.

In this section Tennyson asks the Lord to be near him during his difficult times. For Tennyson these times included growing old, struggling spiritually, dealing with the loss of his friend and counselor, and dying. But through these dark times and the struggles that ensued, Tennyson discovered the meaning of life, which he expressed in the epilogue of this poem: God lives and loves and is moving his whole creation toward one far-off divine event. That is, the return of his Son, Jesus Christ. In the meantime, Tennyson could take refuge in Christ's presence, trusting the Suffering Servant to comfort him.

Someone once asked Tennyson what Jesus Christ meant to him. Pointing to an open flower, Tennyson responded, "What the sun is to that flower, Jesus Christ is to my soul." We have the same need for Jesus—not just for the dark days of life but for all our days on earth. May Christ illumine our days with his presence.

Jesus said to the people, "I am the light of the world. If you follow me, you won't be stumbling through the darkness, because you will have the light that leads to life." John 8:12

Because I Could Not Stop for Death—

Because I could not stop for Death—
He kindly stopped for me—
The Carriage held but just Ourselves—
And Immortality.

We slowy drove—He knew no haste
And I had put away
My labor and my leisure too,
For His Civility—

We passed the School, where Children strove
At Recess—in the Ring—
We passed the Fields of Gazing Grain—
We passed the Setting Sun—

Or rather—He passed Us—
The Dews drew quivering and chill—
For only Gossamer, my Gown—
My Tippet[a]*—only Tulle*[b]*—*

We paused before a House that seemed
A Swelling of the Ground—
The Roof was scarcely visible—
The Cornice—in the Ground—

Since then—'tis Centuries—and yet
Feels shorter than the Day
I first surmised the Horses' Heads
Were toward Eternity—

EMILY DICKINSON (1830–1886)

[a]a shoulder cape [b]a sheer silk net

DEATH fascinated Emily Dickinson. Many of her 1,775 poems pertain to the subject. She did not view death, however, as morbid, macabre, or annihilistic. She thought of death as passing from one phase of existence to the next, as illustrated in this poem.

Dickinson portrays death as a chauffeur who transports the poet from this life to the next. On this "carriage" ride from mortality to immortality, she passes the things of this world—children, grain, and setting sun—until she goes beyond them into eternity. This journey was not something she had been planning on or preparing for. It came at Death's timing, not the poet's. But she peacefully complies—there is no sense of panic or alarm—and accepts that her time has come.

Like the poet, we do not know when our last day will come. We can plan for it and prepare for it, but we cannot predict it. The best way to prepare for that day is to accept Christ as our Savior and live our life for him. Doing so will ensure that we are ready for the journey into eternity.

God has made everything beautiful for its own time. He has planted eternity in the human heart, but even so, people cannot see the whole scope of God's work from beginning to end. Ecclesiastes 3:11

My Baptismal Birth-Day

God's child in Christ adopted,—Christ my all,—
What that earth boasts were not lost cheaply, rather
Than forfeit that blessed name, by which I call
The Holy One, the Almighty God, my Father?—
Father! in Christ we live, and Christ in Thee—
Eternal Thou, and everlasting we.
The heir of heaven, henceforth I fear not death:
In Christ I live! in Christ I draw the breath
Of the true life!—Let then earth, sea, and sky
Make war against me! On my heart I show
Their mighty master's seal. In vain they try
To end my life, that can but end its woe. —
Is that a death-bed where a Christian lies?—
Yes! But not his—'tis Death itself there dies.

SAMUEL TAYLOR COLERIDGE (1772–1834)

BAPTISM is not a ritual by which we join a church. It is so much more. The day of your baptism was when you publicly identified yourself with Christ. This is a high purpose for what can be a messy, sometimes embarrassing experience. All that water soaks you to the skin in front of everyone. Your hair gets plastered to your head. You sputter and spit as you come out of the water. Then you head backstage for a change of clothes.

Coleridge calls baptism his birth—another messy and difficult event. Paul gave us the opposite perspective when he wrote that baptism is a burial (Romans 6:4). Within the visible procedure of baptism is a profound, unseen reality: You unite with Christ in his death, burial, and resurrection (Romans 6:5). Coleridge knew these truths and wove them into his sublime poem.

Day by day, we see creation in bondage to decay (Romans 8:20-21). Our own body displays this truth. It is certain because we are flesh and blood, and one day we will die. But Coleridge leads us into the joy of our baptism in Christ—the one who himself shared in our flesh and blood. In this baptism we have become victors over death because we died with Christ who destroyed the one who has the power over death (Romans 6:3; Hebrews 2:14). Coleridge glories in these truths: "Is that a death-bed where a Christian lies?—Yes! But not his—'tis Death itself there dies."

Or have you forgotten that when we became Christians and were baptized to become one with Christ Jesus, we died with him? For we died and were buried with Christ by baptism. And just as Christ was raised from the dead by the glorious power of the Father, now we also may live new lives. Romans 6:3-4

The Harp

Some may occasion snatch to carp,
Saying that I have sung to Nero's harp,
And therefore am for David's most unfit,
Which piety requires, as well as wit:
But thus, I my defence prepare,
Showing how I have travelled far,
And by the streams of Babylon have sate,[a]
Where I deplored my sad, and wretched state;
Upon a willow there I hung
That harp, to which I whilome[b] *sung:*
This tree, which neither blossoms yields, nor fruit,
Did with this instrument unhappy suit:
There let it hang, consume, and rot
Since I a better harp have got,
Which doth in worth as far surpass the other,
As Abel in devotion, did his brother.

RALPH KNEVET (1601–1671)

[a]sat [b]at one time, formerly

THIS POEM is a defense of the poet's conversion. Knevet's critics accused him of being worldly—of singing to Nero's harp—and therefore judged him unfit to sing to David's. "After all," they say, "this requires piety as well as wit."

A paraphrase of Knevet's defense might sound like this: "I have been around the block a couple of times. I know my way in the world. But I found it to be a prison. By being worldly, I learned that my condition as a human is sad and wretched. You say that I sing to a worldly tune. I once did, but I hung up that harp there on the fruitless willow tree and never sang by it again. Let it hang there forever and rot away! I now play a harp that is far more valuable."

In the last two lines Knevet makes an interesting comparison: The worth of his new harp is greater than that of the old, just as Abel's devotion to God surpassed Cain's (Genesis 4:1-5). What is the difference between the two? Abel was a herdsman; Cain, a farmer. Both made offerings to God, but God accepted Abel's and refused Cain's. In anger over his rejection, Cain murdered Abel. Through this simile, Knevet contrasts the law (Cain) and grace (Abel). The worldly way is to work hard for acceptance and success. This isn't bad except in relation to God. Cain the farmer worked hard to produce crops. But Abel only had to pick his offering from his flock.

This describes the Christian gospel. No amount of hard work or good behavior earns our salvation. The Bible says, "Look! There is the Lamb of God who takes away the sin of the world!" (John 1:29). Salvation is God's gift to us in grace. We cannot work for it. Thus, true believers sing to the harp of Abel.

Beside the rivers of Babylon, we sat and wept as we thought of Jerusalem. We put away our lyres, hanging them on the branches of the willow trees. Psalm 137:1-2

Yet a Little While . . . VERSES 1, 4–6

The day grows old, the low-pitched lamp hath made
No less than treble shade,
And the descending damp doth now prepare
T' uncurl bright Titan's[a] *hair;*
Whose western wardrobe now begins t' unfold
Her purples, fringed with gold;
To clothe his evening glory, when th' alarms
Of rest shall call to rest in restless Thetis'[b] *arms.*

Our wasted taper now hath brought her light
To the next door to night;
Her spriteless flame grown great with snuff, doth turn
Sad as her neighboring urn:
Her slender inch, that yet unspent remains,
Lights but to further pains,
And in a silent language bids her guest
Prepare his weary limbs to take eternal rest.

Now careful age hath pitched her painful plough
Upon the furrowed brow;
And snowy blasts of discontented care
Have blanched the falling hair:
Suspicious envy mixed with jealous spite
Disturbs his weary night:
He threatens youth with age; and now alas,
He owns not what he is, but vaunts[c] *the man he was.*

Gray-hairs, peruse thy days, and let thy past
Read lectures to thy last:
Those hasty wings that hurried them away
Will give these days no day:
The constant wheels of Nature scorn to tire
Until her works expire:
That blast that nipped thy youth, will ruin thee;
The hand that shook the branch will quickly strike the tree.

FRANCIS QUARLES (1592–1644)

[a]the son of Uranus and Gaea in classical mythology [b]the mother of Achilles in Greek mythology [c]brags; boasts

A SINGLE poem can tell many tales. Today's describes:

• The beauty of the close of day—"Whose western wardrobe now begins t' unfold her purples, fringed with gold."

• The pain and sadness of growing old—"Her slender inch, that yet unspent remains, lights but to further pains."

• The self-deception that may come as one approaches death—"He owns not what he is, but vaunts the man he was."

• The brevity of human life—"Those hasty wings that hurried them away will give these days no day."

Among the images in this poem are used-up candles, weary limbs, and eternal rest; the furrowed brow, falling white hair, and sleepless nights; the tireless wheels of nature, and a storm-toppled tree. All this is not so cheerful. Is this the poem's only message—everyone grows old and eventually dies? No. The message is in the poem's title—"Yet a Little While Is the Light with You." The entire poem is intended to help us read with fresh eyes the following words of Jesus Christ:

Jesus replied, "My light will shine out for you just a little while longer. Walk in it while you can, so you will not stumble when the darkness falls. If you walk in the darkness, you cannot see where you are going. Believe in the light while there is still time; then you will become children of the light." After saying these things, Jesus went away and was hidden from them. John 12:35-36

Dear Lord and Father of Mankind

Dear Lord and Father of mankind,
Forgive our fev'rish ways!
Reclothe us in our rightful mind;
In purer lives Thy service find,
In deeper rev'rence, praise.

In simple trust like theirs who heard,
Beside the Syrian Sea,
The gracious calling of the Lord,
Let us, like them, without a word,
Rise up and follow Thee.

O Sabbath rest by Galilee!
O calm of hills above,
Where Jesus knelt to share with thee
The silence of eternity,
Interpreted by love.

Drop Thy still dews of quietness
Till all our strivings cease;
Take from our souls the strain and stress,
And let our ordered lives confess
The beauty of Thy peace.

Breathe thru the heats of our desire
Thy coolness and Thy balm;
Let sense be dumb, let flesh retire;
Speak thru the earthquake, wind, and fire,
O still small voice of calm!

JOHN GREENLEAF WHITTIER (1807–1892)

JOHN GREENLEAF WHITTIER, a Quaker, is one of America's best-loved poets. Many admired his poetry for its piety, compassion, and commendation of goodness. The height of his fame came in the 1880s. It was then that the country began to regard Whittier as one of the "schoolroom poets"; student readers studied his writings in classrooms everywhere because they could readily understand them.

This poem (which later became a hymn), "Dear Lord and Father of Mankind," is the twelfth stanza (and following) of "The Brewing of Soma." In the earlier stanzas, Whittier wrote about an intoxicating drink called soma, which Hindu worshipers drank "to bring the skies more near, or lift men up to heaven."

To Whittier, the emotionalism that sometimes accompanies Christian worship was similar to drinking Hindu soma. It is a vain attempt to get closer to God. "Forgive our fev'rish ways," he prayed and then asked God to "drop Thy still dews of quietness" so that we might enjoy "the beauty of Thy peace." In the final lines, he draws upon the image of God communicating with Elijah—not by "earthquake, wind, and fire" but by a "still small voice of calm." How many times do we miss God's voice because we are caught up in feverish activity, whether in worship or at work? May God "breathe thru the heats of our desire" his cool balm so we can hear him speaking.

After the wind there was an earthquake, but the Lord was not in the earthquake. And after the earthquake there was a fire, but the Lord was not in the fire. And after the fire there was the sound of a gentle whisper. When Elijah heard it, he wrapped his face in his cloak and went out and stood at the entrance of the cave. 1 Kings 19:11-13

To St John Baptist

As Anne long barren, Mother did become
of him, who last was Judge in Israel:
Thou last of prophets born like Samuel
didst from a womb past hope of issue come.
His mother silent spake: thy father dumb
recovering speech, God's wonder did foretell:
he after death a prophet was in hell:
and thou unborn within thy mother's womb:
He did annoint the king, whom God did take
from charge of sheep, to rule his chosen land:
But that high king who heaven and earth did make
Received a holier liquour from thy hand,
When God his flock in human shape did feed,
as Israel's king kept his in shepherd's weed.

HENRY CONSTABLE (1562–1613)

HENRY CONSTABLE was an English poet who worked to develop the English sonnet "Diana" (1592). Today's sonnet studies the similarities between Samuel and John the Baptist. Samuel, the last judge of Israel, and John, the last prophet of Israel, were both born to barren women (1 Samuel 1:2; Luke 1:7). Samuel's mother prayed silently for a son; John's father was struck mute until it was time to name John (1 Samuel 1:12-13; Luke 1:67-79). Samuel prophesied after he was dead; John rejoiced before he was born (1 Samuel 28:15-19; Luke 1:41). Samuel anointed the shepherd David to become king; John announced the coming of the Messiah, who became our spiritual shepherd (1 Samuel 16:13; Mark 1:7-8).

What do these interesting observations mean to us today? They illustrate the way God acted to advance his purpose before the coming of Christ—miracles performed through specially anointed people. But since the Lord's coming things have changed. Hebrews 1:1-2 says: "Long ago God spoke many times and in many ways to our ancestors through the prophets. But now in these final days, he has spoken to us through his Son." These verses echo God's words in Matthew 17:5: "This is my beloved Son, and I am fully pleased with him. Listen to him."

In this era of personality worship, men like John and Samuel would most likely attract a following. Charismatic individuals can easily capture our heart and devotion with captivating words and amazing feats. While God may still use specially anointed people to accomplish his work today, his Son completed the most important task—dying for our sins. He alone should be the focus of our praise and devotion.

Then his father, Zechariah, was filled with the Holy Spirit and gave this prophecy: "Praise the Lord, the God of Israel, because he has visited his people and redeemed them. He has sent us a mighty Savior from the royal line of his servant David." Luke 1:67-69

The Book of Books

Within this ample volume lies
The mystery of mysteries.
Happiest they of human race
To whom their God has given grace
To read, to fear, to hope, to pray,
To lift the latch, to force the way;
But better had they ne're been born
That read to doubt or read to scorn.

SIR WALTER SCOTT (1771–1832)

SIR WALTER SCOTT was one of the foremost literary figures of the romantic period. He achieved unprecedented popularity during his lifetime with his narrative poems and historical romances. His first narrative poem, *The Lay of the Last Minstrel* (1805), was a great success. Following that, he wrote a series of romantic poems, including *The Lady of the Lake* (1810) and *The Lord of the Isles* (1815).

As a novelist, Scott re-created periods of history through accurate description and skillful characterization. He was among the first writers who stressed the relationship of characters to their environment. His novels include *Waverley* (1814), *Rob Roy* (1818), *The Bride of Lammermoor* (1819), and *Ivanhoe* (1820).

Today's short poem tells us how much Scott appreciated the Word of God. He wrote, "Happiest they of human race to whom their God has given grace to read." These words show the author's understanding of God's ways.

What does a person need to understand the Bible? Scott does not say that we need a high IQ like his or deep insight, which he doubtless possessed. What about a high level of education? Or ordination as a minister or pastor? No. None of these.

When Paul wrote to Timothy he said, "You have been taught the holy Scriptures from childhood" (2 Timothy 3:15). Who taught Timothy? His mother, Eunice, and his grandmother, Lois (1:5). They may not have been extraordinary women, but they taught the Scriptures to Timothy, a future apostle of God. Clearly they were, like Sir Walter Scott, among the happiest of the human race to whom God had given grace to read and understand his Word.

➻ *All Scripture is inspired by God and is useful to teach us what is true and to make us realize what is wrong in our lives. It straightens us out and teaches us to do what is right. It is God's way of preparing us in every way, fully equipped for every good thing God wants us to do.*
2 Timothy 3:16-17

Earth's Answer

Earth raised up her head
From the darkness dread and drear.
Her light fled,
Stony dread!
And her locks covered with grey despair.

"Prisoned on watery shore,
"Starry Jealousy does keep my den:
"Cold and hoar,[a]
"Weeping o'er,
"I hear the Father of the ancient men.

"Selfish father of men!
"Cruel, jealous, selfish fear!
"Can delight,
"Chained in night,
"The virgins of youth and morning bear?

"Does spring hide its joy
"When buds and blossoms grow?
"Does the sower
"Sow by night,
"Or the plowman in darkness plow?

"Break this heavy chain
"That does freeze my bones around.
"Selfish! vain!
"Eternal bane!
"That free Love with bondage bound."

WILLIAM BLAKE (1757–1827)

[a]frost

WILLIAM BLAKE speaks as earth's voice after Adam's fall. It is afflicted, imprisoned, jealous, cold, and weeping. Blake imagines in verses 3 and 4 that creation hears God, "the Father of the ancient men," speaking to Adam, the "selfish father of men."

Finally the earth pleads, "Break this heavy chain that does freeze my bones around." Blake vividly and eloquently paraphrases Paul's words: "All creation anticipates the day when it will join God's children in glorious freedom from death and decay. For we know that all creation has been groaning as in the pains of childbirth right up to the present time" (Romans 8:21-22).

When Adam fell away from God, everything on earth experienced God's curse (8:20). This is why creation groans (8:22). The wonder and beauty of nature may cause us to question whether this is really true. But natural disasters, death, and decay give us a definite answer to our inquiry. There is good news, however. When Christ died, he reconciled us to God (5:10). In other words, he brought us into harmony with God. Through Christ, "God reconciled everything to himself. He made peace with everything in heaven and on earth by means of his blood on the cross" (Colossians 1:20).

As we continue in the faith, we too will groan for release from the Curse's consequences. But God has promised to release us from this "heavy chain" and make all things new (2 Peter 3:13). Therefore, let us "wait anxiously for that day when God will give us our full rights as his children, including the new bodies he has promised us. Now that we are saved, we eagerly look forward to this freedom" (Romans 8:23-24).

➻ *The Lord God called to Adam, "Where are you?" He replied, "I heard you, so I hid. I was afraid because I was naked."* Genesis 3:9-10

Of Human Knowledge PART ONE, LINES 1–40

Why did my parents send me to the schools
That I with knowledge might enrich my mind?
Since the desire to know first made men fools,
And did corrupt the root of all mankind.

For when God's hand had written in the hearts
Of the first parents all the rules of good,
So that their skill infused did pass all arts
That ever were, before or since the flood,

And when their reason's eye was sharp and clear,
And, as an eagle can behold the sun,
Could have approached th' eternal light as near
As the intellectual angels could have done,

Even then to them the spirit of lies suggests
That they were blind, because they saw not ill,
And breathes into their incorrupted breasts
A curious wish, which did corrupt their will.

For that same ill they straight desired to know;
Which ill, being nought but a defect of good,
And all God's works the devil could not show
While man their lord in his perfection stood.

So that themselves were first to do the ill,
Ere they thereof the knowledge could attain;
Like him that knew not poison's power to kill,
Until, by tasting it, himself was slain.

Even so by tasting of that fruit forbid,
Where they sought knowledge, they did error find;
Ill they desired to know, and ill they did,
And to give passion eyes, made reason blind.

(continued in next day's reading)

SIR JOHN DAVIES (1569–1626)

SIR JOHN DAVIES was an English jurist and poet. He served as attorney general for Ireland and sought to establish Protestantism in Ulster. He was Speaker of the Irish Parliament, sat in English Parliament, and was appointed lord chief justice (1626) but died before entering office. Davies is known for his philosophical poems *Orchestra* (1596), *Nosce Teipsum* (1599), and *Hymnes of Astraea* (1599).

In today's poem Davies puzzles over the primal event of human history—the eating from the tree of the knowledge of good and evil. At that time Adam and Eve "could have approached th' eternal light as near as the . . . angels could have done." But they believed the lie that since they did not know good and evil, they were actually blind. So they ate of the wrong tree and as a result were cut off from the tree of life.

The tree of life and the tree of the knowledge of good and evil—one gives life, the other causes death. One is of life, the other of good and evil. This simple comparison reveals what is missing in our world. We have plenty of evil, and there is also much good. But we don't have much life—eternal life, that is.

Enter Jesus Christ, saying, "I am . . . the life" (John 11:25; 14:6) and "I am the bread of life" (6:35). To "eat" Jesus Christ—to believe and receive him—brings eternal life (6:54). Adam and Eve did not eat the life that God provided them, and human history got off to a bad start. So Jesus came to make this same life available again. All a person needs to do is eat—that is, believe in Christ. "Taste and see that the Lord is good. Oh, the joys of those who trust in him!" (Psalm 34:8).

Then the Lord God said, "The people have become as we are, knowing everything, both good and evil. What if they eat the fruit of the tree of life? Then they will live forever!" Genesis 3:22

Of Human Knowledge PART TWO, LINES 149-180

If aught[a] can teach us aught, affliction's looks,
Making us look into ourselves so near,
Teach us to know ourselves beyond all books,
Or all the learnëd schools that ever were.

This mistress lately plucked me by the ear,
And many a golden lesson hath me taught;
Hath made my senses quick and reason clear,
Reformed my will and rectified my thought.

So do the winds and thunders cleanse the air;
So working lees[b] settle and purge the wine;
So lopped and prunëd trees do flourish fair;
So doth the fire the drossy gold refine.

Neither Minerva[c] nor the learnëd muse,
Nor rules of art, nor precepts of the wise,
Could in my brain those beams of skill infuse,
As but the glance of this dame's angry eyes.

She within lists[d] my ranging mind hath brought,
That now beyond myself I list[e] not go;
Myself am center of my circling thought,
Only myself I study, learn, and know.

I know my body's of so frail a kind
As force without, fevers within, can kill;
I know the heavenly nature of my mind,
But 'tis corrupted both in wit and will;

I know my soul hath power to know all things,
Yet is she blind and ignorant in all;
I know I am one of nature's little kings,
Yet to the least and vilest things am thrall.

I know my life's a pain and but a span,
I know my sense is mocked with everything;
And to conclude, I know myself a man,
Which is a proud and yet a wretched thing.

SIR JOHN DAVIES (1569–1626)

[a]anything [b]sediment in fermenting wine [c]the goddess of wisdom, technical skill, and invention in Roman mythology [d]boundaries [e]desire

AFTER reading this portion of today's poem, one could be comfortable in this English jurist's court. Someone who, through suffering, knows himself is someone who is trustworthy.

Davies likens affliction to a schoolteacher who pinched his ear to focus his attention on his lessons. The mistress affliction worked in the poet's life like a rainstorm cleanses the air, like settling sediment clarifies wine, like pruning causes a tree to be fruitful, like fire separates dross from gold. He knew that nothing but the "glance of this dame's angry eyes" could have taught him to know himself.

When the poet says, "Myself am center of my circling thought, only myself I study, learn, and know," he sounds self-centered. But he means that he has learned not to focus on other people's weaknesses and failures; he has learned that his own body is frail and his soul is blind.

When the serpent tempted Eve to eat from the tree of the knowledge of good and evil, he said, "Your eyes will be opened, and you will be like God" (Genesis 3:5, NRSV). Indeed, the Fall has made us like gods of our own personal universe, looking out judgmentally on everyone else. Davies testifies that affliction cured him of that and concludes, "I know myself a man, which is a proud and yet a wretched thing."

Lord, remind me how brief my time on earth will be. Remind me that my days are numbered, and that my life is fleeing away. My life is no longer than the width of my hand. An entire lifetime is just a moment to you; human existence is but a breath. Psalm 39:4-5

On the Two Great Floods

Two floods I read of; water, and of wine;
The first was Noah's; Lot, the last was thine:
The first was the effect; the last, the cause
Of that foul sin, against the sacred laws
Of God and nature, incest: Noah found
An ark to save him, but poor Lot was drowned;
Good Noah found an ark; but Lot found none:
We're safer in God's hands than in our own:
The former flood of waters did extend
But some few days; this latter has no end;
They both destroyed, I know not which the worst;
The last is even as general, as the first:
The first being ceased, the world began to fill;
The last depopulates, and wastes it still:
Both floods o'erwhelmed both man and beast
together;
The last is worst, if there be best of either:
The first are ceased: Heaven vowed it by a sign;
When shall we see a rainbow after wine?

FRANCIS QUARLES (1592–1644)

THE BIBLE does not explicitly forbid the consumption of alcoholic beverages. What it does say is, "And be not *drunk* with wine, wherein is excess" (Ephesians 5:18, KJV, italics added). There has been an emphasis on temperance among Christians, but here is what C. S. Lewis once said on this subject:

> One great piece of mischief has been done by the modern restriction of the word Temperance to the question of drink. It helps people to forget that you can be just as intemperate about lots of other things. A man who makes his golf or his motor-bicycle the center of his life, or a woman who devotes all her thoughts to clothes or bridge or her dog, is being just as "intemperate" as someone who gets drunk every evening. Of course, it does not show on the outside so easily: bridge-mania or golf-mania do not make you fall down in the middle of the road. But God is not deceived by externals.[a]

Francis Quarles speaks of two floods—one of water in Noah's time and the other of wine in Lot's time. But we shouldn't let ourselves off the hook if we aren't drowning in a flood of alcohol as did Lot. We need to look at drunkenness in a broader sense and understand that nearly everything in the world can lead to some sort of excess. So what are we to do? "Be not drunk with wine, . . . *but be filled with the Spirit*" (Ephesians 5:18, KJV, italics added).

Afterward Lot left Zoar because he was afraid of the people there, and he went to live in a cave in the mountains with his two daughters. One day the older daughter said to her sister, "There isn't a man anywhere in this entire area for us to marry. . . . Come, let's get him drunk with wine, and then we will sleep with him. That way we will preserve our family line through our father." Genesis 19:30-32

[a]*Mere Christianity* (New York: Macmillan, 1952).

Genesis XXIV PART ONE

Who is this Man
that walketh in the field,
O Eleazar,
steward to my lord?

And Eleazar
answered her and said,
Daughter of Bethuel,
it is other none
But my lord Isaac,
son unto my lord;
Who, as his wont is,
walketh in the field
In the hour of evening
meditating there.

Therefore Rebekah
hasted where she sat,
And from her camel
lighting to the earth
Sought for a veil,
and put it on her face.
Wherefore he came,
and met them on the field,
Whom, when Rebekah
saw, she came before,
Saying, Behold
the handmaid of my lord,
Who for my lord's sake
travel from my land.

(continued in next day's reading)

ARTHUR HUGH CLOUGH (1819–1861)

THIS POEM recasts an interesting tale of faith from Genesis 24. Abraham's servant Eleazar travels to northwest Mesopotamia to find a wife for Isaac because Abraham did not want his son to marry a local Canaanite woman. Aware of the importance of his task, Eleazar asks God for a sign. Rebekah is God's answer; she not only gives Eleazar a drink but waters his camels as well.

After her family extends hospitality to Eleazar and makes a dowry payment, Rebekah willingly goes with him to meet her new husband. In those days it was common for a bride to leave her parents when she married and live with her husband's clan. Rebekah did this without seeing Isaac. This took faith and courage, because it was also common for husbands to think of their wives as property. However, she felt that Isaac would be different because he was a distant family member. Rebekah's father, Bethuel, was Abraham's nephew (Genesis 22:20-23), making her Abraham's great-niece and eventually daughter-in-law.

Rebekah married into a family of faith. Her willingness to trust God—evident in her words, "Behold, the handmaid of my lord"—made this possible.

Imagine if Rebekah and Eleazar had not been willing to trust and obey God. Instead of participating in God's divine plan, they might have lived ordinary, uneventful lives. Instead of having their stories recorded in God's Word, they might have been just people lost in the sea of time. But Rebekah and Eleazar believed God and obeyed his will. And the rest is history.

Faith and obedience certainly have their privileges.

Then I [Eleazar] bowed my head and worshiped the Lord. I praised the Lord, the God of my master, Abraham, because he had led me along the right path to find a wife from the family of my master's relatives.
Genesis 24:48

Genesis XXIV PART TWO

But he said, O
thou blessed of our God,
Come, for the tent
is eager for thy face.
Shall not thy husband
be unto thee more than
Hundreds of kinsmen
living in thy land?

And Eleazar answered,
Thus and thus,
Even according
as thy father bade,
Did we; and thus and
thus it came to pass;
Lo! is not this
Rebekah, Bethuel's child?

And as he ended
Isaac spoke and said,
Surely my heart
went with you on the way,
When with the beasts
ye came unto the place.
Truly, O child
of Nahor, I was there,
When to thy mother
and thy mother's son
Thou madest answer,
saying, I will go.
And Isaac brought her
to his mother's tent.

ARTHUR HUGH CLOUGH (1819–1861)

THE STORY of Rebekah and Isaac in Genesis 24 is wonderful yet seemingly impossible. Abraham sent his trusted servant Eleazar into a distant land to find a wife for his son, Isaac. At a spring, Eleazar prayed that God would grant him success on his mission. Before he had finished his prayer, a lovely woman came to the spring to draw water. Eleazar asked her for a drink, and she complied without hesitation, even going so far as to water his camels too. He knew then that God had answered his prayer. She was the one for Isaac.

This account is symbolic of another story that continues today. Like Abraham, God the Father has sent his representative—the Holy Spirit—to our far-off land, seeking a bride for the Son. Doesn't it seem impossible that humanity could become the bride of divinity? Nonetheless, this is God's desire as seen in Ephesians 5:31-32 when Paul advises husbands and wives: "'A man will leave his father and mother and be joined to his wife, and the two will become one flesh.' This is a great mystery, and I am applying it to Christ and the church" (NRSV). The wedding ceremony between Christ and the church appears in Revelation: "For the time has come for the wedding feast of the Lamb, and his bride has prepared herself. She is permitted to wear the finest white linen" (Revelation 19:7-8).

Obviously, theirs is not a literal marriage between a husband and wife. But their relationship is so intimate that it serves as an example of how husbands and wives should love one another. Thus, Paul wrote, "As the church submits to Christ, so you wives must submit to your husbands in everything. And you husbands must love your wives with the same love Christ showed the church" (Ephesians 5:24-25).

➻ *And Isaac brought Rebekah into his mother's tent, and she became his wife. He loved her very much, and she was a special comfort to him after the death of his mother.* Genesis 24:67

The Scribe

What lovely things
Thy hand hath made:
The smooth-plumed bird
In its emerald shade,
The seed of the grass,
The speck of stone
Which the wayfaring ant
Stirs—and hastes on!

Though I should sit
By some tarn in thy hills,
Using its ink
As the spirit wills
To write of Earth's wonders,
Its live, willed things,
Flit would the ages
On soundless wings
Ere unto Z
My pen drew nigh;
Leviathan told,
And the honey-fly:

And still would remain
My wit to try—
My worn reeds broken,
The dark tarn dry,
All words forgotten—
Thou, Lord, and I.

WALTER DE LA MARE (1873–1956)

THE POET is admiring what God has created. Sitting near a tarn, a steep-banked mountain lake or pool, he admires "the smooth-plumed bird in its emerald shade, the seed of the grass, the speck of stone which the wayfaring ant stirs."

But as the poem continues, the poet expresses what many writers go through when they try to put down in words what they see and feel in creation. Writers never feel that they have adequately described a sunset, a sunrise, a living creature crawling by, or a bird flying in the wind. Just when we think we have captured the image, it evades us. We can't express what we view in creation because creation is alive with the life of God. It is in motion—always moving forward, always active. By the time a writer expresses the first glow of sunrise, the beams have already begun to break out. This poet laments that the ages would "flit" by before he had a chance to fully describe the largest creature, the Leviathan (a sea monster) or even a small creature like a honey fly.

The poet also laments that he could write and write—exhausting his entire wit and draining the tarn dry—and still not be able to describe God's creation: "And still would remain my wit to try—my worn reeds broken, the dark tarn dry."

How amazing the ordinary can be! We see elements of God's creation every day and take them for granted. Yet if we look at a meadow or a tree or a bird or a sunset through the eyes of a poet, we might gain a renewed appreciation for the miracle of life and creation and even the Creator. What aspect of creation will you look at today with new eyes? How can you praise God creatively for his creativity?

The heavens are yours, and the earth is yours; everything in the world is yours—you created it all. Psalm 89:11

If Only

If I might only love my God and die!
But now He bids me love Him and live on,
Now when the bloom of all my life is gone,
The pleasant half of life has quite gone by.
My tree of hope is lopped that spread so high;
And I forget how Summer glowed and shone,
While Autumn grips me with its fingers wan,
And frets me with its fitful windy sigh.
When Autumn passes then must Winter numb,
And Winter may not pass a weary while,
But when it passes Spring shall flower again:
And in that Spring who weepeth now shall smile,
Yea, they shall wax who now are on the wane,
Yea, they shall sing for love when Christ shall come.

CHRISTINA ROSSETTI (1830–1894)

CHRISTINA ROSSETTI'S poetry is often easy to understand, yet it is also quite elegant and profound. In this poem Rossetti makes a startling comment: "If I might only love my God and die! But now He bids me love Him and live on." In two short lines she uncovers a major struggle of the Christian life—living for Christ.

Have you ever thought the same thing? Wouldn't it be simpler to die for Christ in an instant than live for him day after day until we die? We could complain that Jesus' death on the cross took only six hours, while our crucifixion lasts a lifetime. But Jesus didn't deserve to die—he did it for our sake. We need to live a crucified life. Paul realized this: "I have been crucified with Christ. I myself no longer live, but Christ lives in me. So I live my life in this earthly body by trusting in the Son of God, who loved me and gave himself for me" (Galatians 2:19-20).

If we are serious about following Christ, we must come to this same realization. We must be willing to lay aside our personal ambitions, dreams, and desires to serve Christ, living a life of total obedience to him. May God grant us the grace to live a crucified life—not on our own but through the power of Christ who died for us and now lives in us.

For you died when Christ died, and your real life is hidden with Christ in God. And when Christ, who is your real life, is revealed to the whole world, you will share in all his glory. Colossians 3:3-4

Our Journey Had Advanced—

Our journey had advanced—
Our feet were almost come
To that odd Fork in Being's Road—
Eternity—by Term—

Our pace took sudden awe—
Our feet—reluctant—led—
Before—were Cities—but Between—
The Forest of the Dead—

Retreat—was out of Hope—
Behind—a Sealed Route—
Eternity's White Flag—Before—
And God—at every Gate—

EMILY DICKINSON (1830–1886)

EMILY DICKINSON often contemplated what the passage from life through death to eternity would be like. In this poem she expresses a corporate pilgrimage toward the afterworld. The pilgrims want to make it to the city of God but know that they must pass through "the Forest of the Dead" to get there. There's no turning back, even though they thought about it.

Christians have mixed feelings about death. On one hand, they welcome it because it will usher them into the eternal presence of God. On the other hand, they fear it because it is unknown and because it will separate them from their loved ones on earth. Paul had these ambivalent thoughts while he was in prison—potentially awaiting execution. He experienced two compelling desires: to die and be with Christ (which was far better) or to remain alive for the sake of his fellow Christians who needed him on earth (see Philippians 1:19-24).

The journey of Abraham also depicts the pilgrimage from earth to heaven. When Abraham left his homeland, he didn't know where he was going. But he trusted God to guide him (Genesis 12:1-7). Likewise, we don't have to fear the unknown. We can trust God as we pass from this life to the next, knowing that he will meet us at every gate in the new Jerusalem.

So he took me in spirit to a great, high mountain, and he showed me the holy city, Jerusalem, descending out of heaven from God. It was filled with the glory of God and sparkled like a precious gem, crystal clear like jasper. Its walls were broad and high, with twelve gates guarded by twelve angels. And the names of the twelve tribes of Israel were written on the gates. There were three gates on each side—east, north, south, and west. Revelation 21:10-13

The Pillar of the Cloud

Lead, Kindly Light, amid the circling gloom,
Lead Thou me on!
The night is dark, and I am far from home—
Lead Thou me on!
Keep Thou my feet; I do not ask to see
The distant scene,—one step enough for me.

I was not ever thus, nor prayed that thou
Shouldst lead me on!
I loved to choose and see my path; but now
Lead Thou me on!
I loved the garish day, and, spite of fears,
Pride ruled my will: remember not past years.

So long Thy power hath blest me, sure it still
Will lead me on,
O'er moor and fen,[a] *o'er crag and torrent, till*
The night is gone;
And with the morn those angel faces smile
Which I have loved long since, and lost awhile.

JOHN HENRY, CARDINAL NEWMAN (1801–1890)

[a]low land covered with water

RECENTLY, an eighty-four-year-old mission worker sprained her ankle and cracked a bone on the way to her birthday celebration. She lay on a couch at the party and opened her gifts while awaiting a ride to the doctor's office.

Well-meaning guests came to her, inquiring, "Why do you think the Lord would have you sprain your ankle on your birthday?" or "What does the Lord want to teach you through this?" The godly woman answered, "All I know is that I love God and I sprained my ankle." After a few days of being unable to walk, this intrepid missionary-mother was up and about with the aid of an inflatable cast and a cane.

Cardinal Newman wrote, "Keep Thou my feet; I do not ask to see the distant scene,—one step enough for me." How true these words became for this woman. One wrong step injured her ankle, generating interest from others as to why this had happened. Then came the cane—a real blow to the pride of this stalwart daughter of American pioneers. Yet in following the Lord step-by-step, she suddenly found that she could only walk with the aid of a cane.

It is amazing to ponder just how much each of us relies on God and his grace for even the most simple things, such as walking. Even more amazing is how symbolic physical realities can be of the spiritual. From time to time, we may all take our spiritual walk for granted. But then God gets our attention and helps us realize how greatly we depend on him.

The cane is long gone for this woman, but the lesson remains in her heart: "I loved to choose and see my path; but now lead Thou me on!"

The Lord guided them by a pillar of cloud during the day and a pillar of fire at night. That way they could travel whether it was day or night. Exodus 13:21

On God's Law

Thy sacred law, O God,
Is like to Moses' rod:
If we but keep it in our hand,
It will do wonders in the land;
If we slight and throw it to the ground;
Twill turn a serpent, and inflict a wound;
A wound that flesh and blood cannot endure,
Nor salve, until the brazen serpent cure:
I wish not, Lord, thou shouldst withhold it;
Nor would I have it, and not hold it:
O teach me then, my God,
To handle Moses' rod.

FRANCIS QUARLES (1592–1644)

THE FINAL two lines of today's poem are reminiscent of Psalm 119:34: "Give me understanding and I will obey your law." Both are marvelous prayers that alert us to the importance of understanding the law and its place in God's eternal purpose.

Case in point: Religious leaders accused Jesus of breaking a cardinal law of Judaism—working on the Sabbath. Jesus told his accusers, "The Sabbath was made for man, not man for the Sabbath" (Mark 2:27, NIV). God intended for the law to serve humanity, not the other way around. The religious leaders misunderstood the law.

But how does the law serve us? First, the law given to Moses (Exodus 31:18) testifies to the nature and person of God. Under the new covenant—that is, faith in Christ—God writes the law on our heart as the subjective testimony of who and what he is: "This is the covenant, . . . I will put my laws in their minds and write them on their hearts. . . . They shall not teach one another or say to each other, 'Know the Lord,' for they shall all know me, from the least of them to the greatest" (Hebrews 8:10-12, NRSV; Jeremiah 31:33-34).

But Scripture also says, "If it had not been for the law, I should not have known sin" (Romans 7:7, NRSV). In other words, it teaches us what God is *not.* This is the law's second purpose. So the law not only teaches us who God is but also who he is not. With this understanding we can handle the law carefully, like Moses handled his rod. Failure to do so could result in a poisonous bite.

Then the Lord asked him, "What do you have there in your hand?" "A shepherd's staff," Moses replied. "Throw it down on the ground," the Lord told him. So Moses threw it down, and it became a snake! Moses was terrified, so he turned and ran away. Exodus 4:2-3

from Moses His Birth and Miracles

In time the Princess playing with the child,
In whom she seemed her chief delight to take,
With whom she oft the weary time beguiled,
That as her own did of this Hebrew make:
It so fell out as Pharaoh was in place,
Seeing his daughter in the child to joy,
To please the Princess, and to do it grace,
Himself vouchsafes to entertain the boy:
Whose shape and beauty when he did behold
With much content his princely eye that fed,
Giving to please it, any thing it would,
Set his rich crown upon the infant's head,
Which this weak child regarding not at all
(As such a baby carelessly is meet)
Unto the ground the diadem let fall
Spurning it from him with neglectful feet.
Which as the priests beheld this ominous thing
(That else had passed unnoted as a toy)
As from their skill report unto the King,
This was the man that Egypt should destroy.
Told by the Magi that were learn'd and wise,
Which might full well the jealous King enflame,
Said by th'Egyptian ancient prophecies
That might give credit eas'lier to the same.
She as discreet as she was chaste and fair,
With princely gesture and with countenance mild
By things that hurtful and most dangerous were
Shows to the King the weakness of the child:
Hot burning coals doth to his mouth present,
Which he to handle simply doth not stick,
This little fool, this reckless innocent
The burning gleed with his soft tongue doth lick:
Which though in Pharaoh her desire it wrought,
His babish imbecility to see,
To the child's speech impediment it brought,
From which he after never could be free.

MICHAEL DRAYTON (1563–1631)

MICHAEL DRAYTON was an English lyric poet. His *Harmonie of the Church* (1591), a rendering of scriptural passages in verse, offended the archbishop of Canterbury, who had the work publicly burned. But thereafter Drayton published many works of fine poetry.

In today's poem Drayton imagines an event in Pharaoh's household. Pharaoh—pleased that his daughter delighted in Moses—decided to entertain the child by placing his own crown on Moses' head. The infant Moses paid no attention to it, letting it fall to the ground. The priests of the royal house said this was an ominous sign, citing ancient Egyptian prophecies that said the child must die.

The princess, attempting to prove that the child was not a threat to the kingdom, put hot coals to Moses' mouth, and he licked them. This proved to Pharaoh that the child was no threat, but it also injured Moses, causing him to speak with an impediment "from which he after never could be free."

This sounds like a folk tale and certainly isn't true. But it does focus our attention on a fact that we often overlook about the first leader of Israel: Moses had difficulty speaking. At the burning bush "Moses pleaded with the Lord, 'O Lord, I'm just not a good speaker. I never have been, and I'm not now, even after you have spoken to me. I'm clumsy with words'" (Exodus 4:10). But when Moses stopped making excuses and simply obeyed, God used him in powerful ways.

Making excuses not to do something is always easier than obeying. But doing so can cause us to miss the work that God desires to do in us and through us. In what area of your life is God asking you to obey him today?

As the princess opened it, she found the baby boy. His helpless cries touched her heart. "He must be one of the Hebrew children," she said. . . . The princess named him Moses, for she said, "I drew him out of the water." Exodus 2:6, 10

The Church of a Dream

Sadly the dead leaves rustle in the whistling wind,
Around the weather-worn, grey church, low down
the vale:
The Saints in golden vesture shake before the gale;
The glorious windows shake, where still they dwell
enshrined;
Old Saints by long-dead, shrivelled hands, long
since designed:
There still, although the world autumnal be, and
pale,
Still in their golden vesture the old Saints prevail;
Alone with Christ, desolate else, left by mankind.
Only one ancient Priest offers the Sacrifice,
Murmuring holy Latin immemorial:
Swaying with tremulous hands the old censer of
spice,
In gray, sweet incense clouds; blue, sweet clouds
mystical:
To him, in place of men, for he is old, suffice
Melancholy remembrances and vesperal.

LIONEL JOHNSON (1867–1902)

IN THIS sonnet the poet creates a scene of desolation. The old church has been abandoned for quite a while. The designers of its stained-glass windows have long been dead, and no human beings frequent this church anymore. But the saints, depicted in the stained-glass windows, are still present. One can imagine portraits of Peter, John, and James—among many others—encased in the windows, clattering in the wind. Christ is present with them. He is the ancient High Priest offering up the Sacrifice.

In a dreamy, almost surreal way, the poet has portrayed the church abandoned by the earthly believers, yet still alive because it is not abandoned by Christ and the saints of old. The idea seems to be that even if the modern world abandoned Christ's church, Christ could not abandon it, nor could the saints of old. After all, the church was built upon Christ, the cornerstone, and upon the foundation of the early apostles, who were Christ's first witnesses (Ephesians 2:19-22).

The poem also suggests Christ's high priesthood is constant. No matter what people on earth do, Christ is still in heaven carrying out his eternal priesthood. Having made a perfect, once-for-all sacrifice to God by offering his body on the cross for the sins of the world, he now appears before God as our compassionate and stable high priest. As such, he never sleeps or grows weary of remembering us before God—even if earthly priests fail to do so.

Only one ancient Priest offers the Sacrifice, . . .
In gray, sweet incense clouds; blue, sweet clouds mystical:
To him, in place of men, for he is old, suffice
Melancholy remembrances and vesperal.

But Jesus remains a priest forever; his priesthood will never end. Therefore he is able, once and forever, to save everyone who comes to God through him. He lives forever to plead with God on their behalf.
Hebrews 7:24-25

Glory to Thee, My God, This Night

Glory to thee, my God, this night
For all the blessings of the light;
Keep me, O keep me, King of kings,
Beneath thy own almighty wings.

Forgive me, Lord, for thy dear Son,
The ill that I this day have done,
That with the world, myself, and thee
I, ere I sleep, at peace may be.

Teach me to live, that I may dread
The grave as little as my bed;
Teach me to die, that so I may
Rise glorious at the awful day.

O may my soul on thee repose,
And with sweet sleep mine eyelids close,
Sleep that may me more vigorous make
To serve my God when I awake.

When in the night I sleepless lie,
My soul with heavenly thoughts supply;
Let no ill dreams disturb my rest,
No powers of darkness me molest.

Praise God, from whom all blessings flow,
Praise him, all creatures here below,
Praise him above, ye heavenly host,
Praise Father, Son, and Holy Ghost.

THOMAS KEN (1637–1711)

"PRAISE God, from whom all blessings flow, praise him, all creatures here below." In 1709 Thomas Ken wrote these wonderful words that many of us still recite today. Ken spent his entire life serving God in the Church of England. At one point, he was chaplain to the king, who eventually appointed Ken as bishop of Bath and Wells.

When Ken writes of sleep he also writes of death. The Scripture also speaks of death as sleep. Lazarus had been dead for three days when Jesus said, "Our friend Lazarus has fallen asleep; but I am going there to wake him up" (John 11:11, NIV). In Acts Paul says, "When David had served God's purpose in his own generation, he fell asleep; he was buried with his fathers and his body decayed" (13:36, NIV). The definitive chapter on the resurrection of the dead—1 Corinthians 15—refers to death as sleep four times. Concerning Christ it says, "Christ has indeed been raised from the dead, the firstfruits of those who have fallen asleep" (15:20, NIV).

What do the Bible and Ken mean by *sleep?* What happens when we die? Scripture says death is like falling asleep: "Brothers, we do not want you to be ignorant about those who fall asleep, or to grieve like the rest of men, who have no hope" (1 Thessalonians 4:13, NIV). What is the Christian hope? Resurrection morning (1 Corinthians 15:12-21)!

Hardly anyone is afraid to go to sleep at night because there is nothing to fear. This is why Christians don't grieve over death like people who have no hope in the resurrection. Hallelujah! We know that the morning will come when "the Lord himself will come down from heaven . . . and the dead in Christ will rise first" (1 Thessalonians 4:16, NIV).

We believe that Jesus died and rose again and so we believe that God will bring with Jesus those who have fallen asleep in him.
1 Thessalonians 4:14, NIV

from Taylor's Arithmetic . . .

The 10 Commandments, are the Law Divine,
(To keep those laws, Good Lord our hearts incline;)
But from those 10, should 10 men each pluck one,
Tis to be feared that left we should have none.
The atheist (which the Psalmist fool doth call)
As he believes will have no God at all.
Th' idolater will stock, block, idols have
To save him, though themselves they cannot save.
The roarer that delights to damn and swear,
From the Commandments he the third would tear,
The Sabbath-breaker would pluck out the fourth,
The fifth (with rebels) is of little worth,
The sixth the murderer would stab and wound,
The seventh the hot adult'rer would confound,
The thief would steal the eighth away, and then
False witness spoil the ninth: and for the ten,
The wretch that's covetous would rend and bite,
And pluck the rest in pieces if he might.
Thus would there 10 (this cursed catalogue)
Each 'rase[a] *out one, and spoil the Decalogue.*[b]

JOHN TAYLOR (C. 1578–1653)

[a]erase [b]the Ten Commandments

PROBABLY all of us have attempted to pluck some commandment out of God's law. Why? Because it is impossible to keep that law. Paul explains: "We know that the law is spiritual; but I am of the flesh" (Romans 7:14, NRSV). We cannot keep God's law because it is spiritual and we are flesh. So what are we to do about the law? Ignore it? Change it? Eradicate it like the characters in John Taylor's poem? No.

Scripture gives us a better option: "God has done what the law, weakened by the flesh, could not do: by sending his own Son in the likeness of sinful flesh . . . he condemned sin in the flesh, so that the just requirement of the law might be fulfilled in us" (Romans 8:3-4, NRSV). Jesus confirmed this: "I did not come to abolish the law of Moses or the writings of the prophets. No, I came to fulfill them" (Matthew 5:17). Jesus fulfilled the law because we could not. When we believe in him, the just requirement of the law becomes fulfilled in us.

The apostle Paul preached this to the believers in Galatia. But when they began to keep the Jewish law, he wrote: "Let me ask you this one question: Did you receive the Holy Spirit by keeping the law? Of course not, for the Holy Spirit came upon you only after you believed the message you heard about Christ. Have you lost your senses? After starting your Christian lives in the Spirit, why are you now trying to become perfect by your own human effort?" (Galatians 3:2-3).

Thank God that anyone can receive salvation by believing the message of Jesus Christ! Any other way is impossible. That is why Paul wrote, "If anyone preaches any other gospel than the one you welcomed, let God's curse fall upon that person" (Galatians 1:9).

Jesus told him, "I am the way, the truth, and the life. No one can come to the Father except through me." John 14:6

The Dark Angel PART ONE

Dark Angel, with thine aching lust
To rid the world of penitence:
Malicious Angel, who still dost
My soul such subtile violence!

Because of thee, no thought, no thing
Abides for me undesecrate:
Dark Angel, ever on the wing,
Who never reachest me too late!

When music sounds, then changest thou
Its silvery to a sultry fire:
Nor will thine envious heart allow
Delight untortured by desire.

Through thee, the gracious Muses turn
To Furies, O mine Enemy!
And all the things of beauty burn
With flames of evil ecstasy.

(continued in next day's reading)

LIONEL JOHNSON (1867–1902)

SOME people don't believe in the devil. This poet does! He has experienced the devil's powers. And his experience matches many of ours. This is what the devil does to us.

First, the poet recognizes the motivation behind the Dark Angel's actions, which is to "rid" the world of penitence. In addition, the Dark Angel seeks to corrupt the souls of those who have turned their hearts from sin to God. He works his violence upon our souls subtly. Never late—in fact, always just in time—he comes to desecrate (make unholy) what first begins as innocuous. For example, the poet says, we hear some nice "silvery" (light and fine) music. Before we know it, the tune becomes "sultry," changing simple delight to fiery desire. Perhaps this has happened to us when we listen to a song on the radio! Before we know it, a simple tune has inflamed lustful thoughts.

The devil can turn good into evil. We look at beauty in a woman or a work of art, and instead of just letting us admire the beauty, the devil inflames desire within us—lust for the woman and covetousness for the art. He makes us want what we see; he turns the Muses (inspiring spirits) to Furies (enticing spirits):

Through thee, the gracious Muses turn
To Furies, O mine Enemy!
And all the things of beauty burn
With flames of evil ecstasy.

We cannot escape the workings of the devil. But if we are knowledgeable about his workings and on guard against his tactics, we can expose his work in our life and arm ourselves against his powers.

➻ *Satan will not outsmart us. For we are very familiar with his evil schemes.* 2 Corinthians 2:11

The Dark Angel PART TWO

Because of thee, the land of dreams
Becomes a gathering-place of fears:
Until tormented slumber seems
One vehemence of useless tears.

When sunlight glows upon the flowers,
Or ripples down the dancing sea:
Thou, with thy troop of passionate powers,
Beleaguerest, bewilderest me.

Within the breath of autumn woods,
Within the winter silences:
Thy venomous spirit stirs and broods,
O Master of impieties!

The ardour of red flame is thine,
And thine the steely soul of ice:
Thou poisonest the fair design
Of nature, with unfair device.

Apples of ashes, golden bright;
Waters of bitterness, how sweet!
O banquet of a foul delight,
Prepared by thee, dark Paraclete.

Thou art the whisper in the gloom,
The hinting tone, the haunting laugh:
Thou art the adorner of my tomb,
The minstrel of mine epitaph.

I fight thee, in the Holy Name!
Yet, what thou dost, is what God saith:
Tempter! should I escape thy flame,
Thou wilt have helped my soul from Death:

The second Death, that never dies,
That cannot die, when time is dead:
Live Death, wherein the lost soul cries,
Eternally uncomforted.

Dark Angel, with thine aching lust!
Of two defeats, of two despairs:
Less dread, a change to drifting dust,
Than thine eternity of cares.

Do what thou wilt, thou shalt not so,
Dark Angel! triumph over me:
Lonely, unto the Lone I go;
Divine, to the Divinity.

LIONEL JOHNSON (1867–1902)

THE POET continues to rail against the devil, the Dark Angel. Johnson blames the devil for turning sweet anticipation into fearful dread by increasing our anxiety and ruining our best plans, so that our dreams turn into nightmares. For example, we may look forward to a wonderful vacation with our family, but one small, unpleasant occurrence—such as a wrong word said to a spouse, or even a wrong look—could ruin everything. We all know how it goes. Each one of us can cause trouble at times.

The Dark Angel delights in being the spoiler, as we see in stanza 2. Just when everything seems so pleasant—with sunlight glowing upon the flowers and rippling down the dancing sea—the devil brings his "troop of passionate powers" to ruin the moment. *Beleaguerest* means "to surround with an army to prevent escape." The devil can beleaguer our thinking—he and his host of demons want to oppress and ruin us.

We must beware of this Dark Angel; his "venomous spirit stirs and broods" everywhere—just waiting to strike an unwary victim and poison someone with his venom that produces impiety (that is, ungodliness). We should not be ignorant of his crafty ways, and we should arm ourselves, especially our minds, to fight against him. Scripture says:

➺ *Use every piece of God's armor to resist the enemy in the time of evil, so that after the battle you will still be standing firm. . . . Put on salvation as your helmet, and take the sword of the Spirit, which is the Word of God.* Ephesians 6:13, 17

A Spirit Passed before Me

A spirit passed before me: I beheld
The face of immortality unveiled—
Deep sleep came down on every eye save mine—
And there it stood,—all formless—but divine;
Along my bones the creeping flesh did quake;
And as my damp hair stiffened, thus it spake:

'Is man more just than God? Is man more pure
Than he who deems even seraphs insecure?
Creatures of clay—vain dwellers in the dust!
The moth survives you, and are ye more just?
Things of a day! you wither ere the night,
Heedless and blind to wisdom's wasted light!'

LORD BYRON (1788–1824)

THE BOOK of Job is not the most popular book in the Bible, but it teaches many valuable lessons about suffering, good and evil, and the character of God. Throughout the book Job refutes his so-called friends' explanations as to why he is suffering. As the debate heats up, Job comes dangerously close to questioning God's goodness and wisdom. God ultimately answers Job from the whirlwind with a slew of questions.

In today's poem, Byron imagines what Job experienced in his encounter with God. The experience was frightening: "Along my bones the creeping flesh did quake; . . . my damp hair stiffened." Be honest. How would you feel if God appeared to you and asked, "Is man more just than God? Is man more pure than he who deems even seraphs insecure?"

Although Job couldn't answer God's questions, he did endure the inquisition, which ultimately changed his attitude about God (Job 38–42). Job said, "I know that you can do anything, and no one can stop you. You ask, 'Who is this that questions my wisdom with such ignorance?' It is I. And I was talking about things I did not understand, things far too wonderful for me" (Job 42:2-3).

We should all keep Job's response in mind, especially when we go through hard times. For it is then that we face the greatest temptation to question God's goodness and wisdom. But God never changes; he is always good and wise. Rather, it is we who need a change in attitude and perspective when we suffer, so when all is said and done, we won't have to "take back everything [we] said, and . . . sit in dust and ashes to show [our] repentance" (42:6).

What are mere mortals, that you should make so much of us? For you examine us every morning and test us every moment. Job 7:17-18

Elijah's Wagon Knew No Thill

Elijah's Wagon knew no thill[a]
Was innocent of Wheel
Elijah's horses as unique
As was his vehicle—

Elijah's journey to portray
Expire with him the skill
Who justified Elijah
In feats inscrutable—

EMILY DICKINSON (1830–1886)

[a]either of the two shafts between which a horse is hitched to a wagon

SINCE ELIJAH was transported to heaven before he died, there has never been another person like him. Whatever he had been disappeared in the whirlwind that day, including his skill in miracles. During his lifetime Elijah multiplied a widow's food, brought the widow's son back to life, called down fire from heaven, and restored the rains. His skill was as unique as his personality.

The Bible records only a few periods marked by multiple miracles and miracle workers: the Exodus, the time of Elijah and Elisha, the years of Christ's ministry on earth, and the early days of the church.

In Scripture, the apostle Paul was the last person to perform a miracle, which happened in Ephesus: "When handkerchiefs or cloths that had touched his skin were placed on sick people, they were healed of their diseases, and any evil spirits within them came out" (Acts 19:12).

Dickinson writes, "Who justified Elijah in feats inscrutable—." The answer is God, who also justified the church in its early days through the display of miracles. Thus no one could effectively oppose the apostles because of the veracity of their miracles. And we see that the name of Jesus could not be used for any other purpose but God's.

Since that time, God has established the gospel by his Word and Spirit. Multiple miracles and miracle workers are no longer commonplace today, because God uses other means to advance his purposes.

But the church hasn't seen the last of God's miracles. Revelation 11:3-6 shows that miracles will return in God's time and for God's purpose. In the meantime, let us be satisfied with the testimony of the Bible as the Holy Spirit brings its truth to light.

As they were walking along and talking, suddenly a chariot of fire appeared, drawn by horses of fire. It drove between them, separating them, and Elijah was carried by a whirlwind into heaven. 2 Kings 2:11

Job. I

Out of my mother's womb
All naked came I lo:
And naked shall I turn again
To earth that I came fro.

The Lord gave at the first,
As his good pleasure was,
And at his will did take again,
As it is come to pass.

The Lord his holy name
Be praised now therefore,
As it hath been, as it is now,
And shall be evermore.

JOHN HALL (1529–1566)

JOB'S identity is lost in the mists of time. All we know about him comes from the book that bears his name. He was the "finest man in all the earth" (Job 1:8). He owned 7,000 sheep, 3,000 camels, 500 yoke of oxen (two oxen per yoke), 500 donkeys, and employed enough servants to care for and use these animals (1:3). But Job was not only rich, he was also a loving father (1:2, 4) who cared for the spiritual lives of his children (1:5).

One day, however, Job lost it all—possessions, family, health—everything. Today's poem versifies Job's response to this archetypical tragedy: "The Lord gave at the first, as his good pleasure was, and at his will did take again."

In the difficulties of life, people often say, "Why is this happening to me?" Christians sometimes answer by quoting Romans 8:28: "We know that God causes everything to work together for the good of those who love God and are called according to his purpose for them." The problem with this answer is that it raises another bigger question: What is God's purpose for me? But Scripture certainly answers this one: "For those whom he foreknew he also predestined to be conformed to the image of his Son" (8:29, NRSV).

God's ultimate purpose is to transform us into the image of his Son. Trials are just one tool he uses to accomplish this purpose (1 Peter 1:7). Although trials are never pleasant, we can endure them with joy (James 1:2) because of what God is doing in us, and we can say with Job, "The Lord his holy name be praised now."

[Job] said, "I came naked from my mother's womb, and I will be stripped of everything when I die. The Lord gave me everything I had, and the Lord has taken it away. Praise the name of the Lord!" In all of this, Job did not sin by blaming God. Job 1:21-22

Grace

My stock lies dead, and no increase
Doth my dull husbandry improve:
O let thy graces without cease
Drop from above!

If still the sun should hide his face,
Thy house would but a dungeon prove,
Thy works nights' captives: O let grace
Drop from above!

The dew doth every morning fall;
And shall the dew out-strip thy dove?
The dew, for which grass cannot call,
Drop from above.

Death is still working like a mole,
And digs my grave at each remove:
Let grace work too, and on my soul
Drop from above.

Sin is still hammering my heart
Unto a hardness, void of love:
Let suppling[a] *grace, to cross his art,*
Drop from above.

O come! for thou dost know the way.
Or if to me thou wilt not move,
Remove me, where I need not say,
Drop from above.

GEORGE HERBERT (1593–1633)

[a]supplying

THE POET'S situation is bleak. All his cattle are dead, and he finds no comfort in God's house, which "would but a dungeon prove." Even the beauty of creation becomes dull to him. But he is not without hope. He knows that God can rescue him by grace. So the poet makes his supplication to God: "O let thy graces without cease drop from above!"

The phrase "drop from above" appears throughout this poem and is key to understanding the poet's view of grace. He compares grace to dew. Just as dew refreshes the grass that passively receives it, so grace refreshes the believer's soul. But grace is not something believers can attain by their own efforts. Christians must wait on God to grant it to them. This is the hard part. As the poet points out, "The dew doth every morning fall; and shall the dew out-strip thy dove?" How long must one wait to receive God's grace? At times the dew seems to fall faster than the dove—that is, God's Spirit.

God, however, is not slow in responding. Sometimes he withholds his grace, waiting for the right time or the right response from his children. Thus the poet asks to be moved closer to God, if God will not move closer to him: "O come! for thou dost know the way. Or if to me thou wilt not move, remove me." Here is true humility—the response God desires from all of his followers. Whether or not the poet was to blame for his circumstances, he made the right decision by turning to God for relief and humbling himself before the Almighty.

We have two choices in times of trouble: We can become angry, turn away from God, and try to solve our problems on our own. Or we can turn to God in faith and humility, trusting that his grace will "drop from above."

Humble yourselves, therefore, under God's mighty hand, that he may lift you up in due time. 1 Peter 5:6, NIV

On the Gospel

When two Evangelists shall seem to vary
In one discourse, they're diverse, not contrary;
One truth doth guide them both, one spirit doth
Direct them; doubt not, to believe them both.

FRANCIS QUARLES (1592–1644)

HAVE you ever wondered about this? Matthew's Gospel says, "When Jesus arrived on the other side of the lake in the land of the Gadarenes, two men who were possessed by demons met him" (8:28). Mark's Gospel says, "So they arrived at the other side of the lake, in the land of the [Gadarenes]. Just as Jesus was climbing from the boat, a man possessed by an evil spirit ran out from a cemetery to meet him" (5:1-2). Matthew has two demon-possessed men while Mark has only one. Why?

Some people use this discrepancy to argue that the Bible isn't authoritative because it contains mistakes. Others say that these are two different incidents so there is no conflict. But there are other similarities in the stories that argue against the latter. In both cases Christ sends demons into a herd of pigs, which then rush into the water and drown. Discussing the discrepancy problem could become detailed and technical and yield no satisfactory explanation for the difference between the accounts. But we do know that "all Scripture is inspired by God and is useful to teach us what is true" (2 Timothy 3:16). The purpose of the Bible is to reveal the truth.

Some say that Pilate was a bitter cynic when he asked Jesus, "What is truth?" (John 18:38). Who can really say? In his political position, Pilate had probably heard so many lies that he could no longer discern the truth. Or maybe someone had broken his heart with deceit. Whatever the case, Pilate did not know that the man he was speaking to had once said, "I am . . . the truth" (John 14:6).

For believers, minor discrepancies in the Gospel accounts are not an issue, because, as Francis Quarles says, "One truth doth guide them both." This truth is a person, Jesus Christ, who gives eternal life.

➻ *This is the way to have eternal life—to know you, the only true God, and Jesus Christ, the one you sent to earth.* John 17:3

Nahum 2.10

She's empty: hark, she sounds: there's nothing there
But noise to fill thy ear;
Thy vain enquiry can at length but find
A blast of murmuring wind:
It is a cask, that seems as full as fair
But merely tunned[a] *with air:*
Fond youth, go build thy hopes on better grounds:
The soul that vainly founds
Her joys upon this world but feeds on empty sounds.

She's empty: hark, she sounds: there's nothing in't
The spark-engendering flint
Shall sooner melt, and hardest raunce shall first
Dissolve and quench thy thirst;
Ere this false world shall still thy stormy breast
With smooth-faced calms of rest:
Thou mayst as well expect Meridian[b] *light*
From shades of black-mouthed night,
As in this empty world to find a full delight.

She's empty: hark, she sounds; 'tis void and vast;
What if some flattering blast
Of flatuous[c] *honor should perchance be there,*
And whisper in thine ear:
It is but wind, and blows but where it list,
And vanishes like a mist:
Poor honor earth can give! What generous mind
Would be so base to bind
Her Heaven-bred soul a slave to serve a blast of wind?

She's empty: hark, she sounds; 'tis but a ball
For fools to play withal:
The painted film but of a stronger bubble,
That's lined with silken trouble:
It is a world, whose work and recreation
Is vanity and vexation?
A hag, repaired with vice-complexion, paint,
A quest-house of complaint:
It is a saint, a fiend; worse fiend, when most a saint.

FRANCIS QUARLES (1592–1644)

[a]filled [b]of or at noon [c]windy or empty in speech; pompous; pretentious

FOUR TIMES we read "She's empty: hark, she sounds." In Quarles's day, to measure the depth of a body of water you had to "sound" it, using a line with a weight on the end. A well-known American novelist took his pen name while listening to boatmen sound the depth of the Mississippi River. The pilot called out, "Mark?" and the sounder answered, "Twain."

So what is Quarles "sounding"? He sounds the world by comparing it to a cask—a barrel. To learn if a barrel is full or empty, we must sound it by rapping on its side with our knuckles. If it sounds hollow, then it is empty. That is what the poet finds as he sounds the world—emptiness.

Today's poem is similar to Ecclesiastes, which begins "Vanity of vanities; all is vanity" (1:2, KJV). The word *vanity* means "vacant, empty, meaningless." What is meaningless? "Everything done here under the sun" (2:17). What is "under the sun"? Everything except God, who is above all.

Like this Hebrew author and English poet, we all must live in this world, "under the sun." But our life does not have to be meaningless. We can "have peace with God through our Lord Jesus Christ" (Romans 5:1, NRSV), which is meaningful and satisfying. Quarles instructs us to build our hopes on this ground. To build elsewhere will only lead to disappointment. So the poet warns, "Thou mayst as well expect Meridian light from shades of black-mouthed night, as in this empty world to find a full delight."

Loot the silver! Plunder the gold! There seems no end to Nineveh's many treasures—its vast, uncounted wealth. Soon the city is an empty shambles, stripped of its wealth. Hearts melt in horror, and knees shake. The people stand aghast, their faces pale and trembling.
Nahum 2:9-10

The Altar

A broken ALTAR, *Lord, thy servant rears,*
Made of a heart, and cemented with tears:
Whose parts are as thy hand did frame;
No workman's tool hath touched the same.
A HEART *alone*
As such a stone,
As nothing but
Thy power doth cut.
Wherefore each part
Of my hard heart
Meets in this frame,
To praise thy name.
That if I chance to hold my peace,
These stones to praise thee may not cease.
O let thy blessed SACRIFICE *be mine,*
And sanctify this ALTAR *to be thine.*

GEORGE HERBERT (1593–1633)

"If you build altars from stone, use only uncut stones. Do not chip or shape the stones with a tool, for that would make them unfit for holy use" (Exodus 20:25). This verse illustrates that humans cannot improve on what God has done. The stones for Israel's altars were fine the way God had made them. Cutting or shaping them might make a neat-looking altar. But doing so would defile the Israelites' worship because the altar would have been built to please the human eye, not the divine.

Herbert compares the worshiper's heart to an Old Testament altar in today's poem. Herbert knew that his heart was so hard that only God's power could cut it. Attempting to use tools on his own heart—such as self-denial, outward adjustments, or overt sanctity—would turn him into a performer rather than a worshiper.

Nothing we offer on or from the altar of our heart will curry God's favor, for God has already made the perfect offering for us—Jesus Christ. We simply need to accept his sacrifice for our sins. This is the message of Hebrews, because Jewish believers attempted to earn God's salvation through animal sacrifices and keeping the law. While this made a good show of holiness, the author of Hebrews reminds believers that "a righteous person will live by faith. But I [God] will have no pleasure in anyone who turns away" (10:38).

God doesn't want us to work for his acceptance. We cannot make our heart—through self-effort—an altar that pleases him. Instead, we must follow Herbert's example and pray, "O let thy blessed Sacrifice be mine, and sanctify this Altar to be thine."

This is the new covenant I will make with my people on that day, says the Lord: I will put my laws in their hearts so they will understand them, and I will write them on their minds so they will obey them.
Hebrews 10:16

The world's a floor, whose swelling heaps retain
The mingled wages of the ploughman's toil;
The world's a heap, whose yet unwinnowed grain
Is lodged with chaff and buried in her soil;
All things are mixed, the useful with the vain;
The good with bad, the noble with the vile;
The world's an ark,[a] *wherein things pure and gross*
Present their lossfull gain, and gainfull loss;
Where every dram[b] *of gold contains a pound of dross.*[c]

This furnished ark presents the greedy view
With all that earth can give, or Heaven can add;
Here, lasting joys; here, pleasures hourly new,
And hourly fading, may be wished and had:
All points of honor, counterfeit and true,
Salute thy soul, and wealth both good and bad:
Here mayst thou open wide the two-leaved door
Of all thy wishes, to receive that store
Which being empty most, does overflow the more.

(continued in next day's reading)

FRANCIS QUARLES (1592–1644)

[a] a trunk or chest used for storage [b] ⅛ ounce [c] waste matter

HE IS ready to separate the chaff from the grain with his winnowing fork. Then he will clean up the threshing area, storing the grain in his barn but burning the chaff with never-ending fire" (Matthew 3:12). Thus John the Baptist introduced Jesus Christ to the world.

Francis Quarles uses the image of a threshing floor in today's poem. In the ancient Middle East, threshing floors were flat open spaces, usually on the tops or sides of high hills where strong winds blew. Here farmers would haul harvested grain and crush it with wooden flails or weighted sleds drawn back and forth by animals. The farmer then tossed the crushed grain into the air with a winnowing fork. The heavier grain fell in a heap, while the wind blew the chaff and lighter straw away.

Significant events in the Old Testament often occurred at a threshing floor: The Temple was built on the threshing floor of Araunah the Jebusite (1 Chronicles 21:15-25). In the New Testament the whole world is God's threshing floor, on which Quarles sees unwinnowed grain lodged with chaff. "All things are mixed, the useful with the vain; the good with bad, the noble with the vile." But in this odd mixture, he saw a crucial choice between life and death that everyone must make. So he titled his poem "Deuteronomy 30.19."

Daily we choose between "all that earth can give, or Heaven can add." We can choose "lasting joys" or "pleasures hourly new, and hourly fading." Meanwhile, the Divine Farmer stands ready with his winnowing fork. When the wind of judgment blows, the living grain—those who have chosen life—will remain on his threshing floor, while all else will blow away like useless chaff. Therefore, let us choose wisely. May we choose life.

Today I have given you the choice between life and death, between blessings and curses. . . . Oh, that you would choose life, that you and your descendants might live! Deuteronomy 30:19

The worldly wisdom of the foolish man
Is like a sieve, that does alone retain
The grosser substance of the worthless bran:
But thou, my soul, let thy brave thoughts disdain
So coarse a purchase; O be thou a fan[a]
To purge the chaff, and keep the winnowed grain:
Make clean thy thoughts, and dress thy mixed desires,
Thou art Heaven's tasker;[b] *and thy God requires*
The purest of thy floor, as well as of thy fires.

Let grace conduct thee to the paths of peace,
And wisdom bless thy soul's unblemished ways;
No matter then, how short or long's the lease,
Whose date determines thy self-numbered days:
No need to care to wealth's or fame's increase,
Nor Mars his palm, nor high Apollo's bays.
Lord, if thy gracious bounty please to fill
The floor of my desires, and teach me skill
To dress and choose the corn, take those the chaff that will.

FRANCIS QUARLES (1592–1644)

[a]a winnowing fork with wooden tines configured in the shape of a fan, which is why it is sometimes called a winnowing fan [b]worker

HERE Quarles moves from describing the choice we all have between life and death to his own personal decision. What does he choose? Quarles chooses life. Following through on his decision won't be easy though, as Quarles is aware of: "The worldly wisdom of the foolish man is like a sieve, that does alone retain the grosser substance of the worthless bran." As humans, we often pursue the worthless chaff of worldly things. But not Quarles; he chides his soul to "disdain so coarse a purchase." Instead, he instructs his soul to be "a fan to purge the chaff, and keep the winnowed grain: Make clean thy thoughts, and dress thy mixed desires, thou art Heaven's tasker."

The poet's task is not as impossible as it seems. Grace will guide "Heaven's tasker" to the paths of peace, and wisdom will bless his soul's unblemished ways. God will equip the poet with all he needs to stay the course of life.

Choosing life/following Christ is never easy. Things of this world constantly war against our soul, not to mention "evil rulers and authorities of the unseen world" (Ephesians 6:12). We must reaffirm our choice to follow Christ day after day. Christ gives us everything we need to remain faithful to him. He wants us to choose life, and he will help us stay on the right path. Christ desires to teach us the skill to "dress and choose the corn," leaving the chaff of this world to those who will take it.

Choose to love the Lord your God and to obey him and commit yourself to him, for he is your life. Then you will live long in the land the Lord swore to give your ancestors Abraham, Isaac, and Jacob. Deuteronomy 30:20

Numeri XIII

Let now thy power be great O Lord,
Like as thy lips did once repeat:
And as we find it in thy word,
Thy suffrance long, thy mercy great.

For as thou dost our sins forgive
And trespasses, when we repent:
So are we sure no man alive
From sin is free and innocent.

And of their father the misdeed
Thou visitest upon the child,
His generation and his seed,
In four degrees therewith defiled.

But now oh Lord be gracious
Unto thy flock and their offence:
And of thy mercy bounteous
Remember not our negligence.

Thy people as thou didst forbear,
From Egypt into wilderness,
We thee beseech in like manner,
That we may taste thy gentleness.

JOHN HALL (1529–1566)

ISRAEL was in a mess, as we see in Numbers 14:1-4. God wanted them to enter the Promised Land, but they refused because of their unbelief. So God was ready to destroy them. But Moses reminded God of the divine testimony, saying, "What will the world say about you if you destroy Israel?" (Numbers 14:14-16, paraphrase). Today's poem is Moses' plea for mercy on behalf of God's people.

The Israelites' problem was their lack of faith and their ingratitude. Both were an offense to God after the incredible mercy he had shown them. How could they not believe God after all he had done? God had delivered them from Egypt, parted the Red Sea, provided manna and quail from heaven and water from a rock, and spared their lives at Sinai. How could Israel be so ungrateful? Their lack of faith caused fear, and their fear left little room for gratitude. Thus, Moses begged God to spare the lives of these untrusting, ungrateful people: "But now oh Lord be gracious unto thy flock and their offense."

We should never take God's mercy for granted. Doing so shows that we do not truly understand God or the significance of his mercy. It may even point out that we lack faith. What can we do to appreciate God and be grateful for his mercy? Meditating on what he has done for us through his Son, Jesus, is a good start. We can also pray for ourselves as Moses prayed for Israel: "Please pardon the sins of this people because of your magnificent, unfailing love, just as you have forgiven them ever since they left Egypt" (Numbers 14:19).

Please, Lord, prove that your power is as great as you have claimed it to be. For you said, "The Lord is slow to anger and rich in unfailing love, forgiving every kind of sin and rebellion. Even so he does not leave sin unpunished, but he punishes the children for the sins of their parents to the third and fourth generations." Numbers 14:17-18

Proverb. XXX

O Lord two things I thee require,
That thou me not deny,
But that I may the fruit thereof
Receive before I die.

The first shall be that vanity
Thou wilt from me restrain,
And eke[a] *the lips that lust to lie,*
To flatter, glose[b] *and feign.*

The second that thou make me not
Too poor in any wise,
Ne yet too rich: but mean living,
Of necessary size.

Lest when I am too full of wealth
I thee forget and say:
What fellow is the Lord? when I
Forgotten have thy way.

And likewise lest that poverty
Constrain me out of frame,
And me provoke to steal O God
And to forswear thy name.

JOHN HALL (1529–1566)

[a]also [b]be garrulous; talk too much, especially about unimportant things

PROVERBS 30:6 says:"Do not add to his words, or he may rebuke you, and you will be found a liar." This is, and has always been, a serious problem in the church. The epistle to the Galatians deals with this almost exclusively. "I am shocked," wrote Paul, "that you are turning away so soon from God. . . . You are being fooled by those who twist and change the truth concerning Christ" (Galatians 1:6-7).

In Galatia Jewish believers added their law and lifestyle to the simple gospel. They told Gentile believers that they could not obtain salvation without keeping this law. The New Testament clearly condemns this: "Let God's curse fall on anyone, including myself, who preaches any other message than the one we told you about" (1:8). So Proverbs teaches us to pray specifically about watching what we say. As John Hall paraphrases, "Restrain . . . the lips that lust to lie, to flatter, glose, and feign."

Today we often struggle with denominational styles, ministry preferences, so-called biblical principles that vary and change, and peripheral teachings, doctrines, and practices. These facts lend significance to the second part of this prayer in Proverbs: "Give me just enough to satisfy my needs" (30:8).

The truth of the gospel is exactly enough for us. It is not flashy, fulsome, or overdressed. But today exists the somber danger that the church has become like the one in Laodicea, which said, "I am rich. I have everything I want. I don't need a thing!" And Lord replied: "You don't realize that you are wretched and miserable and poor and blind and naked" (Revelation 3:17). Let us pray then this simple prayer from Proverbs 30, and may God graciously answer it.

Every word of God proves true. He defends all who come to him for protection. Do not add to his words, or he may rebuke you, and you will be found a liar. Proverbs 30:5-6

The Rabbi's Song

If thought can reach to Heaven,
On Heaven let it dwell,
For fear thy Thought be given
Like power to reach Hell.
For fear the desolation
And darkness of thy mind
Perplex an habitation
Which thou hast left behind.

Let nothing linger after—
No whimpering ghost remain,
In wall, or beam, or rafter,
Of any hate or pain.
Cleanse and call home thy spirit,
Deny her leave to cast,
On aught thy heirs inherit,
The shadow of her past.

For think, in all thy sadness,
What road our griefs may take;
Whose brain reflect our madness,
Or whom our terrors shake:
For think, lest any languish
By cause of thy distress—
The arrows of our anguish
Fly farther than we guess.

Our lives, our tears, as water,
Are spilled upon the ground;
God giveth no man quarter,
Yet God a means hath found,
Though Faith and Hope have vanished,
And even Love Grows dim—
A means whereby His banished
Be not expelled from Him!

RUDYARD KIPLING (1865–1936)

THE ENGLISH novelist and poet Rudyard Kipling was a literary giant in his time. He is best known for *Jungle Book* (1894) and *The Second Jungle Book* (1895). He wrote imaginatively on many subjects. Kipling used a variety of settings—India, London, the sea, the jungle—to convey his ideals of duty and self-abnegation as well as the importance of law and of action. His verse displays a great range of technical achievement. His works include *Barrack-Room Ballads* (1892), *The Seven Seas* (1896), and *The Five Nations* (1903).

Today's poem is based on a relatively obscure verse in 2 Samuel 14. This chapter concerns a complex ruse hatched by Joab to convince David to forgive his son Absalom. The climax comes in verse 14: "All of us must die eventually. Our lives are like water spilled out on the ground, which cannot be gathered up again. That is why God tries to bring us back when we have been separated from him. He does not sweep away the lives of those he cares about—and neither should you!" Joab was telling David, "Since God forgives, so should you."

Isn't this the prayer most of us pray every week ("forgive us our sins, just as we have forgiven those who have sinned against us," Matthew 6:12)? Scripture allows us no excuse for holding a grudge. When Peter asked, "Lord, how often should I forgive someone who sins against me? Seven times?" Jesus replied, "No! Seventy times seven!" (Matthew 18:21-22).

Since God has forgiven our million-dollar debt, we should forgive the few dollars another owes us (18:23-35). After all, "The arrows of our anguish fly farther than we guess."

For we must needs die, and are as water spilt on the ground, which cannot be gathered up again; neither doth God respect any person: yet doth he devise means, that his banished be not expelled from him.
2 Samuel 14:14, KJV

David in the Cave of Adullam

David and his three captains bold
Kept ambush once within a hold.
It was in Adullam's cave,
Nigh which no water they could have,
Nor spring, nor running brook was near
To quench the thirst that parched them there.
Then David, king of Israel,
Straight bethought him of a well,
Which stood beside the city gate,
At Bethlem; where, before his state
Of kingly dignity, he had
Oft drunk his fill, a shepherd lad;
But now his fierce Philistine foe
Encamped before it he does know.
Yet ne'er the less, with heat oppressed,
Those three bold captains he addressed;
And wished that one to him would bring
Some water from his native spring.
His valiant captains instantly
To execute his will did fly.
The mighty Three the ranks broke through
Of armed foes, and water drew
For David, their beloved king,
At his own sweet native spring.
Back through their armed foes they haste,
With the hard-earned treasure graced.
But when the good king David found
What they had done, he on the ground
The water poured. "Because," said he,
"That it was at the jeopardy
Of your three lives this thing ye did,
That I should drink it, God forbid."

CHARLES LAMB (1775–1834)

SINCE David valued the lives of his compatriots, why did he mention to them his longing for water from Bethlehem's well? Although David was a great and well-loved leader, he was, after all, only human. He was simply expressing a wistful thought, much like our longing for a warm sunny beach in the middle of winter.

But weren't these men obligated to obey David? After all, he was their military leader. Yes, they were to obey him, but for the purpose of military victory only, not for his own personal comfort. When these three men risked their lives for water, they took their relationship with David to a personal extreme. Because David was a great leader, he repented that he had allowed this to happen.

Scripture admonishes us to obey authority for two clear reasons—one spiritual, the other civil. Hebrews 13:17 says, "Obey your spiritual leaders and do what they say." Romans 13:1 says, "Obey the government, for God is the one who put it there." But Scripture also puts limits on how far we are to carry our obedience to those in authority. We exceed that limit anytime we obey human authority above God (Acts 4:19), and we must never compromise our obedience to God.

David's men carried out a beautiful act of devotion, but their devotion was misdirected. The risk they took was too high for the objective. May we, unlike them, never risk our life or soul for something so trivial.

David remarked longingly to his men, "Oh, how I would love some of that good water from the well in Bethlehem, the one by the gate." So the Three broke through the Philistine lines, drew some water from the well, and brought it back to David. But he refused to drink it. Instead, he poured it out before the Lord. 2 Samuel 23:15-16

The World

By day she wooes me, soft, exceeding fair:
But all night as the moon so changeth she;
Loathsome and foul with hideous leprosy
And subtle serpents gliding in her hair.
By day she wooes me to the outer air,
Ripe fruits, sweet flowers, and full satiety:
But thro' the night, a beast she grins at me,
A very monster void of love and prayer.
By day she stands a lie: by night she stands
In all the naked horror of the truth
With pushing horns and clawed and clutching hands.
Is this a friend indeed; that I should sell
My soul to her, give her my life and youth,
Till my feet, cloven too, take hold on hell?

CHRISTINA ROSSETTI (1830–1894)

MOST of Christina Rossetti's poetry is religious in nature. Today's poem is no exception. Here Rossetti reveals the dark struggle every man, woman, and child must face, regardless of his or her faith. That struggle is against the seductive enticements of this world. Like a mistress, the world woos all with its attractions, which appear "exceeding fair" and are like "ripe fruits, sweet flowers." But Rossetti, knowing that the true nature of these things is "loathsome and foul," resolved to resist the world and its enticements. She knew that to give in would bring grave consequences—the loss of her very soul.

Rossetti's view has biblical roots. The apostle John warned us about the world's attractions when he wrote: "Stop loving this evil world and all that it offers you, for when you love the world, you show that you do not have the love of the Father in you" (1 John 2:15). The world is the morally evil, satanic system that opposes Christ's kingdom on earth (John 12:31; 15:18; Ephesians 6:11-12; James 4:4; 1 John 2:16; 3:1; 4:4; 5:19). God and the world are so opposite that we cannot possibly love both at once.

In 1 John 2:16 John describes three things we need to be wary of: (1) "the lust for physical pleasure," (2) "the lust for everything we see," and (3) "pride in our possessions." Satan used these three enticements to tempt Eve (Genesis 3:6) and Christ (Luke 4:1-12). The difference in the outcome (that is, our eternal destiny) shows the importance of heeding God's command in 1 John. May God grant us the strength and wisdom to stand against the trickery of the devil so we don't sell our soul to gain the world (Matthew 16:26).

A final word: Be strong with the Lord's mighty power. Put on all of God's armor so that you will be able to stand firm against all strategies and tricks of the Devil. Ephesians 6:10-11

It Is an Honorable Thought

It is an honorable Thought
And makes One lift One's Hat
As One met sudden Gentlefolk
Upon a daily Street

That We've immortal Place
Though Pyramids decay
And Kingdoms, like the Orchard
Flit Russetly away.

EMILY DICKINSON (1830–1886)

THE MIDDLE child of Edward Dickinson, a prominent lawyer, Emily attended Amherst Academy and spent one year at Mount Holyoke Female Seminary in nearby South Hadley. When asked about her education, Dickinson replied, "I went to school—but in your manner of phrase—had no education."

Though Dickinson humbly said she was not educated, she was an excellent poet, a master at catching a glimpse of eternity and expressing it in verse. In simple style, Dickinson utters what many believers often also see: that we all are coheirs of that which is immortal, while all around us we see and even experience mortality. It is a thought that—as Dickinson puts it—is honorable, inspiring us to tip our hat, so to speak, when we pass fellow believers on the street.

Perhaps as Dickinson contemplated the temporal nature of this world, she also thought about how Christians should love one another while here, treating each other with kindness and courtesy. Thus, the courteous gesture of tipping one's hat to another.

As we look at this world and all that people have built—its pyramids and kingdoms—we should realize that all of it will "flit russetly away." Only God's kingdom endures forever. Therefore, let us not only strive to enter his kingdom but to love one another along the way.

God blesses those who are gentle and lowly, for the whole earth will belong to them. Matthew 5:5

Stanzas on the Psalms

Not the songs that nobly tell,
How Troy was sacked, and Rome began,
Not the numbers that reveal
The wars of Heaven to falling man;

Can boast that true celestial fire,
That equal strength and ease,
Or with such various charms conspire,
To move, to teach, to please.

Those complaints how sadly sweet,
Which weeping seraphim repeat;
Those prayers how happily preferred,
Which God himself inspired and heard.

Ye partial wits no longer boast
Of Pindar's fire in David's lost!
Who to the Hebrew harp must yield,
As Jove[a] *by great Jehovah is excelled.*

THOMAS WARTON THE ELDER (1688–1745)

[a]also called Jupiter, the supreme deity of the ancient Romans

POETS have produced many great literary works throughout history. One such poet was Pindar, a major lyric poet of ancient Greece, whose works have survived in larger quantity than those of any other poet of ancient times. Pindar's poetry celebrates the values of an aristocratic society. He took the commonplace Homeric celebration of competition and raised it to a primary moral commitment—the pursuit of excellence.

In this poem Warton proclaims the power and superiority of the psalms over other ancient verse. He states that Pindar's fire has been lost in David's true celestial fire. The Grecian lyre yields to the Hebrew harp just as Jove succumbs to Jehovah's greatness.

The psalms are superior because they reveal the one and only living God, whom the poets celebrate for his many attributes: his creative power (33:6-9; 95:3-7), faithfulness (18:25-28; 89:5-8; 145:13-16), love (36:5-7; 63:3-5), mercy (28:6-7; 30:8, 10; 86:15-17), righteousness (11:4-7; 145:17-21), and sovereignty (47:7-9; 96:10-13).

The psalms also reflect universal experiences and emotions that speak to everyone's dreams, hopes, concerns, and fears, all the while directing people to the one who cares for them deeply. As the psalmist Asaph rejoiced: "I still belong to you; you are holding my right hand. You will keep on guiding me with your counsel, leading me to a glorious destiny" (Psalm 73:23-24).

Reading poetry can do so much for us—teaching us about life and broadening our perspective. But reading the psalms—that is even better. For within this body of poetry we meet the one true God who is worthy of our devotion and praise.

➽ *Whom have I in heaven but you? I desire you more than anything on earth.* Psalm 73:25

King Solomon and the Ants PART ONE

Out from Jerusalem
The King rode with his great
War chiefs and lords of state,
And Sheba's queen with them;

Comely, but black withal,
To whom, perchance, belongs
That wondrous Song of songs,
Sensuous and mystical,[a]

Whereto devout souls turn
In fond, ecstatic dream,
And through its earth-born theme
The Love of loves discern.

Proud in the Syrian sun,
In gold and purple sheen,
The dusky Ethiop[b] *queen*
Smiled on King Solomon.

(continued in next day's reading)

JOHN GREENLEAF WHITTIER (1807–1892)

[a]Song of Songs 1:5 [b]Ethiopian

WHO WAS this queen of Sheba? John Greenleaf Whittier says she may be the maiden from the Song of Songs: "Comely, but black withal, to whom, perchance, belongs that wondrous Song of Songs, sensuous and mystical." This echoes Song of Songs 1:5: "I am dark and beautiful . . . tanned as the dark tents of Kedar. Yes, even as the tents of Solomon!"

First-century Jewish authorities debated whether they should include Song of Songs in Holy Scripture because it is explicit about sexual attraction. Some rabbis even went so far as to keep younger men from reading it. For scholars the Song is a collection of love poems to be recited during ancient Near Eastern wedding festivities.

Many Christians interpret the Song's poetry symbolically. Expositors find the Song symbolic of Christ's love for his church, as well as the love between God and an individual. So sections of these love songs have found their way into Christian worship. Charles Wesley's hymn "Jesus, Lover of My Soul" contains references to the Song, as does Bernard of Clairvaux's "Jesus, the Very Thought of Thee."

"My lover is mine," sings the maiden, "and I am his" (Song of Songs 2:16). This is the assurance of God's beloved. The apostle Paul expressed this assurance in 2 Timothy 1:12: "I know the one in whom I trust, and I am sure that he is able to guard what I have entrusted to him until the day of his return." As we wait for that blessed day, let us pray like the maiden: "Before the dawn comes and the shadows flee away, come back to me, my love" (Song of Songs 2:17).

When the queen of Sheba realized how wise Solomon was, and when she saw the palace he had built, she was breathless. She was also amazed at the food on his tables, the organization of his officials and their splendid clothing, the cup-bearers and their robes, and the burnt offerings Solomon made at the Temple of the Lord. 1 Kings 10:4-5

King Solomon and the Ants PART TWO

Wisest of men, he knew
The languages of all
The creatures great or small
That trod the earth or flew.

Across an ant-hill led
The king's path, and he heard
Its small folk, and their word
He thus interpreted:

"Here comes the king men greet
As wise and good and just,
To crush us in the dust
Under his heedless feet."

The great king bowed his head,
And saw the wide surprise
Of the Queen of Sheba's eyes
As he told her what they said.

"O king!" she whispered sweet,
"Too happy fate have they
Who perish in thy way
Beneath thy gracious feet!"

(continued in next day's reading)

JOHN GREENLEAF WHITTIER (1807–1892)

NEWSPAPERS report that students in the United States score lower on standardized tests in math and science than do students from many other countries. Yet some reports pointed out that the United States still exceeds the rest of the world in technical innovation. Why?

Whittier's poem about the ants tells us why. Solomon is seen with the queen of Sheba proceeding with his entourage out of Jerusalem. The queen had heard of Solomon's reputation as a very wise man, so she had come to Jerusalem to test him with hard questions (1 Kings 10:1). The queen talked with Solomon about everything on her mind. Solomon answered all her questions (10:2-3).

The record of her visit continues: "When the queen of Sheba realized how wise Solomon was, and when she saw the palace he had built, she was breathless. She was also amazed at the food on his tables, the organization of his officials and their splendid clothing, the cup-bearers and their robes, and the burnt offerings Solomon made at the Temple of the Lord. She exclaimed to the king, 'Everything I heard in my country about your achievements and wisdom is true! I didn't believe it until I arrived here and saw it with my own eyes' " (10:4-7).

Wisdom is not the same as knowledge. Wisdom is knowledge combined with creativity and insight and applied to real life. This is why Matthew says, "Wisdom is shown to be right by what results from it" (11:19). The queen of Sheba knew that Solomon was wise not because of what he knew but by what he did—his actions. He could pass the standardized test and apply his knowledge to real-life problems. May God grant us this same kind of wisdom.

The queen of Sheba will also rise up against this generation on judgment day and condemn it, because she came from a distant land to hear the wisdom of Solomon. And now someone greater than Solomon is here—and you refuse to listen to him. Matthew 12:42

"Thou of the God-lent crown,
Shall these vile creatures dare
Murmur against thee where
The knees of kings kneel down?

"Nay," Solomon replied,
"The wise and strong should seek
The welfare of the weak,"
And turned his horse aside.

His train, with quick alarm
Curved with their leader round
The ant-hill's peopled mound
And left it free from harm.

The jewelled head bent low;
"O king!" she said, "henceforth
The secret of thy worth
And wisdom I well know.

"Happy must be the state
Whose ruler heedeth more
The murmurs of the poor
Than the flatteries of the great."

JOHN GREENLEAF WHITTIER (1807–1892)

KING SOLOMON represents the paragon of wisdom. James says, "If any of you lacks wisdom, he should ask God, who gives generously to all without finding fault, and it will be given to him" (1:5, NIV). James surely knew that everyone could use more wisdom. If we were to ask for it every time we need it, such prayer would become habitual.

The Lord personally gave us two patterns for prayer—the Lord's Prayer in Matthew 6:9-13 and the prayer in the Garden of Gethsemane in Matthew 26: 39-44. The Epistles also have two patterns for prayer—the prayer for wisdom and revelation in Ephesians 1:17-23 and the prayer for a strengthened inner being in Ephesians 3:16-19.

The Lord's Prayer is universally known among Christians and frequently invoked. Think about how lives would change if we just as frequently prayed according to Ephesians:

> I pray that the God of our Lord Jesus Christ, the Father of glory, may give [me] a spirit of wisdom and revelation as [I] come to know him, so that, with the eyes of [my] heart enlightened, [I] may know what is the hope to which he has called [me]. (1:17-18, NRSV)

Try this prayer for a few weeks. As you pray and as God works according to your prayer, remember that the wisdom God gives is nothing like wisdom that has its source in the world. Such wisdom is not automatically bad, but it is certainly inadequate for God's purposes. First Corinthians 1:24 says that Christ is God's wisdom. So when you pray for wisdom, don't be surprised to encounter Christ.

Since God in his wisdom saw to it that the world would never find him through human wisdom, he has used our foolish preaching to save all who believe. . . . But to those called by God to salvation, both Jews and Gentiles, Christ is the mighty power of God and the wonderful wisdom of God. 1 Corinthians 1:21, 24

Hezekiah's Display

When Heaven in mercy gives thy prayers return,
And Angels bring thee treasures from on high,
Shut fast the door, nor let the world discern,
And offer thee fond praise when God is nigh.

In friendly guise, perchance with friendly heart,
From Babel, see, they haste with words of love:
But if thou lightly all thy wealth impart,
Their race will come again, and all remove.

Ill thoughts, the children of the King of Pride,
O'er richest halls will swarm, and holiest bowers,
Profaning first, then spoiling far and wide:—
Voluptuous sloth make free with Sharon's flowers.

Close thou the garden-gate, and keep the key,
There chiefly, where the tender seedlings fold
Their dainty leaves—a treasure even to thee
Unknown, till airs celestial make them bold.

When sun and shower give token, freely then
The fragrance will steal out, the flower unclose:
But busy hands, and an admiring ken,[a]
Have blighted ere its hour full many a rose.

Then rest thee, bright one, in thy tranquil nook,
Fond eyes to cherish thee, true arms to keep,
Nor wistful for the world's gay sunshine look;—
In its own time the light will o'er thee sweep.

Think of the babes of Judah's royal line:—
Display but touched them with her parching glare
Once, and for ages four they bare the sign,
The fifth beheld them chained in Babel's lair.

JOHN KEBLE (1792–1866)

[a]glance

THE ENGLISH theologian and poet John Keble was ordained in the Church of England in 1815. In 1827 he published a volume of poems, *The Christian Year,* which went through ninety-five editions during his lifetime and led to a professorship in poetry at Oxford. In his poetry Keble exhibited fervent faith in the authority of the church and its sacraments and is said to have begun the Oxford movement with a sermon on "National Apostasy," preached on July 14, 1833.

Keble uses an Old Testament story about a king's foolishness in an interesting way. Playing off Hezekiah's display of wealth, Keble advises us not to display or brag about our spiritual riches. This concept is reminiscent of Jesus' words: "But when you pray, go away by yourself, shut the door behind you, and pray to your Father secretly. Then your Father, who knows all secrets, will reward you" (Matthew 6:6).

As Christ commanded, we should not make a show of our relationship with him. We should not pray in public simply to impress others. Prayer is sacred communion with our Creator, Lord, and Savior. To abuse this privilege is akin to divulging marital secrets or violating a sacred trust. No wonder Christ had such scathing comments about the Pharisee (6:5).

Rather, we should pray: *Father, I repent for ever praying publicly for the wrong reasons. I am sorry that we spend so little time together in secret. Now I know that these times are important not only to me but also to you. Please increase my desire to spend more time alone with you in prayer. And in public prayer may my motivations always be to glorify you, not me. Amen.*

Hezekiah welcomed the Babylonian envoys and showed them everything in his treasure-houses—the silver, the gold, the spices, and the aromatic oils. He also took them to see his armory and showed them all his other treasures—everything! There was nothing in his palace or kingdom that Hezekiah did not show them. 2 Kings 20:13

Psalm XXIII

The sheep-keepin o' the Lord's kind an' canny,
wi' a braw howff at lang last:
David keeps his sheep; the Lord keeps David.
An heigh-lilt o' David's.

The Lord is my herd, nae want sal fa' me:
He luts me till lie amang green howes; he airts me
atowre by the lown watirs:
He waukens my wa'-gen saul; he weises me roun,
for his ain name's sake, intil right roddins.
Na!, tho' I gang thro' the dead-mirk-dail; e'en thar,
sal I dread ane skaithin:
for yersel are nar-by me; yer stok an' yer stay haud
me baith fu' cheerie.
My buird ye hae hansell'd in face o' my faes; ye hae
drookit my head wi' oyle;
my bicker is fu' an' skailin.
E'en sae, sal gude-guidin' an' gude-gree gang wi'
me, ilk day o' my livin;
an' evir mair syne, i' the Lord's ain howff, at
lang last, sal I mak bydan.

P. HATELY WADDELL (1817–1891)

P. HATELY WADDELL was a disciple of Robert Burns. One of his major accomplishments was translating the psalms from Hebrew into Scottish. This poem is his version of Psalm 23. While the text is quite difficult to read, let alone understand, the poem has great value in two respects. First, it represents God's Word. As such, it communicates the eternal truths of Psalm 23 for the Scottish people to understand.

Second, it shows us another important but often overlooked aspect of poetry. We all know that poetry is more than words on a page. It may tell a story or convey a meaningful message or sentiment. But it does even more than this. Poetry is also pure sound, created through patterns of words in meter, rhyme, and rhythm. In this respect, poetry is not always about communicating ideas or truths. Sometimes it's just about experiencing language in a new, vibrant way. That is one reason poetry is so ineffable that we must also call it art.

What has Waddell done to our beloved Psalm 23? Well, it's not ours. This psalm belongs to poetry. It is English and Scottish, Hebrew and many other languages. Read it aloud in Waddell's Scottish version. How fresh it is! The joy, the hope, the divine, and the human are all there in power. This is a poem!

The Lord is my shepherd; I shall not want. He maketh me to lie down in green pastures: he leadeth me beside the still waters. He restoreth my soul: he leadeth me in the paths of righteousness for his name's sake. Yea, though I walk through the valley of the shadow of death, I will fear no evil: for thou art with me; thy rod and thy staff they comfort me. Thou preparest a table before me in the presence of mine enemies: thou anointest my head with oil; my cup runneth over. Surely goodness and mercy shall follow me all the days of my life: and I will dwell in the house of the Lord for ever. Psalm 23, KJV

On Balaam's Ass

The ass, that for her slowness, was forbid
To be employed in God's service, did
Perform good service now, in being slow:
The ass received stripes, but would not go:
She balked the way, and Balaam could not guide her:
The ass had far more wisdom than the rider:
The message being bad, the ass was loth
To be the bearer: 'Twas a happy sloth;
'Twas well for Balaam: had his ass but tried
Another step, Balaam had surely died:
Poor ass! And was thy faithful service paid
With oft-repeated strokes? Hadst thou obeyed,
Thy Lord had bought thy travel, with his blood:
Such is man's payment, often bad for good:
The ass begins to question with his master,
Argues the case, pleads why he went no faster:
Nay, shows him mysteries, far beyond his reach;
Sure, God wants prophets, when dull asses preach:
The ass perceives the angel, and falls down;
When Balaam sees him not; or sees, unknown:
Nor is 't a wonder: for God's spirit did pass
From blindfold Balaam, into Balaam's ass.

FRANCIS QUARLES (1592–1644)

ISRAEL had completed the forty-year trek through Sinai and now camped across the Jordan River on the plains of Moab. Balak, the pagan king of Moab, was terrified. So he sent for help from the Gentile prophet Balaam (Numbers 22–24).

Balaam practiced divination (Joshua 13:22) and was not a prophet in the biblical sense. He combined worship of Jehovah with occult practices. Balak believed that particular incantations could constrain an enemy or drain the power of a nation, so he hired Balaam to bring such a curse on Israel.

Because God told Balaam not to go to Moab (Numbers 22:12), the prophet refused to go with Balak's messengers (22:13-14). But Balak persisted, sending more officials (and money) to Balaam. This time God told him to go (22:16-21). Thus we come to Quarles's poem and this amazing miracle. Balaam's donkey not only saves her master from being killed by the Lord's angel but also speaks to Balaam. During their conversation, the Lord opens Balaam's eyes to the truth about the donkey's actions. Balaam then realizes that he has sinned.

This story contains many lessons for Christians. For example, we should never attempt to bend God's divine will to our own or disobey God out of greed. But as Quarles points out, it also tells us of a tragic human response: "Such is man's payment, often bad for good." How easy it is to treat others poorly when we think they have offended us. Naturally, we feel terrible when we discover the truth. But we would be better off if we used God-given wisdom and discernment to seek the truth before we react, instead of acting like Balaam.

Then the Lord caused the donkey to speak. "What have I done to you that deserves your beating me these three times?" it asked Balaam.
Numbers 22:28

Epitaph

Stop, Christian passer-by!—Stop, child of God,
And read with gentle breast. Beneath this sod
A poet lies, or that which once seemed he.
O, lift one thought in prayer for S. T. C.;
That he who many a year with toil of breath
Found death in life, may here find life in death!
Mercy for praise—to be forgiven for fame
He asked, and hoped, through Christ. Do thou the
same!

SAMUEL TAYLOR COLERIDGE (1772–1834)

THIS POEM is a fitting epitaph for a poet who had gained fame for his poetry and later realized that his achievements meant nothing if he did not have Christ.

Coleridge's achievements as a poet began after he met the English poet William Wordsworth in 1795. Their association resulted in a collaboration to publish the *Lyrical Ballads* (1798), a landmark in literary history. Coleridge's most significant contribution to the volume was "The Rime of the Ancient Mariner," an eerie ballad of the supernatural that concludes with the ancient mariner teaching reverence for all things created by God.

In 1798 Coleridge toured Europe with William and Dorothy Wordsworth. The next year he attended the University of Göttingen (Germany), where he mastered the German language and absorbed German Romanticism and the philosophy of Immanuel Kant.

Coleridge's return to England coincided with the decline of his poetic powers. He became addicted to opium. Although he was able to diminish his addiction, his creative work was permanently hampered. In spite of the high quality of his poetry, his overall output was disappointingly low. "Dejection: An Ode" (1802) and "Youth and Age" (1828–1832) depict his realization of and disillusionment over his impeded abilities.

Coleridge spent his remaining years working on a variety of literary and philosophical projects but writing only a few more poems. After being attracted to Unitarianism and to German mystical pantheism, he returned to the Christian faith. This poem—written one year before his death—reflects his return to Christ and serves as a living gospel for all who would seek fame but miss Christ, the giver of eternal life.

➾ *[The Lord said,] "You thought you could get along without me, so you trusted instead in your fame."* Ezekiel 16:15

Naaman's Song

"Go wash thyself in Jordan—go, wash thee and be clean!"
Nay, not for any Prophet will I plunge a toe therein!
For the banks of curious Jordan are parcelled into sites,
Commanded and embellished and patrolled by Israelites.

There rise her timeless capitals of Empires daily born,
Whose plinths[a] *are laid at midnight, and whose streets are packed at morn;*
And here come hired youths and maids that feign to love or sin
In tones like rusty razor-blades to tunes like smitten tin.

And here be merry murtherings,[b] *and steeds with fiery hooves;*
And furious hordes with guns and swords, and clamberings over rooves;
And horrid tumblings down from Heaven, and flights with wheels and wings;
And always one weak virgin who is chased through all these things.

And here is mock of faith and truth, for children to behold;
And every door of ancient dirt reopened to the old;
With every word that taints the speech, and show that weakens thought;
And Israel watcheth over each, and—doth not watch for nought. . . .

But Pharpar—but Abana[c]*—which Hermon launcheth down—*
They perish fighting desert sands beyond Damascus-town.
But yet their pulse is of the snows—their strength is from on high—
And, if they cannot cure my woes, a leper will I die!

RUDYARD KIPLING (1865–1936)

[a]the square block at the base of a column [b]murders [c]rivers in Syria—see 2 Kings 5:12

NAAMAN was a powerful, desperate man. He was the commander of the Syrian army but also a leper. During a time of uneasy peace between Syria and Israel, Naaman learned that there was a prophet in Israel who could cure him. So he went seeking a cure. Israel's king thought the Syrians were trying to resume warfare (2 Kings 5). But the prophet Elisha sent a message to the king: "Send Naaman to me, and he will learn that there is a true prophet here in Israel" (5:8). Naaman visited Elisha but became furious when told to wash seven times in the Jordan River.

You would have been angry if you were in Naaman's place. Just think: You are the commander of the world's most powerful army, and you have fought against this despised country. You travel with a huge entourage, carrying hundreds of pounds of silver and gold. In all your power and with your incurable, excruciating leprosy, you arrive at Elisha's little house. You expect Elisha to emerge, bow down to you, pronounce some incantation, offer a sacrifice, anoint you with spiced oils, and you will be cured. Instead, a servant comes from the prophet with a message about washing in the Jordan River. You deserve more honor than this. What an insult! Wash in the Jordan? You have bigger and better rivers back in Syria!

Let's apply Naaman's song to the present, but the disease isn't leprosy, it's sin. In place of Israel and the prophet stand the church of God and the gospel of Jesus Christ. Only one thing remains the same—the obstacle to healing—human pride. God's cure seems too simple. The homeless are saved the same way as the powerful—they wash in the river of faith. No other river will cure sin.

But Naaman became angry and stalked away. "I thought he would surely come out to meet me!" he said. "I expected him to wave his hand over the leprosy and call on the name of the Lord his God and heal me!" 2 Kings 5:11

The Destruction of Sennacherib

The Assyrian came down like the wolf on the fold,
And his cohorts were gleaming in purple and gold;
And the sheen of their spears was like stars on the sea,
When the blue wave rolls nightly on deep Galilee.

Like the leaves of the forest when summer is green,
That host with their banners at sunset were seen:
Like the leaves of the forest when autumn hath blown,
That host on the morrow lay withered and strown.

For the Angel of Death spread his wings on the blast,
And breathed in the face of the foe as he passed;
And the eyes of the sleepers waxed deadly and chill,
And their hearts but once heaved—and for ever grew still!

And there lay the steed with his nostril all wide,
But through it there rolled not the breath of his pride;
And the foam of his gasping lay white on the turf,
And cold as the spray of the rock-beating surf.

And there lay the rider distorted and pale,
With the dew on his brow, and the rust on his mail;
And the tents were all silent, the banners alone,
The lances unlifted, the trumpet unblown.

And the widows of Ashur are loud in their wail,
And the idols are broke in the temples of Baal;
And the might of the Gentile, unsmote by the sword,
Hath melted like snow in the glance of the Lord!

LORD BYRON (1788–1824)

BYRON'S poem is a magnificent depiction of a biblical event rarely talked about: God's miraculous rescue of Jerusalem from certain destruction at the hands of Sennacherib, king of the Assyrian Empire (705–681 B.C.)

Shortly after Sennacherib became king he encountered a rebellion from the western provinces. It is likely that Hezekiah, king of Judah, joined Egypt and other Palestinian nations and led this insurrection (2 Kings 18:7–19:37). Sennacherib led his armies against this Palestinian alliance. Sennacherib captured the cities of Tyre and Sidon and continued southward. Several Philistine cities submitted before the Assyrian onslaught, but Ashkelon, Bethdagon and Joppa resisted, so Sennacherib's army captured and plundered these towns. In Ekron, the Assyrians killed the city's leaders by skinning them alive. Sennacherib then besieged the Judean city of Lachish and captured forty-six other towns, taking 200,150 Jewish captives. Jerusalem was next.

Realizing his desperate situation, Hezekiah was about to surrender. But God sent the prophet Isaiah to inform Hezekiah that he—the Lord—would humble Sennacherib and spare Jerusalem for David's sake. The next morning as Sennacherib's troops awoke, they found 185,000 of their fellow soldiers dead from a miraculous plague. Sennacherib abandoned plans to take Jerusalem and returned to Assyria. "The might of the Gentile, unsmote by the sword, hath melted like snow in the glance of the Lord!"

This is what the Lord says about the king of Assyria: His armies will not enter Jerusalem to shoot their arrows. They will not march outside its gates with their shields and build banks of earth against its walls. The king will return to his own country by the road on which he came. 2 Kings 19:32-33

The Heart Is Deep

He that can trace a ship making her way,
Amidst the threatening surges on the sea;
Or track a towering eagle in the air,
Or on a rock find the impressions there
Made by a serpent's footsteps; who surveys
The subtle intrigues that a young man lays,
In his sly courtship of an harmless maid,
Whereby his wanton amours are conveyed
Into her breast; 'tis he alone that can
Find out cursed policies of man.

ROGER WOLCOTT (1679–1767)

ROMANS 12:17-19 is full of good advice: Don't pay back evil for evil, live in peace with everyone, and never avenge yourself—leave that to God. The reason this is sound counsel is that we never know what is really happening in another person's life. God, on the other hand, has the insight to trace the path of a snake on a rock. In other words, God knows everything.

Roger Wolcott had a distinguished career in public service. He was an American colonial administrator from Windsor, Connecticut. He also served as deputy governor of Connecticut and governor of Connecticut (1751–54), and authored *Poetical Meditations* (1725), the first volume of verse published in Connecticut.

Roger's son, Oliver (1726–1797), was also prominent in colonial and early national politics. He was a member of the Continental Congress and a signer of the Declaration of Independence. He commanded the Connecticut militia on the Hudson River and led a volunteer army against British General John Burgoyne in the Revolutionary War.

As a politician, Wolcott witnessed firsthand the "cursed policies of man." But through today's poem, we know he understood that only God can truly perceive the truth behind these "policies." Perhaps Wolcott knew the trustworthiness of the advice from Romans 12.

As believers, we can trust the Lord to "repay those who deserve it" (Romans 12:19). Our part is to do what Scripture says: "If your enemies are hungry, feed them. If they are thirsty, give them something to drink, and they will be ashamed of what they have done to you. Don't let evil get the best of you, but conquer evil by doing good" (12:20-21).

➻ *O God, listen to my complaint. Do not let my enemies' threats overwhelm me. Protect me from the plots of the wicked, from the scheming of those who do evil.* Psalm 64:1-2

Times Go By Turns

The loppèd[a] tree in time may grow again;
Most naked plants renew both fruit and flower;
The sorriest wight[b] may find release of pain,
The driest soil suck in some moistening shower;
Times go by turns and chances change by course,
From foul to fair, from better hap[c] to worse.

The sea of fortune doth not ever flow,
She draws her favors to the lowest ebb;
Her tide hath equal times to come and go,
Her loom doth weave the fine and coarsest web;
No joy so great but runneth to an end,
No hap[c] so hard but may in time amend.

Not always fall of leaf nor ever spring,
No endless night yet not eternal day;
The saddest birds a season find to sing,
The roughest storm a calm may soon allay;
Thus with succeeding turns God tempereth all,
That man may hope to rise yet fear to fall.

A chance may win that by mischance was lost;
The net that holds no great, takes little fish;
In some things all, in all things none are crossed,
Few all they need, but none have all they wish;
Unmeddled[d] joys here to no man befall,
Who least hath some, who most hath never all.

ROBERT SOUTHWELL (1561–1595)

[a]trimmed, pruned [b]any living being, a creature [c]an occurrence or happening [d]not mixed, pure

ROBERT SOUTHWELL was a Jesuit poet and martyr of the Elizabethan period. After studying in France and Rome, he was ordained in 1584 and returned to London to serve as missionary to the oppressed Roman Catholics. During this time Southwell lived in hiding. In 1592 he was arrested, tortured, and executed three years later for being Catholic.

Today's poem is Southwell's version of Ecclesiastes 3:1-8. Many scholars attribute the writing of Ecclesiastes to Solomon—David's son, who reigned in Israel 970–940 B.C. This book is a philosophical search for life's meaning.

There are two keys to understanding Ecclesiastes: (1) The writer relies only on human reason ("explore by wisdom," 1:13), and (2) he considers only data available within the created universe ("under the sun," 1:14). This explains why the writer is despondent and says that life is meaningless. Although this view is repeated throughout Ecclesiastes, it is *not* the view of Scripture. It is, however, the conclusion that even the wisest people come to if they use only human reason and if they assume that life in this world is all there is. Such despair is seen in the conclusions of modern philosophers.

But despair and hopelessness are not what Ecclesiastes 3:1-8 is about. The passage is about the repeated cycles that control life. Hence, there is nothing new. Southwell views these cycles that balance life as God's way of tempering humanity so that we "may hope to rise yet fear to fall." Southwell saw life through the eyes of faith, in the wisdom of the Spirit.

As we experience life's seasons, let us remember: "Unmeddled joys here to no man befall." We look forward to when the downward cycles of life will vanish, and "there will be no more death or sorrow or crying or pain" (Revelation 21:4).

There is a time for everything, a season for every activity under heaven. Ecclesiastes 3:1

Lucifer in Starlight

On a starred night Prince Lucifer uprose.
Tired of his dark dominion swung the fiend
Above the rolling ball in cloud part screened,
Where sinners hugged their spectre of repose
Poor prey to his hot fit of pride were those.
And now upon his western wing he leaned,
Now his huge bulk o'er Afric's[a] *sands careened,*
Now the black planet shadowed arctic snows.
Soaring through wider zones that pricked his scars
With memory of the old revolt from awe,
He reached a middle height, and at the stars,
Which are the brain of heaven, he looked, and sank.
Around the ancient track marched, rank on rank,
The army of unalterable law.

GEORGE MEREDITH (1828–1909)

[a]Africa's

GEORGE MEREDITH was a major literary figure of the English Victorian age. A poet and novelist, his best-known works are *Modern Love and Poems of the English Roadside* (1862), *The Egoist* (1879), and *Diana of the Crossways* (1885). Brilliant psychological insights, carefully chosen diction, and powerful imagery characterize his work.

Such imagery is seen in "Lucifer in Starlight." Lucifer soars above the earth, leans westward over North Africa, and casts his dark shadow across the arctic snow. He enters the area where battles occurred during the angelic rebellion (Isaiah 14:12-17), when God cast him and a third of the angels out of heaven (2 Peter 2:4; Jude 1:6). Next Lucifer pauses to look at the stars, which represent the faithful angels of God. At this sight the devilish heart sinks at the thought of defeat.

What is this defeat? Perhaps the angelic rebellion, but given God's "unalterable law," Lucifer may have known there would be future defeats as well. The first came when Jesus died on the cross, through which "God disarmed the evil rulers and authorities. He shamed them publicly by his victory over them on the cross of Christ" (Colossians 2:15). These rulers and authorities are the angels that rebelled. Also, remember that the eternal fire has been prepared for the devil and his demons (Matthew 25:41). The Bible records that in the end, "The Devil . . . was thrown into the lake of fire that burns with sulfur . . . [and] tormented day and night forever and ever" (Revelation 20:10).

No wonder Meredith sees Lucifer's heart sink! "The army of unalterable law" that he sees marching rank on rank around the ancient track is God's army of angels who will carry out his judgment upon the evil one.

How you are fallen from heaven, O shining star, son of the morning! You have been thrown down to the earth, you who destroyed the nations of the world. Isaiah 14:12

Of Paul and Silas It Is Said

Of Paul and Silas it is said
They were in Prison laid
But when they went to take them out
They were not there instead.

Security the same insures
To our assaulted Minds—
The staple must be optional
That an Immortal binds.

EMILY DICKINSON (1830–1886)

SECURITY. It's something just about everyone desires. And some people will do anything for it, including sacrificing their freedom.

In today's poem Dickinson writes that security insures to our minds that what God binds is optional. What does this mean? One way of looking at it is that God requires his followers and those who seek him to step outside of their comfort zones. Sometimes he even asks them to leave behind those people and things that give them security in order to follow him more closely. But the desire for security often interferes with the call to obedience. To justify our disobedience, we allow security to whisper in our ear, "The staple must be optional that an Immortal binds."

This was not the case for Paul and Silas. They chose obedience to Christ over security, and their obedience cost them dearly—here on earth. For the cause of Christ Paul and Silas endured beatings and imprisonment. Once while they were imprisoned, the Lord caused a great earthquake to shake the foundations of the jail, opening the cell doors and causing the prisoners' chains to fall off (Acts 16:16-34).

During Paul's time, when Roman guards placed a prisoner in a cell, they would attach the prisoner's chains to a long spike secured in the ground. This is what Dickinson means by "staple." But in the account in Acts, God did not bind the staple that confined Paul and Silas. God removed their chains and created an opportunity for them to share the gospel, the true staple that bound Paul and Silas.

As their example shows us, the staple not bound by the Immortal is the only staple that is optional. May we never allow security to hinder our obedience to God.

A mob quickly formed against Paul and Silas, and the city officials ordered them stripped and beaten with wooden rods. They were severely beaten, and then they were thrown into prison. Acts 16:22-23

Sonnet 146

Poor soul, the centre of my sinful earth,
Fooled by these rebel powers that thee array,
Why dost thou pine within and suffer dearth,
Painting thy outward walls so costly gay?
Why so large cost, having so short a lease,
Dost thou upon thy fading mansion spend?
Shall worms, inheritors of this excess,
Eat up thy charge? Is this thy body's end?
Then, soul, live thou upon thy servant's loss,
And let that pine to aggravate thy store;
Buy terms divine in selling hours of dross;
Within be fed, without be rich no more:
  So shalt thou feed on death, that feeds on men,
  And death once dead, there's no more dying then.

WILLIAM SHAKESPEARE (1564–1616)

IN THIS sonnet Shakespeare echoes 1 Corinthians 15:50: "Flesh and blood cannot inherit the Kingdom of God. These perishable bodies of ours are not able to live forever." Shakespeare asks, Why do you paint "thy outward walls so costly gay? Why so large cost, having so short a lease, dost thou upon thy fading mansion spend?" After all, says Scripture, "our perishable earthly bodies must be transformed into heavenly bodies that will never die" (15:53). This is not a work that we can do. Yes, we should take care of our body and dress appropriately. But eventually we will die. And just as surely, we will all resurrect at the end of time.

Someone once asked the apostle Paul how Christ will raise the dead and what kind of body he will give them (15:35). Paul answered with the example of sowing seed: "What you put in the ground is not the plant that will grow, but only a dry little seed of wheat or whatever it is you are planting. Then God gives it a new body—just the kind he wants it to have. A different kind of plant grows from each kind of seed" (15:37-38).

"It is the same way for the resurrection of the dead," the apostle continues. "Our earthly bodies, which die and decay, will be different when they are resurrected, for they will never die" (15:42).

Therefore, we who are living "upon thy servant's loss"—that is, putting our faith in Christ—have nothing to fear. For one day, Christ will return and transform our earthly bodies into heavenly ones. On that day, death itself will die.

In Jerusalem, the Lord Almighty will spread a wonderful feast for everyone around the world. It will be a delicious feast of good food, with clear, well-aged wine and choice beef. In that day he will remove the cloud of gloom, the shadow of death that hangs over the earth. He will swallow up death forever! Isaiah 25:6-8

If I Could Shut the Gate

If I could shut the gate against my thoughts
And keep out sorrow from this room within,
Or memory could cancel all the notes
Of my misdeeds, and I unthink my sin:
How free, how clear, how clean my soul should lie,
Discharged of such a loathsome company!

Or were there other rooms without my heart
That did not to my conscience join so near,
Where I might lodge the thoughts of sin apart
That I might not their clam'rous crying hear;
What peace, what joy, what ease should I possess,
Freed from their horrors that my soul oppress!

But, O my Saviour, who my refuge art,
Let thy dear mercies stand 'twixt them and me,
And be the wall to separate my heart
So that I may at length repose me free;
That peace, and joy, and rest may be within,
And I remain divided from my sin.

ANONYMOUS

THIS anonymous writer eloquently deals with a question found in the heart of every lover of God. How can I be separated from sin? Some seek refuge from sin in monasticism, locking themselves away from outside influences. Others employ asceticism, severely denying themselves physical comforts and pleasures. People eschew the conveniences and fashions of the world, cleave to outdated doctrines and practices, or invent teachings to excise their sin. But none of this will stand between us and sin.

"The world around us is under the power and control of the evil one" (1 John 5:19). So we cannot escape sin by taking refuge *in* the world. No matter if something is old-fashioned or modern, it is still of the world. All lifestyles have their origin in the world that is under the power of the evil one. So what is a Christian to do?

We don't have to look any further than the first epistle of John to find the answer: "God sent his only Son into the world so that we might live through him" (1 John 4:9, NRSV). This is good news! We don't have to escape the world to find refuge from sin because "the Father sent his Son to be the Savior of the world" (4:14). John continues: "All who proclaim that Jesus is the Son of God [that is, Christians] have God living in them, and they live in God" (4:15). Although we reside in the world like everyone else, by faith in Jesus Christ we are actually living in God. In him we find peace and joy and rest because we remain separated from sin. "So we will not be afraid on the day of judgment, but we can face him with confidence because we are like Christ here in this world" (4:17).

For every child of God defeats this evil world by trusting Christ to give the victory. And the ones who win this battle against the world are the ones who believe that Jesus is the Son of God. 1 John 5:4-5

from Last Verses

The seas are quiet when the winds give o'er;
So calm are we when passions are no more.
For then we know how vain it was to boast
For fleeting things, so certain to be lost.
Clouds of affection from our younger eyes
Conceal that emptiness which age descries.[a]
The soul's dark cottage, batter'd and decay'd,
Lets in new light through chinks that time has made;
Stronger by weakness, wiser, men become
As they draw near to their eternal home.
Leaving the old, both worlds at once they view
That stand upon the threshold of the new.

EDMUND WALLER (1606–1687)

[a]discerns

FIRST CORINTHIANS 13 is about love, but it also contains Paul's thoughts on spiritual gifts. Note Paul's introduction to 1 Corinthians 13: "Is everyone a prophet? No. . . . Does God give all of us the ability to speak in unknown languages? No! . . . First, however, let me tell you about something else that is better than any of them!" (12:29-31).

Today's poem helps us understand Paul's thoughts in this chapter. The poet writes, "For then we know how vain it was to boast for fleeting things, so certain to be lost." Couldn't these things be prophecy and speaking in unknown languages, which will all disappear (13:8)?

When Waller writes, "Clouds of affection from our younger eyes conceal that emptiness which age descries," he could be rephrasing Paul: "When I was a child, I spoke and thought and reasoned as a child does. But when I grew up, I put away childish things" (13:11).

Waller also speaks of "the soul's dark cottage, batter'd and decay'd." Over time our bodies decline, leaving cracks and clefts through which God's light intrudes upon our soul to show us more about his divine way—love. What does God teach us about love? For one thing, he shows us what love is: "Jesus Christ laid down his life for us" (1 John 3:16, NIV). He teaches us about love's endurance. It is not only one of three things that will last, but it is the greatest of the three (1 Corinthians 13:13). Why? Because God's nature is to love (1 John 4:16). As we become more like him, everything we do will reveal his nature.

Lord, my heart is not proud; my eyes are not haughty. I don't concern myself with matters too great or awesome for me. But I have stilled and quieted myself, just as a small child is quiet with its mother. Yes, like a small child is my soul within me. Psalm 131:1-2

To St. Michael the Archangel PART ONE

When as the prince of Angels puffed with pride
stirred his seditious spirits to rebel:
God choose for chief, his champion Michael:
and gave him charge the host of heaven to guide.
And when the Angels of the rebel's side
vanquished in battle from their glory fell,
the pride of heaven became the Drake of hell,
and in the dungeon of despair was tied.

(continued in next day's reading)

HENRY CONSTABLE (1562–1613)

HENRY CONSTABLE was an English poet who wrote a sonnet sequence titled *Diana* (1592). This collection helped develop the poetic genre of the sonnet in English. A Roman Catholic, Constable spent much of his life in Paris. His *Spiritual Sonnets* remained unpublished until 1815, though several of his pastoral poems appear in *England's Helicon* (1605), an important collection of Elizabethan poetry.

In "To St. Michael the Archangel" the poet addresses a popular topic these days—angels. Books and seminars on the subject are common. But do these books teach that Lucifer (Satan) was an angel? Or that Michael contends with Lucifer over the bride of Christ? Are there workshops about how "the prince of Angels puffed with pride stirred his seditious spirits to rebel," as Constable says? This is doubtful.

The Bible is the best source for information on angels. They are mentioned about 180 times in the New Testament—75 times in the book of Revelation alone. They appear almost exclusively in the following key periods: the birth and resurrection of Christ (Matthew 1:20-25; Luke 1:26-28; John 20:11-14), the beginning of the church (Acts 12:6-10), and the end times and judgment (Revelation 8:3).

Angels are not simply helpful men with wings. They are powerful agents of God: "Suddenly there was a great earthquake, because an angel of the Lord came down from heaven and rolled aside the stone and sat on it. His face shone like lightning, and his clothing was as white as snow. The guards shook with fear when they saw him, and they fell into a dead faint" (Matthew 28:2-4). Angels do the heavy lifting in God's eternal purpose and must not be taken lightly.

Then there was war in heaven. Michael and the angels under his command fought the dragon and his angels. And the dragon lost the battle and was forced out of heaven. Revelation 12:7-8

To St. Michael the Archangel PART TWO

This Dragon since let loose, God's Church assailed,
and she by help of Michael's sword prevailed.
Who ever tried adventures like this knight?
Which general of heaven, hell overthrew;
for such a Lady as God's spouse did fight:
and such a monster as the Devil subdue.

HENRY CONSTABLE (1562–1613)

JESUS once told a parable about the weeds of the field (Matthew 13:36-43). Angels play an important role in this story. Although it is not quite so dramatic as Constable's poem, this parable is a serious warning to the church and the world. Jesus says that some people are true children of the kingdom. Others are like weeds in a field; they belong to the evil one. These people will experience angels as the reapers on Judgment Day, who will throw them into a furnace and burn them. As the Lord so often said, "Anyone who is willing to hear should listen and understand" (13:43).

Thankfully, angels serve another important role in God's plan. They are "servants . . . spirits sent from God to care for those who will receive salvation" (Hebrews 1:14). The author of Hebrews asks the church—you and me—this question: "What makes us think that we can escape if we are indifferent to this great salvation that was announced by the Lord Jesus himself?" (2:3). Angels first care for those who receive God's great salvation and afterward reap the harvest of God's judgment.

In light of this, let's pray: *O God, save me from misunderstanding your will. Keep me from romanticizing the role of angels. I pray that my heart's understanding will be enlightened to know you more. May I receive the blessings of your angels' ministry in my life. Amen.*

The weeds are the people who belong to the evil one. The enemy who planted the weeds among the wheat is the Devil. The harvest is the end of the world, and the harvesters are the angels. . . . I, the Son of Man, will send my angels, and they will remove from my Kingdom everything that causes sin and all who do evil, and they will throw them into the furnace and burn them. Matthew 13:38-42

Meditation 17 PART ONE

Nunc lento sonitu dicunt, morieris.

Now this bell tolling softly for another, says to me, Thou must die.

Perchance he for whom this bell tolls may be so ill as that he knows not it tolls for him; and perchance I may think myself so much better than I am, as that they who are about me and see my state may have caused it to toll for me, and I know not that. . . . All mankind is of one author and is one volume; when one man dies, one chapter is not torn out of the book, but translated into a better language; and every chapter must be so translated. God employs several translators; some pieces are translated by age, some by sickness, some by war, some by justice; but God's hand is in every translation, and his hand shall bind up all our scattered leaves again for that library where every book shall lie open to one another. As therefore the bell that rings a sermon calls not upon the preacher only, but upon the congregation to come, so this bell calls us all; but how much more me, who am brought so near the door by this sickness. . . . No man is an island, entire of itself; every man is a piece of the continent, a part of the main. If a clod be washed away by the sea, Europe is the less, as well as if a promontory were, as well as if a manor of thy friend's or of thine own were. Any man's death diminishes me because I am involved in mankind, and therefore never send to know for whom the bell tolls; it tolls for thee.[a]

(continued in next day's reading)

JOHN DONNE (1572–1631)

[a]This selection was included because it bears the marks of a prose poem—poetry having a high incidence of sight and sound and voice devices, but with no formal line arrangements.

IN THE novel *For Whom the Bell Tolls,* Ernest Hemingway tells of a band of guerrilla soldiers in the Spanish Civil War. As Fascist soldiers close in on this little group, the mortally wounded Robert Jordan tells his lover Maria, "We will not go to Madrid now but I go always with thee wherever thou goest. Understand? . . . As long as there is one of us there is both of us. Do you understand?" Is this mere fiction? sheer fantasy?

About twenty years after the death and resurrection of Jesus Christ, the apostle Paul visited Athens. "He was deeply troubled by all the idols he saw everywhere in the city" (Acts 17:16). As Paul encountered Epicurean and Stoic philosophers, he told them about Jesus and his resurrection. They disdained Paul, calling him a "babbler" who pushed some foreign religion (17:18). Did Paul respond in kind? Did he scorn and divide himself from them? No. He said, "From one man [God] created all the nations throughout the whole earth" (17:26). John Donne wrote in today's selection, "No man is an island entire of itself; every man is a piece of the continent, a part of the main."

There is one God and one human race. Paul continued, "For in him we live and move and exist. As one of your own poets says, 'We are his offspring' " (17:28). It is this truth that inspired Donne to write, "Never send to know for whom the bell tolls; it tolls for thee," which in turn inspired Hemingway to express the oneness of two people in his novel so aptly titled.

Many things connect people to each other, transforming individual "clods" into a continent. But the one main connector is our loving God, who presides over us all, offering us peace, joy, and salvation.

From one man he created all the nations throughout the whole earth. He decided beforehand which should rise and fall, and he determined their boundaries. Acts 17:26

Meditation 17 PART TWO

Affliction is a treasure, and scarce any man hath enough of it. No man hath affliction enough that is not matured and ripened by it and made fit for God by that affliction. If a man carry treasure in bullion, or in a wedge of gold, and have none coined into current money, his treasure will not defray him as he travels. Tribulation is treasure in the nature of it, but it is not current money in the use of it, except we get nearer and nearer our home, heaven, by it. Another man may be sick too, and sick to death, and this affliction may lie in his bowels as gold in a mine and be of no use to him; but this bell that tells me of his affliction digs out and applies that gold to me, if by this consideration of another's dangers I take mine own into contemplation and so secure myself by making my recourse to my God, who is our only security.

JOHN DONNE (1572–1631)

A RECENT best-selling book, *When Bad Things Happen to Good People,* brings to mind the age-old complaint, "Why is this happening to me?" John Donne expresses the Christian attitude toward this problem: "Affliction is a treasure, and scarce any man hath enough of it. No man hath affliction enough that is not matured and ripened by it, and made fit for God by that affliction." How is this treasure, this "wedge of gold," coined into current money for use as we travel home toward God?

Why do bad things happen to good people? Here is a surprising though Christian answer: So that good people will know they are bad. This does not mean *bad* in the sense of socially unacceptable. Good people are not chronic shoplifters, drunk drivers, or pornographers. But good people *are* sinners. The Bible clearly says, "For all have sinned; all fall short of God's glorious standard" (Romans 3:23). Even the apostle Paul—who was not only a very good man but among the greatest in human history—suffered so that he would not be proud.

John Donne—himself no stranger to suffering—provides us with the most effective response to affliction: "I take mine own into contemplation and so secure myself by making my recourse to my God, who is our only security." Turn to God and by doing so, convert the raw gold of tribulation into "current money" useful for this human journey.

I was given a thorn in my flesh, a messenger from Satan to torment me and keep me from getting proud. Three different times I begged the Lord to take it away. Each time he said, "My gracious favor is all you need. My power works best in your weakness." So now I am glad to boast about my weaknesses, so that the power of Christ may work through me. Since I know it is all for Christ's good, I am quite content with my weaknesses and with insults, hardships, persecutions, and calamities. For when I am weak, then I am strong. 2 Corinthians 12:7-10

Let Us with a Gladsome Mind

Let us with a gladsome mind
Praise the Lord, for He is kind:
For His mercies shall endure,
Ever faithful, ever sure.

Let us sound His name abroad,
For of gods He is the God:
For His mercies shall endure,
Ever faithful, ever sure.

He, with all-commanding might,
Filled the new-made world with light:
For His mercies shall endure,
Ever faithful, ever sure.

All things living He doth feed;
His full hand supplies their need:
For His mercies shall endure,
Ever faithful, ever sure.

Let us then with gladsome mind
Praise the Lord, for He is kind:
For His mercies shall endure,
Ever faithful, ever sure.

JOHN MILTON (1608–1674)

JOHN MILTON, a devoted Christian and outstanding writer, has blessed the Christian church immensely with his literary works. A poet of incredible talent, he ranks second only to Shakespeare among the English writers of all time.

Milton exhibited his talent early in life, and by age twenty-four he had written three excellent poems: "On the Meaning of Christ's Nativity," "L'Allegro," and "Il Penseroso." In the next few years he wrote poems that would guarantee his immortality in literature—among them, "Lycidas."

In addition to poetry, he wrote scholarly and polemical essays on religious, social, and educational issues in England. Between 1655 and 1661, Milton—now blind—completed *De Doctrina Christiana,* an exposition of Christian doctrine derived from his interpretation of the Bible. As this work proved, Milton didn't let his disability slow him down. He continued to write with the help of people who read to him and took dictation from him. Milton devoted the last years of his life to his greatest works.

The epic *Paradise Lost* (1667), his version of man's creation and fall; *Paradise Regained* (1671), the temptation of Jesus, who unlike Adam, would not fall; and *Samson Agonistes* (1671), Samson's tribulation and triumph in the form of Greek tragedy, assured Milton's reputation as a great poet.

Today's poem is one of Milton's earliest works. At the age of fifteen, he penned this metrical version of Psalm 136, in which each verse ends with "For his mercy endureth for ever" (KJV). Perhaps, when Milton composed these verses, he couldn't have imagined the depth of reality that lay behind them, especially since he still had his sight. But the trials he faced—including blindness—were opportunities for God to show him just how faithful and kind the Lord truly is. His mercies do indeed endure forever.

Give thanks to him who alone does mighty miracles. His faithful love endures forever. Psalm 136:4

Pied[a] Beauty

Glory be to God for dappled things—
For skies of couple-color as a brinded[b] cow;
For rose-moles all in stipple[c] upon trout that swim;
Fresh-firecoal chestnut-falls; finches' wings;
Landscape plotted and pieced—fold, fallow, and plough;
And áll trádes, their gear and tackle and trim.

All things counter, original, spare, strange;
Whatever is fickle, freckled (who knows how?)
With swift, slow; sweet, sour; adazzle, dim;
He fathers-forth whose beauty is past change:
Praise him.

GERARD MANLEY HOPKINS (1844–1889)

[a]having two or more colors, in patches or blotches [b]brownish orange in color with streaks of gray [c]speckle; fleck

WE SAY that beauty is in the eye of the beholder. Why do we never say that it is in the eye of the Creator? That is what Hopkins suggests indirectly in this poem as he praises God for the diversity of color in creation.

As we might expect, Hopkins praises God for the aspects of creation that we all find beautiful, such as the sky at sunrise or sunset, a rainbow trout, autumn colors, and finches' wings. But he doesn't stop there. He also praises God for things most of us may not find beautiful. Hopkins points to the "brinded cow"; a plotted, fallow landscape; dappled things; and "all things counter, original, spare, strange; whatever is fickle, freckled (who knows how?)." Why does Hopkins find beauty in the unattractive? Simply because all creation comes from God and displays the diversification of his being. That is not to say that God has an ugly side to his appearance or character. We have a distorted view of beauty that is similar to our culture's view of life, which doesn't appreciate the unborn, the disabled, or the elderly. But all life has worth because it comes from God. Likewise, all creation is in some way beautiful because God made it.

As we look at God's handiwork, let us view it with an open mind and praise God for everything in his creation—especially things striped, streaked, and spotted. God did not paint an unblemished creation; the blemishes are what beautify it.

And God said, "Let the earth bring forth every kind of animal—livestock, small animals, and wildlife." And so it was. God made all sorts of wild animals, livestock, and small animals, each able to reproduce more of its own kind. And God saw that it was good. Genesis 1:24-25

Of the Father's Love Begotten

Of the Father's love begotten,
Ere the worlds began to be,
He is Alpha and Omega,
He the source, the ending He;
Of the things that are, that have been,
And that future years shall see,
Evermore and evermore.

O ye heights of heaven, adore Him;
Angel hosts, His praises sing;
Powers, dominions, bow before Him,
And extol our God and King;
Let no tongue on earth be silent,
Every voice in concert ring,
Evermore and evermore.

Christ, to Thee with God the Father,
And, O Holy Ghost, to Thee,
Hymn and chant and high thanksgiving,
And unwearied praises be:
Honor, glory, and dominion,
And eternal victory,
Evermore and evermore.

AURELIUS CLEMENS PRUDENTIUS (348–c. 410)
Translated by John Mason Neale (1818–1866) and Henry W. Baker (1821–1877)

BORN in Spain, Prudentius trained to become a lawyer and rose high in the civil service as a provincial governor of his country. He ended his career at the age of fifty-seven to devote his life to Christ. At this time he published his writings, which had a great influence on subsequent Christian poetry.

Three of his prose works dealt with apologetical and theological themes: the *Apotheosis* (on the divinity of Christ), the *Hamartigenia* (on the origin of sin), and the *Contra Symmachum* (against a brief reappearance of paganism in Rome). He modeled his poetic style after classical Latin forms as an attempt to take the best of Roman culture and consecrate it to the church.

In this poem Prudentius affirms the orthodox position concerning Christ's eternal deity. This position counters an ancient heresy known as Arianism, which promoted the erroneous view that the Son of God was not coeternal with the Father and therefore was a lesser deity. This heresy developed from a misconception of the phrase *only begotten* as applied to the Son of God. The term "only begotten Son of God" does not mean that God the Father sired his Son, Jesus. Rather, "only begotten Son" in Greek indicates that Jesus was especially dear to the Father—"his one and only."

This is another great mystery of the godhead. How can a son exist without being sired? But Christ did and does. The apostle John wrote: "In the beginning the Word already existed. He was with God, and he was God. He was in the beginning with God. He created everything there is. Nothing exists that he didn't make" (John 1:1-3). Let us in awe and wonder praise Christ, the Eternal One, the Alpha and Omega.

See, I am coming soon, and my reward is with me, to repay all according to their deeds. I am the Alpha and the Omega, the First and the Last, the Beginning and the End. Revelation 22:12-13

Do People Moulder Equally

Do People moulder[a] equally,
They bury, in the Grave?
I do believe a Species
As positively live

As I, who testify it
Deny that I—am dead—
And fill my Lungs, for Witness—
From Tanks—above my Head—

I say to you, said Jesus—
That there be standing here—
A Sort, that shall not taste of Death—
If Jesus was sincere—

I need no further Argue—
That statement of the Lord
Is not a controvertible—
He told me, Death was dead—

EMILY DICKINSON (1830–1886)

[a]decay

EMILY DICKINSON has posed a question few would think to ask. It takes a poet to consider if the dead decay equally. But then again, such thoughts are not even possible without a Savior to first declare, "Some . . . shall not taste of death" (Matthew 16:28).

Dickinson answers her own question. She believes that some people who are in the grave are as alive as she. In fact, she testifies that she draws her life from a divine source—the "Tanks" above her head. The third stanza repeats the promise of Matthew 16:28. And finally the poet declares that there can be no argument against the Lord's word. Death indeed is dead.

The King James version of the Bible refers to believers as "peculiar people" (1 Peter 2:9). Today translators have given us a more accurate rendering of this verse. But Emily Dickinson's sketch of the moldering dead agrees with the antiquated translation. She says that there is a certain "species" of the dead who are as alive as she. There is a "sort" of person who will not taste death.

Did you ever know someone who is color blind? In the course of everyday conversation you realize that what you see as green he may guess is brown. How peculiar this is! They sense color differently than the rest of us. Similarly, there is a peculiar species of people who sense death differently than others. For these people (that is, the redeemed) death is not a bitter poison. Their faith transforms their taste. Their crucified and resurrected Savior, Jesus Christ, has swallowed up the fearful flavor of death forever.

For the Son of Man is to come with his angels in the glory of his Father, and then he will repay everyone for what has been done. Truly I tell you, there are some standing here who will not taste death before they see the Son of Man coming in his kingdom. Matthew 16:27-28, NRSV

The Harp . . . PART ONE

The harp the monarch minstrel swept,
The king of men, the loved of Heaven,
Which music hallowed while she wept
O'er tones her heart of hearts had given,
Redoubled be her tears, its chords are riven![a]
It softened men of iron mould,
It gave them virtues not their own;
No ear so dull, no soul so cold,
That felt not, fired not to the tone,
Till David's lyre grew mightier than his throne!

(continued in next day's reading)

LORD BYRON (1788–1824)

[a]torn apart; shattered

IF DAVID had been a president of the United States instead of a king of Israel, how would the newspaper headlines have read? "Warlord Wins Election!" or "President Despised by Wife"; David's Son Rapes Sister" or "President Caught in Adultery." These are among the scandals that dogged David throughout his life. But when Byron commemorated this Israelite king, he wrote of the harp David played. Today few people even know who David was much less that his sons rebelled or that he foolishly brought a great plague on Israel. Yet millions can recite from memory his Psalm 23: "The Lord is my shepherd; I shall not want" (KJV).

Why do we make mistakes, pursue bad decisions, and fall into sin? For the same reason David did: We are human. This is not an excuse; it is a fact. Only one human being never made a mistake. He is Jesus Christ. David wasn't chosen king of Israel because he was perfect. Remember what God told Samuel when David was anointed king? "People judge by outward appearance, but the Lord looks at a person's thoughts and intentions" (1 Samuel 16:7).

So we make mistakes, sin, repent, and try again as David did. Did he stop playing his harp at any time in his life? We don't know. But David wrote many psalms. He was likely an accomplished musician and may have frequently stopped to tune his instrument and sing praises to God. So we remember him less for his sins than for his songs.

We too can stop in the midst of life's tumult and disappointment and offer this prayer: "Come, thou fount of ev'ry blessing, tune my heart to sing thy grace."[a]

But if we confess our sins to him, he is faithful and just to forgive us and to cleanse us from every wrong. 1 John 1:9

[a]from the hymn "Come, Thou Fount of Every Blessing" by Robert Robinson

It told the triumphs of our king,
It wafted glory to our God;
It made our gladdened valleys ring,
The cedars bow, the mountains nod;
Its sound aspired to heaven and there abode!
Since then, though heard on earth no more,
Devotion and her daughter Love
Still bid the bursting spirit soar
To sounds that seem as from above,
In dreams that day's broad light can not remove.

LORD BYRON (1788–1824)

MOST prominent of the English romantic poets, Lord Byron had a profound effect on the literature of Europe. His adventures were equally prominent. For example, in 1823 he joined the Greek insurgents, recruited a regiment for the cause of Greek independence, and contributed large sums of money to it. The Greeks made him commander in chief of their forces in January 1824. The poet died at Missolonghi three months later.

Byron filled his short life with romance and adventure. The poet was a model of the romantic hero. In today's poem Byron writes of another hero, not romantic, but real—David, king of Israel.

Those of us who lead ordinary lives can hardly comprehend David's life—exploits, riches, intrigue, warfare, rebellion, death! But there is one thing we share with this extraordinary man—faith. So we are his companions as he writes, "Yea, though I walk through the valley of the shadow of death, I will fear no evil: for thou art with me" (Psalm 23:4, KJV). We have no idea what ancient modal tune David may have played on his harp while singing these words. But as Byron wrote, "Since then, though heard on earth no more, devotion and her daughter Love still bid the bursting spirit soar."

Devotion and love will indelibly mark our lives when we accept Christ as our Savior. With David, we share the assurance that God forgives our sins, and so we can sing with him, "Surely goodness and mercy shall follow me all the days of my life: and I will dwell in the house of the Lord for ever" (23:6, KJV).

Have mercy on me, O God, because of your unfailing love. Because of your great compassion, blot out the stain of my sins. Wash me clean from my guilt. Purify me from my sin. Psalm 51:1-2

Muse in Late November

I greet you, son, with joy and winter rue:[a]
For you the fatted calf, the while I bind
Sackcloth against my heart for siring you
At sundown and the twilight. Child, you find
A sire sore tired of striving with the winds;
Climbing Mount Nebo with laborious breath
To view the land of promise through blurred lens,
Knowing he can not enter, feeling death.

And, as old Israel called his dozen sons
And placed his withered hands upon each head
Ere he was silent with the skeletons
In Mamre[b] *of the cold, cave-chambered dead,*
So would I bless you with a dreamer's will:
The dream that baffles me, may you fulfill.

JONATHAN HENDERSON BROOKS (1904–1945)

[a]remorse [b]the burial place of the patriarchs Abraham, Isaac, Jacob, and Joseph

THIS POEM moves between extremes: joy and remorse, the fatted calf and the sackcloth, a child and a sire, silent skeletons and a dreamer's will. A parent speaks to a child. The poet likens this parent to Moses whom God denied entrance into the Promised Land (Deuteronomy 32:48-52) and to Jacob, who blessed his sons on his deathbed (Genesis 49:1-27). Yet, ultimately, it is a poem about hope—the hope of one generation's dreams fulfilled in the next.

The poet realizes that he will die before he fulfills his dream. Yet his hope is that his son will achieve what he could not. Thus, like Moses, who views the Promised Land from Mount Nebo, or Jacob, who blesses his sons and dies in a foreign land, the poet passes on his dream to his heir.

The book of Hebrews touches upon the kind of hope that the poet has. The writer lists God's faithful ones, including Abraham, who "died without receiving what God had promised them, but they saw it all from a distance and welcomed the promises of God" (11:13). The promise, the dream they desired to see fulfilled, was the heavenly home God was preparing for them (11:16).

As Christians we have this hope too. We anticipate the day when Christ will return to take us home with him. We can wait patiently and confidently, trusting God who alone knows the hour of his Son's return. So what can we do while we wait, while we witness the passing of our lifetime without Christ appearing? We can pass on our hope, our dream, blessing others with a dreamer's will. We can pray that the dream that baffles us will be fulfilled in our children's lifetime.

[Jacob said,] "Soon I will die. Bury me with my father and grandfather in the cave in Ephron's field. This is the cave in the field of Machpelah, near Mamre in Canaan, which Abraham bought from Ephron the Hittite for a permanent burial place." Genesis 49:29-30

The Tree of Knowledge

The sacred tree midst the fair orchard grew;
The Phoenix Truth did on it rest,
And built his perfumed nest.
That right Porphyrian tree which did true logic shew,
Each leaf did learnëd notions give,
And th' apples were demonstrative.
So clear their color and divine,
The very shade they cast did other lights out-shine.

Taste not, said God; 'tis mine and angels' meat;
A certain death does sit
Like an ill worm i'th' core of it.
Ye cannot know and live, nor live or know and eat.
Thus spoke God, yet man did go
Ignorantly on to know;
Grew so more blind, and she
Who tempted him to this, grew yet more blind than he.

The only science man by this did get,
Was but to know he nothing knew;
He straight his nakedness did view,
His ignorant poor estate, and was ashamed of it.
Yet searches probabilities,
And rhetoric, and fallacies,
And seeds by useless pride
With slight and withering leaves that nakedness to hide.

Henceforth, said God, the wretched sons of earth
Shall sweat for food in vain
That will not long sustain,
And bring with labor forth each fond abortive birth.
That serpent, too, their pride,
Which aims at things denied,
That learned and eloquent lust
Instead of mounting high, shall creep upon the dust.

ABRAHAM COWLEY (1618–1667)

ABRAHAM COWLEY uses two images that convey the horror of the tree of knowledge. First is the phoenix named Truth, who sits near his perfumed nest, in the tree that poisoned the entire human race. Egyptian mythology says the phoenix was a beautiful bird that lived in the Arabian desert for five or six hundred years. He set himself on fire and rose, renewed from the ashes, to start another long life. It is symbolic of immortality.

Cowley calls the tree of knowledge "that right Porphyrian tree," referring to a method of logic—developed by the Greek philosopher Porphyry—that attempts to explain our existence. The word *Being* appears at the top of Porphyry's tree, from which extend ten branches named for Aristotle's ten supreme predicaments. These each have two branches named material substance and immaterial substance.

Porphyry saw philosophy as a means to salvation just as many today see knowledge as a means of salvation and/or immortality. However, the branches of the tree of knowledge are impossible to ascend. One never can find the way to the top—the immortal rest in the phoenix's nest. From Eve's day to the present, our race has been hopelessly entangled in the deadly grasp of this thorny maze.

But there is hope. Another tree grew in the Garden called the tree of life. This tree grows along the banks of the river of life in the new Jerusalem (Revelation 22:1-2). By faith in Jesus Christ we will taste of this tree, and our Savior will usher us into the joy of the long-lost garden, where we can live "in the hope of eternal life that God, who never lies, promised before the ages began" (Titus 1:2, NRSV).

Then the Lord God said, "The people have become as we are, knowing everything, both good and evil. What if they eat the fruit of the tree of life? Then they will live forever!" Genesis 3:22

Love Divine, All Loves Excelling

Love Divine, all loves excelling,
Joy of heaven, to earth come down,
Fix in us thy humble dwelling,
All thy faithful mercies crown.
Jesu, thou art all compassion,
Pure unbounded love thou art;
Visit us with thy salvation,
Enter every trembling heart.

Breathe, O breathe thy loving Spirit
Into every troubled breast,
Let us all in thee inherit,
Let us find that second rest:
Take away our power of sinning,
Alpha and Omega be,
End of faith as its beginning,
Set our hearts at liberty.

Come, almighty to deliver,
Let us all thy life receive;
Suddenly return, and never,
Never more thy temples leave.
Thee we would be always blessing,
Serve thee as thy hosts above,
Pray, and praise thee without ceasing,
Glory in thy perfect love.

Finish then thy New Creation,
Pure and spotless let us be;
Let us see thy great salvation
Perfectly restored in thee,
Changed from glory into glory
Till in heaven we take our place,
Till we cast our crowns before thee,
Lost in wonder, love, and praise!

CHARLES WESLEY (1707–1788)

CHARLES WESLEY was a prolific hymn writer, writing nearly eight thousand hymns during his lifetime! He wrote hymns to provide material for public worship, especially among the Methodists. He brought to his writing a rich understanding of Scripture, filling many of his hymns with scriptural quotations or allusions. He also brought his knowledge of literature in English, Latin, and Greek, which helped him write elevated and often exquisite verse—even though he wrote for the common man and woman.

Among the hymns most noted for its poetic beauty is "Love Divine, All Loves Excelling." This poem celebrates God's love, which he demonstrated by sending his Son to live among humanity *on* earth and then *in* the hearts of those who believe in him. Stanza by stanza, the poem dwells on the theme of the indwelling Christ: "Fix in us thy humble dwelling, . . . Enter every trembling heart." Then again in the second stanza we read: "Breathe, O breathe thy loving Spirit into every troubled breast."

The indwelling of Christ through his Spirit commences the Christian life. From thereon, Christ's goal is to sanctify us and purify us:

> *Finish then thy New Creation,*
> *Pure and spotless let us be;*
> *Let us see thy great salvation*
> *Perfectly restored in thee.*

When Christ changes us into his glorious image (2 Corinthians 3:17-18), we will become temples for him to live in forever. The poet exclaims: "Suddenly return, and never, never more thy temples leave." May we prepare our hearts for Christ's return, looking forward to the day when we "cast our crowns before thee, lost in wonder, love, and praise!"

➾ *Look! The virgin will conceive a child! She will give birth to a son and will call him Immanuel—"God is with us."* Isaiah 7:14

To God

AN ANTHEM, SUNG IN THE CHAPEL
AT WHITE-HALL, BEFORE THE KING

Verse. My God, I'm wounded by my sin
And sore without, and sick within:
Ver. Chor. I come to Thee, in hope to find
Salve for my body, and my mind.
Verse. In Gilead though no balm be found,
To ease this smart, or cure this wound;
Ver. Chor. Yet, Lord, I know there is with Thee
All saving health, and help for me.
Verse. Then reach Thou forth that hand of
Thine,
That pours in oil, as well as wine.
Ver. Chor. And let it work, for I'll endure
The utmost smart, so thou wilt cure.

ROBERT HERRICK (1591–1674)

GILEAD is the biblical name of the region east of the Jordan River and northeast of the Dead Sea. It is an area of rugged highlands, known for its pastures, vineyards, and olive groves. Today this region lies in Jordan. The balm of Gilead, an aromatic honey-colored resin, comes from the Mecca balsam found in this area and was used for incense and medicinal purposes.

Robert Herrick uses this substance to contrast superficial or physical healing to the spiritual healing that only Christ can perform in the hearts of sinners. Herrick proclaims that his sin has wounded him, making him "sore without, and sick within." But he has hope of being cured because he knows whom to go to for treatment: "I come to Thee, in hope to find salve for my body, and my mind."

Why did the poet approach God? Why didn't he look for an earthly cure to his problem? Herrick knew that he needed more than physical healing, which the balm of Gilead supposedly offered. He needed spiritual healing. Since there is no physical cure for this spiritual malady, the prophet Jeremiah despaired of the existence of such a balm (Jeremiah 8:22; 46:11), which Herrick echoes: "In Gilead though no balm be found, to ease this smart, or cure this wound."

Herrick's illness infects all of humanity. The Bible diagnoses it as sin: "For all have sinned; all fall short of God's glorious standard" (Romans 3:23). Unfortunately, many do not recognize how serious their condition is. They look for a cure in possessions, pleasure, relationships—whatever will ease their pain. But nothing except the blood of Christ cures our sinful condition. That is why we should ask God to "reach Thou forth that hand of Thine, that pours in oil, as well as wine. And let it work . . . so thou wilt cure."

➺ *Is there no medicine in Gilead? Is there no physician there? Why is there no healing for the wounds of my people?* Jeremiah 8:22

The Holy Scriptures II

Oh that I knew how all thy lights combine,
And the configurations of their glory!
Seeing not only how each verse doth shine,
But all the constellations of the story.
This verse marks that, and both do make a motion
Unto a third, that ten leaves off doth lie:
Then as dispersed herbs do watch a potion,
These three make up some Christian's destiny:
Such are thy secrets, which my life makes good,
And comments on thee: for in every thing
Thy words do find me out, and parallels bring,
And in another make me understood.
Stars are poor books, and oftentimes do miss:
This book of stars lights to eternal bliss.

GEORGE HERBERT (1593–1633)

THE WORDS of the Bible, says George Herbert, are not only like stars in the sky but also like herbs dispersed in a potion or stew. With this image he brings Scripture and its effectiveness close to our lives.

The poet mentions three typical Bible verses. The first verse points to a second and these two motion toward a third. For example: John 14:6 says, "I am . . . the life." This verse points us to Colossians 3:4, which says, "Christ . . . is your real life." Jesus is the life and not only so, he is *our* life. Now these two verses direct us to the following destination: "This is what God has testified: He has given us eternal life, and this life is in his Son. So whoever has God's Son has life; whoever does not have his Son does not have life" (1 John 5:11-12).

Imagine these three verses as the poet's herbs dispersed into the stew of our life. What do they do there? Herbert says that they watch. This could mean that they are guardians standing watch over our soul. But Herbert's insight is deeper, more subjective. He was an early seventeenth-century poet, an expert in language and words. His understanding of the word *watch* comes from the Germanic word that shares its origin with *vigor.* A vigorous person is healthy, full of life, wide awake. So in the Germanic languages this began to mean *wakefulness,* thus *watch.*

In this poem the herbs that watch a potion invigorate it. They strengthen its flavor, giving it life. This is exactly how Scripture functions in a Christian. We do not go about spouting Bible verses aloud, nor do we tell everyone we meet that we are Christians. Yet we have an unmistakable flavor and vigor that comes from the Lord's word invisibly dispersed in our soul like herbs in a savory stew.

Your words are what sustain me. They bring me great joy and are my heart's delight, for I bear your name, O Lord God Almighty. Jeremiah 15:16

Ruth

She stood breast high amid the corn,
Clasped by the golden light of morn,
Like the sweetheart of the sun,
Who many a glowing kiss had won.

On her cheek an autumn flush,
Deeply ripened;—such a blush
In the midst of brown was born,
Like red poppies grown in corn.

Round her eyes her tresses fell,
Which were blackest none could tell,
But long lashes veiled a light,
That had else been all too bright.

And her hat, with shady brim,
Made her tressy forehead dim;—
Thus she stood amid the stooks,[a]
Praising God with sweetest looks:—

Sure, I said, heaven did not mean,
Where I reap thou shouldst but glean;
Lay thy sheaf adown and come,
Share my harvest and my home.

THOMAS HOOD (1799–1845)

[a] a shock of sheaves

DID YOU ever say to yourself, "I'm not good enough. I wish I'd come from a better background"? You may have variations on this thought, such as wishing for a better education, an improved job history, or a finer family name. But no one can change his or her past.

Consider Ruth from Moab. The Moabites descended from the son of Lot, who was the offspring of Lot's incest with his elder daughter (Genesis 19:30-38). Hardly a promising beginning. Many negative prophecies were spoken against Moab, such as "No Ammonites or Moabites, or any of their descendants for ten generations, may be included in the assembly of the Lord" (Deuteronomy 23:3). They were thoroughly cut off from the God of Israel.

Ruth was so poor that in order to eat she followed behind harvesting crews and picked up the grain they missed. Today, such people gather discarded food from Dumpsters behind grocery stores and restaurants. Their plight sounds something like Paul's description of our former spiritual condition: "In those days you were living apart from Christ. . . . You lived in this world without God and without hope" (Ephesians 2:12). Even with a good name, the best education, and a successful career, we are all like Moabites as far as God's inheritance is concerned. At best, we try to glean spiritual nourishment from among the dry stubble of earthly idols.

But this is no longer our lot. Instead, we seek the rich and glorious inheritance God has given us (Ephesians 1:18). And so give "all honor to the God and Father of our Lord Jesus Christ, for it is by his boundless mercy that God has given us the privilege of being born again. . . . For God has reserved a priceless inheritance for his children" (1 Peter 1:3-4).

Boaz ordered his young men, "Let her gather grain right among the sheaves without stopping her. And pull out some heads of barley from the bundles and drop them on purpose for her. Let her pick them up, and don't give her a hard time!" Ruth 2:15-16

from Hezekiah

From the bleak beach and broad expanse of sea,
To lofty Salem, thought direct thy way;
Mount thy light chariot, move along the plains,
And end thy flight where Hezekiah reigns.
How swiftly thought has passed from land to land,
And quite outrun time's measuring glass of sand,
Great Salem's walls appear and I resort
To view the state of Hezekiah's court.
Well may that king a pious verse inspire,
Who cleansed the temple, who revived the choir,
Pleased with the service David fixed before,
That heavenly music might on earth adore.
Deep-robed in white, he made the Levites stand
With cymbals, harps, and psalteries in their hand;
He gave the priests their trumpets, prompt to raise
The tuneful soul, by force of sound to praise.
A skillful master for the song he chose,
The songs were David's these, and Asaph's those.
Then burns their offering, all around rejoice,
Each tunes his instrument to join the voice;
The trumpets sounded, and the singers sung,
The people worshipped and the temple rung.
Each while the victim burns presents his heart,
The priest blesses, and the people part.
Hail sacred music! since you know to draw
The soul to Heaven, the spirit to the law,
I come to prove thy force, thy warbling string
May tune my soul to write what others sing.

THOMAS PARNELL (1679–1718)

DAVID prepared Jerusalem to be the site of the Temple—the unique place of worship for the Jews. He made a place for the Ark of God and carefully arranged for the proper handling and transport of this most important ceremonial object (1 Chronicles 15:1-15). Next he turned to another vital part of the worship of God—music (15:16).

Music permeated Israel's daily life: at family parties (Luke 15:25), in celebration of war heroes (Judges 11:34), in coronations (1 Kings 1:39-40), for entertainment (Isaiah 24:8-9), for work (Isaiah 16:10), and for mourning (Matthew 9:23).

David's careful organization of Temple musicians and singers reflects the importance of music in Hebrew worship. Scholars believe the superscriptions of the psalms contain musical notations (see, for example, Psalms 4–7). The familiar word *selah* found throughout the psalms may have been a direction to the conductor, indicating a segue or a pause. The Old Testament contains various references to instruments used for worship and other purposes—cymbals (Nehemiah 12:27), flute (Job 21:12), harp (Genesis 31:27), lyre (Psalm 33:2), ram's horn (Exodus 19:13), tambourine (Psalm 149:3), and trumpet (Numbers 10:5-10).

Today's poem tells of Hezekiah's revival of worship and its vital musical accompaniment (see 2 Chronicles 29:25-30). He calls upon this music—"Hail sacred music!"—to draw his soul to heaven and his spirit to God's law. "I come to prove thy force," he sings. And forceful it is to lift the heart to celebrate divine goodness and call to mind the mighty acts of God. Let us not neglect our need for worship.

The entire assembly worshiped the Lord as the singers sang and the trumpets blew, until all the burnt offerings were finished. . . . King Hezekiah and the officials ordered the Levites to praise the Lord with the psalms of David and Asaph the seer. So they offered joyous praise and bowed down in worship. 2 Chronicles 29:28, 30

Jeremie .17

O Lord I shall be whole in deed,
If I be healed of thee:
If thou vouchsafe now me to save,
Then shall I saved be.

Thou art my prayer and my praise,
I have none other fort:
To give thee thanks for all my help,
To thee I must resort.

Behold those men that say to me
In mockage and in scorn,
Where is the word of God say they?
Let it come us beforne.

Though not withstanding when I led,
Thy flock in godly train,
Into thy ways by violence
I did them not constrain.

Ne yet the death of any man,
I never did desire,
Thou knowst right well that before thee
My tongue was not a liar.

Be not to me too terrible
O Lord, but me refrain:
For thou art he in whom I hope
In peril and in pain.

Confound me not, but confound them
That do my life pursue:
Nor fear me not, but make thou them
To fear and eke[a] *to rue.*[b]

And pour on them their painful plague
When thou shalt see the time,
And them destroy that have thee done
So detestable crime.

JOHN HALL (1529–1566)

[a]also [b]regret bitterly

INTO thy ways by violence I did them not constrain. Ne yet the death of any man, I never did desire, Thou knowst right well that before thee my tongue was not a liar." John Hall paraphrases Jeremiah 17:16. Jeremiah, while shepherding Israel, did not use threats to bring the people into God's way. We gather from his words that there are two ways to relay God's message—God's way and humanity's way.

The Lord's way involves love, mercy, and grace: "The Lord, the Lord, a God merciful and gracious, slow to anger, and abounding in steadfast love and faithfulness, keeping steadfast love for the thousandth generation" (Exodus 34:6-7, NRSV). God does not manipulate people to do his will nor command his servants to do so.

Fanny Crosby once said, "Don't tell a man he's a sinner; he knows that already. Tell him there is pardon and love waiting for him . . . and never give him up! People want and need love." We could take a cue from Ms. Crosby and pray: *Dear Savior, I pray that you will rescue the perishing and care for the dying. Snatch them in pity from sin and the grave. Lord, look upon the human heart crushed by the tempter; feelings lie buried there that your grace can restore. Praise to you, Jesus. You are merciful; you will save.*[a]

O Lord, you alone can heal me; you alone can save. My praises are for you alone! People scoff at me and say, "What is this 'message from the Lord' you keep talking about? Why don't your predictions come true?" Lord, I have not abandoned my job as a shepherd for your people. I have not urged you to send disaster. It is your message I have given them, not my own. Jeremiah 17:14-16

[a]adapted from Crosby's hymn "Rescue the Perishing"

Sion Lies Waste

Sion lies waste and thy Jerusalem
O Lord, is fallen to utter desolation.
Against thy prophets and thy holy men
The sin hath wrought a fatal combination:
Profaned thy name, thy worship overthrown,
And made thee, living Lord, a God unknown.

Thy powerful laws, thy wonders of creation,
Thy word incarnate, glorious heaven, dark hell,
Lie shadowed under man's degeneration,
Thy Christ still crucified for doing well.
Impiety, O Lord, sits on thy throne,
Which makes thee, living light, a God unknown.

Man's superstition hath thy truths entombed,
His atheism again her pomps defaceth;
That sensual unsatiable vast womb
Of thy seen church thy unseen church disgraceth.
There lives no truth with them that seem thine own,
Which makes thee, living Lord, a God unknown.

Yet unto thee, Lord, mirror of transgression,
We who for earthly idols have forsaken
Thy heavenly image, sinless, pure impression,
And so in nets of vanity lie taken
All desolate implore that to thine own,
Lord, thou no longer live a God unknown.

Yet, Lord, let Israel's plagues not be eternal,
Nor sin forever cloud thy sacred mountains,
Nor with false flames, spiritual but infernal,
Dry up thy mercy's ever springing fountains.
Rather, sweet Jesus, fill up time and come
To yield the sin her everlasting doom.

FULKE GREVILLE, 1ST BARON BROOKE (1554–1628)

BARON BROOKE despairs that God is unknown. First he cites the desolation of Jerusalem; second, the shadow of the degeneration of humanity. Then in stanza 3 he describes the disgraceful superstition of the "sensual insatiable . . . seen church." In Brooke's day this probably referred to Roman Catholicism.

Next are the vanities of earthly idols that have defaced the Lord's heavenly image—the materialistic distractions in each of our hearts that veil the Lord's face.

But why should Brooke care? After all, he is a prominent figure in the courts of Elizabeth I and James I, a foreign diplomat, a member of Parliament four times, treasurer of the navy, and Chancellor of the Exchequer (the accounting and auditing department of the British treasury). Consider how formidable he would be in today's world. We might well ask how all his power and prestige did not come to fill his heart and deface the heavenly image. Somehow, thankfully, "infernal false flames" did not dry up the ever-springing fountain in Baron Brooke, and so he prayed for the return of Christ.

"One day Jesus told his disciples a story to illustrate their need for constant prayer and to show them that they must never give up" (Luke 18:1). Jesus told of a powerless woman in a hopeless situation who persisted in appealing for justice and finally received it. Today's poem describes a world that has made the living Lord a God unknown. So what are we to do if we, like Baron Brooke, still have a perpetual spring within us giving eternal life (John 4:14)? Like the poet, we can pray and hope in the Lord's second coming. This is the faith that Christ desires to find when he returns (Luke 18:8).

Then the Lord said, "Learn a lesson from this evil judge. Even he rendered a just decision in the end, so don't you think God will surely give justice to his chosen people who plead with him day and night?"
Luke 18:6-7

For the Baptist

The last and greatest herald of Heaven's King,
Girt with rough skins, hies[a] *to the deserts wild,*
Among that savage brood the woods forth bring,
Which he than man more harmless found and
mild:
His food was blossoms, and what young doth
spring,
With honey that from virgin hives distilled;
Parched body, hollow eyes, some uncouth thing
Made him appear, long since from Earth exiled.
There burst he forth; All ye, whose hopes rely
On God, with me amidst these deserts mourn,
Repent, repent, and from old errors turn.
Who listened to his voice, obeyed his cry?
Only the echoes which he made relent,
Rung from their marble caves, repent, repent.

WILLIAM DRUMMOND OF HAWTHORNDEN
(1585–1649)

[a]to hurry or hasten

OUR WORLD is far removed from the times and events surrounding God's coming in Christ. So we find it difficult to appreciate the impact of John the Baptist appearing in Israel. After eight hundred years Isaiah's ancient utterance came alive in this new prophet. Why did God send John declaring, "Prepare the way of the Lord, make his paths straight" (Mark 1:3, NRSV; Isaiah 40:3)? Because this was the signal to Jerusalem that "she [had] served her term, that her penalty [was] paid" (Isaiah 40:2, NRSV). John emerged from the wilderness with God's charge to "Comfort, O comfort my people. . . . Speak tenderly to Jerusalem, and cry to her" (40:1-2, NRSV). "People from the whole Judean countryside and all the people of Jerusalem were going out to him, . . . confessing their sins" (Mark 1:5, NRSV), electrified by John's proclamation that their Messiah was at long last about to arrive.

The millennia prophets predicted the arrival of Christ. But none of these prophets lived to see the day of the Lord. When Malachi wrote, "I am sending my messenger to prepare the way before me" (3:1, NRSV), he was referring to the final prophet of the Old Testament age—John the Baptist, who prepared a straight, smooth path for Christ's arrival.

John personally greeted Christ and baptized him. Jesus said that no one was greater than John. "Yet," he added, "the least in the kingdom of heaven is greater than he" (Matthew 11:11, NRSV). This is why Jesus says to believers, "Blessed are your eyes, for they see, and your ears, for they hear. Truly I tell you, many prophets and righteous people longed to see what you see, but did not see it, and to hear what you hear, but did not hear it" (Matthew 13:16-17, NRSV).

Listen! I hear the voice of someone shouting, "Make a highway for the Lord through the wilderness. Make a straight, smooth road through the desert for our God. Fill the valleys and level the hills. Straighten out the curves and smooth off the rough spots." Isaiah 40:3-4

Two Went Up into the Temple to Pray

Two went to pray? o rather say
One went to brag, th'other to pray:

One stands up close and treads on high,
Where th'other dares not send his eye.

One nearer to God's altar trod,
The other to the altar's God.

RICHARD CRASHAW (C. 1613–1649)

"I WILL DO whatever you ask in my name" (John 14:13, NRSV). This promise is both encouraging and puzzling. We could all be assured of answered prayer if we knew what it means to ask in the Lord's name. Could it be as simple as tagging on "in Jesus' name, amen" at the end of a prayer? This is doubtful. If the Pharisee in Luke 18 had ended his prayer this way, do you think God would have accepted him? Not a chance. Why? Luke says that Jesus told the story paraphrased opposite to people who trusted in themselves and their own righteousness (18:9). This man was praying for himself. In other words, he prayed in his own name. He qualifies as one of the hypocrites in Matthew 6:5 who "love to stand and pray in the synagogues and at the street corners, so that they may be seen by others" (NRSV).

As children, many of us ran errands for our mother. Knocking at a neighbor's door, we would say, "My mother sent me to borrow a cup of sugar." The neighbor gladly gave us the sugar because we asked for it in our mother's name. The sugar was not for our use but for our mother's purpose. This analogy describes prayer in the Lord's name.

The praying Pharisee thought he was righteous. He trusted in himself and prayed for his own purpose—so he would be seen by others and glorified in their sight. But whatever we ask in the Lord's name will be answered not because of who we are but because of who Christ is. The main reason God answers our prayers is to fulfill his purpose—so that the Father will be glorified through the Son (John 14:13).

I tell you, this sinner, not the Pharisee, returned home justified before God. For the proud will be humbled, but the humble will be honored. Luke 18:14

The Pulley

When God at first made man,
Having a glass of blessings standing by,
Let us (said he) pour on him all we can;
Let the world's riches, which dispersèd lie,
Contract into a span.

So strength first made a way;
Then beauty flowed, then wisdom, honour,
pleasure.
When almost all was out, God made a stay,
Perceiving that alone of all his treasure
Rest in the bottom lay.

For if I should (said he)
'Bestow this jewel also on my creature,
He would adore my gifts instead of me,
And rest in Nature, not the God of Nature:
So both should losers be.

Yet let him keep the rest,
But keep them with repining restlessness;
Let him be rich and weary, that at least,
If goodness lead him not, yet weariness
May toss him to my breast.

George Herbert (1593–1633)

EDUCATED at Westminster and Trinity College, Cambridge, George Herbert became praelector in rhetoric in 1618 and public orator to the university in 1620. His career took a sudden turn when he became priest of a village parish at Bemerton. His small book on the duties of his new life, *A Priest to the Temple,* expresses both the joys and sorrows of this position. In chronic bad health, Herbert spent his final three years at Bemerton performing pastoral duties while writing and revising his poems.

The point of this poem is that God gave human beings every blessing (strength, beauty, wisdom, honor, and pleasure) except one: rest. He withheld rest so that human beings in their restlessness would seek him. Had God given humans rest, their contentment would have blinded them to their need for God.

In the last years of his life, Herbert knew what it meant to be restless and uneasy. Bad health and pastoral obscurity forced him to come to God again and again. This restlessness "pulled" him to God—hence the title "The Pulley."

We all experience this restlessness. It is the common lot of humanity. Nothing and no one except Jesus Christ can give us rest. May our weariness and our need for rest motivate us to come to Christ.

Jesus said, "Come to me, all of you who are weary and carry heavy burdens, and I will give you rest. Take my yoke upon you. Let me teach you, because I am humble and gentle, and you will find rest for your souls. For my yoke fits perfectly, and the burden I give you is light."
Matthew 11:28-30

Te Martyrum Candidatus

Ah, see the fair chivalry come, the companions of
Christ!
White Horsemen, who ride on white horses, the
Knights of God!
They, for their Lord and their Lover who sacrificed
All, save the sweetness of treading, where He first trod!

These, through the darkness of death, the dominion
of night,
Swept, and they woke in white places at morning tide:
They saw with their eyes, and sang for joy of the sight,
They saw with their eyes the Eyes of the Crucified.

Now, whithersoever He goeth, with Him they go:
White Horsemen, who ride on white horses, oh, fair
to see!
They ride, where the Rivers of Paradise flash and flow,
White Horsemen, with Christ their Captain: for
ever He!

LIONEL JOHNSON (1867–1902)

THIS POEM recasts the vision recorded in Revelation 19:11-16, where John sees Jesus riding on a white horse, symbolic of victory. He goes forth in righteousness to judge and make war against the evil forces and to establish his kingdom of glory.

In this vision Jesus bears the name "Word of God." Elsewhere, John had called God's Son "the Word" (John 1:1) and "the Word of life" (1 John 1:1)—the personal expression of God in the flesh. In this vision the Word of God dips his clothing in blood as he "treads the winepress of the fierceness and wrath of Almighty God" (Revelation 19:15, NKJV), executing vengeance on God's enemies (see Isaiah 63:2-4). The poet says of this, "All, save the sweetness of treading, where He first trod!"

John also sees heavenly armies riding white horses and following Jesus. These, the poet says, are "the companions of Christ! White Horsemen, who ride on white horses, the Knights of God!" Who are these heavenly armies? Some think they are angels. But the poet considers them to be martyrs for Christ—hence the title of the poem. The book of Revelation mentions the martyrs throughout. These are men and women who testified for Christ and consequently lost their lives. Their reward is to be with Christ forever, to follow him wherever he goes, and their first great task is to join him in his conquest of God's enemies. Christ and his heavenly horsemen sweep down from heaven against the armies of the beast, the false prophet, and the kings of the earth.

This conquest is only the beginning. When Christ defeats his enemies, he and his companions will ride forever "where the Rivers of Paradise flash and flow." Martydom for Christ is a small price to pay for such a glorious privilege.

He was clothed with a robe dipped in blood, and his title was the Word of God. The armies of heaven, dressed in pure white linen, followed him on white horses. Revelation 19:13-14

What We, When Face to Face

What we, when face to face we see
The Father of our souls, shall be,
John tells us, doth not yet appear;
Ah! did he tell what we are here!

A mind for thoughts to pass into,
A heart for loves to travel through,
Five senses to detect things near,
Is this the whole that we are here?

Rules baffle instincts—instincts rules,
Wise men are bad—and good are fools,
Facts evil—wishes vain appear,
We cannot go, why are we here?

O may we for assurance' sake,
Some arbitrary judgement take,
And wilfully pronounce it clear,
For this or that 'tis we are here?

Or is it right, and will it do,
To pace the sad confusion through,
And say:—It doth not yet appear,
What we shall be, what we are here?

Ah yet, when all is thought and said,
The heart still overrules the head;
Still what we hope we must believe,
And what is given us receive;

Must still believe, for still we hope
That in a world of larger scope,
What here is faithfully begun
Will be completed, not undone.

My child, we still must think, when we
That ampler life together see,
Some true result will yet appear
Of what we are, together, here.

ARTHUR HUGH CLOUGH (1819–1861)

ARTHUR HUGH CLOUGH explores the question, Why are we here? He unsuccessfully seeks an answer in John's contemplation of what we will be in the coming age: "When he comes we will be like him, for we will see him as he really is" (1 John 3:2).

So Clough attempts to answer his own question, running the gamut of reasons people have offered since time began. Are we here to think, to love, to sense? If so, why do rules baffle our instincts and vice versa?

"For assurance' sake" we desire and accept some arbitrary judgment as to why we are here. But this too falls short of answering the question. Refusing to seek answers or concluding there is no answer is also unsatisfactory. Thus Clough cannot answer his own question.

He does, however, come to a wise conclusion. The reason for our existence will not be clear until we see God face-to-face. Here is where faith comes in: "Still what we hope we must believe, and what is given us receive." What have we received? God's Holy Spirit, which "is God's guarantee that he will give us everything he promised" (Ephesians 1:14). What God has "faithfully begun will be completed, not undone."

Did you ever go into the kitchen to find out what's for dinner? What you're really after is a little taste of the meal to come. This taste is a guarantee in kind that the meal is not only coming but will be worth the wait. So it is with us. "We Christians, . . . have the Holy Spirit within us as a foretaste of future glory," which will be ours when we are face-to-face with God (Romans 8:23).

Yes, dear friends, we are already God's children, and we can't even imagine what we will be like when Christ returns. But we do know that when he comes we will be like him, for we will see him as he really is.
1 John 3:2

The Meaning of the Look

I think that look of Christ might seem to say,
"Thou Peter! Art thou then a common stone
Which I at last must break my heart upon,
For all God's charge to his high angels may
Guard my foot better? Did I yesterday
Wash thy feet, my beloved, that they should run
Quick to deny me 'neath the morning sun?
And do thy kisses, like the rest, betray?
The cock crows coldly.—Go, and manifest
A late contrition, but no bootless fear!
For when thy final need is dreariest,
Thou shalt not be denied, as I am here;
My voice to God and angels shall attest,
'Because I KNOW *this man, let him be clear.'"*

ELIZABETH BARRETT BROWNING (1806–1861)

WHEN Elizabeth Barrett Moulton published *Poems* in 1844, she became one of the most popular writers in England and inspired Robert Browning to write to her of his love for her poems. They met in May 1845 and eloped in 1846.

We consider her poem on what is perhaps the lowest point in the gospel story during the season of highest Christian joy. Why? Because Peter was tremendously enthusiastic for the Lord. Special seasons or ceremonies—such as Christmas or baptism—can produce similar enthusiasm for Christ in any one of us. But as Peter's experience teaches us, enthusiasm can blind us to our weaknesses.

When Jesus told his disciples that he was going away and they could not go with him, Peter asked, "But why can't I come now, Lord? . . . I am ready to die for you" (John 13:36-37). In a moment of enthusiasm, Peter vowed to do more than he possibly could in his own strength. Jesus responded to Peter's zealous devotion with his characteristic truthfulness: "Die for me? No, before the rooster crows tomorrow morning, you will deny three times that you even know me" (13:38). Of course this happened, and we see it as Peter's failure. But it is not only his.

Peter illustrates the failure of all humanity to be faithful to God. Like Peter, we sometimes allow our enthusiasm to get the best of us. Then when the moment of truth comes, we may prove unfaithful, failing God miserably.

Fortunately, God is not like us in this respect. He is faithful. His love and fidelity are seen not only in his birth as a human infant but also in his death as a man. He has redeemed us, failures though we are.

About an hour later someone else insisted, "This must be one of Jesus' disciples because he is a Galilean, too." But Peter said, "Man, I don't know what you are talking about." And as soon as he said these words, the rooster crowed. Luke 22:59-60

Mary and Gabriel PART ONE

Young Mary, loitering once her garden way,
Felt a warm splendour grow in the April day,
As wine that blushes water through. And soon,
Out of the gold air of the afternoon,
One knelt before her: hair he had, or fire,
Bound back above his ears with golden wire,
Baring the eager marble of his face.
Not man's or woman's was the immortal grace
Rounding the limbs beneath that robe of white,
And lighting the proud eyes with changeless light,
Incurious. Calm as his wings, and fair,
That presence filled the garden.
She stood there,
Saying, "What would you, Sir?"
He told his word,
"Blessed art thou of women!" Half she heard,
Hands folded and face bowed, half long had known,
The message of that clear and holy tone,
That fluttered hot sweet sobs about her heart;
Such serene tidings moved such human smart.
Her breath came quick as little flakes of snow.
Her hands crept up her breast. She did but know
It was not hers. She felt a trembling stir
Within her body, a will too strong for her
That held and filled and mastered all. With eyes
Closed, and a thousand soft short broken sighs,
She gave submission; fearful, meek, and glad.

(continued in next day's reading)

RUPERT BROOKE (1887–1915)

RUPERT BROOKE was an English poet. His sonnet series *1914 and Other Poems* (1915) expresses the patriotism and romantic optimism of the early years of World War I. But the handsome and talented Brooke became a symbol of youth wasted in war. On his way to serve in the Dardanelles, he died of blood poisoning.

In this poem Brooke writes of Mary, one of the most amazing people in the Bible. Many Christians, however, fail to appreciate her because of the tendency of some to worship her as a member of the godhead. But the reason she is remarkable is that God didn't give her divinity, but he used her obedience to give his Son humanity.

We speak of the mystery of Christ's person. We say he is entirely God and thoroughly man. Where did he obtain that humanity? It didn't come through a snap of the fingers but through a woman's pregnancy and labor pains.

G. K. Chesterton thought that we cannot understand Christ if we don't understand Mary. He said, "You cannot visit the child without visiting the mother; you cannot in common human life approach the child except through the mother. . . . We must either leave Christ out of Christmas, or Christmas out of Christ, or we must admit, if only as we admit it in an old picture, that those holy heads are too near together for the halos not to mingle and cross."[a]

As we remember the birth of Christ, it is not improper to also remember the woman who gave him birth.

[a]from *The Everlasting Man*

In the sixth month of Elizabeth's pregnancy, God sent the angel Gabriel to Nazareth, a village in Galilee, to a virgin named Mary. She was engaged to be married to a man named Joseph, a descendant of King David. Gabriel appeared to her and said, "Greetings, favored woman! The Lord is with you!" Luke 1:26-28

Mary and Gabriel PART TWO

She wished to speak. Under her breasts she had
Such multitudinous burnings, to and fro,
And throbs not understood; she did not know
If they were hurt or joy for her; but only
That she was grown strange to herself, half lonely,
All wonderful, filled full of pains to come
And thoughts she dare not think, swift thoughts and dumb,
Human, and quaint, her own, yet very far,
Divine, dear, terrible, familiar . . .
Her heart was faint for telling; to relate
Her limbs' sweet treachery, her strange high estate,
Over and over, whispering, half revealing,
Weeping; and so find kindness to her healing.
'Twixt tears and laughter, panic hurrying her,
She raised her eyes to that fair messenger.
He knelt unmoved, immortal; with his eyes
Gazing beyond her, calm to the calm skies;
Radiant, untroubled in his wisdom, kind.
His sheaf of lilies stirred not in the wind.
How should she, pitiful with mortality,
Try the wide peace of that felicity
With ripples of her perplexed shaken heart,
And hints of human ecstasy, human smart,
And whispers of the lonely weight she bore,
And how her womb within was hers no more
And at length hers?
Being tired, she bowed her head;
And said, "So be it!"
The great wings were spread
Showering glory on the fields, and fire.
The whole air, singing, bore him up, and higher,
Unswerving, unreluctant. Soon he shone
A gold speck in the gold skies; then was gone.

The air was colder, and grey. She stood alone.

RUPERT BROOKE (1887–1915)

GABRIEL was busy in Luke 1. First he appeared to the old priest Zechariah (1:11-20) and later to the young woman Mary (1:26-38). The responses of these two are as different as their ages. Zechariah asked, "How can I know this will happen? I'm an old man" (1:18). Mary asked, "But how can I have a baby? I am a virgin" (1:34). Both knew they were unable to do what Gabriel said they would. One was too old; the other too young.

Mary believed the angel's message and wondered how *God* was going to accomplish it. Mary responded with faith, the faith that can verify the unseen things of God (Hebrews 11:1). She said, "May everything you have said come true" (1:38) and became one of "those who through faith and patience inherit the promises" (Hebrews 6:12, NRSV).

Zechariah's response to Gabriel was that of a lawkeeper. Such people think that the responsibility for accomplishing God's desire falls on their shoulders. Gabriel told the old man that his barren wife would have a child who would grow up to prepare Israel for the arrival of Christ (Luke 1:17). This seemed impossible, so Zechariah asked for a sign to prove that the angel's words were true. This is unbelief (1:19-20).

Have you ever read the New Testament and said, "This seems impossible!"? For example, Romans 13:8 may leap up and say, "Pay all your debts, except the debt of love for others. You can never finish paying that!" How will you respond? You must choose either the way of Zechariah according to the law, or the way of Mary according to faith.

Mary responded, "I am the Lord's servant, and I am willing to accept whatever he wants. May everything you have said come true." And then the angel left. Luke 1:38

Annunciation

Salvation to all that will is nigh;
That All, which always is All every where,
Which cannot sin, and yet all sins must bear,
Which cannot die, yet cannot choose but die,
Lo, faithful Virgin, yields himself to lie
In prison, in thy womb; and though he there
Can take no sin, nor thou give, yet he will wear
Taken from thence, flesh, which death's force may
try.
Ere by the spheres time was created, thou
Wast in his mind, who is thy Son, and Brother;
Whom thou conceiv'st, conceived; yea thou art now
Thy Maker's maker, and thy Father's mother;
Thou hast light in dark; and shut'st in little room,
Immensity cloistered in thy dear womb.

JOHN DONNE (1572–1631)

IN THIS POEM John Donne struggles to comprehend the fact that Mary gave birth to "that All, which always is All every where"—that is, our eternal God. Without the insight of faith that is the evidence of things we cannot see (Hebrews 11:1), this is indeed incomprehensible. Look again at this poem. Notice how the poet wrests our language into a form that will express the mystery of Incarnation.

John the apostle may have struggled—like Donne—to express the Incarnation in the same way: "In the beginning the Word already existed. He was with God, and he was God. He was in the beginning with God. He created everything there is. Nothing exists that he didn't make. Life itself was in him, and this life gives light to everyone. . . . So the Word became human and lived here on earth among us" (John 1:1-4, 14).

This Word came to bring "salvation to all." But how the Son of God would accomplish salvation was—at that time—still a mystery. As the apostle Peter wrote, "This salvation was something the prophets wanted to know more about. They prophesied about this gracious salvation prepared for you, even though they had many questions as to what it all could mean. . . . They wondered when and to whom all this would happen" (1 Peter 1:10-11). Even the prophets inspired by the Spirit to foretell the Good News did not entirely grasp the meaning of their own prophecy.

What mystery! Is it any wonder Donne struggled to express the paradox of the Incarnation? Today as you ponder *"Immensity cloistered in [that] dear womb,"* think also about the prophets' own wonder. Then praise God, whose ways and thoughts are far above and beyond our own (Isaiah 55:8-9).

Mary asked the angel, "But how can I have a baby? I am a virgin." The angel replied, "The Holy Spirit will come upon you, and the power of the Most High will overshadow you. So the baby born to you will be holy, and he will be called the Son of God." Luke 1:34-35

The Song of the Virgin Mary

My soul doth magnify the Lord,
My spirit rejoiceth greatly
In God my Savior and his word:
For he hath seen the low degree
Of me his handmaiden truly.
Behold now, after this day,
All generations shall speak of me,
And call me blessed alway.

For he that is only of might
Hath done great things for me;
And holy is his name by right:
As for his endless mercy,
It endureth perpetually,
In every generation,
On them that fear him unfeignedly
Without dissimulation.

He showeth strength with his great arm,
Declaring himself to be of power;
He scattereth the proud to their own harm,
Even with the wicked behavior
Of their own hearts every hour
He putteth down the mighty
From their high seat and great honor,
Exalting them of low degree.

The hungry filleth he with good,
And letteth the rich go empty,
Where his own people want no food:
He thinketh upon his mercy,
And helpeth his servant truly,
Even Israel, as he promised
Unto our fathers perpetually,
Abraham and to his seed.

MILES COVERDALE (1488?–1569)

MILES COVERDALE was an eminent Bible translator, second only to William Tyndale. Coverdale was a Cambridge graduate who fled England because he (under Luther's influence) boldly preached against Roman Catholic doctrine. While abroad, he met Tyndale and served as his assistant, helping Tyndale translate the first five books of the Old Testament. By the time Coverdale produced a complete translation (1537), the king of England, Henry VIII, had broken all ties with the pope and was ready to see the appearance of an English Bible. Thus, the Coverdale Bible became the first English Bible printed in England.

Here we see Coverdale's talent in recasting a beautiful portion of Scripture, namely "Mary's Song" (Luke 1:46-55), often called the "Magnificat" after the first word in the Latin translation. Mary's song greatly resembles that of Hannah, the mother of Samuel (see 1 Samuel 2:1-10). Both women glorified God for the promised birth of a son and thanked God for taking care of the poor, oppressed, and despised.

Mary's song outshines Hannah's in that Mary rejoiced about the birth of "God my Savior"—Jesus, the Son of God. Mary greatly anticipated his coming, because he would put down the mighty and exalt the lowly, and because he would bring salvation to his people Israel. Little did Mary imagine that this salvation meant that Jesus would have to die for the sins of Israel and the whole world.

We must never forget why Christ was born—to die.

Oh, how I praise the Lord. How I rejoice in God my Savior! For he took notice of his lowly servant girl, and now generation after generation will call me blessed. Luke 1:46-48

Christmas Day: . . . PART ONE

In the days of Caesar Augustus
There went forth this decree:
Si quis rectus et justus
Liveth in Galilee,
Let him go up to Jerusalem
And pay his scot to me.

There are passed one after the other
Christmases fifty-three,
Since I sat here with my mother
And heard the great decree:
How they went up to Jerusalem
Out of Galilee.

They have passed one after the other,
Father and mother died,
Brother and sister and brother
Taken and sanctified,
I am left alone in the sitting,
With none to sit beside.

On the fly-leaves of these old prayer-books
The childish writings fade,
Which show that once they were their books
In the days when prayer was made
For other kings and princesses,
William and Adelaide.

(continued in next day's reading)

JOHN MEADE FALKNER (1858–1922)

HAVE YOU ever walked through an open field where grasshoppers abound, sending thousands of these little green creatures into the air? Big-eyed and bent-legged they hop and fly, cling to your clothes, and spit the summer's green on your hands. As autumn begins, this bounding population disappears. But sometimes in October you find one venerable old grasshopper slowly crawling across your path. Not a hop left in him—the remnant of his race. Little did you know that you are looking at your future.

Ecclesiastes 12:5 (NRSV) describes old age this way: "When one is afraid of heights" (picture an elderly person at the top of a staircase) "and terrors are in the road" (not robbers, but little things on the floor that may cause a trip, a fall, a broken hip), "the almond tree blossoms" (white as an old man's hair), and "the grasshopper drags itself along."

Given this background, let's look at Falkner's poignant thoughts about his Christmases. How sobering to realize that if you live a long life you may outlive your loved ones and friends. All that will remain are memories and perhaps some old books or keepsakes. Yet Falkner finds meaning in the old story of the first Christmas, a hint of the hope that helps him through the sadness of loss and loneliness. His hope is the same as Abraham's, who "was confidently looking forward to a city with eternal foundations, a city designed and built by God" (Hebrews 11:10).

One day Christ will call us up from this Galilee of labor and loneliness. He will bring us home to the eternal city that John described:

Then I saw a new heaven and a new earth, for the old heaven and the old earth had disappeared. And the sea was also gone. And I saw the holy city, the new Jerusalem, coming down from God out of heaven like a beautiful bride prepared for her husband. Revelation 21:1-2

The pillars are twisted with holly,
And the font[a] *is wreathed with yew.*
Christ forgive me for folly,
Youth's lapses—not a few,
For the hardness of my middle life,
For age's fretful view.

Cotton-wool letters on scarlet,
All the ancient lore,
Tell how the chieftains starlit
To Bethlehem came to adore;
To hail Him King in the manger,
Wonderful, Counsellor.

The bells ring out in the steeple
The gladness of erstwhile,
And the children of other people
Are walking up the aisle;
They brush my elbow in passing,
Some turn to give me a smile.

Is the almond-blossom bitter?
Is the grasshopper heavy to bear?
Christ make me happier, fitter
To go to my own over there:
Jerusalem the Golden,
What bliss beyond compare!

My Lord, where I have offended
Do Thou forgive it me.
That so when, all being ended,
I hear Thy last decree,
I may go up to Jerusalem
Out of Galilee.

JOHN MEADE FALKNER (1858–1922)

[a]fountain

ANYONE can easily sentimentalize Falkner's topic here. In an elderly voice, he remembers and describes the sights and decorations of Christmases past and regrets his "youth's lapses" and the hardness of middle age.

In stanza 3 the poet describes a Christmas you may recognize. Do you see Falkner sitting on the aisle at a Christmas Eve service, his hair white with age? His body is thinner than it was in his prime and dressed in an out-of-fashion suit. He sees the sparkling eyes of children as they process toward the dais that signals the start of the pageant. A youngster bumps his elbow along the way. This experience causes the poet to wonder about his hope, about the passing of this life to the next.

So what is our hope? Ecclesiastes 12:5 says if we live long enough we become like grasshoppers who can no longer hop. But the verse continues: "all must go to their eternal home." So Falkner, sitting in that church pew, asks the Lord for forgiveness so when he hears the last decree calling him "up to Jerusalem out of Galilee," he will be prepared to die and experience eternal "bliss beyond compare!"

The holidays that are usually joyous can be sad and lonely for some. How can you spread the joy and peace of Christ to those who are especially lonely this time of year?

So he took me in spirit to a great, high mountain, and he showed me the holy city, Jerusalem, descending out of heaven from God. . . . The wall of the city had twelve foundation stones, and on them were written the names of the twelve apostles of the Lamb. Revelation 21:10, 14

In the Bleak Midwinter

In the bleak midwinter,
Frosty wind made moan,
Earth stood hard as iron,
Water like a stone;
Snow had fallen, snow on snow,
Snow on snow,
In the bleak midwinter,
Long ago.

Our God, heaven cannot hold Him,
Nor earth sustain;
Heaven and earth shall flee away
When He comes to reign;
In the bleak midwinter
A stable place sufficed
The Lord God Almighty,
Jesus Christ.

Angels and archangels
May have gathered there,
Cherubim and seraphim
Thronged the air;
But His mother only,
In her maiden bliss,
Worshiped the Beloved
With a kiss.

What can I give Him,
Poor as I am?
If I were a shepherd,
I would bring a lamb;
If I were a wise man,
I would do my part;
Yet what I can I give Him:
Give my heart.

CHRISTINA ROSSETTI (1830–1894)

THROUGHOUT Christian history, hymn writers have taken excellent poems, such as Rossetti's "In the Bleak Midwinter," and set them to music. Perhaps you are familiar with this one, singing it in church during Advent season.

The beauty and excellence of this poem lies in its stark contrasts and message. Rossetti imagines the conditions surrounding Christ's birth. Outside, the wind moans, the earth is as hard as iron, the frozen water is as hard as stone, and snow piles up "snow on snow"—hardly fitting conditions for the Savior of humanity to be born. Inside, Joseph and Mary, finding no room in the inn, had to make a stable for animals suffice.

But despite these poor surroundings, Christ didn't enter this hostile world alone. Rossetti imagines that a heavenly host of "Angels and archangels may have gathered there, cherubim and seraphim thronged the air." The one giving birth to God's Son "worshiped the Beloved with a kiss."

Later, shepherds and wise men visit the child, bearing gifts for this tiny king. As Rossetti contemplates this scene, she wonders what she would have brought this newborn Messiah. Having no gifts or a lamb, she decides to give him the only thing she can—her heart.

Perhaps if we could go back in time and experience this blessed event, we would bring Jesus gifts of gold or silver, clothing, or blankets. Today we give Jesus our tithe and offering, our time, even our praise. But these gifts, as nice as they are, pale in comparison to giving him what he really wants—our heart.

They entered the house where the child and his mother, Mary, were, and they fell down before him and worshiped him. Matthew 2:11

Nativity

Angels, from the realms of glory,
Wing your flight o'er all the earth,
Ye who sang creation's story,
Now proclaim Messiah's birth;
Come and worship,
Worship Christ the new-born King.

Shepherds, in the field abiding,
Watching o'er your flocks by night,
God with man is now residing,
Yonder shines the infant-light;
Come and worship,
Worship Christ the new-born King.

Sages, leave your contemplations,
Brighter visions beam afar;
Seek the great Desire of nations;
Ye have seen His natal star;
Come and worship,
Worship Christ the new-born King.

Saints before the altar bending,
Watching long in hope and fear,
Suddenly the Lord, descending,
In His temple shall appear;
Come and worship,
Worship Christ the new-born King.

Sinners, wrung with true repentance,
Doom'd for guilt to endless pains,
Justice now revokes the sentence,
Mercy calls you,—break your chains;
Come and worship,
Worship Christ the new-born King.

JAMES MONTGOMERY (1771–1854)

JAMES MONTGOMERY'S parents, who were missionaries to the West Indies, died while he was young. After living through some difficult years, he became a journalist in England. Later he became owner of a press, through which he championed many causes.

Montgomery's writing skills were also manifest in his poetry and hymns. On Christmas Eve of 1816, he published "Nativity," which later was put to music and became the well-known hymn "Angels, from the Realms of Glory."

The poem's structure is noteworthy. The five stanzas address angels, shepherds, sages, saints, and sinners. The first three stanzas recall the events of Christ's birth by referring to the angels' announcement and to the wise men's journey (see Luke 2:8-20; Matthew 2:1-12). These stanzas also call on the present-day angels, shepherds, and sages to come and worship Christ, the newborn king. The emphasis is on the "now-ness" of the event: "Now proclaim Messiah's birth." Christ's birth is ever alive because Christ is alive: "God with man is now residing."

The poet calls on "sages" or "learned individuals" to leave their "contemplations" because "brighter visions beam afar." They should seek Christ, who is the light and wisdom of God. A modern-day bumper sticker says it well: "Wise Men Still Seek Him."

Christians ("saints") must be ready to receive Christ when he comes again. As predicted by the prophet Malachi, this coming will be sudden (3:1), so all must be watchful and prepared.

Sinners "doom'd for guilt to endless pains" can have their sentences revoked by turning to Christ and worshiping the newborn King.

The angel reassured [the shepherds]. "Don't be afraid!" he said. "I bring you good news of great joy for everyone! The Savior—yes, the Messiah, the Lord—has been born tonight in Bethlehem, the city of David! Luke 2:10-11

Nativity

Immensity cloistered in thy dear womb,
Now leaves his well-beloved imprisonment,
There he hath made himself to his intent
Weak enough, now into our world to come;
But Oh, for thee, for him, hath th' Inn no room?
Yet lay him in this stall, and from the Orient,
Stars, and wisemen will travel to prevent
Th' effect of Herod's jealous general doom.
Seest thou, my Soul, with thy faith's eyes, how he
Which fills all place, yet none holds him, doth lie?
Was not his pity towards thee wondrous high,
That would have need to be pitied by thee?
Kiss him, and with him into Egypt go,
With his kind mother, who partakes thy woe.

JOHN DONNE (1572–1631)

IMMENSITY emerges from that dear womb. And look! God is no longer immense. "There he hath made himself to his intent weak enough, now into our world to come." What would it have been like had God come to earth without passing through Mary's womb—in other words, if the Word had not been made flesh? What if the one who already existed had not become weak enough to enter our world as a man?

Maybe instead of a babe in a manger he would have been the Ancient of Days (Daniel 7:9) with hair white like wool, his eyes bright like flames of fire, his feet as bright as bronze refined in a furnace, his voice thundering like mighty ocean waves, and his face as bright as the brilliant sun (Revelation 1:13-16). Who knows? But it is certain that God would have been our judge, not our Savior.

To become our Savior "he did not demand and cling to his rights as God. He made himself nothing; he took the humble position of a slave and appeared in human form. And in human form he obediently humbled himself even further by dying a criminal's death on a cross" (Philippians 2:6-8).

Some people prefer to think that Jesus was not God in human form. But they cannot imagine the terror of facing a god who has not been cloistered in a woman's womb. So God is patient for their sake. "He does not want anyone to perish, so he is giving more time for everyone to repent" (2 Peter 3:9). How else could he have shown us such wondrous pity?

While they were there, the time came for her baby to be born. She gave birth to her first child, a son. She wrapped him snugly in strips of cloth and laid him in a manger, because there was no room for them in the village inn. Luke 2:6-7

A Hymn on the Nativity of My Savior

I sing the birth, was born tonight,
The author both of life, and light;
The angels so did sound it,
And like the ravished shepherds said,
Who saw the light, and were afraid,
Yet searched, and true they found it.

The Son of God, th' Eternal King,
That did us all salvation bring,
And freed the soul from danger;
He whom the whole world could not take,
The Word, which heaven, and earth did make,
Was now laid in a manger.

The Father's wisdom willed it so,
The Son's obedience knew no No,
Both wills were in one stature,
And as that wisdom had decreed,
The Word was now made Flesh indeed,
And took on him our nature.

What comfort by him do we win?
Who made himself the prince of sin,
To make us heirs of glory?
To see this babe, all innocence;
A martyr born in our defence;
Can man forget this story?

BEN JONSON (1572–1637)

DRIVING on US Route 3 through New Hampshire's north country toward Quebec, you enter the northernmost town in the state—Pittsburg. There in someone's dooryard is a small shed of weathered wood with an open front covered with chicken wire. Its year-round occupants—a man and a woman made of plastic, kneeling at a manger. These half-sized figures make up a very familiar nativity scene. Hunters and fishers, loggers and truckers, natives and tourists pass here all the time.

This display is most visible in the summer when no colored lights surround the shed and no one's playing "Jingle Bells." It is most conspicuous in the bright sun and green grass—a permanent reminder of the birth of Jesus Christ.

Theologians call his birth the Incarnation. The apostle John says, "The Word became human and lived here on earth among us" (1:14). Ben Jonson sings, "Was born tonight, the author both of life, and light." Our children carol, "Away in a manger no crib for a bed," and a citizen of Pittsburg, New Hampshire, puts together old planks, colored plastic, and chicken wire to tell of Immanuel—God with us. But, from the simplest to the most sublime, nothing we can do or say or sing can adequately represent this event.

The creator became a creature! Crude chicken wire and well-crafted phrases are equally impotent to explain this. *The living God lives a human life!* Use plastic, use poetry—try as you might nothing will do. *The immortal dies!* Combine the voices of apostles, poets, theologians, and every children's choir on earth to sing the significance of Jesus Christ. Silence works as well.

Construct a cathedral or cobble together a crèche—God knows this is the best we can do. So let's praise him with our whole being!

Oh, what a wonderful God we have! How great are his riches and wisdom and knowledge! Romans 11:33

Hymn 32

The Nativity of Our Lord and Savior Jesus Christ

Where is this stupendous stranger,
Swains of Solyma, advise,
Lead me to my Master's manger,
Show me where my Savior lies.

O MOST *Mighty!* O MOST HOLY*!*
Far beyond the seraph's thought,
Art thou then so mean and lowly
As unheeded prophets taught?

O the magnitude of meekness!
Worth from worth immortal sprung;
O the strength of infant weakness,
If eternal is so young!

If so young and thus eternal,
Michael tune the shepherd's reed,
Where the scenes are ever vernal,[a]
And the loves be love indeed!

See the God blasphem'd and doubted
In the schools of Greece and Rome;
See the pow'rs of darkness routed,
Taken at their utmost gloom.

Nature's decorations glisten
Far above their usual trim;
Birds on box and laurels listen,
As so near the cherubs hymn.

Boreas[b] *now no longer winters*
On the desolated coast;
Oaks no more are riv'n in splinters
By the whirlwind and his host.

Spinks[c] *and ouzles*[d] *sing sublimely,*
'We too have a Saviour born,'
Whiter blossoms burst untimely
On the blest Mosaic thorn.

[a]fresh and new like the spring [b]Greek god of the North wind [c]small bird, sparrow
[d]blackbirds

God all-bounteous, all-creative,
Whom no ills from good dissuade,
Is incarnate, and a native
Of the very world he made.

CHISTOPHER SMART (1722-1771)

CHRISTOPHER SMART published a few significant volumes of poetry. One of his most original and powerful poems was "A Song to David" (1763). Smart wrote many of his poems, such as this one, in stream of consciousness, where one thought leads to another without bridging the thoughts logically.

The poet calls upon the "Swains of Solyma" (the wisemen or magi) to lead him to the manger, to see the Christ child, his Savior. In stanza 2 he breaks out in praise: "O MOST Mighty! O MOST HOLY! Far beyond the seraph's thought, Art thou then so mean and lowly."

He marvels that the most high God has become so mean (so humble) and lowly. The prophet Isaiah had predicted that the Messiah would be lowly and despised (see Isaiah 53). The poet continues his praise: "O the magnitude of meekness! . . . O the strength of infant weakness, if eternal is so young!"

Struck with the paradox of incarnation—the Immortal One becoming a weak infant and the Eternal One becoming young—the poet has more to sing. So he asks Michael (the archangel) to tune the shepherd's reed.

Smart sees the incarnate God conquering the pagan world empires (Rome and Greece). He also sees the entire creation taking on a new glint of joy and celebration because *"God all-bounteous, all-creative, . . . is incarnate, and a native of the very world he made."*

Look! The virgin will conceive a child! She will give birth to a son, and he will be called Immanuel (meaning, God is with us). Matthew 1:23

The Burning Babe

As I in hoary winter's night
Stood shivering in the snow,
Surprised I was with sudden heat
Which made my heart to glow;
And lifting up a fearful eye
To view what fire was near,
A pretty babe all burning bright
Did in the air appear;
Who, scorchèd with excessive heat,
Such floods of tears did shed,
As though His floods should quench His flames,
Which with His tears were bred:
'Alas!' quoth He, 'but newly born
In fiery heats I fry,
Yet none approach to warm their hearts
Or feel my fire but I!

'My faultless breast the furnace is;
The fuel, wounding thorns;
Love is the fire, and sighs the smoke;
The ashes, shames and scorns;
The fuel Justice layeth on,
And Mercy blows the coals,
The metal in this furnace wrought
Are men's defilèd souls:
For which, as now on fire I am
To work them to their good,
So will I melt into a bath,
To wash them in my blood.'
With this He vanish'd out of sight
And swiftly shrunk away,
And straight I callèd unto mind
That it was Christmas Day.

ROBERT SOUTHWELL (1561–1595)

THE TITLE of this poem is as unusual as the poem itself. On a wintry night near Christmas the poet stood shivering. Suddenly, he was greatly warmed. Fearful, he looked around and saw a most unusual vision—a burning baby in the air. This baby, hotter than a furnace, was crying so profusely that the poet thought its tears would put out the fire. But they didn't. As he cried, the baby spoke: "In fiery heats I fry, yet none approach to warm their hearts or feel my fire but I!" The baby complains that he is on fire, but no one draws near to get warm.

In the next stanza the poem takes on a metaphysical tone, meaning that each physical object has spiritual significance. The furnace is Christ's faultless breast; the fuel is the wounding thorns; the fire is God's love; the smoke is sighs; the ashes are shames and scorns; and the metal wrought in this furnace are men's defiled souls.

We realize that the burning babe is a vision of the Christ child come to die for the sins of the world and to purify human souls. The poet may have drawn on a saying of Jesus from the Gospel of Luke: "I have come to bring fire to the earth, and I wish that my task were already completed!" (12:49). When Christ went to the cross, he was "set on fire"—a fire that spread to the whole world.

The paradox of the poem is that we usually think of babies as innocent, as in unaware or unknowing. Here, however, the baby is aware. He knows—even from the day of his birth—that he has come to die.

He [God] paid for you with the precious lifeblood of Christ, the sinless, spotless Lamb of God. God chose him for this purpose long before the world began, but now in these final days, he was sent to the earth for all to see. And he did this for you. 1 Peter 1:19-20

The Incarnation

Glory be to God on high,
And Peace on Earth descend:
God comes down: He bows the Sky:
He shows himself our Friend!
God th'Invisible appears,
God the Blest, the Great I AM
Sojourns in this Vale of Tears,
And JESUS *is his Name.*

Him the Angels all ador'd
Their Maker and their King:
Tidings of their Humbled LORD
They now to Mortals bring:
Emptied of his Majesty,
Of His dazzling Glories shorn,
Beings Source begins to BE
And GOD *himself is* BORN*!*

See th'Eternal Son of GOD
A Mortal Son of Man,
Dwelling in an Earthly Clod
Whom Heaven cannot contain!
Stand amaz'd ye Heavens at This!
See the LORD *of Earth and Skies*
Humbled to the Dust He is,
And in a Manger lies!

We the Sons of Men rejoice,
The Prince of Peace proclaim,
With Heaven's Host lift up our Voice,
And shout Immanuel's Name;
Knees and Hearts to Him we bow;
Of our Flesh, and of our Bone
JESUS *is our Brother now,*
And GOD *is All our own!*

CHARLES WESLEY (1707–1788)

ONE OF the greatest hymn writers of all time was Charles Wesley, the brother of John Wesley and cofounder of Methodism. Many of his hymns rank among the best of Christian poetry.

In this poem Wesley captures our attention about the Son of God's incarnation through paradoxical statements. The first two paradoxes are in stanza 1: "God on high" (who lives in heaven) comes to live on earth. How can a dweller of heaven also dwell on earth? The second paradox follows shortly: "God th'Invisible appears." How can one who is invisible appear? The third paradox occurs in stanza 2: "God himself is BORN!" How can God, the eternal one, experience birth? The fourth paradox quickly follows:

> *See th'Eternal Son of GOD*
> *A Mortal Son of Man,*
> *Dwelling in an Earthly Clod*
> *Whom Heaven cannot contain!*

How can an immortal one (incapable of dying) become mortal? Can God die? And how can one whom heaven itself cannot contain (see 1 Kings 8:27) live within a small earthly body? These are the mysteries of the Incarnation. Wesley exclaims: *"See the LORD of Earth and Skies humbled to the Dust He is, and in a Manger lies!"*

The mystery and paradoxes of the Incarnation prompt praise, rather than inquiry. How can we ever fathom an eternal, heaven-dwelling, immortal God becoming a mortal human being? It is beyond our comprehension, but not beyond our praise. "Stand amaz'd ye Heavens at This!"

But will God really live on earth? Why, even the highest heavens cannot contain you. How much less this Temple I have built!
1 Kings 8:27

Upon Christ His Birth

Strange news! a city full? Will none give way
To lodge a guest that comes not every day?
No inn, nor tavern void? yet I descry
One empty place alone, where we may lie:
In too much fullness is some want: but where?
Men's empty hearts: let's ask for lodging there.
But if they not admit us, then we'll say
Their hearts, as well as inns, are made of clay.

SIR JOHN SUCKLING (1609–1642)

WHATEVER became of the inn—the one whose keeper could not receive Mary and Joseph on the eve of Christ's birth? Someone, way back when, built it of stone or brick. Perhaps the builder mixed and spread stucco across its walls for a smooth appearance and then hung shutters to cover its windows. He tamped down the dirt floor, firm and level, and attached the door.

A man and a woman had made it their home, raised children there, prepared food and drink, and took in guests. Was it the only inn in Bethlehem? If so, its proprietors were well known in town. Perhaps he was prominent in the synagogue and she was sought out by the women at the well. They had children and grandchildren of their own. Could they have been pleased to turn away the man from Nazareth with his pregnant wife?

And then, long after Mary's child had been born in one of their outbuildings, when Herod's soldiers came to kill all the little boys in town, whom did the innkeepers lose to this slaughter? Grandsons, sons, nephews, and cousins all fell beneath the Roman blades. Their family blood dampened the dust, and tears fell to the floor.

Whatever became of that inn? It is gone; it is dust. Suckling observes that our hearts, like this inn, are made of clay. The Bible, as well as science, tells us we are made of dust: "Then you will return to the ground from which you came. For you were made from dust, and to the dust you will return" (Genesis 3:19). Not only is the inn dust, but the innkeepers have returned to dust along with all the jars in their kitchen.

This story can serve to remind us that sometimes our hearts are like this inn—too full to house the most important being in the universe, Jesus Christ, God's only Son. Without Christ living in us, we are no better than clay.

Look, you and I are the same before God. I, too, was formed from clay. Job 33:6

Journey of the Magi PART ONE

"A cold coming we had of it,
Just the worst time of the year
For a journey, and such a long journey:
The ways deep and the weather sharp,
The very dead of winter."
And the camels galled, sore-footed, refractory,
Lying down in the melting snow.
There were times we regretted
The summer palaces on slopes, the terraces,
And the silken girls bringing sherbet.
Then the camel men cursing and grumbling
And running away, and wanting their liquor and women,
And the night-fires going out, and the lack of shelters,
And the cities hostile and the towns unfriendly
And the villages dirty and charging high prices:
A hard time we had of it.
At the end we preferred to travel all night,
Sleeping in snatches,
With the voices singing in our ears, saying
That this was all folly.

(continued in next day's reading)

T. S. ELIOT (1888–1965)

T. S. ELIOT, who penned this poem, is generally regarded as the greatest poet of the twentieth century. Since this poem reflects the personal pilgrimage of the poet, it is necessary to understand something of his life. American born and educated at Harvard, he moved to London and became a British citizen. He began to write and publish poetry. He achieved fame with the publication of "The Love Song of J. Alfred Prufrock" (1911). What made this poem unique—and others that followed—was Eliot's use of images rather than statements to suggest meaning. His next poem, "The Waste Land" (1922), depicted a morally wasted age and became tremendously popular.

In the late 1920s Eliot declared that he was a classicist with respect to literature, a Tory (conservative) with respect to politics, and an Anglo-Catholic with respect to religion. The first glimmers of his faith came in "Journey of the Magi." Imagine that Eliot visualizes himself as one of the magi, making the journey to see the baby Jesus. Magi were the wise men, the scholars, of their day. Eliot identified with them.

Eliot does not romanticize the magi's journey. He depicts the hassles and their regrets for having left a comfortable life: "There were times we regretted the summer palaces on slopes, the terraces, and the silken girls bringing sherbet." They traveled by faith. They did not know exactly where they were going or what they would find. The journey could have been for nothing. Voices in their heads mocked them, "saying that this was all folly."

It is likely that the intellectual Eliot once thought it futile to pursue a relationship with Christ, which requires faith not reason. Likewise, our minds will never take us to Jesus. Faith is the motivator; faith is the way.

Since God in his wisdom saw to it that the world would never find him through human wisdom, he has used our foolish preaching to save all who believe. 1 Corinthians 1:21

Then at dawn we came down to a temperate valley,
Wet, below the snow line, smelling of vegetation;
With a running stream and a water-mill beating the darkness,
And three trees on the low sky,
And an old white horse galloped away in the meadow.

Then we came to a tavern with vine-leaves over the lintel,
Six hands at an open door dicing for pieces of silver,
And feet kicking the empty wine-skins.
But there was no information, and so we continued
And arrived at evening, not a moment too soon
Finding the place; it was (you may say) satisfactory.

All this was a long time ago, I remember,
And I would do it again, but set down
This set down
This: were we led all that way for
Birth or Death? There was a Birth, certainly,
We had evidence and no doubt. I had seen birth and death,
But had thought they were different; this Birth was
Hard and bitter agony for us, like Death, our death.
We returned to our places, these Kingdoms,
But no longer at ease here, in the old dispensation,
With an alien people clutching their gods.
I should be glad of another death.

T. S. ELIOT (1888–1965)

TODAY we discover that the magi from the east came to a temperate climate where they smelled vegetation, saw three trees (a foreshadowing of Golgotha, where Jesus was crucified with two thieves), and a old white horse galloping away. Eventually, they found the place at evening, and this place "was (you may say) satisfactory." Oddly, that is all that is said about their visitation to the Christ child. Why? Because it is not the event itself that was significant but what the experience did to them.

This visitation profoundly affected these great men, so much so that they thereafter pondered if they had been "led all that way for Birth or Death." Seeing the newborn King humbled them tremendously; it caused them to question the meaning of their lives: "I had seen birth and death, but had thought they were different; this Birth was hard and bitter agony for us, like Death, our death."

Never again would the magi be the same. Never again would they enjoy their old way of life in their old kingdoms, "in the old dispensation, with an alien people clutching their gods." Christ's birth had become a death to them—a death to their life on earth: "I should be glad of another death." Then, and only then, would he be released into the eternal kingdom of Christ. May we all anticipate the day when we enter into Christ's eternal kingdom.

I have been crucified with Christ. I myself no longer live, but Christ lives in me. So I live my life in this earthly body by trusting in the Son of God, who loved me and gave himself for me. Galatians 2:19-20

The Flight into Egypt

Through every precinct of the wintry city
Squadroned iron resounds upon the streets;
Herod's police
Make shudder the dark steps of the tenements
At the business about to be done.

Neither look back upon Thy starry country,
Nor hear what rumors crowd across the dark
Where blood runs down those holy walls,
Nor frame a childish blessing with Thy hand
Towards that fiery spiral of exulting souls!

Go, Child of God, upon the singing desert,
Where, with eyes of flame,
The roaming lion keeps thy road from harm.

THOMAS MERTON (1915–1968)

THOMAS MERTON had an interesting upbringing. He was born in France; his mother was an American Quaker, and his father was an English landscape painter. In 1938 he became a Roman Catholic and soon thereafter joined a Trappist monastery in Kentucky. He wrote about his early spiritual experiences in a volume called *The Seven Story Mountain* (1941), which he followed up with a collection of poems entitled *Thirty Poems.*

In this poem he addresses the Christ child as his parents take him to Egypt to avoid Herod's soldiers. After Herod learned that the wise men had come to worship the newborn king of Israel, he ordered the killing of all male infants in Bethlehem who were under two years old to get rid of any competition to the throne. But Joseph had been warned about this in a dream. So he took Jesus to Egypt to save him from this attack. Merton begins his poem here.

How dreadful the scene that was about to take place. Roman soldiers would rip babies from their mothers' arms and slaughter them.

Merton then focuses on the fleeing family. He warns them not to look back at the "starry country" (Bethlehem) because now its walls run with the blood of slaughtered infants. Rather, the family should hasten to Egypt, where "the lion" (a symbol of Egypt's power) will protect them.

Throughout his life, Jesus faced many death threats. But God protected him from harm until the time of his crucifixion. During this Christmas season, let us thank God not only for sending Jesus but also for protecting him from harm before he accomplished the Father's purpose.

After the wise men were gone, an angel of the Lord appeared to Joseph in a dream. "Get up and flee to Egypt with the child and his mother," the angel said. "Stay there until I tell you to return, because Herod is going to try to kill the child. Matthew 2:13

Tomorrow (Mañana)

Lord, what am I, that, with unceasing care,
Thou didst seek after me, that thou didst wait,
Wet with unhealthy dews, before my gate,
And pass the gloomy nights of winter there?
Oh, strange delusion, that I did not greet
Thy blest approach! and oh, to Heaven how lost,
If my ingratitude's unkindly frost
Has chilled the bleeding wounds upon thy feet!
How oft my guardian angel gently cried,
"Soul, from thy casement look, and thou shalt see
How he persists to knock and wait for thee!"
And, oh! how often to that voice of sorrow,
"To-morrow we will open," I replied,
And when the morrow came I answered still,
"To-morrow."

LOPE DE VEGA (1562–1635)
Translated by William Wordsworth (1770–1850)

TOMORROW, tomorrow, I'll do it tomorrow." How often have we said this to ourselves and to others? Procrastination—putting off until tomorrow what we should do today—is a common human fault. It produces many problems, the most serious being to put off Christ's offer of salvation for a later date. This poem provides a poignant reminder concerning the dangers of this choice.

The poet grieves and laments—even castigates himself—for not having welcomed the Savior who suffered for him and entreated him persistently to open the door of his heart. How much this sounds like Jesus' appeal in Revelation 3:20 to those who have shut him out: "Look! Here I stand at the door and knock. If you hear me calling and open the door, I will come in, and we will share a meal as friends." In context, this appeal is not an explicit invitation to the sinner to receive Christ but an invitation to the lukewarm Christian to be open to Christ, allowing him to make his home in the believer's heart (see Ephesians 3:17) and enjoying intimate fellowship with the Savior. However, the implict message applies to all: Christ stands outside every person's heart, asking each one to let him enter.

None of us knows when our last day or hour will come. In addition, we don't know when Christ will return. Christ offers salvation today. Tomorrow may be too late. Let us heed the words of the Lord:

For God says, "At just the right time, I heard you. On the day of salvation, I helped you." Indeed, God is ready to help you right now. Today is the day of salvation. 2 Corinthians 6:2

INDEX OF POEM TITLES

INDEX OF FIRST LINES

INDEX OF POETS

TOPICAL INDEX OF POEM TITLES